THE IMPACT OF WESTERN
NATIONALISMS

The Impact of Western Nationalisms
Edited by
Jehuda Reinharz and George L. Mosse

Essays dedicated to
Walter Z. Laqueur on the
occasion of his 70th birthday

SAGE Publications

London ● Newbury Park ● New Delhi

SAGE Publications Ltd
6 Bonhill Street
London EC2A 4PU

SAGE Publications Inc
2111 West Hillcrest Drive
Newbury Park, California 91320

SAGE Publications India Pvt Ltd
32, M-Block Market
Greater Kailash - I
New Delhi 110 048

British Library Cataloguing in Publication data

Impact of Western Nationalisms
    I. Reinharz, Jehuda II. Mosse, George L. 320.5

ISBN 0-8039-8766-8

Library of Congress catalog card number 92-050374

Typeset by Megaron, Cardiff, Wales
Printed in Great Britain by J. W. Arrowsmith Ltd, Bristol

Contents

Notes on Contributors follow each paper

Preface

Nationalism has proved the most lasting world view of modern times. After the second world war many had pronounced it dead, and yet some fifty years later it is still alive, determining the fate of people and nations. Nationalism in the past had many layers of meaning: it could be liberal, conservative, even socialist, respecting diversity within the nation and the rights of other states. But in the twentieth century, especially after the first world war, nationalism tended to become a prisoner of the far right, suppressing dissent and encouraging violence among nations. A nationalism dedicated to power and force seemed to triumph over the patriotism of earlier times.

For the historian the task of explaining this foreclosing of nationalism is ever present, and it is to this task that Walter Laqueur has made his unique contribution. At a time when specialization remains the hallmark of the historical profession, his vast knowledge enables him to transcend such confines, to see the whole picture rather than just one of its parts. Russia and Germany have been the European nations which have engaged most of his attention, together with the various nationalisms of the Near East. Such breadth gives his work depth and relevance. His analyses based upon common sense have enabled him to disentangle the communist and the populist elements which were embraced by nationalism in Russia, or to focus upon the idealism and commitment of youth which played a major role in both fascism and bolshevism. Walter Laqueur's unobstructed view of the essentials of a historical period or problem forms a vital part of his work. For example, where other historians have been mesmerized by the brilliance of Weimar culture, he wrote about the culture of the average German during this period and how it determined the future.

Zionism is one of the national movements which captured Laqueur's imagination. When he wrote his *History of Zionism* in the late 1960s it was a daring enterprise. The last time such a synthetic work was attempted was in the 1930s. This did not deter Walter Laqueur who, in a period of four years, mastered the subject in all its intricacies. Owing to the anomalies of the Jewish position in the diaspora, Jewish ideologies since the eighteenth-century enlightenment had to redefine cultural, social and economic as well as purely political aims, and adopt a variety of strategies to accomplish them. This caused not only Zionism but all modern Jewish ideologies to assume a distinctly different character from comparable movements among other people. In his study, Walter Laqueur outlined the variety of competing ideologies within the Jewish world and within the Zionist movement in the context of European and Middle Eastern history. Twenty years later, his book is still the standard work in courses in the United States and Israel and has been translated into many languages.

But Walter Laqueur's importance as a historian cannot be confined in this manner. He has dealt with terrorism, more often than not itself an outgrowth of nationalism, but he is also a peerless historical detective, the discoverer of hitherto hidden connections. Thus he found out that it was the Russian far right in flight from bolshevism who introduced the *Protocols of the Elders of Zion* to Germany, just as he was instrumental in discovering the most effective way in which the terrible secret of the Holocaust was revealed to the world. His explanations of how the radical right worked in Germany and Russia, his deep understanding of bolshevism, reinforced his analyses of nationalism.

When it came to prepare a special tribute to all he has taught us, it seemed only natural to synthesize the various nationalisms discussed in the essays which follow, which alert us to a world view which, though it provided a hope for many people, in the end proved also their misfortune.

George L. Mosse
Jehuda Reinharz

Irving Louis Horowitz

Anti-Modernization, National Character and Social Structure

What I should like to do in this tribute to the work and life of Walter
Laqueur is examine the question of modernity and its limits, or more
precisely, fundamentalist assaults on modernization. In his strong
emphasis on Europe, America and Israel, it is too easily forgotten
that Laqueur has also been a powerful student of the Third World
nationalisms and revisionist socialisms. The revolt against modernity, which sometimes comes as reaction and other times as revolution,
is basic to our understanding of political cleavage in portions of the
Third World and Second World, and no less than to sociological
cleavage in advanced industrial centres. Walter Laqueur reminds us
that national character remains important, and that no revolutionary
approach has emerged that sheds a clearer light or gives more
dramatic insights into so-called laws that 'lay hid in the night'.[1]

To raise the issue of modernity and its discontents is to enter the
heart and soul of current debates on the structure and purpose of
social life in historical settings. It is also at the centre of so much
discussion as to what constitutes a national entity. For despite 150
years of communist ideology, and nearly half that amount of regimes
professing communist practice, nationalism, far from being liquid-
ated or subsumed under categories of class struggle, remains a
powerful force, if not the most independent single factor, in defining
relations amongst peoples.[2] And in consequence, the work of Walter
Laqueur remains central to all contemporary debates on the
relationship of nationalism to modernity. In this, he is not only an
analyst of, but part of the great twentieth-century European
migration of Hans Kohn, Hans Kelsen, George Mosse, Jacob
Talmon and Henry Pachter, among others.[3]

The sense of the limits of modernity has structural no less than
historical roots. One of the very few 'iron laws' of development is that

peoples and leaders of less developed areas observe the material consequences of development, but not necessarily the extremely difficult and complex processes of 'getting there'. Leaders in the Middle East in particular, by virtue of the pot of black gold called petroleum, can realize the fruits of advanced development without incurring the social and material costs of older developed societies. Hence, there arises a severe imbalance between advanced commodities and technology, and the infrastructure in which they can be used, an imbalance that persists over time. The resentments toward those who use that which others are blessed with possessing is no small factor in the current Third World revolt against modernization.

A second element in the revolt against modernity is inspired by socialist societies, especially Soviet society, in which materialism is not simply a fact of empirical life but the organizing belief system of the whole society. Given the extraordinary force of religious fundamentalism within Islamic societies, and to a lesser but still noticeable degree within largely Catholic societies, ranging from Poland in the Soviet orbit, to Brazil in the Western camp, this emphasis on materialism leads not so much to a 'new man' as to a rather bizarre recycling and retooling of old capitalist man: venality, greed and dishonesty are not so much overcome by socialist systems or even advanced free-market systems as they are hidden from sight and filtered through much-abused humanitarian rhetoric. The equation of capitalism and democracy may have force in advanced economies, but less pulling power in backward and less developed economies.

A third structural source of the new fundamentalism is the perception that economic development is a segmented activity; it is a phenomenon that stimulates only certain kinds of growth. However, such asymmetry also creates wide disparities within the national culture. As a result, far from being an integrating mechanism, as it was in the industrial process, development may also function as a disintegrating machinery in pre-industrial societies. Costs of development are borne disproportionately, and, worse, rewards are also disbursed disproportionately. Arguments from defenders of Western culture that such disparities are necessary to maintain innovation, industry and invention tend to fall on deaf ears; they confirm the belief that the developmental ideologies are intrinsically materialistic, and hence evil.

A fourth factor is the concern that any authentic egalitarian model must reject notions of change that permit, even encourage, a variety of theories concerning political vanguards and/or intellectual élites. The urge toward development is too often seen as a revolution from above. The new fundamentalism claims that such developmental ideologies widen the sense and reality of disparities between élites and masses, proletariats and peasants, urban cosmopolitans and rural locals, and so on. In short, the developmental process encourages class differentiation and poses a serious threat to national hegemony in ethnic and religious terms. This argument suggests that only religion and not production can create the foundations of national solidarity.

The developmental model promotes a wide array of dualisms that may negate the value of the model. It so isolates the spiritual life from the political or material life as to foster needlessly sharp and antagonistic differentiations between church and state, clerical and lay forces. In political terms, therefore, the developmental impulse isolates a series of rational measures and models that deprive social life of spiritual meaning, or a sense of teleological purpose.

These then are the five constituent elements that appear in the assault on modernity — an assault likely to increase as the states of the Third World assess the meaning of the current rapprochement of the United States and the Soviet Union — along with their respective allies in Europe and America.

The ideological groundwork for an assault on modernity, criticism of development per se, is in no small measure a result of the quixotic nature of the developmental process itself, not simply or primarily a Third World conspiracy against modernization. Development has reached such 'high' levels that it has come to depend, in a kind of economic irony, upon 'low' forms of energy to make the engines of change work. Development has occurred, on the one hand, with the assistance of advanced technology, computerization and miniaturization; but, on the other hand, development can be frustrated by bedouin tribes controlling major sources of the world's fuel energy. And without such energy this modernization process could not occur.[4]

Within the context of pan-Arabism for example, the empirical paradox of military might and economic impotence has taken on a metaphysical character. Ultimately there was a crisis about what really counted. Providence, not socialism, was said to account for the monopoly of fuel energy in the hands of have-nots, energy without which the entire developmental process would come to a crashing halt. Such monopoly, furthermore, did not make it necessary for such nations to employ the equivalent of bows and arrows against atomic weapons. The disparity between military power and economic domination itself became a proof of divine support for the anti-modernist vision.

A serious consequence of viewing any commodity as a pot of gold is that it has limited economic characteristics. An agricultural or commercial system creates a business civilization, but oil creates only revenues. As a result, an economy based on a commodity can afford the luxury of anti-developmentalism as an ideology, since it can import from abroad the sorts of managerial and organizational skills Western societies must generate from within. Beyond that, pot-of-gold economics precludes the sort of developmental regimes found earlier among the Japanese Shogunate and the German Hohenzoll-erns. The maintenance of a pot-of-gold economy permits sheikdoms lacking mass support to retain power. But traditional tribal forms of rule can maintain their varieties of Islamic fundamentalism only for that period of time in which the commodity can be held in short supply and replenished. The structural fragility and temporal limits of an economy based on raw materials has cast a long shadow over the revolt against modernity in these cultures.[5]

The basis of ideology in the early 1990s is a sense of the limits of modernity and development. Once a revolution in the distribution of goods was achieved, and once an absolute paralysis in the fuelling mechanism or triggering mechanism of the advanced sector could be produced, if need be, a shift in the theory and practice of development became inevitable. For the first time the modern world is being attacked for its industrializing premises as such, and not, as in earlier radical critiques, for its excesses and inequities.

The decisive point is not the role of religion in the organization of state power but, rather, the uses of religious symbolism to confound the notion of development. In earlier epochs, whether in Germany, France or England, religious fervour was used to organize state power to enhance the developmental process. What uniquely char-acterizes the current era is *the organization of religious forces either through or against the mechanism of state power* to frustrate the developmental process. This is an important difference, since it thoroughly confounds the Weberian notion of the chiliastic vision as a handmaiden to economic progress. Religious fundamentalism has come to characterize the present period and current mood in many portions of the less developed areas.

Religious fundamentalism is not confined to the Middle East.

Poland is proto-typical in this regard. Few photographs of the workers' strikes of the 1980s failed to show a group of workers displaying a crucifix or in the background a picture of the current Pope. The organizing premise, the ideological formation, was not only more money and less work — ordinary working-class demands — but a strong ideological commitment to Christianity as an answer to the industrializing theories of Marxism. The same condition prevailed in many of the nations involved in the anti-communist revolutions of 1989. The Church displaced the Party as the centre of political gravity. And for the Church the nation rather than class has historically been the key to national integration. The use of religion, or the use of traditionalism if one prefers, is aimed directly at the heart of the concept of development — capitalist and socialist formations alike.

What shibboleths of development went unquestioned in the past? First, the need to sacrifice for the next generation and, in the process, to display a primitive accumulation of wealth. Demands were confounded. On the one hand came the call to sacrifice, on the other the assertion that material goods were not worth the sacrifice, that they were shabby and had no ultimate worth. A second shibboleth is that a society is defined by the character of its developmental process. The counter-argument is that society is not defined by the developmental process, but that the developmental process tends to wash away the unique characteristics of each society or each civilization. A conflict between traditionalism and modernity is emerging that threatens the developmental process itself. This is much more than a theological phenomenon. The zero-growth movement, the limits-to-growth movement, the idea of zero-growth as a positive good — each of these assert that there are abstract values, goods, and services quite beyond those resulting from concrete development.

What potential do these movements have for frustrating further industrial innovation? How seriously should they be taken? What are the relationships between developmentally oriented regimes or developmentally oriented sectors within developing societies and the traditional elements or theocratic elements within these societies? In certain parts of Latin America a tremendous struggle may be taking shape between a military sector that is oriented toward development and a religious sector that is oriented toward traditional values. The issue is akin to the argument concerning indigenous folklore, about the relationship between the international environment and its folkloristic roots. The entire direction of the twentieth century is in question. The measurement of society or civilization by a gross national product, by levels of industrial output, or by levels of consumptive activity has come under tremendous criticism. At some level, the consequences will be a redefinition of what constitutes value as such; what constitutes the relationships of base and superstructure as such; and what constitutes the relationship of state power and religious power as a mobilizing force.

The ability of this new anti-modernization movement to survive is not likely to rest primarily on the structure of economic productivity but more decisively on the character of nationalist impulse. For the weakening of the modernizing sector also implies a lessening of the militarizing sector, and that means the essential pillar of power upon which modernization-states rest is much more subject to external threat and military adventure. In Iran, the main danger to the rule of the religious mullahs came not from the modernizing forces, which were overthrown, but from rival regimes in the area such as Iraq or the Kurd separatists, who saw the opportunity to chip away at what has been a major force in the area. Whether religious fundamentalism can withstand an impairment of nationalism is an essential touchstone both of the depth of feeling involved in this revolt against modernity and the survival capacities of the counter-revolutionary regime which seizes power.

What is the impact on the United States of this revolt against modernity? This question concerns not only the United States but, in part, the Soviet Union as well. The post-war environment was shaped by the struggle between the United States and the Soviet Union, involving competing concepts of development between the Keynesian concept in the West of modernization based upon consumer satisfaction and the Marxist concept of industrialization based upon the principle of national security and self-sufficiency. The entire post-war dialogue has been about which type of development should be implemented. No question has been raised about whether development is good per se, only about which form of development is admissible.

The rise of a special Third World segment, high in energy resources and low in developmental skills, has had a very profound impact on American society. For the first sustained period of time in its more than 200-year history, overseas reality is affecting everyday life in America. Unlike Europe, the United States has never been affected directly by war or famine or any other ravage. Even the first and second world wars, the Korean War and the Vietnam War were essentially overseas events. People lost loved ones, and war politicized the domestic climate of opinion, but essentially these wars had no mass impact on American life. The material life of American society remained largely unaffected by events that took place overseas.

This changed dramatically with the infusion of the politics of petroleum; with the 1973 oil embargo, the 1978–9 oil crises and the 1990 Iraqi occupation of Kuwait and threat to Saudi Arabia, the ordinary American felt that foreign affairs were real, more so than they had been at any previous time. The relationship between what went on abroad and what was going on at home became direct in its reality, in its impact and in its consequences. What began as a strategy and a tactic of Middle East regimes and the OPEC cartel became a world-historic event in American life. For the first time Americans understood that they were not self-sustaining. Even the Vietnam War, which challenged the concept of American invincibility, had not shaken that feeling of self-sufficiency. Furthermore, North Vietnam as a communist state shared the premises of modernization, albeit of the Marxian rather than capitalist sort. This is not the case with the Middle East — where the very premises of non-traditional views of social structure and economic aims are under profound attack.

Every Soviet leader — Lenin, Stalin, Khrushchev, Brezhnev and now Gorbachev — has aspired to the United States' level of self-sufficiency. The idea of self-sufficiency is the ultimate metaphysical pay-off of the developmental process. Why develop? Why accelerate development? The answer is always that self-sufficiency is desirable. The nation will no longer be beholden to, no longer be dependent upon, other nations. The events within Middle Eastern societies like Iran or Saudi Arabia or other OPEC nations provide the framework within American life for challenging the developmental thesis in its essential form — the doctrine of national self-sufficiency.

Early challenges to modernity took a secular form in the West. One such challenge might be identified as environmentalism, which asserted that the environment had to be preserved, even at the cost of economic growth. Industrial waste and industrial diseases were too high a risk factor; nature had its own value. The early phases of the environmental movement, for instance, were relatively innocuous. There was nothing particularly theocratic about the concept of small as beautiful; the environmental impulse was, if anything, naturalistic. Environmentalism embodied a belief that somehow the relationship between environment and industrialism had to be dealt with in an entirely new way. Admittedly, there were special problems involved:

labour reallocation, increased fuel costs, increased costs of goods. The presumption was that these problems, as well as reduced industrial development and modernization, were worth it because nature had its own value.

The second round of the challenge to modernity moved beyond the environmental and beyond the purely secular. The rise of religious cults and of fundamentalist movements meant that the rejection of modernism had extended to an evaluation of the notion of what constitutes a good world. Limited growth was quickly translated into zero-growth. Spiritual values were emphasized over material values. Millions of people within American society began to participate in religious fundamentalism. The origins of these sentiments were not so much anti-developmentalism as a spiritual answer to the externally imposed limits to further material growth. No growth became better than slow growth because it was easier to assert as a metaphysical first principle. The naturalistic impulses of the environmental movement of the 1970s were transformed into an aggressive spiritual revolt against modern values, not infrequently involving the same fears of advanced technology and the same appeals to puritan values of self-discipline.

A third level was a kind of right-wing impulse toward anti-modernism, akin to isolation from the world at large and from America's problems in particular. What has evolved within the United States is unadorned anti-developmentalism akin to chiliastic visions in the Middle East, and no less demanding in ideological terms. What remains to be examined is how the new fundamentalism relates to engineering, science and research. How does biblical literalism connect with advanced forms of development within American culture and society? Further, what is the response of such Christian doctrinaire visions to Islamic concerns? That such questions can even be asked, much less take a front and centre position is indicative of just how pervasive and widespread is the revolt against modernity.[6]

There is a gigantic national struggle under way: the science of development versus the culture of the spiritual; the culture of the traditional versus the culture of the modern. We are experiencing a new version of the nineteenth-century struggle between science and religion.[7] It is not so much restricted to general ideological formations as it is focused on the consequences of this ideology for economic development in the world. The consequences of this revolt against modernity are taking a broad and dangerous shape, for while the curses of industrialism are under constant attack, the demands for a share of the products these accursed societies produce have not abated. Not only does this produce a volatile political environment, it also makes for a cul-de-sac that enlarges prospects for international conflict. As a result, the new rapprochement between East and West does little to enhance prospects for peace between North and South.

One response within the United States to this paradoxical situation may be a kind of renewed isolationism. Within the United States, we may experience a period in which these new movements — whether they be pentecostal, environmental or libertarian — create dogged and determined neo-isolationism, while the nation protects itself through advanced technology and advanced systems design. The divisions between the scientific and the spiritual allow American society to develop what may be called capital-intensive militarization through advanced forms of scientific endeavour. On the other hand, they also encourage mass participation in theological and neo-isolationist movements, in reaction to this increasing sophistication. Among the masses, non-participation and non-commitment have become normative. Even under the most extreme provocation, US political leadership, whether Democratic or Republican, must be cautious about extending its claims. The polarization of scientific and religious culture and the assault on a development severely limit any claims the leadership can make on the masses. The cult of expertise may itself come to be viewed as part and parcel of the curse of modernity.

A potential outcome of any widespread revolt against modernity within the United States is authoritarian domestic politics. The character of American society is shaped by mass forces. Fundamentalist frameworks have to be expressed and could take the form of a protest not only against modernism but against presumed excesses of sexual liberation or excess personal freedom in general. At some level, the new fundamentalism may challenge the pluralistic value base of American society.

Even if American society does not move readily in an authoritarian direction, tendencies toward a revolt against modernity will increase if there is an economic slow-down coupled with a steady rate of high unemployment. Such factors, coupled with very high equity demands, produce high demands on the system. Within a stern moralistic value system, obligations to the system are emphasized over rights within it. The consequence may well be an exaggerated turn to the right. What limits such fundamentalism is the huge shift from rural to urban patterns, and the general secularization of culture in personal habits and decisions. Still, there is no incongruity between an authoritarian-bureaucratic orientation domestically and a neo-isolationist foreign policy; they may work very well in tandem. Shrinking power is increasingly focused on domestic rather than foreign policy.[8]

Anti-modernity, anti-developmentalism, and anti-industrialism are phenomena that could lead to an American society increasingly insular in character, isolated from world patterns and subjected to the same internal pressures that have led to 'Finlandization' in some parts of Europe,[9] and 'Hollanditis' in others.[10] A revolt against a complex present leads to policy-making unilateralism, disregard of the 'other' side and the sentimental view that all real problems are negotiable between 'men of good will', whatever the nature of the social system. Even those actions taken by the United States on a world scale have, since the débâcle in Vietnam, tended to be limited, sporadic and indecisive.

The secular traditions, including French Enlightenment, German Romanticism and American Modernism, have experienced a peculiar crisis. Requirements for personal achievement have become increasingly complicated. There is a systems overload within modern culture (and here I include the Soviet Union as well), because each generation must confront so much information, digest so much material, absorb so much innovation and store so much scientific knowledge. The overload tends to produce an opposite result: namely, an impulse to disgorge or empty out. The developmental model came upon hard times not so much because of its negative consequences but through its positive results. Managing these developmental processes has proven to be so complex that they became problems instead of solutions.[11]

Take one small example. The phonograph machine is an entirely twentieth-century artefact. It began as a simple, hand-driven turntable, coupled with a record made of shellac which at best gave modest sound reproduction. Digital recordings are now so precise that recordings only three years old have become obsolete. The sophistication in equipment makes what we generated a decade ago appear primitive in comparison. Word-processing equipment requires almost professional-level knowledge to assemble the equipment necessary to achieve the desired results. The very ability to manage what has been created itself becomes a triumph of sorts. Similarly, in the developmental process, an enormous case of information overload occurs, resulting in an incapacity to enjoy the results of the developmental process or a much higher level of coping, as with the vast network of home computerization.

Anti-developmentalism becomes a critique of complexity as such. It is not only an attack on the notion of gross national product but a response to the difficulty of absorbing the language of mathematics and computer science or the methods of research and theories of evidence. The world of science and technology has become exceedingly difficult. The fact that significant numbers of people are unable to absorb large chunks of information has created a special problem within American culture, especially since it stands as the most advanced 'modern' society. A rebellion thus arises not just against the developmental, but against complexity and difficulty. The failure to establish a firm set of answers produces frustration. A world in quest of certainty is denied answers. Instead, the developmental paradigm presents problems to be researched and policies to be evaluated. Teleological resolutions of life arise as a challenge to the new technology necessary to cope with the continuation of the developmental impulse.

It is extremely difficult to develop a scientific or technological style that encourages a developmental process within a society. In American society, development has too readily become an élitist concept, a slogan put forward in the name of the people by bureaucratic and administrative élites. And as Laqueur has pointed out, the social scientific model, far from giving a populist twist to developmental impulses, has only deepened the sense of remoteness ordinary people experience in confronting the policy-making arena.

Development remains a vision held by those at the top who have a sense of the national conscience and the national consensus. The cult of the traditional is a rebellion against such élitism. It is a demand for simplification, for a world in which answers are known. The current wave of fundamentalism in American life rests on ideology based on solutions — truth through Providence. In this sense, the fundamentalism of the Middle East may have a direct relationship to similar events in American society. The assault on modernity within American life and elsewhere should be taken with absolute seriousness. It affects the character of individual life, community values and ultimately the nature of state power.

The depth and breadth of this new fundamentalism, whatever varieties it takes, will be determined by the character and consistency of the response from the scientific and secular communities. One big new factor in this struggle are changes in the structure of Soviet practice and ideology. Laqueur is probably correct to note that the Soviet Union is prepared 'to rejoin the common culture after its lapse into barbarism' or 'the organizing values of social myths should not be minimized'. Less certain is whether powerful segments within the Third World are also prepared to participate in this shared consensus. The risks of proceeding in the same technological directions without regard to the needs and wishes of ordinary people, who are by no means certain that modernity is a higher value than tradition, even of obscurantist sorts, are substantial.[12]

The question of historical moment is whether democratic, modernizing societies have the same sustaining power as their adversaries — authoritarian, traditionalist societies. The struggle between developmental, modernizing, scientific ideologies and traditional, moralizing, theological ideologies has entered an advanced stage. As Laqueur well understands, we are not simply locked into a world of intellectual continuities and discontinuities, but into quite practical and painful national choices about whether to go forward, stand still or move backward. 'No advance can be made so long as the West does not muster the courage to stop talking to demagogues with no genuine interest in economic and social improvement.'[13] These words are uttered by a scholar not given to hyperbole or exaggeration. What is at stake in this struggle between modernity and tradition, again to conclude with Laqueur's powerful phrase, is nothing less than 'the torch of civilization' itself.[14]

Notes

1. Walter Laqueur, *Communism and Nationalism in the Middle East* (London 1956); and *The Fate of the Revolution: Interpretations of Soviet History* (New York 1967).

2. Walter Laqueur, 'National Bolshevism' in *Young Germany: A History of the German Youth Movement* (New Brunswick and London 1984), 179–87; *Looking Forward, Looking Backward: A Decade of World Politics* (New York 1983); and *Soviet Union 2000: Reform or Revolution?* (New York 1990).

3. Walter Laqueur, *The Left-Wing Intellectuals Between the Wars: 1919–1939* (New York 1966); and *A Continent Astray: Europe 1970–1978* (New York 1979).

4. Irving Louis Horowitz, *Three Worlds of Development: The Theory and Practice of International Stratification* (New York and London 1965 and 1972); and also *Beyond Empire and Revolution: Militarization and Mobilization in the Third World* (New York and London 1982).

5. Walter Laqueur, *Confrontation: The Middle East War and World Politics* (London 1974); *The Struggle for the Middle East* (New York 1969); and *The Middle East in Transition* (London 1958).

6. Daniel Bell, 'Contradictions of Modernity', *Society*, 27, 3 (March/April 1990), 43–50; and 'Modernity and Modernism', *Society*, 27, 4 (May/June 1990), 66–75.

7. Eric Rouleau, 'Khomeini's Iran', *Foreign Affairs*, 59, 1 (Autumn 1980), 1–20.

8. Karl W. Deutsch and Andrei S. Markovits, *Fear of Science and Trust in Science* (Cambridge 1980), 230–5.

9. Walter Laqueur, 'Fascism: The Second Coming', in *The Political Psychology of Appeasement: Finlandization and other Unpopular Essays* (New Brunswick and London 1980), 208–10.

10. Walter Laqueur, 'Hollanditis: A New Stage in European Neutralism' in *America, Europe and the Soviet Union* (New Brunswick and London 1983), 33–47.

11. Daniel Pipes, *The Long Shadow: Culture and Politics in the Middle East* (New Brunswick and London 1988), 320pp.

12. Walter Laqueur, *A World of Secrets: The Uses and Limits of Intelligence* (New York 1985).

13. Walter Laqueur, 'Third World Fantasies' and 'Fascism: The Second Coming' in *The Political Psychology of Appeasement: Finlandization and other Unpopular Essays*, op. cit., 189–210.

14. Walter Laqueur, *The Rebirth of Europe: Europe Since Hitler* (New York and London 1970, revised edition 1982). See also Walter Laqueur, *Inter Nationes Prize* (Bonn 1985), 58–60.

Irving Louis Horowitz
is Hannah Arendt Professor of Sociology
and Political Science at Rutgers University.
He also serves as President of a social
scientific activity, Transaction Publishers,
located at Rutgers. He is the author and
editor of numerous books, including *Three
Worlds of Development* (1965, 1972);
Ideology and Utopia in the United States
(1976); *Beyond Empire and Revolution*
(1982); and *Winners and Losers* (1984).

Gordon A. Craig

On the Pleasure of Reading Diplomatic Correspondence

Some years ago, in an article in the *American Historical Review*, I suggested various reasons for the relative lack of interest in diplomatic history among young historians. In particular, I noted that precisely because diplomatic history, with political history in general, had for so long been the principal form of historical research and teaching, it had come to appear old-fashioned and lacking in either the glamour associated with the new deconstructionist theories of intellectual history or the excitement with which mechanical techniques of measurement and analysis were now investing economic and social history. The fact that it was associated with international friction and violence did not help diplomatic history either, making it appear, indeed, to be a preoccupation appropriate only for superannuated cold warriors. What Charles S. Maier has called 'a bad conscience about the legitimacy of American power' after Vietnam contributed to this feeling, making the study of the relationships and rivalries of the Great Powers distasteful to many scholars.[1]

There is some indication that the strength of these prejudices is beginning to wane, in part because of changes in the job market. There are already more gender specialists and social historians doing computerized research projects than the traffic will bear, whereas the marked revival of undergraduate interest in international relations suggests that this may be the new area of opportunity for aspiring teachers. It is possible that there would already have been a perceptible swing towards diplomatic history among candidates for degrees, if it were not for the widespread conviction that to commit oneself to this field is to consign oneself to a lifetime of reading diplomatic correspondence, regarded as a form of literature scarcely more exciting than seed catalogues.

The origin of this notion, which is implausible on the face of it, given the importance of the matters discussed and the interests at stake in diplomatic exchanges, to say nothing of the rigorous intellectual standards that have governed the appointment and promotion of career diplomats in most countries in the modern period, is mysterious. But there is no doubt that it is pervasive and should be corrected. A possible way of correcting it is to present a rebuttal in the form of examples of diplomatic literature that not only fulfil the purpose for which they were written, which is, after all, the prime consideration, but do so in a way that cannot help but give the sensitive reader deep aesthetic and intellectual pleasure.

Everyone who has studied diplomatic history for any length of time has his own list of favourite notes and dispatches that have provided such pleasure. Wicquefort, the author of the greatest seventeenth-century treatise on ambassadorial functions and a diplomat of long, if somewhat chequered, experience himself,[2] reserved his greatest admiration for the instructions that Queen Elizabeth gave to Francis Walsingham when he was sent to France in 1570.[3] The ostensible purpose of the mission was to seek an alliance, although in a highly dilatory manner; the real one was to discover 'all manner of their doings which may be prejudicial to [the Queen's] estate', and particularly whether the French government was considering intervention in either the Netherlands or Scotland. Wicquefort was impressed by the force with which the Queen, in an instruction that would seem laconic by later standards, delineated the ambiguous functions of her envoy; and — coining a phrase that impressed later writers on diplomacy — he wrote: 'In these few lines you find the two principal functions of the ambassador, who is represented there as a messenger of peace on the one side and an honourable spy on the other.'[4]

Charles de Martens, who filled the second volume of his *Guide Diplomatique* with what he considered to be models of diplomatic writing, had a preference for French correspondence of the eighteenth century, and particularly for the often spirited dispatches of diplomats on mission, like Breteuil's fascinating reports in the late 1770s of his conversations with Maria Theresa, Kaunitz and Joseph II concerning Austrian intentions in Poland and the German states.[5] D.P. Heatley, in his unjustly neglected book *Diplomacy and the Study of International Relations* (1919) found his choicest pieces, like Wicquefort, in the Tudor period, specifically Thomas Cromwell's instruction in October 1537 to Sir Thomas Wyatt about how to sound the Emperor out concerning a recent offer of mediation by Henry VIII:

> ... Your parte shal be nowe like a good oratour, both to set furthe the princely nature and inclynacion of his highnes with all dexterite, and soo to observe themperours answers to the said overture and to the rest of the pointes in the same letteres expressed, as you may therebye fishe the botom of his stomake, and advertise his Majeste how he standeth disposed towardes him, and to the continyuance of thamytie betwene them ...

and the same minister's blistering note to an agent in Rome, accusing him of betrayal:

> No, no, loyaltie and treason dwell seldome togethers. There can be no feithfull subject so long abide the sight of so haynous a traytour to his prince . . . . You have bleared myn yee ones: your credite shall nevermore serve you so farr, to deceyve me the second tyme. I take youe as youe ar.[6]

Charles de Martens once said that the art of diplomatic writing was to say, in the proper order, everything that needed to be said and nothing beyond that.[7] Both Breteuil's and Cromwell's letters conform to that rule but are distinguished in addition by a vigour of expression and a turn of phrase that linger in the mind of the reader. The same felicitous union of clarity and sufficiency in argument and pregnancy and force of style is characteristic of the best of modern diplomatic correspondence, as the following examples show.

The first of these, written by a man who was both a distinguished historian and an eminent statesman, is a brilliant example of a form of communication frequently employed in critical times — the note of protest, written not in the hope of forcing a revocation of the act complained of, but rather to set the record straight, to make the complainant's position unequivocally clear, and to lay the basis for possible retaliatory action at a later time.[8] In November 1846, the Austrian government annexed the Republic of Cracow, with the secret approval of the Prussian and Russian governments, but without any prior consultation with the Western powers. Aware that the action was a violation of the Final Act of the Congress of Vienna and that this, and their sympathy for the Poles, would make it objectionable to the British and French governments, Metternich addressed a long and carefully argued memorandum to the Western capitals.[9] Both governments responded with indignation, and the French note, written by the Premier and Foreign Minister François Guizot, completely demolished Metternich's case.[10]

Guizot began by noting that the Austrian annexation had caused 'profound and grievous surprise' at the French Court, for it had been assured by the Austrian, Prussian and Russian governments, when they had sent troops into Cracow during the disorders that had affected all territories populated by Poles earlier in the year, that the intervention was purely military and without political motive and would cease when order was restored. That promise had now been broken, and, even worse, the Austrian government was seeking to justify this by an argument that was logically unsound, if not disingenuous. It was their contention that only the suppression of the Republic of Cracow would stop endemic disorders in their own Polish provinces and those of their Prussian and Russian allies, a supposition that Guizot describes tartly as *inadmissible*. These provinces were 'dispersed fragments of a great state that had been violently destroyed, and they still agitate and rebel'. The fact that their division had been recognized by the Vienna settlement did not ameliorate 'the anguish and the social wounds' that had resulted from it. 'Only time, equity, a constantly active good will, and prolonged good government could do that, for these are the only means that European civilization today makes possible and practical.' The benefits of these things, Guizot intimated, had been denied the Poles.

The partition of Poland, he continued, had always troubled the conscience of Europe. The idea that it would somehow be made tolerable to the Poles and their friends by the destruction of the Republic of Cracow was a self-defeating illusion. It might eliminate those elements in Cracow who, Metternich claimed, were encouraging and supplying agitators in Galicia, Posen and Russian Poland, but it would almost certainly inflame other subversive elements, while weakening the authority of moderate Poles who believed in accommodation. Moreover, 'it weakens everywhere in Europe . . . the principles of order and conservation to the profit of secret passions and violent designs'. Metternich's resort to extreme means in the hope of averting future troubles would end by encouraging them.

In any case, the decision was not his to make. In matters affecting the future of Cracow, all powers that had signed the treaties of Vienna had a right to be consulted. Metternich's argument that the three Northern Courts had themselves created the Republic, by the treaty of 3 May 1815, and had then presented this instrument to the Congress of Vienna to be 'registered', could find no support in the principles and practices that constituted the public law of Europe; and it was an insult to the Vienna signatories to suggest that they would 'register' decisions in which they had not participated. 'The very text of the treaty of Vienna demonstrates that the fate of Poland was regulated by a European deliberation . . . . Articles 6, 7, 8 and 9 instituted the Republic of Cracow and,' Guizot added with a cut at Austria's allies, 'there is not the slightest difference between these articles and those that gave Prussia a part of the states of the King of Saxony' or drew the boundaries of other kingdoms or recognized the free cities of Germany or created the Germanic Confederation. As for the three-power treaty of May, the Vienna Act had stipulated that its provisions had 'the same force and value as if they were textually inserted in the general Act'. This was not an act of registration; it constituted a guarantee by all signatories of the Vienna Act of the Republic of Cracow's independence.

Guizot concluded with a powerful invocation of the principle *pacta sunt servanda* and an implied warning to the Northern powers.

> After the long and formidable agitations that shook Europe so profoundly, it is only by respect for treaties and for all the rights that they validated that the European order was given substance and the means of maintaining itself. No power can free itself from this obligation without freeing all the others at the same time. France has not forgotten the grievous sacrifices that the treaties of 1815 imposed on her; it is conceivable that she might rejoice in an action that would authorize her, by a just reciprocity, henceforth to consult only a foresighted calculation of her own interests. Yet it is she who calls once more for faithful adherence to these treaties on the part of those powers who have profited most from them; it is she who is preoccupied above all with the maintenance of acquired rights and respect for the independence of states.

The public law that Guizot appealed to in this eloquent passage was severely weakened by the revolutions of 1848 and the Crimean War, which left the old concert in disarray and confronted statesmen with a dangerous and confusing international situation in which it was difficult to know what course was best designed to protect one's interests. This was felt particularly by the Prussian government, conscious of the fact that their country was the weakest of the Great Powers and that its vulnerability had increased as a result of the serious deterioration of its relations with its traditional allies, Austria and Russia, in the years since 1848. One young Prussian diplomat was undaunted by the prevalent uncertainty. In April 1856, Otto von Bismarck, his country's representative at the Diet of the Germanic Confederation, wrote a long report on the European situation that was intended to clarify thinking in Berlin. Because of the incisiveness of its analysis, the daring and accuracy of its predictions, and the

brilliant formulations in which it abounds, it has won the name the
Prachtbericht, or 'magnificent dispatch'.[11]

For the modern reader the most striking aspect of this extended
essay is Bismarck's skill in foreseeing the nature of the changes that
would come in the international system as a result of the Crimean
War. It was clear to him that the conclusion of the pending peace
would make Paris the diplomatic capital of Europe and the French
emperor the arbiter of European affairs. Already Napoleon III was
being wooed by the defeated power Russia, and although it appeared,
Bismarck wrote, that 'the extraordinary efforts of Orlov [the Russian
envoy to Paris] have not succeeded so far in shaking the apple down
from the tree, it will fall by itself when the time is ripe, and at the right
moment the Russians will be there, holding their caps under it'. At the
same time, the official press in Vienna was talking of a new Catholic
league and 'praising the Voltairian Kaunitz as Austria's greatest
statesman, because he made an alliance with France'; while the lesser
German states were acting like candidates for membership in a new
French-dominated Rhine Confederation.

It was unlikely, Bismarck thought, that Napoleon would pursue a
course of aggression and war as long as a policy of peace was
acceptable to the French army and conformable to France's security
needs. 'In case he should in the future need a war,' he always had an
option that would require neither great effort nor difficult justification:
he could intervene in the Italian question, where the intolerable
nature of current conditions, the ambitions of Piedmont, and the
general hatred of Austria would facilitate his operations. But even if
that possibility did not arise, there were sure to be new political
combinations that included the possibility of war, and the most
obvious and unavoidable of these was a Franco-Russian alliance or
collaboration. Such a partnership would pose grave problems for the
German states and particularly for Austria, given the vulnerability of
its position in Italy and the hatred that its conduct during the war had
induced in Russia.

How could Prussia avert the dangers implicit in a Franco-Russian
alliance? A counter-alliance with Austria and the Germanic Bund,
particularly if supported by Great Britain, would be more than
adequate for this purpose, provided all parties devoted their full
resources to defence against aggression. But even if the British could
be relied on, and that would depend upon their willingness to make
new European commitments after the war was over, the members of
the Bund could not. 'I can assure you that there is scarcely any one

among my colleagues [at the Federal Diet] who in the case of serious danger . . . would regard the federal tie of any value.' Unless they were held in line by Prussian bayonets, they would seek security in treaties of neutrality or 'appear against us in the field'.

As for Austria, its strength was not to be scorned when it was on the offensive, but this was less so when it was under attack, and 'the whole artificial architecture of its centralized government of clerks might collapse like a house of cards' at the first enemy thrust. Besides, there was a greater danger, the fact that the very nature of the Austro-Prussian relationship militated against a genuine alliance. Prussia had suffered too often from Austria's superiority complex and its not infrequent perfidy to place much confidence in its traditional rival.

> I could trust the old fox in its new fur no more than I could when it had its mangy summer hair. According to Vienna's policy, Germany is too small for both of us; and so long as an honourable arrangement cannot be worked out, defining the influence of each power in Germany, we will both plough the same contested acre and Austria will remain the only state to which we can suffer lasting losses and from which we can making lasting gains . . . . We have . . . a great number of conflicting interests, which neither of us can give up without giving up the missions in which each of us believes . . . . Even the most severe pressure, the most compelling threat to our mutual existence in 1813 and 1849 could not forge the iron [of unity]. For a thousand years off and on, and since Charles V every century, the German dualism has regularly adjusted its opposed relationships by . . . war, and in this century too no other means is capable of setting the clock of evolution at the right hour.

He was not, Bismarck added, suggesting that Prussia should begin to search for a favourable opportunity for initiating such a conflict, but only that 'at a not too distant time we shall have to fight for our existence against Austria, because the course of things in Germany permits no other issue'. If that was so, and admittedly it was a question of judgment and not susceptible to exact proof, Prussia should certainly not put its own existence at stake to defend Austria, particularly in a hopeless fight, and here Bismarck referred again to his doubts concerning the readiness of England, 'where a newspaper article has more significance than considerations of statecraft', to make new sacrifices on the continent. Alliance overtures would doubtless come from Austria, but a favourable response would almost certainly be used to make an arrangement with France, and possibly with Russia. Austria 'wants to play Don Juan in all cabinets as long as it can produce a Leporello as sturdy of Prussia, and, true to this role, it will always be ready to extract itself from difficulty at our expense and by leaving us in it'.

At the moment, Prussia's position was not unfavourable, as long as the new combinations were not too rigid and their activity remained on the diplomatic level and did not prevent it from having good relations with all powers. The important thing was to keep its options open, which required 'more of the kind of friendship with Louis Napoleon that costs nothing, and the refusal of all attempts to bind us, *gratuitement* and prematurely, to the leading strings of others'.

The *Prachtbericht* was an astonishing forecast of the main developments in European politics in the fifteen years that followed its composition: the Franco-Russian combination that lasted until Bismarck himself helped to undermine it in 1863; the growing isolation of Great Britain that was to weaken the concert and encourage the designs of revisionist powers; the war in Italy, and the looming conflict for the hegemony of Germany. It was also a literary accomplishment of the first order, combining classic plasticity of speech with a talent for the telling phrase and the apt illustration. It deserves its name.

In the seventeenth century, Wicquefort wrote that the most essential and the most difficult of the ambassador's tasks was to win an understanding, and to discover the secret motives and passions, of the head of the government to which he was accredited, so that his own government would be able to anticipate actions that might threaten its security or interests.[12] The twentieth century provides two examples of ambassadors performing this function supremely well. In the first months after Adolf Hitler's coming to power in Germany, there was, both in the press and in parliamentary circles in France and England, a high degree of wishful thinking about the course that the Führer and his party would pursue in foreign policy. This was sharply contested in two reports written by the French and British ambassadors in Berlin, André François-Poncet and Sir Horace Rumbold.

It is interesting to read these together, for they present a marked contrast in style, the former tentative and reflective and filled with psychological nuances and literary allusions, the latter direct and unadorned but rising to eloquence when its author warns of the dangers ahead. François-Poncet's dispatch was written only a week after Hitler's appointment as Reich Chancellor, before the new regime had taken any serious policy initiatives.[13] In writing about what the new regime might do, the ambassador had only Hitler's past career and what he knew of his character and temperament to go on, but he made the most of these, and the shrewdness of his analysis was to be borne out by Hitler's later actions. He argued, for instance, that the customary rules of diplomatic intercourse could not be expected to be effective in negotiations with the new Chancellor, if only because he was not a man who responded to rational argument. An autodidact, he did not possess a critical intelligence, but rather 'the form of intelligence that is most useful to a tribune'. He was not embarrassed to repeat his arguments with wearying insistence because he believed in them, and he had the great strength that comes from 'remaining completely insensible to the arguments of the opposite party'. He had, moreover, successfully overcome so many crises inside his own party and in the struggle with other parties for power that he had acquired a degree of self-confidence that would be difficult to shake.

Moreover, François-Poncet continued, Hitler's success in avoiding the obstacles and snares that his opponents placed in his path had been due not only to his tenacity and stubbornness but to other gifts, particularly 'a political adroitness that has grown steadily with time' and the fact that 'he ignores all respect for his pledged word'.

> This fertility in ruses, this lack of scruple have deceived more than one subtle mind . . . . Moreover, just as Hitler has succeeded by these means in tricking and seducing those with whom he has dealt . . . so, on the other hand, is he difficult to deceive himself. His obstinacy, his studied failure to understand, save him from any dangerous tendency to compromise and concession. When it comes to the time of decision, he takes counsel only with himself and, like the character in André Gide, remains 'like someone who for guidance follows a light that he is holding in his own hand'.

It was too soon to discern the particular course his foreign policy would take, although it should not be forgotten that all of his propaganda in the years 1927–31 had preached hatred of France and called for an end to reparations and the restrictive clauses of the Versailles Treaty. But the important thing to remember at the moment was that 'the eternal agitator [would] not escape the necessity of acting' and that 'he [was] not a man of the past and that his goal [was] not, like that of M. Hugenberg, purely and simply to restore the situation of 1914'.

Sir Horace Rumbold's dispatch of 26th April 1933[14] was written after the Reichstag fire, the beginning of the systematic elimination of Hitler's opponents that the February decrees made possible, and the passage of the Enabling Act of 23 March, which gave the Führer a position of unchallenged supremacy in his country. Rumbold was able, therefore, to report that the supposition of many observers that Hitler would become a tool of the Papens and the Hugenbergs or be

kept in restraint by the army was an illusion. He then proceeded to
deal with two other notions that were current in his own country: the
idea that the atrocities being committed against oppositional
elements in Germany were a purely domestic matter that had no
implications for Hitler's future external behaviour, and the idea that
Hitler's economic problems would prevent him from being a danger
to his neighbours. Rumbold pointed out that if one took *Mein Kampf*
seriously, as it deserved to be taken, one would recognize in the
victims of Hitler's *Gleichschaltung* and his purges the kind of people
whom he described in that book as opponents of Germany's war
effort in 1914–18 and authors of its defeat. 'I cannot help thinking that
many of the measures taken by the new Government in recent weeks
aim at the inculcation of that silence, or *Schweigsamkeit*, which Hitler
declares in his memoirs to be an essential to military preparations.' As
for economic limitations, there was more than one indication in *Mein
Kampf* of Hitler's belief that war was an efficient way of alleviating
stringency by means of the booty won.

The signs of reviving militarism were evident everywhere in
Germany and conscription might not be far off.

> The wireless and other educational propaganda which is now being conducted by
> Dr Goebbels aims at arousing that perfervid patriotism which can only end in a
> militarist revival. Indeed, the political vocabulary of National Socialism is already
> saturated with militarist terms. There is incessant talk of onslaughts and attacks on
> entrenched positions, of political fortresses which have been stormed, of ruth-
> lessness, violence and heroism. Hitler himself has proclaimed that Germany is now
> to enter upon a 'heroic' age, in which the individual is to count for nothing, and the
> weal of the State for everything.

It was true, of course, that military preparations took time and that
Hitler would camouflage his intentions. He would doubtless be glad
to suppress every extant copy of *Mein Kampf*, which was too candid
about the necessity, during the period of rearmament, of lulling
adversaries 'into such a state of coma that they [would] allow
themselves to be engaged one by one' and, failing that, he would seek
to reassure the West that he had changed since his book was written.
But they should not allow themselves to be distracted from his true
intentions.

> The spirit of the moment is definitely disquieting, and the Government of this
> country, for the first time since the war, are giving State sanction and
> encouragement to an attitude of mind, as well as to various forms of military

training, which can only end in one way. I, therefore, feel that Germany's neighbours have reason to be vigilant, and that it may be necessary for them to determine their attitude towards coming developments in this country sooner than they may have contemplated.

One cannot read these fine examples of diplomatic reporting without being impressed by how accurate history has proved their assessments to have been and without a stir of anger at those who disregarded their counsel at so tragic a price.

A quality that does not occur often in diplomatic correspondence is humour, for the matters treated in dispatches are generally so urgent, so technical or so fraught with consequence that the light touch seems inappropriate. Sometimes, however, a situation becomes so depressing that diplomats seek relief in a kind of gallows humour, and this was characteristic of Rumbold's successor in Berlin, Sir Eric Phipps. Phipps found the behaviour of the men around Hitler both ludicrous and frightening, and this mixture of feelings inspired a report that he wrote in June 1934 about a visit he had made, along with the United States, Italian and French ambassadors and various party dignitaries and their wives, to view Hermann Goering's new bison enclosure in the Schorfheide. This dispatch so delighted an unknown reader in the Foreign Office that he mimeographed it and distributed it to friends, so that, for some weeks, it caused a small sensation in political circles.[15]

The central figure in this report was the Head Ranger of the Reich, Hermann Goering, who, in a variety of costumes, ranging from 'aviator's garments of india-rubber with top boots and a large hunting-knife stuck in his belt' to 'white tennis shoes, white flannel shirt, and a green leather jacket [with] a large harpoon-like instrument' in his hand, harangued his guests about the beauties of the primeval German forest, which he intended to restore, the superiority of his shooting-box and the German materials of which it had been constructed, and the durability of the mausoleum he had built for his dead wife among a grove of German elms and druidical stones, which, he boasted, would 'serve for all eternity, as the walls [were] 1 metre 80 centimetres thick'. In the living-room of the shooting-box, the chief decoration, Phipps noted, was 'a bronze medallion of the Führer, but opposite to it was a vacant space, reserved for the effigy of Wotan. A tree grows in the living-room, presumably ready to receive the sword to be placed there by Wotan and eventually to be removed by Siegfried or General Goering.' An additional ornament was the actress Emmy Sonnemann, whom Goering introduced as his 'private secretary'.

The whole proceedings, Phipps concluded, were so strange as to defy reality and yet, perhaps, they opened a window on the nazi mentality.

> The chief impression was that of the almost pathetic naiveté of General Goering, who showed us his toys like a big, fat, spoilt child: his primeval woods, his bison and birds, his shooting-box and lake and bathing beach, his blonde 'private secretary', his wife's mausoleum and swans and sarsen stones, all mere toys to satisfy his varying moods, and all, or so nearly all, as he was careful to explain, German. And then I remembered that there were other toys, less innocent, though winged, and these might some day be launched on their murderous mission in the same childlike spirit, and with the same childlike glee.

A less considerable effort was Phipps's dispatch of 22 March 1935, describing a state banquet presided over by Goering, although this too has its striking features.[16] These include an engaging explanation by the host that the magnificent pictures by old masters hanging on his walls had been requisitioned from the Kaiser Friedrich Museum under the threat that twice as many would be taken away if the Director didn't send them around to Goering's 'palace' immediately, and a description of Goering showing the plans for a new wood-and-thatch residence that he was building on the shore of the Baltic and assuring his guests that it would be entirely safe from the threat of fire, because the thatch, 'of his own brand from his own lake', had resisted his repeated attempts to ignite it. Opposite this last passage an unknown hand in the Foreign Office wrote: 'And he (vide the Reichstag) is no mean fire-raiser.'

American diplomatic correspondence offers many examples of the combination of skilful exposition and rhetorical force, like Robert R. Livingston's report of his negotiations with Talleyrand and Marbois for the sale of Louisiana,[17] and Secretary of State William H. Seward's masterly note of 26 December 1861 on the *Trent* affair.[18] Among twentieth-century dispatches, one may perhaps be singled out as comparing favourably, in its breadth of view, analytical depth, and literary quality, with Bismarck's *Prachtbericht*. This is the so-called 'long telegram' written by George F. Kennan, United States Chargé d'Affaires in Moscow, in February 1946.[19]

The general contents of this dispatch are reasonably well known, since they formed the basis of a widely read article in *Foreign Affairs* in March 1947[20] and were frequently alluded to in subsequent expositions and criticisms of the policy of containment. We can dispense, therefore, with any detailed description. For the admirer of fine diplomatic writing, the striking feature of the 'long telegram' is the thoroughness and authority with which the author analysed the basic features of the post-war Soviet outlook and demonstrated that this was not based on any objective analysis of the situation outside of Russia but arose from a traditional and instinctive Russian sense of insecurity and from the necessities of the Soviet leadership, and how he then moved from this, first, to an account of the way in which these attitudes of suspicion and insecurity were projected on to the field of official and unofficial policy and, second, to a series of suggested implications for American policy. The sweep of the argument is so compelling that one finds it hard to accept Mr Kennan's own contention, expressed in his memoirs,[21] that his dispatch might have been ignored six months earlier or been greeted with a yawn six months later but was read with attention in February 1946 because Washington, for no discernible reason, was at that time in a 'subjective state of readiness' to respond to it.

Like all pieces of distinguished diplomatic writing, the 'long telegram' abounds in formulations that remain in the memory. The description of the way in which the insecurity of the Bolsheviks found its perfect vehicle in the philosophy of Marxism could hardly be improved on.

> In this dogma, with its basic altruism of purpose, they found justification for their instinctive fear of the outside world, for the dictatorship without which they did not know how to rule, for the cruelties that they did not dare not to inflict, for the sacrifices they felt bound to demand.

Nor is it easy not to be moved and persuaded by the author's argument that, in the last analysis, the key to national security lies in the health and vigour of our own society.

> World communism is like a malignant parasite which feeds only on diseased tissue. This is the point at which domestic and foreign policies meet. Every courageous and incisive measure to solve the internal problems of our own society, to improve the self-confidence, the discipline, the morale, and the community spirit of our own people is a diplomatic victory over Moscow worth a thousand diplomatic notes and joint communiqués.

It is hardly necessary to conclude these observations by admitting that not all, or even most, of the communications that pass between the Foreign Offices and the diplomatic missions possess the intellectual and stylistic qualities of the best writing of the diplomats cited here. But anyone who takes the trouble to read an odd volume of the *Documents diplomatiques français* or the *Documents on British Foreign Policy, 1919–1939* or the *Documents on German Foreign Policy, 1918–1945*, to mention only three of the modern series, will find that the average standard is higher than he suspected would be possible and, if he persists, he is bound to make discoveries that more than repay his efforts. Post-Kennan American diplomatic prose has rather fallen off, but in the most recent volumes of *The Foreign Relations of the United States* — those on the Geneva Summit of 1955 and the Suez crisis of the following year — there are other rewards, including some startling revelations of the looseness and lack of precision of the foreign policy statements of President David Dwight Eisenhower and his Secretary of State, John Foster Dulles. It is well known that Dulles's legal training gave a casuistical cast to his pronouncements that sometimes defeated understanding, and that he had a fondness for standing on both sides of any given question. Even so, it is surprising to find that, after leading the British on and then adamantly opposing them in the Suez affair, he could tell the President in November 1956 after the British retreat had begun, that he 'thought that the British having gone in should not have stopped until they had toppled Nasser'.[22] Illustrations of Eisenhower's carefree slipshodness are rife in these volumes, and there is a fine passage — comic in spite of the matter-of-factness of the departmental prose — that describes the row that ensued after the President, before the Geneva Summit, told the press that the neutralization of a unified Germany would be 'open to discussion' — a statement that left a French journalist 'aghast, [while] a TASS man broke into a broad grin'. A livid Konrad Adenauer subsequently demanded that Secretary Dulles tell him who was really making policy in Washington, while Dulles, protesting feebly that he possessed the President's full confidence, denied everything but thanked the angry Chancellor for his 'frankness in having spoken as he had'.[23]

Only someone who is insensitive to the role of the individual in history could be bored by this kind of literature. What better way is there, after all, to learn about the fallacies of appeasement than to read the beautifully phrased but incorrigibly obtuse letters of Neville Henderson from Berlin in 1938?[24] What better way to gain an understanding of the plight of the professional diplomat in a totalitarian state than to read between the lines of the carefully ironical memoranda of Under-Secretary of State Ernst von Weizsäcker of his conversations with Joachim von Ribbentrop?[25] All in all, these forbidding buckram-bound volumes deserve more readers than they get.

Notes

1. Gordon A. Craig, 'The Historian and the Study of International Relations', *American Historical Review*, LXXXVIII, 1 (February 1983). See also Gordon A. Craig, 'Political History', *Daedalus* (Spring 1971); and Charles S. Maier, 'Marking Time: The Historiography of International Relations' in Michael Kammen (ed.), *The Past Before Us* (Ithaca, NY 1980), 356.

2. After serving for thirty years as the Elector of Brandenburg's minister resident in Paris, he was declared *persona non grata* in 1658 because of uncomplimentary references to Cardinal Mazarin in his reports, which were intercepted. Returning to his native land, Holland, he was made historiographer of the Republic but, because he accepted a pension from Louis XIV and also acted as resident at The Hague for the Duke of Luneburg, was accused of treason in 1675 and sent to prison, where he wrote his famous book and then escaped to Hanover. See Henry Wheaton, *History of the Law of Nations* (Boston 1824), 234–5.

3. Calendar of State Papers: Foreign Series of the Reign of Elizabeth, 1569–79, no. 1441 (19 December 1570).

4. Abraham Wicquefort, *L'Ambassadeur et ses fonctions. Dernière edition, augmentée des réflexions sur les mémoires pour les ambassadeurs, etc.* (Cologne 1690), 6. This work was first published in 1679. The 'honourable spy' figure is repeated in François de Callières, *De la manière de négocier avec les souverains* (1716). See the translation by A.F.Whyte, reprinted as *On the Manner of Negotiating with Sovereigns* (Notre Dame 1963), 21f.

5. Charles de Martens, *Le Guide diplomatique. Précis des droits et des fonctions des agents diplomatiques et consulaires* (2 vols, Paris 1832), II, chapter entitled 'Rapports'.

6. D.P. Heatley, *Diplomacy and the Study of International Relations* (Oxford 1919), 46–7.

7. De Martens, *Guide Diplomatique*, 4th edn, ed. M.F.H. Geffcken (Leipzig 1866), II, part 1, 5.

8. During the second world war, the author, as a member of the Special Division of the Department of State, drafted many such notes for transmission to the German, Italian and Japanese governments, protesting against breaches of diplomatic immunity and outrages against the lives or property of American citizens. The law of reciprocity was always emphasized and was sometimes effective, although, in general, the protests served only as the basis for post-war claims.

9. Martens-Geffcken, *Guide Diplomatique*, II, part 2, 8–20.

10. Ibid., 20–4.

11. Bismarck, *Die gesammelten Werke* (2nd edn, 15 vols, Berlin 1924), II (*Politische Schriften*, 1855–1859, ed. H. von Petersdorff), 138–45.

12. Wicquefort, *L'Ambassadeur*, op. cit., 7.

13. *Documents diplomatiques français 1932–1939* (Paris 1949ff.), 1st series, II, 580–5.

14. *Documents on British Foreign Policy, 1919–1939*, ed. E.L. Woodward and Rohan Butler (London 1949ff.), 2nd series, V, 47–55.

15. *British Documents*, 2nd series, VI, 749–51.

16. Ibid., XII, 688–90.

17. See Ruhl T. Bartlett, *The Record of American Diplomacy* (New York 1947), 107–11.

18. Ibid., 289–92.

19. See *The Truman Administration: A Documentary History*, ed. Barton T. Bernstein and Allen T. Matusow (New York 1966), 198–212.

20. 'The Sources of Soviet Conduct' by X, *Foreign Affairs* (March 1947).

21. George F. Kennan, *Memoirs, 1925–1950* (Boston 1967), 294–5.

22. *Foreign Relations of the United States, 1955–1957*, vol. XVI: 'Suez Crisis, July 26–December 31, 1956' (Washington 1990), 1114.

23. Ibid., vol. V: 'Austrian State Treaty; Summit and Foreign Ministers Meetings, 1955' (Washington 1988), 225–6.

24. *British Documents*, 3rd series, II, appendix.

25. *Documents on German Foreign Policy, 1918–1945* (Washington 1949ff.), series D, II, 593 and passim.

Gordon A. Craig
is J.E. Wallace Sterling Professor of Humanities Emeritus at Stanford University and Honorary Fellow of Balliol College. He is the author of numerous works on Germany as well as *War, Politics and Diplomacy* and (with Alexander George) *Force and Statecraft: Diplomatic Problems of Our Time*. He edited, with Felix Gilbert, *The Diplomats, 1919–1939*.

Paul Mendes-Flohr

Rosenzweig and the *Kameraden*:
A Non-Zionist Alliance

In July 1921, Franz Rosenzweig (1886–1929), who had already become the symbol of a spiritual renaissance among German Jewry, received an invitation to be a guest speaker at the first national convention (*Bundestag*) of the Jewish youth movement, *Deutsch-jüdischer Wanderbund 'Kameraden'*.[1] The invitation was extended by Hedwig Rubensohn, the twenty-four-year-old daughter of Rosenzweig's parents' friends and neighbours in Kassel.[2] Though reluctant, he accepted the invitation because, as he acknowledged to a friend, the *Kameraden* were his 'party'.[3] Indeed, a quick and firm alliance was established between the thirty-four-year-old Rosenzweig and the youth of the *Kameraden*, an alliance that provided him with some of his closest associates in the brief but intense years remaining him. When a debilitating and ultimately fatal disease no longer permitted him to continue his administrative duties at the *Freies Jüdisches Lehrhaus*, the school for adult Jewish education which he founded in Frankfurt-am-Main in August 1920, virtually all the administrators who succeeded him at that institution were members of the *Kameraden* or its adult wing.[4] Moreover, under the leadership of Rosenzweig's disciples, the *Kameraden* evolved from a purely recreational framework for youngsters who happened to be Jewish, to a movement with a commitment to renew Jewish cultural and spiritual life; as a further reflection of Rosenzweig's influence, the *Kameraden* abandoned a decidedly hostile attitude toward Zionism and adopted a more accommodating 'non-Zionist' (or 'pro-Palestine') position.

The alliance was unanticipated; indeed despite the vague ideological sympathies he felt toward the *Kameraden* as 'a German Jewish youth movement', Rosenzweig attended their first *Bundestag*, so it seems, solely out of a sense of obligation,[5] and with a certain disdain for the youth whom, beholden as they were to the ideals of the

German *Wandervogel,* he regarded as frivolous and foolishly romantic.[6] Hence, as he told Hedwig Rubensohn, he would come demonstratively wearing the attire of the urban bourgeoisie so detested by the youth, 'for it is against your principles. I don't want to impress you with imitations.'[7] So he purposefully wore a stiff, high-collared shirt and tie then fashionable among urban sophisticates.[8]

Rosenzweig's ambivalence was also reflected — as he himself acknowledged — in the fact that he missed his train,[9] arriving a day late at the conference which took place from Monday, 8 August to Wednesday, 10 August 1921 at a rural village, Metzlersreuth, nestled in the Fichtelgebirge in North-Eastern Bavaria (Franconia).[10] As it turned out, his tardiness was not crucial since, as the featured speaker, he was scheduled to address the gathering first at the end of the proceedings of the day of his arrival. In his speech, he seems to have made no effort to disguise his scorn for his youthful audience. Self-conscious of his high collar and tie, he commenced his remarks to the equally self-conscious bedraggled youth[11] with a defiant declaration, 'I am not one of you, and I am older than you.'[12]

Yet, in spite of himself, Rosenzweig was taken by the youth — by their exuberance and good cheer. The picture of some 300 delegates gathered at the edge of a wood, frolicking and engaging in robust song delighted him: 'It was a beautiful sight,' he wrote.[13] Charmed, he seems to have lost some of his studied distance, and joined his hosts in song and mirthful banter around campfires.[14] Nonetheless, Rosenzweig felt he failed to make contact with the youth, and regarded his appearance at the conference an utter disaster. Thus, early the next morning, a day before the conclusion of the conference, he abruptly departed. 'The Fichtelgebirge were in all their glory — plateaued, wide and wild. But I did not want to face up to my failure (*Niederlage*), so I promptly left.'[15]

The perception of the *Kameraden,* however, seems to have been otherwise. They — at least some of them — were simply exalted by Rosenzweig's attendance at their conference. Though his aloof manner and dress engendered a certain 'mistrust',[16] and his ponderous oratory left them unmoved (indeed, public speaking was not his forte),[17] his very presence as a genuine German Jew — a true German and a true Jew — touched them deeply.[18] He embodied the new type of German Jew many of the youth were seeking to be.[19]

Before meeting Rosenzweig at Metzlersreuth, the *Kameraden* knew Rosenzweig largely as the author of an impressive scholarly tome, *Hegel und der Staat* (published in 1920 with the support of the prestigious Academy of Sciences of Heidelberg), and a Jewish philosophical treatise, *Stern der Erlösung* (published in April 1921) — works which one may assume few, if any of the youth had read; he was also known as the founder of *Lehrhaus*, and perhaps foremostly for his widely discussed essays on Jewish education.[20]

In these essays — the first of which, 'Zeit ists' (It is Time)[21] was published during the war in 1917 — he affirmed the German Jew's attachment to *Deutschtum*, while envisioning a new conception of the relationship between one's Jewish and German sensibilities. In his essay, 'Bildung und kein Ende' (Towards a Renaissance of Jewish Learning),[22] published in 1920, he rejected the conundrum 'Deutschtum und Judentum?', which had plagued German Jewry since the emancipation, as false and misleading. To pit one's Jewish and German loyalties against one another, Rosenzweig argued, is objectionable, for it erroneously suggests that there is tension and perhaps, even, a choice to be made between the two:

> . . . the Jewishness of a Jew is done an injustice if it is put on the same level as his nationality. One's nationality — the German, for instance — is of necessity differentiated from other nationalities. The German nationality of a Jew excludes his being simultaneously of French or British nationality. A German is after all only a German, not a Frenchman or an Englishman too . . . . The relationship between one's German nationality and one's humanity is one that philosophers of history may meditate upon . . . but there is no 'relationship' between one's Jewishness and one's humanity that needs to be discovered, puzzled out, experienced, or created. Here the situation is different: as a Jew one is a human being, as a human being a Jew. One is a *jüdisch Kind* with every breath. It is something that courses through the arteries of our life, strongly or weakly, but at any rate to our very finger tips. It may course very weakly indeed. But one feels that the Jew in oneself is not a circumscribed territory bounded by other circumscribed territories, but a greater or lesser force flooding one's whole being.
>
> Just as Jewishness does not know limitations inside the Jewish individual, so it does not limit that individual himself when he faces the outside world. On the contrary, it makes for his humanity. Strange as it may sound to the obtuse ears of a nationalist [and here Rosenzweig undoubtedly meant both the German and Jewish nationalist], being a Jew is no limiting barrier that cuts Jew off from someone who is limited by being something else. The Jewish human being finds his limitation not in the Frenchman or German but only in another human being as unlimited as himself: the Christian or heathen. Only against them can he measure himself.[23]

As an 'all-embracing' sensibility, Jewishness does not stand at odds with *Deutschtum*, but rather with the universal claims — 'above and beyond all divisions of nationality and state, ability and character (for these too divide human beings from one another)' — of Christianity and heathen humanism.[24]

Deutschtum and Jewishness, then, are not incompatible, for they appertain to two radically different dimensions of existence. The former is a question of culture and nationality, the latter a religious faith bearing upon the ultimate destiny of human beings and the world. One's attachment to *Deutschtum* need not compromise one's Jewishness. To be sure, Rosenzweig acknowledged, since their emancipation Jews had expended such energy to acquire *Deutschtum* that their Jewishness had often become so attenuated that it ceased to be the universal religious sensibility it had been.

The renewal of Jewishness as a universal religious sensibility, Rosenzweig taught, could be achieved through a sustained study of the sacred texts of Judaism and a determination to reappropriate as much traditional religious practice as each individual Jew found existentially possible. These efforts, he emphasized, could be effective only if they were grounded in a resolve to regard 'nothing Jewish as alien to me'.[25] This latter phrase would be adopted by many of the *Kameraden* as a slogan guiding their own appropriation of a spiritually engaging and comprehensive Jewish identity.[26]

The *Kameraden* convened the Metzlersreuth conference[27] in order to debate the problem of 'Deutschtum und Judentum', and to determine whether the movement would remain an organization of mere *Trotzjuden* — Jews who defiantly asserted Jewishness in the face of anti-semitism but were otherwise Jewishly indifferent — or adopt a more positive, committed attitude toward Judaism.[28]

Founded in Breslau in 1916 as a response to the increasing exclusion of Jews from the German youth movement, the *Kameraden* were also eager to provide an alternative to the *Blau-Weiss*, the Zionist youth movement founded in 1912.[29] The initial impulse behind the *Kameraden* came from three distinct groups, namely, Jewish 'refugees' from the German scouts and *Wandervogel* which, especially during the war, became increasingly hostile to the 'non-Aryans' in their ranks;[30] members of the Liberal Jewish youth organization which had a decidedly more intellectual and religious bent than the former group; and individuals close to the C.V. (*Central Verein deutscher Staatsbürger jüdischen Glaubens*) which was dedicated to promoting a German–Jewish symbiosis.[31]

At first, a consensus prevailed around what was understood to be the urgent need to provide a youth movement experience for Jewish children and young adults who, for various reasons, were not prepared to join the Zionist *Blau-Weiss*. The movement grew rapidly and by 1920 it had thirty-five branches throughout Germany with some 3,000 members; by the following year there were seventy-five branches.[32] This impressive growth seems only to have increased the need to clarify some basic ideological issues never properly resolved at the movement's founding. The *Bundestag* at Metzlersreuth was charged with resolving these issues, especially the differences between those who desired to give the movement a more pronounced Jewish identity and those who felt that it should be dedicated primarily to affirming the Jew's place in German culture.

The 'Jewish' faction argued, 'We are manifestly German, and thus need not highlight the *Deutschtum* which surrounds and pervades us. It is Jewishness (*das Jüdische*), on the other hand, that we are lacking; it is what we seek, and it is our cultural and religious task to stress it as our characteristic feature . . . .'[33] In reply, the 'German' faction asserted that 'we are proud of our Jewish origin and wish to take it into account, but we have German tasks. Involvement in matters of German culture, participation in the common goals of the German youth movement, are the essential tasks of the *Kameraden*.'[34]

The divisions were deep, but it appears that the Jewish element had the upper hand at the conference.[35] For whereas the German element would have preferred to change the name of the movement to one that would not underscore the religious and ethnic background of its members, the conference resolved to retain as its official name, *Deutschjüdischer Wanderbund Kameraden*. The conference also passed a resolution stating that the movement regarded it as its task to create a new type of 'German-Jewish person'.[36] Otherwise, the movement remained divided, and the actual content of its declared Jewishness would remain undefined. Indeed, the *Kameraden* remained deeply divided over the issue, and fissures soon surfaced that would eventually lead to the dismemberment of the movement.[37]

The 'Jewish' faction — which was behind the invitation extended to Rosenzweig[38] — was undoubtedly strengthened by his presence at the conference. One sentence in his address in particular apparently evoked a sense of Jewish purpose among the youth who had gathered, stretched out in a field under the Fichtelgebirge evening sky, to listen to him.[39] With his characteristic earnestness and deliberate, slow cadences of speech,[40] Rosenzweig told the *Kameraden* that 'the very fact that you are here as Jews, alone is of significance'.[41]

The 'Jewish' faction was also challenged by Rosenzweig's un-bridled criticism of 'thoughtless speech, and declarations that

crumble with the first encounter with real life'[42] — he obviously was
referring to the romantic rhetoric of the *Wandervogel*.[43] Accordingly,
Rosenzweig called upon the *Kameraden* to assume a serious course of
study. Specifically, he told the stunned youth it was their obligation to
study Hebrew and the literary sources of their tradition.[44] 'Rosenzweig left [Metzelsreuth] alone, but slowly and in ever-increasing
numbers those whom he addressed would follow him . . . .'[45]
Throughout the years, hundreds of *Kameraden* would come to regard
themselves as his disciples.[46]

Heeding Rosenzweig's call, the Jewish faction sought to introduce
into the life of the *Kameraden* Friday evening Sabbath services, study
circles dedicated to Jewish themes, and the study of Hebrew, carefully
adhering to the Ashkenazi system of pronunciation rejected by the
Zionists.[47] In these efforts Rosenzweig's presence was palpable, first in
the many references to him in the publications of the *Kameraden*,[48]
and in the use of translations rendered by Rosenzweig of the
traditional Jewish liturgy and later the translation of the Bible which
he undertook together with Martin Buber.[49]

The *Kameraden* turned to Rosenzweig for he was the one spiritual
leader in German Jewry who effectively spoke to their situation while
sharing some of their basic sensibilities. He was of the same social
background as the majority of the *Kameraden* — a solidly middle-
class, assimilated Jewish family which identified with the programme
of the *Central Verein* affirming the Jew's right to an honoured place in
German society and culture.[50] Yet like the *Kameraden* he was
dissatisfied with what they regarded to be the spiritually dessicated
Judaism of the Liberal synagogues attended by their parents.
Furthermore, despite the difference in age, the *Kameraden*, at
least the leadership, shared with Rosenzweig the *Kriegserlebnis*
— as soldiers in the Kaiser's army they had gone through the
purgatory of the first world war, experiencing its fearsome brutality
and, at the same time, its exalting camaraderie.[51] Many of the
older members of the *Kameraden* participated in the latter years of the
war, and all experienced the Revolution of 1918 that came in its
wake.[52]

Like countless of their non-Jewish and Jewish peers, the future
members of the *Kameraden* emerged from the war and the revolution
with the feeling that they constituted a distinct generation, whose
values and vision were no longer compatible with those of their

elders.[53] The war and its anguished aftermath undermined the confidence and esteem of Germany's bourgeoisie, to which virtually all of the parents of the *Kameraden* belonged.[54] The children of the once buoyantly optimistic urban middle classes were now often driven to search for alternative values and identity. Non-Jewish and Jewish youth — and young adults — increasingly turned to the youth movements.[55] Defiantly free of adult control, and with a distinctive culture, the youth movements provided both an intense sense of community (and thus identity) and a social vision that they regarded as eminently more noble than that of their incorrigibly bourgeois parents. The youth movement experience, as Walter Laqueur has observed, was regarded as 'vastly preferable to life interest-motivated, atomistic, impersonal [urban] society'.[56]

The *Kameraden* was a typical German youth movement in its celebration of nature and the putatively pristine, wholesome culture of the rural, pre-industrial society. Similar to other German youth movements, it sought to foster genuine fellowship, love of the German homeland (*Heimat*), its landscape and *Volk*-culture. Singing German *Volkslieder*, the *Kameraden* would 'ramble' through the German countryside, admiring its flora and fauna. Paradoxically, and often despite themselves, the activities of the *Kameraden* led to a heightened Jewish consciousness. After all, they had come together not only as Germans but as Jews, even though initially many might have attached only incidental significance to that fact.[57]

Inevitably, the question of Jewish identity — 'the subjective Jewish Question'[58] — preoccupied the youthful *Kameraden*. Guided by the principle of 'inner truthfulness' (*innere Wahrhaftigkeit*)[59] — sanctified at the Hohe Meissner in 1913 as the overarching code of the German youth movement[60] — they held that the Jew could only be a free personality if he or she dealt with Jewishness in an open, forth-right manner instead of denying it. It was precisely a denial of the importance of Jewishness that characterized their assimilated parents, beholden as they were to the 'conventional lies' typical of bourgeois culture. Their proud affirmation of Jewishness thus took on an anti-bourgeois quality. In consonance, many — although not all — of the *Kameraden* sought to give their Jewishness authentic (i.e. non-bourgeois) expression. The 'Jewish' faction of the *Kameraden* was, therefore, to become part of the Jewish renaissance that took place in Weimar Germany, a spiritual and cultural renewal which one would be mistaken in regarding as exclusively Zionist-inspired. Indeed, German Jews not willing to endorse Zionism — such as the

Kameraden — found in Rosenzweig, if not a guide, at least a symbol for their quest for a more 'authentic', engaging Judaism.

Rosenzweig's significance for the *Kameraden* was particularly mani-fest among a group of older members, university students in their early twenties. Led by Martin Goldner (1902–87), who was later to serve as the last secretary of Rosenzweig's *Lehrhaus*, they called themselves the *Aelterenbund der Kameraden* (the Association of the Older [Members] of the *Kameraden*).[61] The ascendancy of individuals in the movement who did not share their commitment to Jewish renewal precipitated the secession of the *Aelterenbund* which estab-lished itself as an independent organization. They were soon to face the predicament of many recent graduates of the youth movements. They were no longer youths but at the same time were not ready to abandon the values and fellowship they had come to cherish. The *Aelterenbund* sought to perpetuate the youth movement experience through occasional outings, in which the former *Kameraden* would as before come together to ramble in the countryside, singing *Volks-lieder*.[62]

The pre-eminent concerns of *Aelterenbund*, however, were decid-edly intellectual and spiritual. When they met, these 'older *Kamer-aden*' would engage in intense discussion of matters of Jewish identity, and in the spirit of Rosenzweig's teachings they would study Jewish texts, and explore various avenues to reappropriate (select-ively) traditional Jewish religious practice.[63]

Because of their spiritual orientation, the *Aelterenbund* found themselves in what they regarded an anomalous position. None of the existing Jewish organizations quite suited them. On the face of it, one may have thought they would have sought to join the *Kartel-Convent der Verbindungen deutscher Studenten jüdischen Glaubens*, the university students' organization sponsored by the *Central Verein*, which upheld the ideal of the German–Jewish symbiosis. Yet, despite their continued, indeed passionate, affirmation of this ideal, the *Aelterenbund* found the *Kartel* to be alien. For one, the *Kartel* was purely social and had no interest in Jewish matters, spiritual or otherwise. Moreover, it was a typical German students' fraternity, partaking in rowdy parties, and demonstratively indulging in beer- and wine-drinking — activities which the *Kameraden*, like the members of all youth movements, had come to frown upon.[64] The student organizations, identifying with religious Orthodoxy and

Zionism, were, of course, equally unacceptable to them. As one of the founding members of the *Aelterenbund*, Ernst Seligsohn (1903–83) noted: 'Already at Oberhof [where the organization met in December 1925 to establish itself as an independent body], it was clear to us that the contemporary Jewish parties — Liberal, Orthodox and Zionist — do not adequately capture the "essence" of our *Bund*.'[65] Again their guide was Rosenzweig, whose conception of Jewish community and allegiance would prove to be most congenial to them.

Leading members of the *Aelterenbund* came to Frankfurt to study at Rosenzweig's *Lehrhaus*, each of whom developed a very close relationship with him: Martin Goldner, Rudolf Hallo (1896–1933), Ernst Seligsohn, Rudolph Stahl (b. 1899) and Franz Wolf (b. 1900).[66] Goldner, Hallo and Stahl would each serve as administrators of the *Lehrhaus*, an institution that jealously defied the denominational and ideological boundaries then characteristic of German Jewry.[67]

Theologically, Rosenzweig described himself as a Liberal Jew, while his religious practice was traditional, albeit certainly not Orthodox.[68] He regarded the boundaries between the regnant denominations and ideologies as unnecessarily, indeed as reprehensibly divisive. All Jews, he argued, should regard themselves as having a 'common [spiritual] landscape', bounded by shared memory, teachings, liturgical and ritual traditions and, foremostly, sacred texts.[69] Whereas in the past there was one 'highway' along which all Jews travelled through this landscape, Rosenzweig held, today each Jew must forge his or her own path, and the paths so forged might also shift, and recurrently be demarcated anew. What joined these paths was the common landscape, and the commitment of each Jew to affirm and honour the landscape as his or her own.[70]

Neither a Zionist nor Jewish nationalist,[71] Rosenzweig nonetheless manifested a strong sense of Jewish peoplehood, and acknowledged the religious and moral imperative of universal Jewish unity and solidarity. He thus could not subscribe to the anti-Zionism of most Liberal German Jews who studiously sought to distance themselves from the Zionists and their cause. Ultimately he referred to his position as 'non-Zionist' (as opposed to 'anti-Zionist'),[72] and lent his active support to the *Keren Ha-Yesod* (Palestine Foundation Fund) as a framework for world Jewry's identification with the work of building up Palestine as an economically and culturally vibrant Jewish community.[73]

Keren Ha-Yesod was founded in London in July 1920 by the World
Zionist Organization, meeting in the wake of the recent endorsement
by the League of Nations of the British Mandate of Palestine and the
Balfour Declaration committing His Majesty's government to establishing in the Holy Land a National Home for the Jewish People.
Keren Ha-Yesod was to marshal world-wide Jewish support for this
project by appealing to all Jews, Zionists and non-Zionists alike, to
finance the settlement of Palestine in order to lay the foundations of
the Jewish National Home. Chaim Weizmann, the President of the
World Zionist Organization, as Walter Laqueur has observed,
'realized that . . . the means for building up Palestine could not be
raised by Zionists alone'.[74] Subtly differentiating between an ideological commitment to Zionism and an affirmation of Jewish solidarity and honour, Weizmann presented the building of the Jewish
National Home in Palestine as a humanitarian cause and source of
Jewish pride deserving the loyalty and philanthropic support of all
Jews.[75]

Despite his misgivings regarding Zionism as an ideology, Rosenzweig warmly responded to Weizmann's appeal. He personally
contributed to the *Keren Ha-Yesod* and encouraged others to do so.[76]
The *Aelterenbund* followed suit.[77] In striking contrast to their former
youth movement, which resolutely declined to support the *Keren Ha-
Yesod*,[78] the *Aelterenbund* adopted a position remarkably similar to
Rosenzweig's. At the second national conference of the *Aelterenbund*,
which took place in Dessau in 1927, Seligsohn declared that 'our
circle sees Zionism as a decisive deed on behalf of Jewishness
(*Judenheit*), and for some time has dedicated itself to systematically
supporting the building up of Palestine . . . even when official Liberal
personalities would hear nothing of it'.[79] In the debate that followed,
Seligsohn explained the rather opaque term 'Jewishness', noting that
like Zionists, non-Zionists (such as the *Aelterenbund*) 'know that
Judaism is a religion *sui generis* which has an ethnic (*volklichen*)
character that is manifest in a thoroughly concrete existence'.[80]
Judaism is a living reality that has overlapping religious and ethnic
components.

The *Aelterenbund's* interest in Zionism — like Rosenzweig's —
was, therefore, not merely philanthropic; rather, it stemmed from an
appreciation of Zionist efforts to give Judaism a cultural and social
fullness often deemed to be lacking in the contemporary Diaspora.[81]
On the other hand, the *Aelterenbund* — again like Rosenzweig —
rejected the proposition that there was no alternative to Zionism and

that no genuine Jewish culture was possible in the Diaspora, especially in the modern West. 'Many Liberals,' Seligsohn complained,

> support Palestine in part out of weakness, namely, a lack of confidence in the urgent tasks posed by the '*galut*'. We [of the *Aelterenbund*], however, so I wish to believe, happily affirm the work for the future of Judaism here in Germany and with a full sense of responsibility we reach out to the Zionists, who have embarked on another path to solve the Jewish Question.[82]

Elaborating these sentiments, Rosenzweig would claim that Zionism and the affirmation of Jewish life in the Diaspora were dialectically complementary:

> The Zionists would be lost once they lose touch with the Diaspora. Their contact with the Diaspora is the only thing that makes them hold fast to their *goal*, which means, however, that they must be homeless in time and remain wanderers, even there. Adah Haam's conception of Zionism [as creating in Palestine a 'spiritual centre' for world Jewry] is thus quite (unconsciously) correct; only by realizing its connection with Berlin, Lodz . . . will Palestine remain Jewish and also make life in the Diaspora really possible.[83]

The common ground shared by Rosenzweig and his followers from the *Kameraden* was a quest for a post-assimilatory Judaism, a 'Jewishness' no longer pinioned by bourgeois ambitions and thus free to give expression to the fullness of Jewish experience.

There is an epilogue to the above story that touches upon the life of him whom this *Festschrift* honours. After the *Aelterenbund* broke with its parent body, *Deutschjüdsicher Wanderbund 'Kameraden'*, the younger generation of Jewishly-minded members of the latter movement were without leadership. As a result, they were outmanoeuvred by the 'German faction' — those bent on accentuating the *Kameraden*'s loyalty to German culture — which for a time gained ascendancy in the movement.[84] The Jewish faction eventually regrouped around the person of Hermann (Menachem) Gerson (1908–89), who rekindled the *Kameraden*'s interest in Rosenzweig and his distinctive approach to Jewish renewal.[85]

Under Gerson's inspired leadership, the Jewish element of the *Kameraden* formed its own circle and instituted a programme of 'Jewish learning', principally weekly Bible classes, using, of course, the Buber–Rosenzweig translation. Courses were also given in Jewish history, sociology, and even in Mishnah and Midrashim, employing the methods of study devised by Rosenzweig.[86] Gerson also opened the *Kameraden* to the influence of Martin Buber (1878–1965), which drew them even closer to Zionism than the *Aelterenbund*, although they continued to believe that a full Jewish life was still possible in the Diaspora.

Throughout this period — from 1925 to 1933 — the *Kameraden* remained a brittle but surprisingly resilient alliance of various factions. But it was perhaps inevitable that, with the ever-mounting pressure of anti-semitism and the looming threat of National Socialism, the difference would take on an urgency that quickly led to the movement's dissolution. Meeting during Easter 1932 in Kassel — the city of Rosenzweig's birth — the *Deutschjüdischer Wanderbund 'Kameraden'* formally disbanded.[87] Three separate organizations emerged in its stead: the left-wing *Freie deutsch-jüdishe Jugend*,[88] the *Schwarzes Fähnlein*, identifying with right-wing German nationalism,[89] and the *Werkleute*, led by Gerson.[90]

Under the force of events, the *Werkleute* soon evolved into a Zionist movement with a commitment to socialism and pioneering values. As a youth in Breslau — the birthplace of the *Kameraden* — Walter Laqueur joined the *Werkleute* and, upon his emigration to Palestine in 1938, joined Kibbutz Ha-Zore'a, founded two years earlier by the *Werkleute*.

Notes

1. In the literature on the movement there is a tendency to confuse the *Deutschjüdischer Wanderbund 'Kameraden'* with the *Jugendverband jüdischer Deutscher Kameraden*. The former was founded in 1916, the latter in 1919 as a federation of various Jewish sports and gymnastic clubs, some of which also called themselves *Kameraden*, as well as Jewish youth and hiking groups throughout Germany. The federation was also known as *Reichsverband der Kameraden, Verband jüdischer Wander-, Sport- und Turnvereine*. The *Deutschjüdischer Wanderbund 'Kameraden'*, which is the subject of this essay, was a founding member of the federation, and in fact remained its dominant constituency. Nonetheless, it jealously sought to maintain its distinctive identity. See note 27 below.

2. Hedwig's uncle Moritz Ernst Rubensohn lived with his wife Emmy (née Frank), a cousin of Rosenzweig's mother, at Terrasse Strasse 13, and the Rosenzweigs' palatial villa was at Terrasse Strasse 1, Kassel. Information gathered at Stadtarchiv Kassel. Hedwig extended to Rosenzweig an invitation to attend the *Bundestag*, in a letter dated 18 July 1921. Rosenzweig replied on the 22nd of that month, indicating that he would gladly come but not as a *Schlachtenbummeler*, as a visiting fan. Since he himself

was not a *Kamerad* — 'as far as I am concerned, I could just as well go to any other Jewish conference as to yours' — he would require an official invitation from the leadership of the organization, with 'the signature of the entire executive'. The'official' invitation was promptly dispatched. Interview with Hedwig (née Rubensohn) and Rudolf Stahl, May 1987, New York City. I wish to thank Hedwig Stahl for providing me with a copy of Rosenzweig's letter to her.

3. Rosenzweig to Margrit Rosenstock, letter dated 9 August 1921, unpublished. Eugen Rosenstock-Huessy Archive, Four Wells, Vermont. Rosenzweig actually says, 'the youth of my party', by which he probably meant the *Central Verein deutscher Staatsbürger jüdischen Glaubens*, which was dedicated to the ideal of a German–Jewish symbiosis. Cf. letter to Benno Jacob, 17 May 1927, in which Rosenzweig refers to himself as being raised on 'C.V.' values. Rosenzweig, *Der Mensch und sein Werk. Gesammelte Schriften*, part 1: *Briefe und Tagebücher*, ed. Rachel Rosenzweig and Edith Rosenzweig-Scheinmann with the collaboration of Bernhard Casper (The Hague 1979), 2:1144.

4. In the summer of 1922, Rosenzweig appointed Rudolph Hallo to serve as acting Director of the *Lehrhaus*; when Hallo resigned the following summer, Rudolph Stahl was named the Executive Secretary, and after a year was followed by Martin Goldner, who filled that position until the closing of the *Lehrhaus* in 1927. Goldner attended the *Bundestag* of the *Kameraden*; Stahl joined the *Kameraden* first in 1922, after he met Hedwig Rubensohn, his future wife. Hedwig's older sister Gertrud was married to Rudolf Hallo, a member of the *Aelterenbund der Kameraden*, or at least identified with it by writing for its journal.

5. Cf. 'Ich gehe sehr ungern hin [Metzlersreuth].' Rosenzweig to Margrit Rosenstock, 5 August 1921; and 'Ich fahre also morgen früh [zu Metzlersreuth], alle Instinkte meiner Faulheit sind dagegen; wer weiss auf was für Stroh ich die nächsten 4 Nächte liegen muss.' Unpublished. Eugen Rosenstock-Huessy Archive.

6. Rosenzweig to Margrit Rosenstock, 9 August 1921, unpublished. Eugen Rosenstock-Huessy Archive.

7. Interview with Hedwig Stahl (see note 2 above).

8. Rosenzweig to Margrit Rosenstock, 9 August 1921, unpublished. Eugen Rosenstock-Huessy Archive.

9. Rosenstock to Margrit Rosenstock, 7 August 1921, unpublished. Eugen Rosenstock-Huessy Archive.

10. The dates and programme of the *Bundestag* are given in '*Kameraden*'. *Verbandszeitschrift des Jugendverbandes jüdischer Deutscher 'Kameraden*', 2, nos 7–8 (July–August 1921), 1–2.

11. Martin Goldner in Eugen Mayer (ed.), *Franz Rosenzweig. Eine Gedenkschrift* (Frankfurt a.M.: Vorstand der Israelitischen Gemeinde Frankfurt a.M. 1930), 38.

12. Rosenzweig to Margrit Rosenstock, 9 August 1921.

13. Ibid. The figure of 300 delegates is Rosenzweig's; ibid. Goldner recalls '500 young Jewish people' in attendance at the *Bundestag*. Goldner, *Gedenkschrift*, 38.

14. Cf. 'Mir haben sie übrigens besser gefallen als ich ihnen. Es sind wunderbare Jungens dabei gewesen . . . viel *guter Wandervogel*. Nach Dunkelheit gab es ein Wettsingen der Gruppen, z.T. ganz prachtvoll. Ein famoser Ton, ohne Krampfhaftigkeit. . . .' Rosenzweig to Margrit Rosenstock, 9 August 1921. That Rosenzweig actually joined the youth in song round the camp-fires is reported by one of the former *Kameraden* and organizers of the *Bundestag*, Franz Wolf. Interview, May 1987, Washington DC.

15. Rosenzweig to Margrit Rosenstock, 9 August 1921.

16. Goldner, *Gedenkschrift*, 38.

17. Ibid. Cf. 'On the basis of the Metzlersreuth meeting, I certainly would not have described FR [Franz Rosenzweig] as charismatic. . . .' Franz Wolf to myself, 19 June 1987.

18. Cf. 'It is important to recall that the *Kameraden* was an anti-Philistine, anti-bourgeois movement. It sought to inculcate new values based on friendship and nature. . . . The movement was consciously Jewish and consciously German. It emphasized education and self-education. . . . We were interested in Jewish heritage for the sake of our Jewish identity. . . .[Rosenzweig] was a symbol of the type of Jewish affirmation we had in mind. His very presence made a great impact on us.' Franz Wolf, Interview (see note 14 above). Also cf. ' . . . the fact that FR was not a Zionist played a role in the interest of the *Kameraden* in his work — and, I am sure, played a role in his interest in [us].' Wolf's addenda to the transcript of the interview conducted with him (see note 14 above).

19. Cf. 'We are the youth movement of the German Jews, core and advance troop of the new German-Jewish society.' *Kameraden, Deutschjüdischer Wanderbund* (September 1924), cited in C. Rinott, 'Major Trends in Jewish Youth Movements in Germany', *Leo Baeck Institute Year Book*, XIX (1974), 84.

20. Interviews with Hedwig and Rudolph Stahl (see note 2 above) and Franz Wolf (see note 14 above).

21. Rosenzweig, *Zeit ists. Gedanken über das jüdische Bildungsproblem des Augenblicks. An Hermann Cohen* (Berlin/Munich 1918); 'It is Time: Concerning the Study of Judaism', in F. Rosenzweig, *On Jewish Learning*, ed. N.N. Glatzer (New York 1965), 27–54.

22. *Bildung und kein Ende* (Frankfurt a.M. 1920); 'Toward a Renaissance of Jewish Learning', in *On Jewish Learning*, 55–71.

23. Ibid., 56–7.

24. Ibid., 57.

25. Ibid., 65.

26. Ernst Markowicz, 'Die "Kameraden" ', *Jüdische Rundschau*, XXXVII/45–6 (8 July 1932), 215.

27. The Metzlersreuth conference was the first *Bundestag* of the *Deutschjüdischer Wanderbund 'Kameraden'*; it was preceded by a conference of the larger body to which *D.W. Kameraden* belonged, *Jugendverband jüdischer Deutscher Kameraden*, which took place at Nordhausen am Harz from 29 to 31 July 1921. Indeed, the scheduling of the Metzlersreuth conference was determined so as to allow the *D.W. Kameraden* to head directly from the larger gathering, which was deemed to be both organizationally and ideologically a 'monstrosity', to what promised to be a more intimate and serious affair. See the statement by the leader of the *D.W. Kameraden*, Josef Hirschberg, 'Die Zukunft des Verbandes', *Kameraden*, 2/7–8 (July–August 1921), 39–42. In his extensive discussion of the *Kameraden*, Hermann Meier-Cronemeyer fails to differentiate between the two allied organizations, and thus confounds their ideological positions, especially with regard to the questions of Jewish identity and Zionism. Meier-Cronemeyer, 'Jüdische Jugendbewegung', *Germania Judaica* (Kölner Bibliothek zur Geschichte des Deutschen Judentum), VIII/1–2 (1969), 51–6, part 1; VIII/3–4 (1969), 75–86, part 2.

28. Erich Hirschberg, 'Die Kameraden. Ein Weg ins Judentum', *Der Morgen*, IX/6 (December 1933), 342. See also Josef Hirschberg, 'Aufruf. Jüdischer W.B. "Kameraden" ', *Kameraden*, 2/7–8 (July–August 1921), 35–6; Erwin Lichtenstein, 'Prolog zum Bundestag', *Kameraden*, 2/7–8 (July–August 1921), 2–3.

29. Markowicz, 'Die "Kameraden" ', 215.

30. On the increasing exclusion of Jews from the German youth movements, see Walter Laqueur, 'The German Youth Movement and the "Jewish Question" ', *Leo Baeck Institute Year Book*, VI (1961), 193–205. Cf. the constitution of the *Kameraden*: 'Infolgendessen weist der Verband Bestrebungen, welche die jüdischen Deutschen einem Fremdkorper im deutschen Volke machen wollen, von welcher Seite sie auch kommen mögen, mit aller Entschiedenheit zurück.' Cited as motto to *Kameraden*, 2/7–8 (July–August 1921), 1. Also cf. ' . . . the decision to join a Jewish youth movement was not necessarily motivated by a desire for a Jewish commitment. [Yet] it would be wrong to assume that young Jews only joined a Jewish youth movement because the German movement did not accept them.' Werner Rosenstock, 'The Jewish Youth Movement', *Leo Baeck Institute Year Book*, XIX (1974), 98.

31. On the various constituent groups forming the *Kameraden*, see E. Hirschberg, 'Die "Kameraden" ', 342f.

32. Meier-Cronemeyer, 'Jüdische Jugendbewegung', 52. The December 1920 issue (1/2) of the movement's journal, *Kameraden*, lists ninety branches; the July–August 1921 (II/7–8) issue gives the addresses of ninety-five branches.

33. Markowicz, 'Die "Kameraden" ', 215.

34. Ibid. A protocol of the first day of the *Bundestag*, in which Rosenzweig participated, is provided in *Kameraden*, II/9–10 (September–October 1921), 10–12. I wish to thank Mr Tzvi Ra'anan for locating on my behalf this issue in the archives of the youth movement *Werkleute* housed in his kibbutz, Ha-Zore'a.

35. Meier-Cronemeyer (in 'Jüdische Jugendbewegung') ascribes marginal significance to the Jewish faction, perhaps because he fails to take into consideration the ideological and organizational distinctions suggested in note 27 above. According to the published memoirs of two leading personalities in the movement (by Erich Hirschberg and Ernst Markowicz) and interviews I have conducted (with Martin Goldner, Hedwig and Rudolph Stahl, and Franz Wolf), the Jewish faction did indeed hold sway at the *Bundestag* and for a spell thereafter; further, each attribute to Rosenzweig a major role in crystallizing the resolve of the Jewish faction. It may also be noted that the issues of *Kameraden* immediately following the conference display a greater attention to Jewish matters, which is also reflected in the illustrations and artwork of the movement's journal.

36. Hirschberg, 'Die "Kameraden" ', 342f.; Markowicz, 'Die "Kameraden" ', 215.

37. These divisions and tensions between the various factions of the movement are analysed in detail in Carl J. Rheins, 'The Schwarzes Fähnlein', *Leo Baeck Institute Year Book*, XXIII (1978), 173–9.

38. See note 2 above. Markowicz, apparently one of the activists in the Jewish faction, also takes credit for facilitating Rosenzweig's participation in the conference. Markowicz, 'Die "Kameraden" ', 215.

39. Goldner, *Gedenkschrift*, 38; amplified by an interview with Martin Goldner, Palo Alto, April 1987.

40. Goldner, *Gedenkschrift*, 38.

41. Interview with Hedwig Stahl (see note 2 above).

42. Goldner, *Gedenkschrift*, 38.

43. Other speakers at the *Bundestag* voiced similar criticism of the romantic ethos of the *Wandervogel* that evidently still dominated the movement. The editor of the movement's *Führer-Blatt*, Max Staub, for instance, criticized 'die Romantik und die

Vogelstrauss-Politik des Wandervogels' from a socialist perspective. Excerpts of his address are given in *Führer-Blatt des J.W.B.- 'Kameraden'*, 4 (15 November 1921), 3-4.

44. The published protocol of the conference proceedings summarizes Rosenzweig's address in one sentence: '[Rosenzweig] fordert auf zum eifrigen Lernen auf jüdischem Gebiete', *Kameraden*, II 9-10 (September–October 1921), 12.

45. Goldner, *Gedenkschrift*, 39.

46. Markowicz, 'Die "Kameraden" ', 215. Cf. 'Rosenzweig's personality and entire outlook made an impact on some of the most mature and prominent [*Kameraden*], and was thus that much more lasting.' Ibid.

47. Ibid. Rosenzweig insisted on maintaining the Ashkenazi pronunciation, employed in the liturgical recitation of German and East European Jewry, in order to underscore that his interest in the Holy Tongue was purely religious and not at all national. See my 'Hebrew as a Holy Tongue. Rosenzweig and the Revival of Hebrew', in Lewis Glinert, ed., *Hebrew in Ashkenaz* (London 1992).

48. Cf. e.g. Rudolf Hallo, 'Der Stern der Erlösung. Eine Hinleitung', *Führer-Blatt des J.W.B.-'Kameraden'*. 4 (15 October 1921), 1-3. In this introduction to Rosenzweig's recently published philosophical treatise, Hallo emphasizes his 'proud' affirmation of Judaism.

49. Markowicz, 'Die "Kameraden" ', 215.

50. On the social background of the *Kameraden*, see Eliyahu Maoz, 'The Werkleute', *Leo Baeck Institute Year Book*, IV (1959), 165f.; see also George Gunther Eckstein, 'The Freie Deutsch-Jüdische Jugend (FDJJ) 1932-1933', *Leo Baeck Institute Year Book*, XXVI (1981), 231f.

51. Cf. George L. Mosse, *The Jews and the German War Experience, 1914–1918. The Leo Baeck Memorial Lecture 21* (New York 1977).

52. Rudolph Stahl (b.1899) and Franz Wolf (b.1900), e.g., served as combat soldiers in the last year of the first world war; disqualified because of poor health from military service, Rudolf Hallo served as a volunteer in the medical corps. Rosenzweig himself was a Non-Commissioned Officer in an anti-aircraft unit on the Eastern Front.

53. On the generational conflict generated by the war and the resulting shift of values, see Hans Dieter Hellige, 'Generationskonflikt, Selbsthass und die Entstehung antikapitalistischer Positionen im Judentum', *Geschichte und Gesellschaft*, 5(1979), 516f.

54. Cf. ' . . . the process of the elimination of the Jews from German economic life did not begin with Hitler. The post-war years in Germany brought a steady elimination of the small and medium-sized enterprises in favour of the big trusts and concerns. The middle classes lost more and more of their economic independence and joined the ever-growing ranks of white-collar workers. The German Jews had attained their important position and their wealth as small and middle-class entrepreneurs. It was particularly difficult for these Jews (much more than for the Germans proper) to become reconciled to being middle-ranking clerks in business and government.' Maoz, 'The Werkleute', 165f.

55. Walter Laqueur, *Young Germany. A History of the German Youth Movement* (New York 1962), 155–66.

56. Ibid., 165.

57. Rosenstock, 'The Youth Movement', 98.

58. Rinott, 'Major Trends in Jewish Youth Movements in Germany', 82.

59. This and other terms characteristic of German *Wandervogel* were part of the *Kameraden*'s lexicon. In the Preface to the protocol of the movement's first *Bundestag*, the editor speaks of the need to deal with the questions facing Jewish youth with '*innere*

Wahrhaftigkeit und Selbtsverantwortung'. *Kameraden,* II 9-19 (September–October 1921), 10.

60. The Hohe Meissner, a mountain south of the city of Kassel, was the site of a convention of various youth movements in Germany and Austria, which sought to forge a grand alliance of German youth. See Laqueur, *Young Germany,* 32–8.

61. On the *Aelterenbund,* see Meier-Cronemeyer, 'Jüdische Jugendbewegung', 54-6. Although the majority of the members of the *Aelterenbund* were 'graduates' of the *Kameraden,* isolated individuals from other youth organizations also joined, such as Ernst Heinrich Seligsohn (1903–83), who was active in a youth movement associated with Liberal Judaism in Berlin. The *Aelterenbund* had but 50 to 60 members. See H.M. Graupe, *The Rise of Modern Judaism, An Intellectual History of German Jewry.* (Huntington, NY 1978), p. 302, m. 428.

62. For a description of one of the gatherings of the *Aelterenbund,* see Werner van der Zyl, 'Das aussere Bild', *Um Jüdische Wirklichkeit.* Bericht von Bundestag des Aelterenbundes der Kameraden in Dessau 1927 (Im Selbstverlag des Bundes, 1927), 5–6.

63. Ibid. The description of the religious practice of the *Aelterenbund* was elaborated in interviews with Martin Goldner and Franz Wolf. With respect to the religious quest of the *Kameraden* in general, it has been observed that it 'was based more on romanticism than on a deep religious urge'. Maoz, 'The Werkleute', 167.

64. Meier-Cronemeyer, 'Jüdische Jugendbewegung', 52.

65. Seligsohn, Preface to *Um Jüdische Wirklichkeit,* 4.

66. Each of these individuals came to Frankfurt in order to continue their studies or vocation while attending Rosenzweig's *Lehrhaus.*

67. See note 4 above. Significantly, Rosenzweig also had disciples from among the *Blau-Weiss,* the rival Zionist youth movement (e.g. Erich Fromm, Leo Löwenthal and Ernst Simon). Moreover, he refused to grant the *Kameraden* any special privileges, as Rudolf Stahl explained in a letter to me, dated 22 June 1987; see also Rosenzweig to Rudolf Hallo, 'Anfang Dezember 1922', in *Briefe und Tagebücher,* 2, 859f.

68. On Rosenzweig's unique blend of Liberal theology and traditional practice, see my 'Mendelssohn and Rosenzweig', in Wolfdietrich Schmied-Kowarzik (ed.), *Der Philosoph Franz Rosenzweig. Internationaler Kongress — Kassel 1986* (Munich/Freiburg 1988), 1, 213–23.

69. Rosenzweig to Rudolf Hallo, 27 March 1922, in *Briefe und Tagebücher,* 2, 763.

70. Ibid., 763f.

71. On Rosenzweig's attitude toward Zionism, see Stephane Moses, 'Politik und Religion. Zur Aktualität Franz Rosenzweigs', in Schmied-Kowarzik (ed.), *Der Philosoph Franz Rosenzweig,* 2, 855–75.

72. Cf. Rosenzweig, 'Briefe eines Nichtzionisten an einen Anti-Zionisten', *Der Jude.* Sonderheft zum 50. Geburtstag Martin Bubers (February 1928), 619.

73. Cf. Rosenzweig to Julius Blau (President of *Keren Ha-Yesod* in Frankfurt a.M.), 13 January 1927, *Briefe und Tagebücher,* 2, 1123f.

74. Walter Laqueur, *A History of Zionism* (London 1972), 462f.

75. Franz Wolf, a member of the *Aelterenbund,* served for several years as the Vice-President of the *Keren Ha-Yesod* in Frankfurt. He recalls Weizmann's visit to Frankfurt where he addressed a *Keren Ha-Yesod* meeting. 'Weizmann's argument was two-fold: development of a Jewish/Hebrew culture will benefit all Jews everywhere, and [conversely] the failure of the Zionist endeavour in Palestine will backfire on Jews everywhere.' Franz Wolf addenda to the transcript of an interview with me in May 1987.

76. Interviews with Franz Wolf, Hedwig and Rudolph Stahl, and Toni Simon (widow

of Rosenzweig's close associate, Ernst Simon [1899–1988], Jerusalem, April 1988). Initially, Rosenzweig actually opposed non-Zionist support of the *Keren Ha-Yesod*, fearing that it would deflect German Jewry from contributing to its own institutions. He soon realized that this was not the case, however. Cf. Rosenzweig to his mother, 22 May 1924, *Briefe und Tagebücher*, 2, 964.

77. Erich Hirschberg, 'Der C.V. und Wir', *Um Jüdische Wirklichkeit*, 32.

78. Meier-Cronemeyer, 'Jüdische Jugendbewegung', 52.

79. Ernst Heinrich Seligsohn, 'Die Liberalen', in *Um Jüdische Wirklichkeit*, 27.

80. Ibid., 42.

81. Cf. Rosenzweig to Benno Jacob, 17 May 1927, cited in N. Glatzer, *Franz Rosenzweig*, 357. Cf. 'Ich trage mich sehr mit prinzipiellsten Gedanken zur Palästinapolitik, die ja nun auch unsere Sache geworden ist.' Rosenzweig to Ernst Simon, 30 September 1929. Unpublished. Ernst Simon Archive, Jerusalem. I wish to thank Ms Toni Simon for allowing me to examine her late husband's papers.

82. Seligsohn in debate following his address, p. 42. In the same debate, Martin Goldner added: 'Wir sind alle einig in der Anerkennung und Wertschätzung des Palästina Aufbaues, wir sind bereit auch materielle Hilfe zu leisten und tun es nach Kräften. . . . Wir setzen auch für unser Schicksal Hoffnung und Erwartung auf das Gelingen des Werkes. Aber bei all dieser Palästinaarbeit ist und kann doch unsere Seele nur herzlich wenig berührt sein — und um sie aber geht es doch.' Ibid., 36.

83. Franz Rosenzweig to Gertrud Oppenheim, letter dated 1 May 1917, cited in Glatzer, *Rosenzweig. His Life and Thought*, 54. Rosenzweig would recurrently repeat this thesis in ever new formulations. Cf. e.g. his essay, 'Neuhebraeisch?' *Der Morgen*, 21 (1926); now in Rosenzweig, *Der Mensch und sein Werk. Gesammelte Schriften* (Dondrecht 1984), vol. 3 (*Zweistromland. Kleinere Schriften zu Glauben und Denken*), 723–72, esp., 727f.

84. During the period when the 'German faction' controlled the leadership of the *Kameraden*, it was proposed that non-Jews should be recruited for membership in the movement. Markowicz, 'Die "Kameraden" ', 215.

85. Ibid.

86. Maoz, 'The Werkleute', 170–2.

87. Markowicz, 'Die "Kameraden" ', 215.

88. Meier-Cronemeyer, 'Jüdische Jugendbewegung', 86.

89. Charles J. Rheins, 'The Schwarzes Fähnlein, Jungenschaft, 1932–1934', *Leo Baeck Institute Year Book*, XXIII (1978), 173–97.

90. Maoz, 'The Werkleute'.

Paul Mendes-Flohr
is a Professor in the Department of Jewish
Thought at the Hebrew University of
Jerusalem. Amongst his publications are
*Divided Passions. Jewish Intellectuals and the
Experience of Modernity* (Detroit 1991) and
*From Mysticism to Dialogue. Martin Buber's
Transformation of German Social Thought*
(Detroit 1989). He is currently working on
an intellectual and cultural biography of
Franz Rosenzweig.

Martin van Creveld

The Clausewitzian Universe
and the Law of War

The Clausewitzian Universe, in which we live, is named after the Prussian officer and writer Carl von Clausewitz.[1] As a youth he took part in the campaign of 1793 and later studied at the Berlin War Academy. He went through the disastrous Jena Campaign of 1806, was captured, and upon his release entered the General Staff. In 1812 he joined the so-called German Legion, a body of anti-French officers, and stayed with it throughout the Russian campaign. Re-entering the Prussian service in 1813, he served in the Wars of Liberation. After Waterloo he became director of the *Kriegsakademie* and devoted his leisure to writing. In 1831, he was appointed Chief of Staff to the Prussian army which was deployed in Silesia to observe the Polish rebellion against Russia. Following the death of his superior, General August von Gneisenau, Clausewitz took over. He had only occupied his new position for a few days, however, when there arrived from Berlin another general sent to replace him. Thereupon he too fell ill and died, whether of cholera or heartbreak is not clear.

Clausewitz's writings span a period of almost thirty years. His *magnum opus, Vom Kriege (On War)*, in which he invested some twelve years, was left incomplete and was published posthumously. The book's fame spread slowly at first. However, by the 1860s it had already established itself as a classic and its pre-eminent position was confirmed when Helmut von Moltke called it 'the military work which most influenced my mind'. The work was praised by Engels ('a strange way to philosophize, but, on the matter itself, very good') and read by Marx. During his stay in Zurich, Lenin provided it with perceptive footnotes. Hitler is said to have been able to quote it 'by the yard', and Eisenhower grappled with it during his days at the US Army War College. To this day, it is regarded as the greatest work on war and strategy ever written within Western civilization.[2]

While rivers of ink have been spilt in attempts to interpret and understand *On War*, the work's philosophical essence — as distinct from the numerous operational lessons that it contains — may be summed up very briefly. First, Clausewitz considered war as the continuation of politics — this being perhaps the most famous single sentence of all, familiar even to those who have never read him.[3] Second, as a bold-lettered headline in the first chapter of the first book informs us, it is 'an act of violence carried to its utmost bounds'.[4] Never one to mince his words, Clausewitz used some of the book's most forceful passages to serve emphatic warning against introducing 'moderation' into the 'principle' of war; to him, armed force was subject to no rules except those of its own nature and those of the political purpose for which it was waged. He had no patience with the 'philanthropist' belief that war could (or should) be restrained and waged with a minimum of violence. 'In dangerous things such as war, errors made out of kindness are the worst.'[5] 'Let us hear no more about generals who conquer without bloodshed.'

Consistent with this view, Clausewitz held that the law of war consisted of 'self-imposed restraints, hardly worth mentioning'.[6] If civilized nations no longer exterminated each other in the manner of savages (those were the days before Auschwitz), this was not because of any change in the nature of war but because they had found more effective means of fighting.[7] Thus, *Vom Kriege* dismisses the entire body of international law and custom in a single irreverent sentence. In this it set an example which has been followed by subsequent 'strategic' literature down to the present day, even to the point where works on the law of war are usually stored in some separate, slightly out of the way, library.

The purpose of the present essay is to argue that such an exclusively 'instrumental' view is not correct. War, far from being the province of pure unbridled force, is a cultural activity and has always been subject to limitations pertaining to prisoners, non-combatants, and weapons, *inter alia*. The following first three sections will review some of these limitations, whereas the fourth and final one will discuss the reasons they are needed and the light that they shed on the nature of war.

To understand how wrong Clausewitz's dismissal of international law and custom really is, consider his own fate when captured.[8] Together with Prince August of Prussia, whom he was serving as ADC, he was taken to Berlin where the Prince was interviewed by

Napoleon. The meeting over, the two young noblemen gave their word of honour to abstain from further participation in the war and were sent home. A month later they were ordered to proceed to internment in France. Their journey was leisurely enough for Clausewitz to visit Goethe in Weimar. In France they spent time first in Nancy, then in Soissons, and finally in Paris. Though the authorities kept an eye on them, they moved about freely and frequented the best social circles. The sojourn ended after ten months when, following the Treaty of Tilsit, they were allowed to go home.

Clausewitz, at that time, was a captain. Had he been captured in some modern conflict — say, in Italy or France during the second world war — his fate would have been quite different. He would have been taken to an interrogation centre, possibly after being deliberately starved and roughly handled for a day or two. International law would have required him to disclose his name, rank, serial number and blood type, no more. Nevertheless, had he impressed the interrogators as one in possession of important information they would have tried to wrest it out of him. This phase over, he would have been sent away and locked behind barbed wire in a prisoner of war camp. He would not have been asked to give his word that he would not try to escape: on the contrary, as an officer and a gentleman it would have been his *duty* to try. So long as he did not take up weapons or kill a guard, even repeated attempts to escape would not have constituted an offence and would not have been supposed to be punished.[9]

In practice, German prisoners in Allied camps were reasonably, though by no means luxuriously, looked after. Allied prisoners in German hands generally received similar treatment. In Russia, however, the Germans shot Red Army Commissars out of hand. Other prisoners who survived the subsequent death-marches were herded into the usual camps where hundreds of thousands were deliberately starved and frozen to death.[10] The Soviets also ill-treated German prisoners, but not as much as the Germans had mistreated them; normally it was only captured SS who were killed. Allied personnel in Japanese hands suffered atrociously. Apparently their treatment did not result from systematic brutality ordered by the top, but merely reflected the normal way in which Japanese commanders slapped and kicked their own subordinates. Finally, Japanese servicemen were told that the Allies took no prisoners and often preferred suicide to captivity; Japanese troops who *were* taken prisoner, however, generally received decent treatment.[11]

Had Clausewitz been captured four decades earlier, i.e. during the Seven Years War, his fate would also have been different. Very likely he would still have been well treated, even invited to wine and dine with his opposite numbers.[12] Having promised not to escape, a captive officer would have been free to move about, even contact his friends and relatives on the other side. However, his final release would have had to wait until after the payment of a ransom. The sum involved depended on rank. In Clausewitz's case it might have amounted to a few thousand French *livres*, say up to three years' income for one of his station in life. It was a sign of the growing professionalization of armies that, towards 1789, the question of ransom ceased to concern individuals. Instead it was taken over by governments which negotiated with the enemy, fixed prices, and settled accounts.[13] Had Clausewitz been captured during the War of the Spanish Succession (1701–14), however, the ransom would have had to come out of his own pocket. Nor would he have been reimbursed except, perhaps, by throwing himself on the King's mercy and pleading 'difficult circumstances'.[14]

Looking further back to the early modern period and the late Middle Ages, armies *qua* armies did not take prisoners at all; this was done only by individual soldiers who might or might not grant quarter when asked. Once their surrender had been accepted, the prisoners' persons and property belonged to their captors. A prisoner considered sufficiently important (and rich) might find himself well housed and well looked after; he might be invited to wine and dine at his captor's table where an exchange of elaborate compliments would also take place.[15] At the other end of the scale, captives might be harshly treated, both as a punishment for transgressions committed and in order to make them pay up quickly. Regarded as private property, it was not rare for the 'catch' to become the subject of disputes among different would-be captors. The natural authority to settle such disputes was the commander who, in this way, was able to demand and receive one-third of all ransoms.[16]

Medieval *Livres de chevalerie* and early modern treatises on international law agreed that noble prisoners — the only kind considered worth bothering with — should not be mistreated without cause. Some thought captors were within their rights to apply pressure to captives in order to force them to pay, others not. Scholars debated whether a prisoner might be, to quote Honore Bonet, 'held in a high tower', put in chains, or otherwise constrained.[17] Prisoners caught trying to escape were regarded as having broken their word, though there was no unanimity on the kind of penalty involved. Until about 1450, prisoners who made good their escape might have their arms displayed in reverse, a grievous insult. The act of asking and granting quarter was supposed to establish a treaty akin to an ordinary IOU. Regarded as an investment, prisoners could be sold, bartered or otherwise transferred by one captor to another without their respective rights and duties being affected. Just as today we have the white flag, so the medieval chivalric code had certain widely recognized verbal formulae and signals by which intent to surrender could be conveyed.[18]

The ideas of previous ages concerning prisoners other than officers also differed from our own. Whereas modern international law makes few distinctions between the two categories, pre-democratic societies treated them as if they belonged to two different races. The eighteenth century took the view that uncommissioned personnel had no honour and, accordingly, could not be put on parole. They would be held in the cellars of a fortress and rented out as hired labour if the opportunity presented itself. Thus they were in no position to make arrangements for paying their own ransom; nor was it possible to extract very much from men who were, in the Duke of Wellington's famous phrase, 'the scum of the earth, enlisted for drink'. During the War of the Austrian Succession, a common soldier's ransom was fixed at 4 *livres* as opposed to 250,000 for a *maréchal de France*.[19] Apparently even that sum was paid not by the soldier but, following the general settling of accounts, by the state.

In a period when sieges were more numerous than battles, a soldier's fate might depend on the circumstances under which the surrender had taken place. Particularly during the early eighteenth century, sieges rarely had to be pushed to a bloody conclusion. Vauban, Coehorn, and their colleagues had so perfected siege-warfare that it became a question of scientifically applying cannon to walls. Granted sound logistics, this left little doubt about the outcome, attackers and defenders alike being able to forecast the length of time an operation would last with considerable precision. It became normal practice for the two sides to agree that, if no 'succour' arrived within a given time, the garrison would surrender. The surrender-instrument took the form of a legal document. While terms varied, very often the defending commander undertook to deliver fortress, equipment and stores intact. In return, he and his army were allowed to evacuate the fortress and proceed where they wished. Sometimes they gave their word not to fight again, sometimes not.[20]

The agreement having been signed, a *belle capitulation* was arranged. A mixed party of officers was sent to verify the contents of the fortress's storerooms. The two sides might join forces to enlarge the breach in the wall so as to enable the ceremony to take place in some splendour;[21] often an artist was commissioned to paint the occasion. As the garrison came marching out, drums beating and banners flying, the victors formed a guard of honour. To sweeten the pill, officers were usually allowed to retain their personal effects such as arms, horses, carriages, servants and mistresses. Such arrangements saved the besieged force for fighting another day, or at any rate obviated the need for paying ransom; hence they normally received the blessing of governments. There is even a case on record when Louis XIV threatened to cashier an officer because, alone in his garrison, he 'presumptuously' refused to surrender.[22]

Another factor which shaped attitudes to prisoners was the cosmopolitan character of warfare. Early modern governments down to the eighteenth century gladly employed foreigners in their armed services. Many armies contained entire units consisting of non-nationals. Some were volunteers, but troops might also be sold or rented out *en bloc* by their princes, as happened to the Hessians who did much of Britain's fighting during the War of the American Revolution. When such soldiers and such formations were taken prisoner they were sometimes made to change sides. In 1756, Frederick II impressed an entire Saxon army, promising a bounty to those who joined more or less voluntarily, and making liberal use of the knout to persuade those who did not.[23] This particular case owes its fame to the fact that it was among the last. However, between about 1500 and 1650 it had been standard practice, exciting scant comment.

Still, even during this period there were exceptions. If the war was considered a rebellion, or if religious ideas were at stake, the treatment that prisoners could expect was very different. The Thirty Years War in Germany became notorious for the number of massacres. Often, as in the case of Magdeburg in 1631, they were the handiwork of a blood-crazed soldiery acting in defiance of the commander's wishes. No such explanation can be found for that famous Spanish commander, Fernando Alvarez de Toledo. Campaigning in the Netherlands between 1567 and 1574, he developed the nasty habit of tying the members of defeated garrisons back to back and throwing them into the fortress moat. At the battle of Agincourt (1415), Henry V of England ordered his followers to massacre their prisoners, which order was obeyed with some reluctance because it meant that ransom would be forfeit. The incident caused much bad publicity, and had to be justified by the claim that the French were putting their captors in danger by trying to escape *en masse*.[24]

Whatever the outcome in individual cases, the outstanding fact was that, contrary to the situation today, there was no universal rule obliging the victors to grant quarter if that was asked. Certainly the medieval chivalric code frowned on knights who did not accept an opponent's surrender. However, even in this case the defeated did not have an absolute *right* to be spared. Then as later, he who killed an opponent under such circumstances acquired a sinister reputation. Such a reputation might have its uses in battle, but it also exposed him to similar treatment if his fortune deserted him. Unless the dead opponent happened to be some particularly great baron and thus liable to pay a large ransom, the killer had no fear of being formally reprimanded, let alone brought to justice. As late as the early seventeenth century, wrote Hugo Grotius, it was all that the ordinary members of a defeated force could do to appeal to Christian mercy. We shall soon see that the same applied to people who did not form part of an armed force, but were nevertheless so unfortunate as to be captured. Sometimes the appeal worked, sometimes not. Very often whether it did work depended on whether the side asking for quarter looked as if he was able to pay.

The fate of POWs before 1350 will not be discussed here. This is not because war in those periods was not subject to rules, nor does it mean that those rules were more — or less — important than our own. The point is that the rules exist. To understand their importance, one only needs to watch them change. Today, most people would be outraged by a system that discriminated between individual prisoners of war on the basis of their ability to respond to blackmail. Conversely, our ancestors from about 1650 to 1800 would resent and ridicule the modern system which, unwilling to recognize honour, causes captives to be housed, clothed and fed at their captors' expense. None of this is to deny that the rules of war, those concerning prisoners as well as others, are frequently violated. But they do exist, and once we give up a narrow, contemporary point of view, their role in defining what war is all about turns out to be very great.

What is more, the further back into history we go, the greater the problems of terminology and classification. Our present-day legal distinctions between officers and non-commissioned personnel, soldiers and civilians, combatants and non-combatants, break down.

Not even the category of 'wounded' holds up; though people were always injured in battle, 'the wounded' as a distinct legal category dates back no further than the eighteenth century. Before about 1350, so different were historical circumstances that the modern term 'prisoner' itself does more harm than good. It is therefore proposed to break off the discussion at this point, and devote the next section to the treatment of non-combatants.

Except when war is waged in a desert, non-combatants, also known as civilians or 'the people', constitute the great majority of those affected. Today, the distinction between them and combatants is considered vital; even to the point that we reserve the appellation 'war' for those in which it is observed, whereas the rest are called by other names such as 'insurgency', 'low intensity conflict', 'guerrilla warfare', or 'terrorism'. Therefore, it is all the more remarkable that during much if not most of history such distinctions did not exist.

Take the case of tribal societies of the hunting–gathering and gardening types. Most such societies are organized by sex and age. The fundamental distinction is between males and females. Females do not play an active part in war; their role is to encourage the warriors, participate in the celebration of victory, or be victimized in the case of defeat. Typically the males are divided into children, adolescents, warriors and old men. The name, warriors, speaks for itself. While most tribes include a handful of males, such as the shaman, who do not actually fight, by and large to be a warrior, in other words an adult male, is synonymous with membership.

Tribal warfare usually took one of two forms, the ambush or the raid.[25] Of these the latter was the more lethal and sometimes led to the destruction of entire villages. Whatever the exact tactics used, the role of enemy males was to be killed, either on the spot or later on as part of some cannibalistic rite. Women and young children were normally captured. In the absence of 'government' in our sense of the word, let alone an organized state, captives belonged to individual warriors. Their normal fate was to be adopted into the victorious tribe which treated children as children and women as women. Since institutionalized slavery was unknown, troublemakers aside, after a generation or two captors and captives could no longer be distinguished.[26]

A transitional phase between tribal and 'civilized' society is found in the Book of Deuteronomy. It was ordained that the sons of Israel might come unto captured women and take them for their wives.

They were, however, required to allow the fair captives one month of mourning for their dead relatives. Women who failed to please were to be freed; it was expressly forbidden to sell them or to treat them harshly.[27] The fate of the Trojan women was similar, except that this time there was no Pentateuch to prescribe either the time that sex had to wait or the treatment they should receive after it had taken place. The men of Troy were killed, their children either killed or enslaved. The captives were taken back to Achaea. There such of them as were found suitable performed menial tasks in their master's household as well as sharing his bed when required.[28] However, Achaean society differed from the Biblical one in that it was already monogamous. Hence there was usually no question of marrying captive women. Those heroes who did so — Agamemnon and Achilles' son, Neoptolemus — paid the penalty and were murdered by their original wives.

Modern scholarship regards the time when the Biblical injunctions were composed as roughly contemporary with the Trojan War, placing both in the last third of the second millenium BC. For 3,000 years after that, armed conflict continued to fall naturally into field warfare on the one hand and siege-operations on the other. The division, one of the most persistent in all military history, even survived the gunpowder revolution by several centuries: it held true regardless of whether the heaviest weapons in use were spears, catapults, or cannons. Seen from our special point of view, the outstanding fact about field warfare was that it consisted of tournaments between armies, whatever their organization or the tactics that they used. The rule was that, when a battle took place in the 'open' field, non-combatants were nowhere to be found.

An army around 1200 BC, like its successor in AD 1648, would encounter non-combatants principally in the course of marches or else during foraging operations. Their treatment varied from case to case and also depended on the prevailing social institutions. Operating in friendly or neutral territory, the troops might be ordered to pay for what they took. Sometimes this also applied in enemy territory, but such cases were very rare until the second half of the seventeenth century. Most armies on campaign acted like swarms of locusts, eating all that could be eaten and setting fire to the rest. Members of the population who looked as if they were able to pay were put to ransom or else tortured to reveal their treasure's whereabouts. Where slavery existed, they would be rounded up and sold. Thus, throughout the period, the least that the inhabitants could expect was to be relieved of their possessions. If they tried to resist, and frequently even if they did not, they would be enslaved or killed.

To escape the fate just described, people threatened by invasion took refuge in fortified cities or castles. Hence, when a fortress was captured, large numbers of non-combatants of both sexes and all ages were usually found within its walls. From the days of Greece right down to the Thirty Years War, Xenophon's dictum that 'the losers' life and their property belong to the victors' held good. True, the attackers often entered into negotiations with the defenders, agreeing to spare their lives and (sometimes) their property in return for a speedy capitulation. Even Tamerlane, whose march of conquest was marked by pyramids built out of human skulls, preferred to offer a city terms before engaging in the tedious business of a formal siege. The longer and the more difficult the siege, however, the more likely it was that the troops would wreak vengeance in an orgy of murder, plunder and rape.

Faced by an imminent sack, the position of commanders was ambiguous. A sack might damage their reputation in the face of history, particularly if the place in question was sacred or otherwise famous. Also, it meant that control over the army would be temporarily lost and that much valuable property would be destroyed. Hence many commanders tried to prevent it from taking place, sometimes successfully and sometimes not. In AD 69, Titus did his best to prevent Jerusalem from being sacked, or so Josephus claims.[29] In early modern Europe commanders sometimes paid their troops 'storm money' instead of letting them run amok, the idea being both to prevent disorder and permit organized spoliation. But there were also many cases when commanders made deliberate use of the sack, either to terrorize other cities which might refuse to surrender or else as a reward to their own troops. For example, in 146 BC the Romans sacked and utterly destroyed the city of Corinth. The Crusaders sacked Jerusalem in 1099. Charles V sacked Rome in 1527, the Duke of Alba Naarden in 1571; and so on until the end of the Thirty Years War.

Thus, our modern ideas concerning the difference between combatants and non-combatants only date back to the second half of the seventeenth century. It was in this period that war began to be looked on as the business of states acting through their chosen instruments, i.e. armies. Armies were increasingly defined as separate legal entities which, alone among all the organs of the state, were entitled to wage war. Under modern international law, first codified by Vattel around

1750, people who are not members of armed forces or accountable to an established authority are not supposed to take up arms, fight, or resist in any way. In return, their persons are not supposed to be violated by an invading army. Now this is not to say that today's international law does not permit civilian property to be destroyed or taken away. However, such things are supposed to take place only so long as active operations last, and then only to the extent that 'military necessity' demands.

It is also in keeping with eighteenth-century ideas that the end of hostilities no longer signifies the onset of unlimited license. On the contrary, modern international law treats the inhabitants of occupied territories almost as if they were children temporarily deprived of their political rights and, therefore, all the more in need of care. Public property, but not that of private individuals, may be occupied by the occupiers. Existing law is supposed to remain in force, subject only to such modifications as are needed to ensure public security, read that of the invaders. The latter are supposed to allow the population to lead 'normal' lives. They must institute a government, either military or civilian, whose task is to look after its welfare until peace comes. They are permitted to levy taxes for covering the expenses of the occupation; but they may not forcibly appropriate economic resources, deport manpower, strip away artistic treasures, etc.

The international conventions which embody these ideas mostly date back to the age of 'civilized' warfare between 1859 and 1937. Though both the Franco-Prussian War and the first world war saw them violated on some scale, at least the principles behind them were widely recognized. However, the second world war caused the distinction between combatants and non-combatants to break down in two principal ways. First, 'strategic' bombing destroyed men, women and children — to say nothing of religious and artistic treasures of every sort — indiscriminately. Second, and historically perhaps more important, there was the tendency of occupied peoples in many countries to take up arms again after their governments had surrendered. The Germans, to their credit, usually treated de Gaulle's Free French *as if* they were *bona fide* soldiers serving a legitimate government. The same line was not followed when it came to the resistance movements in various countries, whose members were tracked down, imprisoned, tortured and executed.

The nazis regarded 'unlicensed' attacks on their soldiers by civilians who did not wear a distinguishing mark and did not carry arms openly as murder. From the standpoint of international law as it then stood, they were right. Partly because the absurdity of such a position came to be widely recognized after the war, partly because of the sheer number of 'national liberation' struggles since 1945, international law is slowly being amended. In 1977, a meeting assembled in Geneva decided that 'freedom fighters' would also be granted combatants' rights.[30] Seen from the point of view of humanity at large, this may not have been as positive a development as appears on first sight. First, the new order is easy to evade since each government insists that, whatever the situation elsewhere, their homegrown variety are not freedom fighters but bandits, assassins, terrorists or whatever. Second and possibly more important, if terrorists are entitled to be treated as combatants then combatants may also be treated as terrorists. All in all, it is difficult to see who has benefited from the change, except of course the terrorists themselves.

The rules of war as they exist today are far from perfect, nor can one deny that they are being violated every day. Still, at least they no longer grant the victors automatic access to the losers' persons and property, let alone to their womenfolk. In the second world war, more American servicemen were executed for rape than for any other crime, particularly if they were black and particularly if the victim ended up dead as well as violated.[31] By contrast, the Israelis in the occupied territories may have killed large numbers of Palestinians, but to this day not even Jordan TV has reported a single case of rape. Had these facts been reported to our ancestors, surely they would have wondered why Americans, Germans and Israelis were fighting at all, given that they were not even permitted to indulge their lusts. Thus, it is crystal clear that the distinction between combatants and non-combatants, far from being negligible and irrelevant to the practical business of conducting modern war, defines what that war is all about. This becomes even more evident when we discuss the limitations surrounding another field, namely that of weapons.

In the field of weapons, too, war has always been limited by rules. Had Clausewitz's view of armed conflict as a question of employing whatever force is necessary in order to achieve one's ends been right, then there should have been no such limitations; in fact, however, they exist in every civilization that has known war, including our own.[32]

The list of weapons which have been declared 'unfair' starts in the ancient world. An early example is associated with Paris, the man who abducted Queen Helen. A better lover than a warrior, Paris's preferred weapon was the bow, and he is consequently called names such as 'coward', 'weakling' and 'woman'.[33] Similarly among the two sons of Telamon, Ajax and Teukros, the former fights with the spear and counts as a great hero. The latter is an archer who, though quite effective on the battlefield, shelters behind his larger comrade's shield 'like a child in his mother's dress'. Nor was contempt for the bow limited to the epics. According to Plutarch, Lycurgus forbade the Spartans from using the bow to make them brave.[34]

Greek religion being anthropomorphic, similar distinctions prevailed on Olympus. Eurypides in *Heracles Lost* accuses the hero of cowardice, saying that he prefers shooting from afar to fighting, man to man, in the front row and exposing himself to the gash of the spear.[35] The sea-god Poseidon, whose characteristic weapon was the trident, was much stronger and more manly a figure than Apollo of the silver bow. Goddesses, too, were classified by their weapons. The strongest was Pallas Athene who wore armour and whose weapon was the spear. Her father's favourite, she was much stronger than her sisters, the hunting-goddess Artemis and the love-goddess Aphrodite, both of whom used the bow.[36]

Since missile weapons enabled the weak to wound and kill the strong, they did not constitute a proper test of manhood; whereas the Persians expressed their ideal of virility by saying that a man should ride a horse, shoot the bow and speak the truth, the Western military tradition regarded the bow as sneaky. Though suited for sport and hunting, in war its use could be justified only by the force of circumstances. How persistent such traditions could be is evident from the fact that, throughout antiquity, long-range devices such as bow and sling were considered the poor man's weapons.[37] No self-respecting hoplite or legionary would use them. Units of bowmen and slingers, often even javelin-men, typically consisted of men drawn either from the lowest social classes or from foreign, semi-civilized peoples. In the Roman army such units and such men never even attained proper military status. Though tactically quite important, they were called *auxilia* and made to serve for a longer period, and for less pay, than legionaries.[38]

During the Middle Ages, the bow's fortunes became dependent on geography. The Byzantines, many of whose forces consisted of mercenaries originating in the Russian steppes, adopted the latter's method of fighting on horseback and using long-distance weapons. In the West, the Franks preferred to fight hand to hand using spears, swords and axes. Later, when they took to horse and became knights, they still fought hand to hand. The bow remained a second-class weapon. The *Chanson de Roland* derides the Moslems for refusing to fight at close quarters and relying on missiles instead.[39] The Second Lateran Council in 1139 sought to impose a ban on the crossbow, which was considered too cruel — read, too effective — a weapon for use against Christians.[40] The best way to understand the ban is, however, to examine the social position of the bow. Edward I, Edward III and Henry V — to say nothing of William the Conqueror — owed their victories largely to it. Nevertheless, these monarchs themselves did not use it, nor did other noblemen train with it for any but sporting purposes.[41]

Another indication of the bow's inferior position is its role in games and amusements. Already in the *Iliad* shooting with the bow is the last, and least, among the contests organized by Achilles in honour of the dead Patroclus.[42] Similarly in the tournament, that showpiece *par excellence* of medieval chivalry, the bow's position was ambiguous. Its use in combat of knight against knight was prohibited.[43] True, the days set aside for a tournament often also witnessed competitions in archery. Just as the pause in modern soccer games is sometimes filled by dancing girls, so the function of the bow in the tournament was to fill gaps in the programme or else bring it to an end. Those who competed with the bow were not knights, nor does the record tell us that noble ladies awarded the prizes. Ladies did, however, sometimes use the crossbow for target-practice or hunting; another indication of its problematic nature as a first-class weapon of war.

The story of the early firearms which, by enabling a commoner to kill a knight from afar, threatened the continued existence of the medieval world, is well known. Originating in the fourteenth century, firearms took two centuries to become really respectable. In Mamluk Egypt and Samurai Japan they were regarded as incompatible with the social status of the ruling groups and banned.[44] In Europe, too, they were resisted: Ariosto,[45] Cervantes,[46] Shakespeare[47] and Milton are but four out of a long list of famous names who described them as Satan's special creation. Like the bow, firearms were originally considered low-status weapons, although in this case those who specialized in them were perhaps more akin to technicians or magicians than to mere peasants. These factors explain why those who used firearms in war were sometimes punished. The fifteenth-century Italian *condottiere* Gian Paolo Vitelli blinded and cut off the hands of captured arquebusiers; whereas his near-contemporary

Bayard — the *chevalier sans peur et sans reproche* — had them executed.[48]

The ease with which firearms killed from a distance was not the only reason for disliking them. Early firearms were almost impossible to use on horseback. In Europe, as well as among the Egyptian Mamluks, they threatened to bring to an end an entire social order which for centuries had divided humanity into those who did and did not ride. Firearms were also messy, dirty and dangerous. Firing a weapon was a complicated operation which always fouled the firer and sometimes ended with an explosion in front of his face. Whatever the reason, the prejudice against firearms persisted, in some respects, into the nineteenth century and beyond. Even during the last years before 1914, the European nobility typically preferred the cavalry to any other arm, one reason being that its principal weapon continued to be cold steel.

One very important reason for disliking a weapon was, of course, because it was new. The greater its effectiveness, the more it threatened to upset traditional ideas as to how war should be waged and, indeed, what it was all about. This explains why 'unfair' weapons often appear during periods of rapid technological progress; in modern times, one such period opened around 1850 and ended in 1914. Breechloaders were followed by rifles, repeating guns, and machine-guns firing smokeless powder and spitting out death at 600 rounds a minute. Artillery, too, was revolutionized. Muzzle-loaders with a range of perhaps a mile, scarcely changed for three centuries, turned into breechloading rifled steel monsters weighing up to a hundred tons. By 1914 the largest guns, mounted aboard ship or else on rails, could put one shell a minute, each close to a ton in weight, on a target over fifteen miles away. Their introduction was accompanied by that of ancillary devices, such as the railway and the telegraph, whose origin was not military but whose impact on war was soon felt. The steamship, the submarine, the balloon, dynamite and barbed wire conclude the list, even if we only include the most important devices.[49]

As the new devices multiplied, it was feared lest they would transform war into something new, monstrous and unprecedented. Hence many attempts were made to regulate the new weapons, starting in St Petersburg in 1868 and ending in the Hague in 1907.[50] The key problem was to define what did, and did not, constitute war; for which purpose 'fair' means had to be separated from 'dastardly' ones and measures constituting 'military necessity' from those which would merely cause 'unnecessary suffering'.[51] Since each delegation had its own ideas on these subjects the results were, seen in retrospect, meagre enough. It was agreed to ban explosive projectiles weighing less than 400 grams. It was further agreed that explosives should not be dropped from balloons. Finally, it was agreed that submarines would not use their torpedoes to sink unarmed merchantmen without first warning the crew and allowing them to take to their boats. All three prohibitions were later violated. Nevertheless, the debates which brought them into existence, as well as the rules themselves, provide one very good insight into the contemporary understanding of war.[52]

Another weapon banned at St Petersburg, destined to become more controversial than any other, was gas. Now asphyxiating agents — i.e. smoke — had been used in war since time immemorial without being considered in any way special. Since effectiveness depended on concentration, their use was usually associated with the constricted spaces characteristic of siege warfare, particularly mining and countermining operations. As the nineteenth century witnessed the rise of the modern chemical industry, the nature of the problem changed. Poison gas, which previously could be synthesized only in the laboratory, could now be manufactured in whatever quantity needed to turn it into an effective weapon.[53] Just as today there is sometimes talk of unleashing 'weather warfare' and artificial earthquakes, so a century ago the looming possibilities of chemical warfare frightened the military almost out of their wits. It was therefore agreed that it should be banned, and for close to fifty years the ban was observed.

Those who formulated the conventions were thinking in terms of open warfare of the Napoleonic kind. In 1915, faced with the unprecedented situation of stationary trench warfare, the prevailing ideas changed. The Germans were the first to move, but the fact that they were vehemently denounced on all sides did not prevent others from resorting to gas as well. The war was not yet a year old when both sides raced each other to produce more poisonous chemicals and better protective masks. Even the suspected presence of gas forced men to put on protective gear, immobilizing them and turning them into half-soldiers (conversely, the fact that it did not allow them free play as soldiers was one reason why men disliked gas). It was very effective, particularly when used in combination with high explosive. Though a man going blind or drowning in his own fluids even as he coughed his lungs out constituted an appalling sight, paradoxically gas was a relatively humane weapon. This was because, compared to others, a much lower proportion of those who became casualties died.[54]

The interwar period saw gas employed by the Italians in Abyssinia, and possibly also by the British putting down the rebellions of remote Indian villages. In 1937, with the second world war already looming over the horizon, the ban against its employment was formally reaffirmed. During the war itself both sides produced and stored gas on a massive scale. Their arsenals included not just the former, comparatively primitive, asphyxiating and blistering agents but novel, far more lethal compounds aimed at paralysing the central nervous system. The pros and cons of gas were debated in every country. In the end, perhaps the decisive factor why chemical weapons were not employed was that they are ill-adapted to motorized, mobile warfare. To use gas against a well-defined line of fortified positions is one thing; to drench entire provinces and even countries with it, another.

Today many countries produce and store chemical weapons.[55] Partly because their employment is difficult to verify, however, reliable reports of their use have been comparatively few and far between. During the 1960s, the Egyptians used gas in Yemen. Two decades later their example was followed by the Iraqis who used the weapon first against the Iranians and then against their own Kurdish fellow-citizens. The Americans in Vietnam resorted to defoliating agents to deprive the Viet Cong of cover and also employed chemicals to destroy rice-crops in areas considered to be 'infested' by the enemy; whether this amounted to chemical warfare properly speaking is debatable. The CIA has accused the Chinese and Soviets of using gas in Cambodia and Afghanistan respectively. A few cases may have gone unreported, yet, considering the number of conflicts which have taken place since 1945, the total number is small.

A logical reason for this reluctance is hard to find. Already in the first world war, fear of retaliation did not deter the belligerents from resorting to gas — the Germans in particular ought to have been worried, given that the winds blew mostly from west to east. Nor did developed countries waging Low Intensity Conflicts in faraway colonies have to fear retaliation, given that most guerrillas could not produce chemical weapons even if they had wanted to. Perhaps the best explanation is cultural. While tearing people to pieces by artillery or burning them by napalm is regarded as acceptable, we generally do not like to watch them choking to death. As often happens when imagination has to substitute for reality, dislike may become self-reinforcing. Considered horrible, a weapon is not used. Left unused for any length of time, the horror with which it is regarded tends to grow. Unfortunately, time can make people forget as well as remember, with the result that the cycle may not last. As the twentieth century comes to an end, apparently the horror with which chemical weapons are regarded in much of the modern world is not unmixed with curiosity.

Thus, the distinction between chemical and other weapons exists solely in our minds. It is a convention like any other, neither more logical nor less. Like other such conventions, whether those that pertain to weapons or to any other factor, it is a historical phenomenon with a clear beginning and, most probably, a clear end. It remains, however, to ask what all this teaches us about the nature of war, the things it is all about.

The preceding sections have provided an outline, however brief, on international law and custom associated with prisoners, non-combatants and weapons. Vast as these problems are, they represent only a fraction of a much larger body of conventions and usages. Since the dawn of history, men, far from discarding all restraint when they went to war, have sought to regulate it and subject it to limitations. Even the earliest historical societies surrounded armed conflict by rules which defined the way it should be declared and terminated.[56] The same societies sought to establish procedures by which the two sides could communicate even as they fought (parleys), ways in which the fighting could be temporarily halted (truces), places that would be exempt from it (sanctuaries), and so on *ad infinitum*.

Modern international law originates in the late Middle Ages, which in turn built on Roman and Canon Law. Like some long-lived reef of coral, it is still growing daily, adding layer to layer even as older ones degenerate and are forgotten. Besides covering the above-mentioned problems, it also rules over numerous other issues. The status of enemy diplomats, of enemy citizens, of enemy property, have been subjected to an enormous body of scholarship as well as numerous international agreements. Other laws cover the rights and duties of neutrals, particularly as regards assistance to belligerents, asylum, internment, right of passage and so on. Some rules attempt to prevent the destruction of churches, libraries, cultural monuments, even entire cities. There are rules protecting the wounded, the medical personnel attending them, and the facilities for treating or transporting them. Others forbid shooting at members of the armed forces who are temporarily defenceless, e.g. pilots parachuting to safety and ships' crews taking to their boats. There are also problems such as the right to carry arms and *ruse de guerre*. Merely to catalogue the rules would require several volumes.

Like any law, that which pertains to war is occasionally, perhaps frequently, broken. The mere fact that the law in question pertains to war, however, does not prove that this happens more often than elsewhere, let alone that the law does not exist or does not matter. To select but a single extreme example, the second world war was as 'total' a conflict as has been fought at any time and place. Still, social *mores* change. Not even Hitler, fighting Stalin, followed the example of the Ottoman Sultan who, declaring war against the Habsburg Empire in 1683, threatened to 'bare the breasts' of any German woman coming his way.[57] Though both Hitler and Stalin could be ruthless to their subordinates, apparently neither tried to assassinate the other. Neither used chemical weapons, though both had plenty in store. Neither was considerate in his treatment of enemy non-combatants, yet no Soviet or German city was sacked in the manner that Wellington sacked Badajoz or the Japanese Nanking. Both sides treated prisoners harshly. Still, the great majority were not executed, as would have been their fate if they had been, for example, Dacian tribesmen falling into the hands of that paradigm of civilization, the Roman Emperor Trajan.

Furthermore, and whatever the atrocities committed on the Eastern Front, in the West the struggle, in so far as it pertained to the regular forces, was tolerably clean. Between shipwrecked sailors, shot-down pilots, prisoners, wounded, hospital ships, medical personnel and so on, the number of those who owed their lives to the fact that the law of war was observed probably ran into several millions. Nor is this the end of the story. If today we can enjoy the splendours of Paris, this is partly because in 1940 the French declared it an open city, a declaration which was understood, accepted and respected by the Germans. Again, when in 1944 Hitler ordered the city burnt down, the local Wehrmacht commander hesitated. In the end he refused, declaring Paris an open city and thus saving one of mankind's great cultural monuments.[58]

The 'strategic' view of war sees law as applying largely to marginal groups of people who are weak or *hors de combat* and therefore deserve protection; or else to 'exceptional' weapons such as gas.

However, nothing could be further from the truth. The law of war does not just appease the conscience of a few tender-hearted people. Its real function is to protect the armed forces themselves. This is because war is the domain of uncertainty and agony. Nothing is more likely than combat to cause rationality to go by the board, nor is anything more conducive to make even the most even-minded behave strangely. The paradox is that war, the most confused and confusing of all human activities, is also one of the most organized. If armed conflict is to be successfully waged, then many trained individuals must co-operate. People cannot co-operate, nor organizations exist, unless they obey a common code of behaviour. This code should match the prevailing cultural climate, be clear to all, and capable of being enforced.

As Plato puts it in the *Laws*,[59] obedience has always held and will always hold pride of place among the military virtues. From ancient Rome on, the best armies have been the best disciplined. Nor is it by accident that military law has always sought to be more strict, and military parlance more terse and precise, than its civilian equivalents. War is only possible if participants are given to understand just whom they are (and are not) allowed to kill, for what ends, under what circumstances, and by what means. A body of men which is not clear in its own mind about these things is not an army but a mob. Though there have always been mobs, usually in front of an effective fighting organization they scattered like chaff before the wind.

The need for the law of war, however, goes even further than this. War consists of killing, deliberately shedding the blood of one's fellow-creatures. Now no society can tolerate the shedding of blood and killing unless they are carefully circumscribed by rules which define what is, and is not, allowed. Always and everywhere, only killing done by certain authorized persons, under certain specified circumstances, and in accordance with certain prescribed rules is saved from blame and is regarded as praiseworthy. Conversely, bloodshed which ignores the rules or transgresses them will attract punishment or, in some societies both past and present, atonement. Different societies at different times and places have differed greatly as to where they draw the line between war and murder; however, the line itself is indispensable. Some deserve to be decorated, others hung. Where the distinction is obliterated, society falls to pieces and war, as opposed to indiscriminate violence, becomes impossible.

The last function of the war convention is to influence the outcome by telling the vanquished when to surrender. If the vast majority of conflicts are not fought to the end — if not every enemy person has to be slaughtered — this is because the rules define what does, and does not, constitute 'victory'. For example, ancient Greek armies could 'lose' a battle in one of two ways. Either one side ran, or else it asked the other for a truce to gather up its dead. Since there were occasions when one side escaped and the other asked for a truce, disputes sometimes arose as to who had 'won' an engagement. In so far as medieval encounters were simple tournaments taking place in the open field, the armies of the day faced similar problems. To remove any doubt, chivalrous custom demanded that the victor occupy the battlefield for three consecutive days, as the Swiss did at Sempach in 1315 and Granson in 1476.[60] Finally, early modern commanders used to celebrate victory by having the troops sing *Te Deum*. As Voltaire says, each did so in his own camp.[61]

Today the war convention is alive and well, continuing to rule over the life and death of tens, possibly hundreds, of thousands. True, physical possession of the battlefield is less important than it used to be. Since Napoleon invented 'strategy' in the sense of using battles to win a campaign, war is no longer simply a question of one wrestler throwing the other out of the ring. From Moltke to Liddell Hart, the goal of strategy has been just the opposite: namely, to outflank the enemy, encircle him, cut him off, deprive him of supplies and make him surrender *without* actually having to fight for the ground on which he stood.[62] From the Austrians at Ulm in 1805 to the Egyptian Third Army at Suez in 1973, the story of modern strategy is always the same. Large formations counted as defeated — and regarded themselves as defeated — as soon as they were surrounded and their lines of communication severed.

Under modern rules, fights to the death usually ensue only when the sides find it impossible to cut each other off and thus score 'victory points'. For example, the first world war on the Western Front was, as contemporary wisdom put it, 'not war'. Conditions were such that one side was unable to outflank — let alone encircle — the other, with the result that for four years they engaged in a battle of attrition and wore each other down half to death. Attacking the USSR in 1941, the Germans operated according to standard *Blitzkrieg* doctrine, penetrating into the enemy's rear and creating vast pockets; however, they soon found that the Russians, unlike the French the previous year, refused to surrender when surrounded and had to be rooted out one by one, thus delaying the campaign and causing it to fail.[63] Finally, one reason why today's armies often fail when fighting guerrillas and terrorists is precisely that such opponents have no bases or lines of communication and cannot be 'cut off'. Either they run, in which case nothing is achieved, or they make a stand — with the result that the ensuing fight is apt to be unusually tough and bloody.

All this leads to the conclusion that, in any particular kind of war, the meaning of 'victory' is decided as much by convention — tacit or explicit — as by physical results. Like any other kind of law, the war convention consists partly of explicit rules and regulations and partly of norms which are rooted in the culture. Like any other kind of law, it represents a more or less porous, more or less flimsy, barrier built upon the shifting sands of reality. As circumstances cause one type of conflict to be replaced by another, the existing convention becomes inadequate and new definitions have to be found.

Nor is it difficult to see what will happen to a force which, for one reason or another, violates the rules. One possible outcome is for the army to turn into a deaf and blind mob, running amok in all directions while inflicting tremendous destruction on the environment and itself. So far removed is such uncontrolled violence from war proper that Greek mythology had two different deities to represent the two. The patroness of orderly, regular war was the virgin goddess Athene. Springing directly from Zeus's brain, she was a powerful warrior. The patron of unrestrained violence was Ares, 'mad, fulminating Ares', to quote Homer, an outcast among gods and men. Athene was a great goddess in whose honour the Parthenon was erected. Ares, a minor deity, had few worshippers and fewer temples. The *Iliad* tells how Ares met Athene in battle and was trounced. Bleeding, he ran from the field, ascended to Olympus and complained to Zeus; from whom, however, he received little sympathy.[64]

While armies which become raging, uncontrollable mobs are not rare, in the long run the more likely outcome is somewhat different. In a situation like Vietnam, where regular forces fight guerrillas and terrorists, the distinction between combatants and non-combatants will probably break down. Unable to go by the ordinary war convention as expressed in the 'rules of engagement', all but the most disciplined troops will find themselves violating those rules. Having killed, by the force of circumstances, non-combatants and tortured prisoners, they will go in fear of the consequences if caught. If caught, they are certain to blame their commanders for putting them into a situation where they are damned if they do and damned if they do not. The commanders, in turn, will wash their hands of the whole affair. There will be atrocities, as at My Lai, and attempts to cover them up.

Where the cover-up fails, a few low-ranking members of the military establishment may be turned into scapegoats, enabling their superiors to deny responsibility. As the men cease to trust each other, their commanders and their subordinates, disintegration sets in until, as in Vietnam, tens of thousands went AWOL and an estimated 30 per cent of the forces were on hard drugs. Soon they will cease to fight, each man seeking only to save his conscience and his ass.[65]

Without a law to define what is and is not permitted, there can be no war. Though written international law is comparatively recent, previous ages were no less dependent on the war convention for their ability to fight. Nor does the absence of a formal written code necessarily mean that our ancestors were more (or less) ruthless in their conduct of war than we ourselves. Before there was international law, there were often bilateral treaties between kings. These were preceded by the law of nature, the code of chivalry, the *ius gentium*, Greek religion and custom and, earlier still, by tribal customs and usage. While not all of these codes were laid down in writing, they were supposed to represent reason, God, tradition, even — in the case of primitive tribes — 'reality' itself. In all, they were probably as effective as today's international agreements which, made by man, are also capable of being abrogated by him.

Though the rules of previous ages differed from our own, then as today those who broke them were sometimes brought to justice. Nor was fate necessarily more kind to those, probably the majority, who never stood trial. Western literature as represented by the *Iliad* begins at the point where king Agamemnon was punished by Apollo for violating the law and rejecting the ransom of a young woman whom he had captured.[66] In later Greek mythology, warriors who desecrated temples or committed other excesses were overtaken by nemesis and persecuted by the Erinyes, the monstrous goddesses of revenge. During the Christian Middle Ages, knights who did not respect the rights of monks, nuns and 'innocent people' in general were destined to be hounded by the devil while they lived and carried off to hell after they died.[67]

The fate which the modern world reserves for those who cross the border between war and crime is, in some ways, worse still. Gone are the days when, as in ancient Persia, armies were ceremonially purged of bloodshed by being marched between the two halves of a sacrificial dog. God may still exist, but judging by the frequency of His appearances in the strategic literature He has turned His face away. The breakdown of belief and the absence of religiously sanctioned rites for expiation have made it very difficult for people to come to terms with their transgressions. Visit the Vietnam memorial in Washington DC on any average day and watch the crowd for the effects of repentance and guilt on both combatants and non-combatants who, even after fifteen years, have yet to come to terms with that war.

Notes

1. The best modern biography is P. Paret, *Clausewitz and the State* (Princeton, NJ 1976). See also M. Howard, *Clausewitz* (New York 1983).

2. For quotes comparing Clausewitz to Thucydides, Goethe, Shakespeare, Machiavelli, Bacon, Hobbes, Marx and Adam Smith, see M. van Creveld, 'The Eternal Clausewitz', in M. Handel (ed.), *Clausewitz and Modern Strategy* (London 1986), 49, fn. 1.

3. C. von Clausewitz, *On War* (F.N. Maude [ed.], London 1899), vol. 1, 23.

4. Ibid., 2.

5. Ibid., ibid.

6. Ibid., ibid.

7. Ibid., 3.

8. On this episode see Paret, op. cit., 126ff.

9. Most of the regulations concerning prisoners now in force date from the period between 1874 (the Brussels Conference) and 1907 (the Second Hague Conference). For a short account see G. Best, *Humanity in Warfare* (New York 1980), 154ff.

10. See T.J. Schulte, *The German Army and Nazi Policies in Occupied Russia* (Oxford 1979), 8, and the literature there adduced.

11. On the way both sides treated their prisoners during the Pacific War see J.W. Dower, *War without Mercy, Race and Power in the Pacific War* (New York 1986), 48–52, 60–71.

12. On the principles on which eighteenth-century prisoners of war were supposed to be treated see E. de Vattel, *The Law of Nations* (Philadelphia, PA 1857), 354ff.

13. The last recorded ransom-agreement dates back to 1780 and was signed between England and France.

14. See Ch. de Coynart, *Le Chevalier de Folard* (Paris 1914), 133ff. for an example of the way early eighteenth-century prisoners of war were treated.

15. See, for example, Froissart's account of the treatment of French prisoners by the Black Prince after the Battle of Poitiers in 1356; Froissart, *Chronicles* (Penguin ed., Harmondsworth 1968), 143–4.

16. For a detailed account of the way the prisoners from one campaign were treated by their captors see C. Martin and G. Parker, *The Spanish Armada* (London 1988), 242ff. For a typical late medieval contract regulating the division of booty and ransoms between a commander and his retainers see N. Davis (ed.), *Paston Letters and Papers of the Fifteenth Century* (Oxford 1971 —), vol. 1, 636–8; the contract here reprinted dates back to 1475.

17. H. Bonet, *The Tree of Battles* (Cambridge, MA 1949), part 4, chapter 46.

18. The best modern account of these questions is M. Keene, *The Laws of War in the Late Middle Ages* (London 1965), 25ff., 156–8.

19. See J.G. Hoyers, *Geschichte der Kriegskunst* (Goettingen 1797), vol. II, 2, p. 619. For another such agreement — this one signed between France and Spain in 1674 — H. Delbruck, *History of the Art of War* (Westport, CT 1985), vol. XIV, 236.

20. For a detailed explanation of the rationale behind the system of 'la belle capitulation', see Feuquières, *Memoirs Historical and Military* (Greenwood Press reprint of the 1736 edn., New York 1968), vol. II, 305ff.

21. For example, at Modena in 1706: E.G. Leonard, *L'Armée et ses problèmes au xviiie siècle* (Paris 1958), 31.

22. C.S. de Quincy, *Histoire militaire du règne de Louis le Grand* (Paris 1726), iii, 37.

23. For this episode see C. Duffy, *The Army of Frederick the Great* (London 1974), 168–9.

24. The best modern account of the battle and its ensuing massacre is J. Keegan, *The Face of Battle* (London 1976), 107–12.

25. See, for example, C. Lowman, *Displays of Power, Art and War among the Marings of New Guinea* (New York 1973), 46; B. Malinowski, 'War and Weapons among the Natives of the Trobriand Islands', *Man*, 20, 1920, 10–11; and N.A. Chagnon, 'Yanomamo Social Organization and Warfare' in M. Fried (ed.), *War, the Anthropology of Armed Conflict and Aggression* (Garden City, NJ 1968), 109–59; and W.T. Divale, *Warfare in Primitive Societies* (Santa Barbara, CA 1973), xx–xxii.

26. Much the best modern account of primitive war is J.M. Turney High, *Primitive War, its Practice and Concepts* (Columbia, SC 1971); see in particular pp. 152ff.

27. *Deuteronomy*, chapter 20.

28. For the treatment of prisoners in this period see above all Eurypides, *The Trojan Women* (London 1964), representing a blow-by-blow account.

29. *The Jewish War* (Penguin ed., Harmondsworth 1980), v, 369; vi, 88, 254.

30. See Federal Political Department of Switzerland. *Official Records of the Diplomatic Conference on the Reaffirmation and Development of International Humanitarian Law Applicable in Armed Conflicts, 1974–7* (Bern 1978), 17 vols. For a short summary, Best, op. cit., 300ff.

31. See Historical Brigade, Office of the Judge Advocate General with the US Forces, ETO, 'Statistical Survey — General Courts Martial in the European Theater of Operations', MS 8-3.5 AA, vol. 1, National Archives, Suitland, MD, file 204-58 (87). The table in question is reprinted in M. van Creveld, *Fighting Power, German and US Army Performance 1939–1954* (Westport, CT 1982), 117.

32. For examples as they apply among primitive tribes see M.R. Davie, *The Evolution of War* (Port Washington, NY 1929), 129; also T. Williams, *Fiji and the Fijians* (New York 1977), i, 57. On the whole, the topic of unfair weapons has been neglected by the literature; for a few general remarks see M. van Creveld, *Technology and War* (New York 1989), 70ff.

33. *Iliad* (London, Loeb Classical Library, 1952) xi, lines 386–96.

34. Plutarch, *Lycurgus* (London, Loeb Classical Library, 1934), xix, 4. On at least one occasion in Greek warfare a ban on missiles was arranged; Strabo, *The Geographies* (London, Loeb Classical Library, 1969), x, 1, 12.

35. *Heracles* (G.W. Bond [ed.], Oxford 1981), lines 157–65.

36. In *Iliad* xxi, 481–8, Athene calls Artemis 'a shameless bitch' for precisely this reason.

37. See R. Toelle-Kastenbein, *Pfeil und Bogen im Antiken Griechenland* (Bochum 1980), 51ff.

38. See L. Keppie, *The Making of the Roman Army, from Republic to Empire* (London 1984), 150–2, 182–6.

39. *The Song of Roland* (Penguin ed., Harmondsworth 1959), canto no. 154.

40. See on this episode J.T. Johnson, *The Just War in the Middle Ages* (Princeton, NJ 1981), 128–9.

41. The best general account of this entire question is A.T. Hatto, 'Archery and Chivalry: A Noble Prejudice', *Modern Language Review*, 35 (1940), 40–54.

42. *Iliad*, xxiii, line 850ff.

43. See J.R.V. Barker, *The Tournament in England 1100–1400* (Wolfeboro, NH 1986), chapter 2.

44. D. Ayalon, *Gunpowder and Firearms in the Mamluk Kingdoms* (London 1978), chapter 3.

45. *Orlando Furioso* (J. Hoole trans., London 1783), book I, canto 9.

46. *Don Quixote* (New York 1950), part I, book II, chapter 11.

47. *Henry IV*, I, iii.

48. See J.F.C. Fuller, *Armament and History* (New York 1945), 86. For the entire question, J.R. Hale, 'Gunpowder and the Renaissance', in C.H. Carter (ed.), *From Renaissance to Counterreformation* (London 1966).

49. For a brief account of these advances see B. Brodie, *From Crossbow to H-Bomb* (Bloomington, IN 1973), chapter 6.

50. See Best, op. cit., 159ff. for a short discussion.

51. See L. Friedman (ed.), *The Law of War: a Documentary History* (New York 1972), 192ff.

52. For a contemporary discussion of the entire question of new technologies see T.J. Lawrence, *Principles of International Law* (London 1895), 439–40.

53. For a short history of gas before 1914 see L.F. Haber, *The Poisonous Cloud, Chemical Warfare in World War I* (Oxford 1986), 15ff. This meticulously documented study by the son of the celebrated chemist is the most exhaustive ever done on the subject.

54. Ibid., 283–4. In characterizing gas as a 'failure', however, Haber almost certainly goes too far.

55. For a short, non-technical, survey of the state of the art see J.P. Perry Robinson, 'Recent Developments in the Field of Chemical Warfare' in RUSI (ed.), *Defence Yearbook 1983* (Oxford 1983), 166–84.

56. For example, see the customs associated with the declaration of war among primitive peoples as explained in Turney High, op. cit., 244ff.

57. The declaration is reprinted in C.A. Macarney, *The Habsburg and Hohenzollern Dynasties* (New York 1970), 57–8.

58. See on this episode L. Collins and D. Lapierre, *Is Paris Burning?* (New York 1965).

59. *The Laws* (London, Loeb Classical Library, 1965), xii, 942A.

60. For some other examples when this custom was followed see Ph. Contamine, *War in the Middle Ages* (Oxford 1980), 261.

61. *Candide* (Penguin ed., Harmondsworth 1966), 25.

62. B.H. Liddell Hart, *Strategy* (New York 1967), particularly 338ff.

63. On this episode see M. van Creveld, *Supplying War, Logistics from Wallenstein to Patton* (London 1978), 169.

64. *Iliad*, v, line 826ff.

65. See R.A. Gabriel and P.L. Savage, *Crisis in Command, Mismanagement in the Army* (New York 1978) for a record of the disintegration of the US army; in particular, the tables on p.180ff.

66. *Iliad*, book I.

67. See M. Keen, *Chivalry* (New Haven, CT 1984), 233–5.

Martin van Creveld
is Professor of History at the Hebrew
University, Jerusalem and an expert on
military history. His most recent publication
is *The Transformation of War* (New York
1991).

Richard Breitman

Himmler and the 'Terrible Secret' among the Executioners

In *Why Did the Heavens Not Darken?: The 'Final Solution' in History*,
Arno J. Mayer emphasized the nazi fixation with the destruction of
Soviet communism, a concern which many East Europeans shared.
For Mayer, the Jews represent the exposed wing of a decades-long
'Judeobolshevist' threat to Eastern Europe. In the wake of the nazi
invasion of the USSR, strident nationalists in Latvia, Lithuania,
Byelorussia and the Ukraine used the early moments of 'liberation' to
massacre many thousands of known or suspected Bolsheviks and
Jews, whom they regarded as linked together by the same cause.

Mayer also argued that in Poland, Hungary and Rumania
traditional élites maintained their hold on power by becoming
stridently nationalistic, anti-communist and anti-semitic, with Jews
again serving as the most accessible target after 22 June 1941. In
contrast, Mayer believed that during the early months of Operation
Barbarossa, the German forces merely applauded and encouraged
the widespread assaults against Jews, instigating or masterminding
only a few of them.[1]

Mayer's argument has the virtue of emphasizing the very real links
among nationalism, anti-communism and anti-semitism in Eastern
Europe. At the same time, he misread or ignored substantial evidence
about the subordinate relationship of indigenous Baltic, Byelorussian
and Ukrainian nationalists and activists to German police forces in
the occupied Soviet territories. More important, Mayer failed to
recognize that the SS already had a policy of genocide toward the
Jews during the second half of 1941.

To maintain secrecy, Heinrich Himmler and his key subordinates
generally avoided written orders and certainly dispensed with
detailed blueprints setting out their plans for the Jews. The historian
must reconstruct the chronology of planning the 'Final Solution' of

the Jewish question through less direct sources, such as the testimony of the policemen used as executioners. The primary German executioners in the first wave of the Final Solution were members of mobile police execution units known as *Einsatzkommandos*, Order Police battalions, and select Waffen-SS units which followed the German army into the Soviet territories. Only in the field and shortly before they were to carry out mass executions did these men get some sense of what they were expected to do. Secrecy was necessary not only for security reasons, but also because the massive killings produced some adverse reactions among the executioners themselves.

Some policemen and soldiers suffered qualms of conscience, alcoholism and even nervous breakdowns — a psychic 'inner resistance?' — which have been mentioned in the literature. Raul Hilberg described a tendency for police unit commanders to devise and give specific justifications for carrying out mass executions of Jews — more for themselves than for their superiors — and also mentioned occasional nervous breakdowns and alcoholism among the rank and file.[2] One notable figure in the SS empire — Erich von dem Bach-Zelewski, higher SS and police leader for the central Soviet region — not only observed this problem; he himself later suffered psychological disturbances which the chief SS physician, Ernst Robert Grawitz, diagnosed as resulting from his role in the mass murder of Jews and other difficult experiences in the East.[3]

What is not known is that high SS officials, above all Heinrich Himmler, the archetype of the schoolmaster and organization man, anticipated certain difficulties with the troops used to liquidate Jews, and that he reacted to psychological problems once they occurred. Himmler masked the general policy toward Jews with various measures designed to initiate the killing on a limited basis. Subsequently, he personally explained at least the outlines of policy to some who had to carry out executions, and also passed on suggestions to commanders about how they should help their men cope with the burdens of their task. This story sheds additional light on how orders to eliminate the Jewish race were first concealed, and then unveiled, and on how Himmler sought to manipulate his troops to suppress any feelings of revulsion among those who had to murder men, women and children. It also helps to explain why the nazi forces turned to reliable indigenous volunteers in the occupied Soviet territories to carry the burden of slaughtering Jews.

Well before the campaign in the USSR, Himmler had personally witnessed at least one police liquidation of enemies. According to what his adjutant, Jochen Peiper, told a travel companion, Himmler had actually taken part in an execution of members of the Polish intelligentsia, probably in mid-January 1940; afterwards he supposedly did not speak for several days.[4] In a mid-February 1940 telephone conversation, Himmler's office manager Rudolf Brandt also discussed with another nazi official Himmler's giving a speech to members of an *Einsatzkommando*, and Hanns Johst remembered Himmler telling men serving on the eastern border of the newly conquered territory: 'Remain harsh, but do not become brutal.'[5]

In a secret speech to the Nazi Party *Reichsleiter* and *Gauleiter* at the end of February 1940, Himmler had discussed execution of the enemy leadership 'during' the campaign in Poland. He had noted that others had suggested alternatives to him and warned him that German troops themselves would suffer psychological damage from serving as executioners, but that there was no other way to resolve the problem. He had added that those who presumed to give him advice never actually saw what took place, indicating that he had been there. Himmler had called the scenes hideous and frightful, but had justified the actions on racial-ideological grounds.[6]

If Himmler was well versed in ideological justifications of mass murder, some direct participants were not. The manpower Himmler and Reinhard Heydrich assembled for their liquidation campaign in the USSR included a great many men who were not fanatical nazis. Even in the best known and most 'political' of the execution units, the *Einsatzkommandos* led predominantly by officers from the Security Police and SD, there were many rank-and-file troops from the urban and rural police, the Border Police, and the Waffen-SS.[7] One border policeman later testified that he and his colleagues took a four-month training course at the Border Police school at Pretzsch on the Elbe, where the men for the *Einsatzkommandos* assembled, during which it became clear that they would be used in mobile units in the USSR. The police students received some ideological instruction on the Jewish question: they studied the Nuremberg Laws, and were taught that the Jews must be driven from Europe. But they did not learn that one of their tasks was to execute Jews.[8]

There was probably even less preparation of the Order Police units which moved into the USSR during the summer and autumn of 1941. The German Order Police, under the command of Himmler's old friend Kurt Daluege, consisted of the regular urban police (*Schutz-*

polizei) and rural police (*Gendarmerie*), excluding the political and criminal police. The Order Police also had a nucleus of men with military training, organized into battalions. At least twelve Order Police battalions were assigned, just after the German invasion of the USSR, to the *Kommandostab Reichsführer SS*, in effect a private army under Himmler's direct control used to liquidate perceived nazi enemies.[9] These regular Order Police battalions contained about twice as many men as the roughly 3,000 in the *Einsatzgruppen* and their subdivisions.

Between late 1939 and mid-1941 the Order Police battalions were expanded through the creation of reserve battalions. The officers of the new battalions were experienced order policemen. The rank and file were civilian draftees considered too old for service in the armed forces, which meant that they had received their education and political socialization in the Weimar Republic. Many were not even members of the Nazi Party.[10] The companies of Reserve Police Battalion 9 were distributed to various *Einsatzkommandos*; two other reserve battalions were included in the *Kommandostab Reichsführer SS*; at least one additional reserve battalion went into action in the USSR as a unit and concentrated on the execution of Jews and other perceived enemies.[11]

According to what was called Hitler's Fundamental Order, secret information went only to those who needed to know, who were told only as much as they needed to know, and only when they needed to know it. The commanders of the *Einsatzgruppen, Einsatzkommandos*, and *Sonderkommandos* — many of them professionals and bureaucrats before mid-1941 — had to know a good deal, but only just before the invasion began. Otto Ohlendorf, commander of *Einsatzgruppe* D, later testified that Himmler personally briefed the *Einsatzgruppen* chiefs in early June that an important part of their task was to eliminate Jews — men, women and children — and communist functionaries. There is, however, some question whether Ohlendorf's post-war version was designed to assist his legal strategy.[12]

In any case, multiple sources make it certain that on 17 June 1941 Reinhard Heydrich, chief of the Security Police and SD, briefed the heads of the *Einsatzgruppen, Einsatzkommandos, Sonderkommandos* and a few others, a total of perhaps thirty to fifty men, on the policy of eliminating Jews in the Soviet territories, at least in general terms.[13] One of those present, an SD man named Walter Blume, later testified that Heydrich had told this group that eastern Jewry provided the 'reservoir of intellectuals for Bolshevism', and that the Führer and state leadership held the view that it must be destroyed. According to another account, one of the Gestapo officials present asked: 'We should shoot the Jews?' and Heydrich answered, 'Of course'.[14]

In this instance, as in others, oral instructions to a limited circle of officers usually came first and were more specific than whatever came down in written form. The uncovering and decrypting of orders concerning the Final Solution, therefore, must come not only from surviving documents, but from the accounts of meetings and journeys of Himmler, Heydrich and Daluege, from the statements and orders of officers in the execution units, and from the police activities that followed in their wake.

The heads of the *Einsatzkommandos* gave some advance information to the rank and file about their functions. Just before entering Soviet territory, for example, SS-Standartenführer Paul Blobel, head of *Einsatzkommando* 4a, gave a speech to his men and to one company of Reserve Police Battalion 9 attached to his unit. Blobel told the troops that their task was to cleanse the territory of enemy elements, including potential political enemies. Some men later recalled that Blobel had made it clear that they would have to carry out executions, but that he did not mention the word 'Jews'. Other policemen, however, testified that Blobel had spoken of the task of annihilating Jewry in the Ukraine. The most likely explanation for these discrepancies, supported by the testimony of one Friedrich Puschmann, is that Blobel gave two speeches, the first one general and ambiguous. But when executions of Jews were about to begin in the town of Sokal, Blobel specifically identified the destruction of the Jews as a major priority. Nonetheless, greater discretion was required when writing records. Blobel's instructions to the officer who kept the unit log (*Kriegstagebuch*) were to list the persons killed as communists, partisans, saboteurs, or something along these lines; the word 'Jew' was never to be used without an adjective.[15]

Only Waldemar von Radetzky, head of a *Sonderkommando*, testified that at the start Blobel had told him personally of an order from the Führer for the measures against Jews. Months later, after hundreds of thousands had already been executed, Heydrich told a newly appointed police unit commander that the information about the Führer's order was to go no further than the heads of the *Einsatzkommandos* and *Sonderkommandos*, discretion which seems to have been the practice from the start.[16]

Not every *Einsatzkommando* chief went as far as Blobel. Another company of Reserve Police Battalion 9 was serving under *Einsatz-*

kommando 8a, which moved into Byelorussia. The company commander questioned the orders issued by chief Otto Bradfisch, who claimed superior authority and demanded obedience. Bradfisch informed the company commander that it was necessary to pacify the rear army area by eliminating Soviet commissars, agents and 'those they could catch'. It gradually became clear that the last category meant Jews.[17]

One method to reduce the burden on the German police was to make use of non-Germans to do some of the killing. So one of the earliest tasks of the *Einsatzkommandos* was to incite East European nationalities to carry out pogroms. Franz Walter Stahlecker, chief of *Einsatzgruppe* A which moved into the Baltic states, elaborated on this strategy in an October 1941 report. From the beginning his force was

> determined to solve the Jewish question by any means and with complete resolve. It was desirable, however, that the Jewish question not be raised immediately, as the unusually tough measures would also have created shock in German circles. It had to appear to the outside that the indigenous population itself reacted naturally against the decades of oppression by the Jews and against the terror created by the Communists in recent history, and that the indigenous population carried out these first measures of its own accord. . . . It was the duty of the Security Police [*Einsatzkommandos*] to initiate these self-purging actions and to guide them into the proper channels, so that the goal set for cleaning the area was reached as quickly as possible.[18]

Himmler himself probably dictated this strategy even before Heydrich telegraphed it to the *Einsatzgruppen* on 2 July: the first step was to incite pogroms surreptitiously.[19]

On 25 June in the Lithuanian capital of Kowno (Kaunas), Stahlecker succeeded in contacting the leader of one of the local militias, Klimatis. As a result of the advice the Germans gave him, the latter arranged the first pogrom that night, during which more than 1,500 Jews were killed and several synagogues and some sixty Jewish homes destroyed. Over the next few nights further actions, apparently under the command of a Lithuanian, First Lieutenant Norkus, killed 2,300 Jews, all, as Stahlecker later boasted, 'without any visible indication to the outside world of a German order or of any German suggestion'. (Yet historian Mayer somehow managed to conclude that the Lithuanian forces acted on their own, and that Stahlecker subsequently claimed excessive credit for the actions.)[20]

Since the communists were said to have destroyed the local Latvian establishment, it was not as easy to start a Latvian pogrom,

Stahlecker later explained.[21] Still, after *Einsatzkommando* 1a and part of *Einsatzkommando* 2 entered the Latvian capital, they organized a 400-man Latvian auxiliary police force under Latvian First Lieutenant Weiss. On 3 July the auxiliary police plundered Jewish homes, and two other Latvian groups carried out pogroms, killing some 400 Jews and destroying every synagogue.[22] Stahlecker's men took photographs and even films of the actions in Kowno and Riga, to enable them to prove that Lithuanians and Latvians conducted executions 'spontaneously'.[23]

Pogroms were only credible shortly after the German invasion began. Later, after German forces were in firm control and the existence of civilian and military authorities placed some constraint on the *Einsatzkommandos*, the SS and police could and did make use of select units of native police, former soldiers, and recruits for the defence forces (*Schutzmannschaften*) to carry out executions of Jews secretly or under the guise of anti-partisan activity.[24] But the most striking feature of the pogroms carried out by Eastern Europeans is not the substantial Jewish casualties but the fact that the *Einsatzkommando* officers perceived the results as inadequate.[25] There is also post-war testimony from Bach-Zelewski that Himmler wanted to see more pogroms.

A descendant of impoverished aristocrats, Erich von dem Bach-Zelewski was a long-time soldier. By March 1941 he had learned enough about forthcoming activities in the East to ask for a commission to fight the Russian forces.[26] But Himmler made him higher SS and police leader for central Russia instead, which gave him supreme regional authority over the campaign against racial and political enemies. Several days after the war began, Himmler supposedly summoned Bach-Zelewski to his headquarters and asked why there had been no pogroms in the Bialystok region like those in Latvia and Lithuania. Bach-Zelewski later testified that during his meeting with Himmler, he had not known that the pogroms in the Baltics were German-inspired; he said he had tried to present a historical analysis of popular attitudes toward Jews. Himmler then ordered Bach-Zelewski to execute 2,000 Jews in Bialystok as punishment for looting there, and Bach-Zelewski said that Himmler was present at the executions.[27] This version of events is neither complete nor fully accurate regarding date and substance; it contains dubious exculpatory elements common to war crimes interrogations.[28] Nonetheless, there are now independent, contemporary sources connecting Himmler with Bach-Zelewski and the executions of 'looters' in Bialystok.

On 1 July Order Police Battalion 322, one of the units under the *Kommandostab Reichsführer SS*, raided the Jewish quarter of Bialystok. The police extracted from Jewish and Polish homes twenty truckloads of booty that they assumed had been stolen from shops in the city. The plunder was then stored in the school where the battalion was quartered. In late afternoon Himmler showed up unannounced and unexpected, *in media res*. He inspected the plunder, and that same afternoon SD men and one group of police executed twelve Jews and four Poles who had denied possessing looted goods. That evening Bach-Zelewski hosted a dinner for Himmler. Further police raids and executions in the city followed regularly over the next two and a half weeks, with massive action on 11 July. These shootings were cast in the form of reprisals against Jewish looters.[29]

Another large 'reprisal' came on 1 July in the city of Lemberg (Lvov), where the chief and staff of what was soon to be called *Einsatzgruppe* C had just arrived. The population of this main city in eastern Galicia was a mixture of Poles, Ukrainians, Jews, and ethnic Germans. Commander Dr Otto Rasch informed his men that Jews and some other inhabitants of Lemberg had killed a number of people in the city before the Russian troops retreated. Although this 'crime' did not affect the German forces, that mattered little. The Ukrainians had already created a local militia under a military commandant, which the Germans decided to use. Together with the militia, *Einsatzkommandos* 4a and 6 and a police unit brought in from Cracow rounded up some 3,000 suspects, mostly Jews, in the municipal stadium. The next day Rasch informed the men that he had received an order from Hitler that all those guilty or even suspected of involvement were to be executed. Rasch personally supervised the executions on 2 and 3 July. Moreover, another 5,000 Jews in the city died around the same time as a result of Ukrainian pogroms and police killings on the streets.[30]

It is hard to establish how closely Himmler, Heydrich or Daluege were involved in issuing specific orders for retribution against Jews during the first weeks of the war against the USSR. They clearly were not the only ones responsible; their officers in the field could and did act on their own authority, and even the army made a frequent practice of executing Jews in retaliation for acts of resistance.[31] But the existence of a general policy to murder Jews *tout court* made these specific orders largely redundant.

Besides the need to keep the liquidation policy as secret as possible, the justification of 'reprisal' was designed to enable the rank and file to carry out their duties without suffering any crippling psychological effects. Concern about this psychological dimension emerged in the form of an order first issued in Bialystok by the commander of Police Regiment Centre on 11 July, in the midst of the executions there. Citing an order from Higher SS and Police Leader Bach-Zelewski, the commander required all Jews to be shot, secretly if possible, as plunderers. The battalion and company commanders were to show special concern for the men who carried out these actions, and were to dilute the impressions of the bloody day by holding social gatherings in the evening. The men were also to be continually instructed in the political necessity of these measures. This order has Himmler's trademark all over it.[32]

Authorities such as Bach-Zelewski could and did explain to the officers and troops that Jews were associated not only with looting, but also with acts of resistance and the partisan movement.[33] Orders for mass executions thereby 'became' steps necessary to restore order and provide for security in the rear army areas. But this justification was plausible only with regard to adult Jewish men. A specific order to kill Jewish women and children, however, would have made it plain that the general policy was genocide. So it is not surprising that the expansion of the range of killings to include both sexes and all ages was a particularly sensitive matter that required Himmler's personal attention.

At the end of July, Himmler again went to see Bach-Zelewski in Baranowicze, where the latter had now established his headquarters, with further instructions.[34] Before setting out on his tour, Himmler had ordered two SS cavalry regiments (constituting the SS Cavalry Brigade under the command of Hermann Fegelein, Eva Braun's brother-in-law) to assemble in the Baranowicze area. Such cavalry regiments, Himmler believed, were particularly suited for use in the marshland, where motor vehicles were disadvantaged. Bach-Zelewski was supposed to use them, Himmler ordered, to 'cleanse' the Pripet River region, near the border of Byelorussia and the Ukraine. In the marsh areas, Himmler had concluded, all villages either had to be strongholds for the Germans or for the enemy. Ukrainian villagers or other minorities hostile to the Russians or the Poles might provide friendly bases for German forces, but Poles and Russians were enemies, as were other racially inferior and criminal elements. All people suspected of supporting partisans were to be shot, Himmler had ordered; women and children should be shipped off, food and livestock seized, and the villages burned to the ground.[35]

Himmler's order was a death sentence for all male Jews in the region. His terminology for the treatment of Jewish women and children was more ambiguous, but the policy turned out to be little different. The main reason for the ambiguity — and the reason why Himmler omitted specific mention of Jews in the document — was that he did not wish to commit the most sensitive orders to paper.

After Himmler arrived in Baranowicze, he was willing to be somewhat more specific. The Adjutant of the Second SS Cavalry Regiment radioed to the units in the field Himmler's express (oral) orders: 'All [male] Jews must be shot. Drive Jewish females into the swamps.' Himmler's recourse to the swamps was a means of sparing the police the experience of shooting women and children. Nonetheless, Himmler also entrusted Fegelein to inform his subordinate officers to take it to heart that only 'rigid harshness, severe intervention, and holding fast to the great ideas of the Führer could conquer the Russian empire'. The leadership corps had to 'overcome all small personal and human weaknesses and differences of individual character', and Himmler would be an 'ice-cold' judge of anyone who did not follow orders. On 12 August the SS Cavalry Brigade reported that it had found the swamps too shallow to do the job, and it had had to resort to executions, though it did not have time to finish the murder of Jewish women and children in Pinsk.[36]

Another apparent means of transmission of fundamental orders was Heydrich's arrival in August in Zhitomir for a meeting with *Einsatzkommando* 4a Chief Paul Blobel. Immediately after Heydrich's visit the executions of Jewish women and children, as well as adult male Jews, began. Yet even there the first such execution, carried out by a company of Waffen-SS soldiers, was described as retribution for shots fired by unknown persons at German soldiers. Before leaving Zhitomir, however, *Einsatzkommando* 4a and the Ukrainian militia cleaned out the entire Jewish ghetto. Several thousand men, women and children were shot and buried in a ditch prepared for them outside the city near a forest.[37]

This sequence of meetings, varying orders, and killings in the field allow for more than one interpretation of the pre-war orders from Himmler and Heydrich. Alfred Streim and Helmut Krausnick have engaged in an extended debate over whether Heydrich's oral orders of 17 June included Jewish women and children as targets.[38] If they did not, it is hard to explain why some early orders to kill Jews specifically included women and children,[39] and why some women and children were actually killed during the first six weeks. The evidence of prior

SS plans to destroy the Jewish 'race' is also too strong to accept the notion that Himmler and Heydrich (or Hitler) originally wanted to spare Jewish women and children, but changed their minds.[40] If Heydrich specifically included Jewish women and children as targets on 17 June, however, why was it necessary for Himmler and Heydrich to issue this order again — and in person — in late July and early August?

One of Stahlecker's reports suggests one answer to this problem: the original orders to the *Einsatzgruppen* were to eliminate Jews to the greatest degree possible.[41] What was possible depended partly upon the limited manpower available, partly on local and regional political and military constraints. It depended, moreover, on whether the police and SS troops themselves could handle the experience of killing women and children, who were clearly not an immediate danger.

Contemporary documents as well as post-war interrogations of police and Waffen-SS unit members make it obvious that the killing of women and children was particularly controversial at the time. The district commissioner in Libau (Liepaja), Latvia noted in October 1941 that renewed shootings of Jews in recent weeks had involved primarily women and children and were carried out in violation of an ordinance from Reich Commissioner Hinrich Lohse and without consideration of the repercussions:

> Precisely the shooting of women and small children, who were, for example, led screaming to the execution sites, has created general horror . . . . Officers have asked me whether this gruesome manner of execution was necessary even with children. In every cultured society [*Kulturstaat*] and even in the Middle Ages pregnant women could not be executed. Here one does not take this into consideration.[42]

Such orders prompted occasional, if rare, acts of defiance. The proposed killing of some one hundred Jewish children in an orphanage in Bjala Zerkow in mid-August 1941 led to a clash between the SS and some military authorities (such as Lieutenant Colonel Helmuth Groscurth), with General von Reichenau of the Sixth Army upholding the former. There is also credible testimony that the commander of Order Police Battalion 303, Heinrich Hannibal, refused to carry out orders to kill women and children, that he even ordered his men *not* to kill women and children. He was transferred and later charged with undermining the armed forces, probably as a result.[43] It is not surprising, then, that Himmler and Heydrich had to press subordinates to execute all Jews. What requires more explanation is their timing.

The shift toward express orders to murder Jewish women and children came at the end of July. Himmler and Heydrich had just begun to spread information about the Final Solution, because implementation of the first steps toward a continent-wide programme was to begin soon. In fact, the very day Himmler issued orders to the SS Cavalry Brigade to drive women and children into the swamps, Heydrich was obtaining Göring's approval of a draft authorization for him to proceed with a 'total solution' and a 'final solution' of the Jewish question.[44] After Himmler's mid-July meetings with Rudolf Höss and Otto Globocnik, his meetings with Higher SS and Police Leader Prützmann on 29 July, Higher SS and Police Leader Bach-Zelewski on 31 July, and Higher SS and Police Leader Jeckeln shortly thereafter suggest that he was personally spreading the word about the Final Solution.[45] It certainly made no sense to exempt Jewish women and children in the Soviet territories. In fact, until the extermination camps were ready, selected locations in the east would have to receive and dispose of deported Jews from the west, including women and children.

In early August Himmler reproached the SS Cavalry Brigade for being too weak, for not killing enough Jews.[46] In mid-August the *Reichsführer SS* visited Minsk, then the headquarters of Criminal Police Chief Arthur Nebe, commander of *Einsatzgruppe* B, who had not distinguished himself in the mass murder of the Jews. Nebe had reported, for example, that Byelorussia was so thickly populated with Jews that only mass expulsion after the war could get rid of all of them.[47] Neither the timing nor the goal was what Himmler had in mind.

Minsk, the capital of Byelorussia, had a Jewish population of more than 50,000, few of whom had managed to escape or hide at the outset of the war.[48] There had already been killings of Jews in Minsk, but on a limited scale — primarily the Jewish intelligentsia — as well as communist functionaries, 'Asiatics' and criminals. Jewish doctors had been exempted, as had the mass of the Jewish population.[49] In fact, the nazis had brought in additional Jews from the nearby towns of Igumen, Slutsk and Uzda, so that the total number in Minsk soon reached or exceeded 80,000. The first task was to register all these Jews, and then on 20 July 1941 nazi authorities issued a directive establishing a closed ghetto, which was surrounded by barbed wire rather than brick walls, and guarded by German police and a Jewish order service. Transfer of the Jews into the ghetto lasted until early August.[50]

Minsk was soon to become a dumping ground and killing centre for German Jews, and Himmler probably wanted to see whether the facilities and the authorities were capable of handling the additional numbers. Himmler told Nebe he wanted to see a demonstration of a liquidation. So Nebe picked out at least one hundred alleged partisans from the city's large jail; all but two were men. (By Bach-Zelewski's account, Himmler told Nebe to seduce the two women before shooting them — in order to get information on what the partisans were planning.) There was a blond, blue-eyed youth among the men. Before the shooting began, Himmler asked him:

Are you a Jew?
Yes.
Are both of your parents Jews?
Yes.
Do you have any ancestors who were not Jews?
No.
Then I can't help you![51]

Members of *Einsatzkommando* 8 and one company of Police Battalion 9 had to do the dirty work. One group at a time, the victims were led toward a deep ditch that had been prepared for them. They were forced to climb in and then to lie face down. Then the police unit fired a salvo from above. After each round of killing, the bodies were covered with earth, and the next group, which had been kept waiting at some distance, was brought to the killing and burial site. After one round, Himmler complained that one victim was still alive. The chief of *Einsatzkommando* 8, Dr Otto Bradfisch, placed a gun in the hands of one of the reserve police officers, Paul Dinter, and told him to finish the man off, which he did.[52]

As the executions proceeded, Himmler became more and more uncomfortable. Bach-Zelewski took advantage of his momentary weakness to press the *Reichsführer SS* to spare not the victims, but the policemen. Pointing out how shaken the executioners were, he complained that these men were now finished for the rest of their lives: they would either be neurotics or savages. Himmler, affected by the complaint, gave a short speech in which he explained to the men that nazi Germany would soon extend to the Ural Mountains, and that it had hard tasks to carry out. Himmler said that *he* and not they were responsible — they were simply carrying out a repulsive but necessary duty. They were to obey their orders unconditionally, and in any case, those orders were based on harsh necessity. Combat was a law of nature, and human beings had to defend themselves against vermin, he concluded. Bradfisch later remembered Himmler saying that the orders had come personally from Hitler, and that he and the Führer alone bore responsibility for them. But two other accounts which are quite consistent had Himmler alone taking full responsibility. Such absolution was not quite enough; that evening the men got drunk.[53]

After this execution and a number of smaller ones in Minsk, *Einsatzkommando* 8 and the company of Reserve Police moved on to Mogilev, where they regularly began to shoot Jewish women. As a result, two policemen had breakdowns. One, a man named Gilli, woke up a comrade in the middle of the night and told him they had been ordered to dig another trench for bodies. The second policeman could not have known that Gilli was disturbed; the order was not implausible. The two men then supposedly reported to Bradfisch that same night for duty as executioners. The next day, learning of the incident, the company commander told Bradfisch that his men could no longer be used for executions, but Bradfisch insisted on compliance. As a demonstration that it was possible, he himself operated a machine-gun during the next two executions. Afterwards, schnapps was given out to the men.[54]

It is hard to gauge the frequency of mental problems among the executioners, given the lack of contemporary written evidence. Still, breakdowns seem to have been frequent enough for the SS to establish an institution for those men suffering the effects of having executed women and children in the east. The resistance leader Helmut James von Moltke met a nurse who worked in this hospital, which was established by November 1941;[55] unfortunately further details are lacking.

These problems among the executioners led Himmler, in December 1941, to issue more detailed instructions to all his key subordinates in the east who were responsible for the elimination of enemies. The commanders and officers were to be held personally responsible for ensuring that their men who carried out executions did not suffer damage of spirit or character. Himmler suggested social gatherings in the evening as a way of reinforcing camaraderie, but warned against the abuse of alcohol on such occasions. A good meal, good beverages and music would take the men 'to the beautiful realm of German spirit and inner life'. There was, however, to be no discussion of their daily activities or of the statistics of killing. Their orders and duties were absolutely necessary for the German *Volk*, but they were not to serve as the substance for casual conversation.[56]

This instruction reflected Himmler's long-established view that the critical racial struggle required Germans to use methods which they normally would reject. In November 1938, Himmler had warned the high SS officers that they would have to carry out orders without pity if they were to save the German *Volk*: they might even be astounded when he, acting against his own feelings and conscience, again and again ordered them to eliminate and punish harshly. But it was necessary. What lay ahead was either the greater German Empire or nothingness. If the SS carried out its duty, then the Führer would create the greatest empire the world had ever seen. In 1940 Himmler had rejected the charge that executions of enemies were un-German; it was un-German to allow oneself to be deceived and defeated, he argued.[57]

Secrecy was only one reason for not discussing the extermination policy; it was also necessary to avoid becoming coarsened by the constant bloodletting. Education could at least in general terms make it clear why such measures were necessary, and the pedantic Himmler was alert to this need. Beyond that, Himmler wanted his men to establish bonds among themselves like those of front-line troops, and to avoid immersing themselves in the reality of their functions. Nonetheless, if there were psychic casualties, these men would be cared for.

Himmler later betrayed a certain contempt for the weakness of his fellow Germans — and perhaps his own as well. He told the *SS-Gruppenführer* at Posen in October 1943 that it was one thing to put the phrase 'exclusion of the Jews' or 'extermination of the Jews' in the nazi programme and quite another to carry it out. In principle, Germans supported persecution, Himmler noted with some sarcasm, but then they each tried to save the one good Jew that they knew. These people had no sense of what it was like to see one hundred or five hundred or one thousand bodies lying there. Himmler boasted that the SS had maintained this programme and, apart from some exceptions brought about by human weakness, had remained respectable. It was 'an unwritten and never to be written page of glory in our history'.[58]

Shootings of Jews and other victims into ditches or ravines continued throughout much of the war, but from 1942 on, the dominant practice was to make use of the gas chamber, which was not only more advanced technologically, but also was less demanding upon the executioners, a feature that was probably no coincidence. After the war, Erich von dem Bach-Zelewski explained to his

American interrogators that the extermination camps arose because Germans and central Europeans were not suited to be mass executioners. Stalin, he said, always had people to employ for this purpose; Bach-Zelewski cited the Latvians as an example. Although the nazis found some individuals to serve as killers, there was no collective eagerness to do so. The death camp — Bach-Zelewski said Auschwitz, but used it as a generic term — was something that the Russians could not accomplish: it reflected the German gift for organization. Bureaucrats created it, he concluded.[59]

The nazi concept that certain nations or races were suited to conduct mass murder and that others were not does help to explain the nazi-inspired pogroms carried out by Eastern Europeans, whose nationalism, anti-communism, and anti-semitism were exploited for nazi purposes. SS officials then made use of Latvian, Lithuanian and Ukrainian execution squads inside and outside of their own homelands, and there were Ukrainian guards and gassing technicians at Sobibor and Treblinka. Although some non-Germans undoubtedly persecuted or killed Jews on their own initiative at times, there is compelling evidence that the SS and police authorities controlled the general policy toward Jews in the Soviet territories and elsewhere.

The passage of time is supposed to provide historians with additional perspective, enabling them to acquire a deeper and clearer understanding of their subject. Fifty years after 1941, East European nationalistic resentments of the Soviet Union (and nationalist frustration within the Soviet Union) still sometimes take the form of anti-semitism as well as anti-communism, whereas nazism has vanished. There is a danger of reading present problems and orientations back into the nazi era and missing the unique aspects of the Final Solution.

Notes

1. Arno J. Mayer, *Why Did the Heavens Not Darken?: The 'Final Solution' in History* (New York 1988), esp. 64–89, 258–60.

2. Raul Hilberg, *The Destruction of the European Jews* (New York 1985), I, 328–32.

3. Grawitz to Himmler, 4 March 1942, United States National Archives (hereafter NA), Record Group (hereafter RG) 238, NO-600, cited by Hilberg, *Destruction*, I, 328. Grawitz also found Bach-Zelewski suffering from feelings of inferiority: Grawitz to

Himmler, 9 March 1942, Bach-Zelewski SS File, Berlin Document Centre.

4. This comment was made by Peiper to Ernst Schaefer, one of Himmler's academics, in late January; Himmler had been to Lodz and Lublin two weeks earlier. Interrogation of Ernst Schaefer, 1 April 1947, NA RG 238, Microfilm series M-1019/ Roll 62/frames 636–8, and Himmler's appointment book, NA RG 242, T-581/R 38A, 15 January 1940.

5. 'Obf. Behrends, Ausspr. RF an Einsatzkommando', Brandt's log, NA RG 242, T-581/R 39A, 10 February 1940; Gespräch Hanns Johst, 26 February 1940, NA RG 242, T-175/R 88/2611403.

6. *Heinrich Himmler, Geheimreden 1933 bis 1945*, ed. Bradley F. Smith and Agnes Petersen (Frankfurt 1974), 128.

7. Helmut Krausnick and Hans-Heinrich Wilhelm, *Die Truppe des Weltanschauungskrieges: die Einsatzgruppen der Sicherheitspolizei und des SD 1938– 1942* (Stuttgart 1981), 146–8.

8. Interrogation of Robert Barth, 13 January 1948, NA RG 238, M-1019/R 5/ 153–6.

9. On the police battalions, Feldpostnummerverzeichnis, Kommandostab RFSS, 30 June 1941, Himmler Collection, Box 10, Folder 322, Stanford University. For a discussion of the Kommandostab Reichsführer SS, Yehoshua Büchler, 'Kommandostab Reichsführer SS. Himmler's Personal Murder Brigades in 1941', *Holocaust and Genocide Studies*, I (1986), 11–21.

10. Christopher Browning, 'One Day in Jozefow: Initiation to Mass Murder', paper presented at Lessons and Legacies of the Holocaust, Northwestern University Conference, 12 November 1989, pp. 3–5.

11. Reserve Battalions 45 and 53 are listed as part of the *Kommandostab Reichsführer SS*. Feldpostnummerverzeichnis, 30 June 1941, Himmler Collection, Box 10, Folder 322, Hoover Institution, Stanford University. Reserve Police Battalion 11, originally headquartered in Kaunas, Lithuania, was involved in the execution of tens of thousands of Jews in Byelorussia during the autumn of 1941, most prominently in the city of Slutzk. See Carl to Gebietskommissar Minsk, 30 October 1941, NA RG 238, 1104-PS; Monatsbericht vom Kommandant vom Weissrussland, 10 November 1941, Yad Vashem Archive 0-53/6.

12. Ohlendorf Affidavit, 5 November 1945, NA RG 238, NO-2620, cited by Hilberg, *Destruction*, 290. For a challenge to Ohlendorf's testimony, see Alfred Streim, 'Zur Eröffnung des allgemeinen Judenvernichtungsbefehls', in *Der Mord an den Juden im zweiten Weltkrieg*, ed. Eberhard Jäckel and Jürgen Rohwer (Stuttgart 1984), 112–15.

13. Heydrich referred to his meeting on 17 June and his instructions in memoranda on 29 June and 2 July 1941. See Krausnick and Wilhelm, *Truppe des Weltanschauungskrieges*, 150–1 and 151 n. 229. Various participants at that meeting have given conflicting post-war accounts of it, even of who chaired the meeting. See, for example, interrogation of Walter Blume 29 June 1947, NA RG 238, M-1019/R 7/848; interrogation of Martin Sandberger, 23 May 1947, NA RG 238, M-1019/R 61/683- 685. Sandberger's confusion may have arisen because Streckenbach gave a speech at Pretzsch, which Sandberger later remembered (interrogation of 27 February 1948, NA RG 238, M-1019/R 61/780-81). See also n. 38 below for sources analysing the conflicting testimony.

14. Interrogation of Walter Blume, 29 June 1947, NA RG 238, M-1019/R 7/848. Interrogation of Karl Jäger, 15 June 1959, quoted by Hilberg, *Destruction*, 290.

15. Interrogation of Julius August Bauer, 29 January 1962, p. 6; interrogation of

Ernst Willy Richard Boernecke, 5 November 1965, p. 8. For the testimony on annihilation, interrogation of Hans Konrad August Weirup, 26 November 1963, p. 7; interrogation of Ludwig Maurer, 13 February 1964, p. 6; interrogation of Friedrich Puschmann, 30 January 1963, p. 4; on the war diary, interrogation of Ernst Oscar Consée, 28 February 1962, p. 14: all from Trial of Kuno Callsen, et al., copies from Zentrale Stelle der Landesverwaltungen zur Aufklärung von NS-Verbrechen, Ludwigsburg (hereafter ZSL).

16. Interrogation of Waldemar von Radetzky, 8 September 1965, p. 12; Callsen Trial, copy from ZSL. Interrogation of Erich Naumann, 15 March 1948, NA RG 238, M-1019/R 49/484.

17. Interrogation of Paul Dinter, 3 April 1959, Landgericht Wien, Trial of Dr Egon Schönpflug, 9VR 767/60, pp. 3–4.

11

18. Reprinted in International Military Tribunal, *Trial of the Major War Criminals before the International Military Tribunal* (hereafter IMT) (Nuremberg 1949), vol. 37, 672, doc. 180-L.

19. Heydrich to Jeckeln, Bach, Prützmann, and Korsemann, 2 July 1941, Bundesarchiv Koblenz R 70 Sowjetunion/32, 266. Krausnick/Wilhelm, *Truppe des Weltanschauungskrieges*, 533–4, attribute this strategy to Heydrich, but do not deal with the issue of whether it was planned in advance. For discussion of the significance of the 2 July telegram's instructions regarding the Jews, Krausnick and Wilhelm, *Truppe des Weltanschauungskrieges*, 150–65, and Krausnick, 'Hitler und die Befehle an den Einsatzgruppen', 90–6.

20. IMT vol. 37, 677–8, quote from 682, doc. 180-L; Krausnick and Wilhelm, *Truppe des Weltanschauungskrieges*, 173; on Norkus, Alois Wehner Affidavit, 26 August 1947, NA RG 238, NO-4847. See, however, Mayer, *Why Did*, 259.

21. IMT vol. 37, 683, doc. 180-L.

22. Ereignismeldung UdSSR (hereafter EM) no. 15, 7 July 1941, NA RG 242, T-175/R 233/2721440; interrogation of Martin Sandberger, NA RG 238, M-1019/R 61/789.

23. IMT vol. 37, 682–83, 180-L.

24. A special execution unit in Latvia under the command of Viktor Arajs carried out killings of Jews in various locations. In Vilnius, there was a Lithuanian execution squad known as Ypatinga Buras. On the role of the *Schutzmannschaften* in killings of Jews, see Richard Breitman, 'Himmler's Police Auxiliaries in the Occupied Soviet Territories', *Simon Wiesenthal Center Annual* 7 (1990), 23–39.

25. See, for example, EM no. 47, 9 August 1941; EM no. 67, 29 August 1941: NA RG 242, T-175/R 233/2721847 and 2722114.

26. Interrogation of Bach-Zelewski, 19 June 1947, NA RG 238. M-1019/R 4/133–36, 153. Bach-Zelewski's request for *Fronteneinsatz*, 18 March 1941 in log of Himmler's correspondence, NA RG 242, T-581/R 45A.

27. Interrogation of Bach-Zelewski, 30 October 1945, NA RG 238, M-1270/R 1/420–21. Bach-Zelewski's undated affidavit, NA RG 238, M-1270/R 1/295.

28. Bach-Zelewski claimed that he had quarrelled with Himmler and that Himmler had removed jurisdiction from him and given it to Arthur Nebe, who, conveniently was already dead. There is no supporting evidence for this version, and Bach-Zelewski continued to serve as Higher SS and Police Leader for the central region of the USSR after this supposed quarrel.

29. *Kriegstagebuch* no. 1, Police Battalion 322. Czechoslovakian Military Archive, Prague, A-2-1-3, Kr. 1.

30. Erwin Schulz Affidavit, 13 August 1947, NA RG 238. NO-3644, p. 3 of original, refers to 2,500 to 3,000 killed. EM no. 24, 16 July 1941, NA RG 242, T-175/R 233/2721538 cites an overall total of 7,000 shot by the police and 1,000 beaten and jailed by the Ukrainians during the period 30 June–3 July.

31. On this general topic, see Omer Bartov, *The Eastern Front 1941–1945: German Troops and the Barbarization of Warfare* (London 1985), 83–129.

32. ZSL, CSSR 397, cited and quoted by Ruth Bettina Birn, *Die Höheren SS- und Polizeiführer, Himmlers Vertreter im Reich und in den besetzten Gebieten* (Düsseldorf 1986), 171 n. 2. The order of 11 July, formally given by the commander of Police Regiment Mitte, on the basis of instructions from Bach-Zelewski, may have resulted from Himmler's visit to Bialystok. The order anticipates Himmler's order of 12 December 1941. See note 55 below.

33. Bach-Zelewski and Nebe lectured the army commanders on the Jewish question with special regard to the partisan movement. Krausnick and Wilhelm, *Truppe des Weltanschauungskrieges*, 248.

34. Minsk is indicated in Himmler's itinerary, but Brandt's log confirms the trip to Baranowicze, and Bach-Zelewski, who did not volunteer any information about a meeting with Himmler in Baranowicze at this time, nonetheless confirms that his office was in Baranowicze. NA RG 242, T-175/R 112/2637748; NA RG 242 T-581/R 39A, 31 July 1941; interrogation of Bach-Zelewski, NA RG 238, M-1270/R 1/296. Conclusive evidence also in *Unsere Ehre heisst Treue. Kriegstagebuch des Kommandostabes Reichsführer SS: Tätigkeitsberichte der 1. und 2. SS-Inf. Brigade, der 1. SS-Kav. Brigade und von Sonderkommandos der SS* (Vienna 1965), 23.

35. Kommandobefehl no. 19, NA RG 242, T-175/R 109/2632873; and Himmler telegram to Bach-Zelewski, NA RG 242, T-175/R 109/2632872. *Unsere Ehre*, 20; *Kommandosonderbefehl*, 28 July 1941, NA RG 242, T-175/R 124/2598661-64.

36. Himmler's orders to shoot men and drive women and children into the swamps, Reitende Abteilung, SS-Kav. Rgt. 2, 1 August 1941, NA RG 242, T-354/R 168/3818936. Fegelein's 1 August 1941 instruction to the commanders of the SS Cavalry Brigade in *Justiz und NS-Verbrechen: Sammlung deutscher Strafurteile wegen nationalsozialistischer Tötungsverbrechen 1945–1966* (Amsterdam 1979), vol. 20, 47. On the 12 August report, Adalbert Rückerl (ed.), *NS-Vernichtungslager im Spiegel deutscher Strafprozesse: Belzec, Sobibor, Treblinka, Chelmno* (Munich 1978), 97. On the situation in Pinsk, Büchler, 'Kommandostab Reichsführer SS', 15–17.

37. On Heydrich, interrogation of August Häfner, 6 July 1965, p. 17, Trial of Kuno Callsen et al., copy in ZSL. On retribution, interrogation of Erich Otto Heidborn, 1 November 1963, p. 11, Trial of Kuno Callsen et al., copy in ZSL. On the clearing of the Jewish quarter, interrogation of Heinrich August Bernhard Huhn, 16 March 1966, p. 14, Trial of Kuno Callsen et al., copy in ZSL.

38. See Jäckel/Rohwer (eds), *Der Mord an den Juden*, 88–124; Alfred Streim, 'The Tasks of the SS Einsatzgruppen', *Simon Wiesenthal Center Annual* 4 (1987): 311–16; and Helmut Krausnick and Alfred Streim in the correspondence section, *Simon Wiesenthal Center Annual* 6 (1989): 311–47.

39. See, for example, Stahlecker's order to the police in Tilsit on 23 June, in *Justiz und NS-Verbrechen*, vol. 20, 304–5.

40. See my *The Architect of Genocide: Himmler and the 'Final Solution'* (New York 1991).

41. IMT vol. 37, 687, doc. 180-L.

42. Gebietskommissar Libau to Generalkommissar in Riga, 11 October 1941, Bundesarchiv Koblenz R 92, vol. 467.

43. On Bjala Zerkow, see interrogation of August Häfner, 10 May 1966, pp. 2–7 and interrogation of Julius Bauer, 2 August 1965, Trial of Kuno Callsen et al., ZSL. On Hannibal, interrogation of Heinrich Hannibal, 9 April 1965, pp. 5–9, supported by interrogation of Otto Schmidt, 4 October 1961, p. 4; and interrogation of René Rosenbauer, 5 September 1963, p. 9; all in Trial of Kuno Callsen et al., ZSL.

44. On Heydrich's meeting with Göring, 6:15–7:15 p.m., 31 July (from Göring's appointment book) in Eberhard Jäckel, 'Die Entschlussbildung als historisches Problem', in *Der Mord*, 15.

45. On Himmler's meetings with Höss and Globocnik in mid-July, see Breitman, *Architect of Genocide*, chapter nine. On Prützmann, see Himmler's itinerary in NA RG 242, T-175/R 112/2637747. On Bach-Zelewski, see note 34 above. On Jeckeln, Erwin Schulz Affidavit, 13 August 1947, NA RG 238, NO-3644.

46. *Justiz und NS-Verbrechen*, vol. 20, 82.

47. Himmler's itinerary, NA RG 242, T-175/R 112/2637745-46. EM no. 33, 25 July 1941, NA RG 238, NO-4438.

48. Shalom Cholawsky, 'The Judenrat in Minsk', in Yisrael Gutman and Cynthia Haft (eds), *Patterns of Jewish Leadership in Nazi Europe 1933–1945: Proceedings of the Third Yad Vashem International Historical Conference* (Jerusalem 1979), 115.

49. EM no. 17, 9 July 1941, NA RG 242, T-175/R 233/2721450; Dorsch to Rosenberg, 10 July 1941, NA RG 238, 022-PS; EM no. 21, 13 July 1941, NA RG 242, T-175/R 233/2721493; EM no. 32, 24 July 1941, NA RG 242, T-175/R 233/2721638. Hersh Smolar, *The Minsk Ghetto: Soviet-Jewish Partisans Against the Nazis* (New York 1989), 15–16.

50. Cholawksy, 'The Judenrat', 115. Smolar, *Minsk Ghetto*, 17–21.

51. Bach-Zelewski's undated affidavit, NA RG 238, M-1270/R 1/296. Bach-Zelewski's account in 'Leben eines SS-Generals', *Aufbau*, 23 August 1946, and quoted by Hilberg, *Destruction*, II, 332.

52. Testimony of Paul Dinter, 3 April and 15 April 1959, Hauptverhandlung Dr Egon Schönpflug, Landgericht Wien (Austria), 9Vr 767/60.
                                                       11

53. Bach-Zelewski's account presented in *Aufbau*, 23 August 1946. Testimony of Paul Dinter, 3 April 1959, Hauptverhandlung Dr Egon Schönpflug, Landgericht Wien, 9Vr 767/60.
        11

Bradfisch quoted by Gerald Fleming, *Hitler and the Final Solution* (Berkeley, CA 1984), 51.

54. Testimony of Paul Dinter, 3 April 1959, Hauptverhandlung Dr Egon Schönpflug, Landgericht Wien, 9VR 767/60.
                                                       11

55. Helmuth James von Moltke, *Letters to Freya*. ed. and tr. Beata Ruhm von Oppen (New York 1990), 183 and 183 n. 2.

56. Himmler to all Higher SS and Police Leaders, SS and Police Leaders, 12 December 1941, Latvian State Archives, Riga, Collection P-83, Entry 1, File 80.

57. Himmler's 8 November 1938 speech in *Heinrich Himmler: Geheimreden*, 25–47;
also NA RG 242, T-175/R 90/ summarized portions on 261259-62, 2612582.
Himmler's 29 February 1940 speech in *Heinrich Himmler: Geheimreden*, 128.

58. IMT vol. 29, 115, 1919-PS.

59. Interrogation of Bach-Zelewski, 19 June 1947, NA RG 238, M-1019/R 4/
143–44.

Richard Breitman
is Professor of History at The American
University in Washington DC. His most
recent book is *The Architect of Genocide:
Himmler and the Final Solution* (New York
1991).

Leni Yahil

National Pride and Defeat:
A Comparison of Danish and German Nationalism

One is often struck by the conspicuous reaction of the Danish population during the second world war to the German occupier in general and to his intentions toward Jewish citizens in particular. It seems that in their behaviour the Danes showed some characteristics uncommon among the other European nations that became entangled in Germany's war and in its 'Final Solution' of the Jewish question. Today we know of the different rescue attempts initiated by individuals, groups and organizations who engaged in this complicated and mostly dangerous undertaking with varying success. All those struggling on behalf of the persecuted Jews faced formidable obstacles, factual and spiritual, in the political, social and individual realm.[1] The Danes, on the other hand — officialdom, society and individuals — acted from the beginning as though by pre-established agreement and when the danger for Jews became acute, united with remarkable ease in a national act of deliverance. In addition to the favourable geographical and political circumstances, it was the spontaneity of the unisonous response that engendered its outstanding success.[2]

During the ten years preceding the war, Danish society had by no means been uniform, and the political upheaval and social convulsions which shook the European nations had repercussions in Denmark. In their response to the German occupation, however, the Danes presented a united front, politically and socially. A broad coalition government was formed, assisted by a new body, the Council of Unity. Its founding statement declared:

> The parties represented in the Rigsdag [the parliament], in their desire to preserve the existing constitution as the basis of political life, have decided to enact a measure of national Danish co-operation. The parties lay aside all disagreement and will unite to preserve the independence and integrity of our country, which is the principal wish of our people.

In the social realm, a popular movement sprang up, aimed at consolidating 'the political, intellectual and personal freedom of the people and the special cultural character of Denmark'.[3] The initiators were young people from all strata of Danish society, who formed an umbrella organization called the Union of Danish Youth. They were supported by a Council of Elders to which belonged a number of outstanding cultural and political personalities. The Union's aim was not political, at least not at the outset, but was to strengthen national identity through various cultural activities, i.e. the study of Denmark's nature, people, history and literature, and all other expressions of creativity. This programme was identical to that of the Folk High School which had been founded by N.F.S. Grundtvig in the middle of the nineteenth century. In the course of time, this system underwent different stages of development. Its hour of decisive impact arrived in 1864, after Denmark's defeat in the war with Prussia and Austria, when it lost the southern provinces of Holstein and Slesvig (Schleswig in German). While in 1860 there were ten Folk High Schools, in the decade after the war their number increased to over sixty.[4] This sudden growth was the result of the way the Danish people reacted to defeat, as expressed in the then popular slogan: 'What is lost outwardly shall be won inwardly.'[5]

This singular reaction became the decisive factor in the Danes' self-understanding; and their non-aggressive nationalism stands out in antithesis to the aggressive nationalism which gained pre-eminence in Germany in the second half of the nineteenth century and manifested itself especially in the German right's reaction to defeat in the first world war. This paper examines and compares some of the historical elements and psychological and intellectual components which gave rise to these diverging attitudes in Denmark and Germany.

The outstanding figure in the process of shaping the Danes' national image during the nineteenth century was Nicolai Frederik Severin Grundtvig. 'No man in recent times,' wrote one of his biographers, 'has meant so much to Denmark as N.F.S. Grundtvig — no one had so much all-round significance as he.'[6] During his long life (1783–1872), this multi-faceted and often contradictory personality underwent scores of different spiritual and factual experiences. Always aiming at inner clarity and truth, he also gained an understanding of the surrounding realities and, combining the spiritual with the practical, found meaningful answers to crucial national problems. He was a writer and translator; poet, philosopher and historian; a priest who became a reformer, of the Danish Church as well as of secular education. He was also a sort of politician and, from the drawing-up of the constitution of the parliament in 1849, served for several years as a member of the *Folketing* (Lower House).[7] His many books and articles dealt with fundamental historical and contemporary issues. In addition, he wrote poetry, including approximately 1,500 hymns, and delivered and published about 3,000 sermons. Only part of his enormous literary heritage in papers and letters has been published.[8] In spite of his varying, sometimes self-contradictory opinions, there was a certain continuity running through his life.

The son of a Lutheran Orthodox parish priest in one of the many Danish island villages and reared in his youth by a learned clergyman in another parsonage, he grew up in a pietistic atmosphere, but was also strongly influenced by his mother's admiration for the old Danish legends and traditions: 'It was from her that Grundtvig derived that sense of the living connection between past and present which was of such significance for all his thought.'[9] His formal education was complemented by the common classical studies at the Latin School of Aarhus, preparing him for the theological faculty of the University of Copenhagen which he entered in 1800 and from which he graduated in 1803. However, during that period, the rationalistic foundations of his upbringing, based on the nineteenth-century European Enlightenment, were shaken by two opposing influences — namely German Romanticism, mainly as developed by F.W. Schelling, and the history of the Nordic countries, which he studied by immersing himself in the ancient chronicles and sagas. Aroused by the seemingly hopeless situation of the Danish peasants, he decided to try to improve their lot by dedicating his life to their education.

During the nineteenth century, Denmark was primarily a rural country. At the end of the eighteenth century, the peasants composed 85 per cent of the population and it was only in 1788 that the medieval system of feudal tenure under which they laboured was broken up. When the old system of communal tillage was also abolished, the peasants were able to acquire the ownership of their small farms. However, the era of the Napoleonic Wars had disastrous consequences for Denmark, and politically as well as economically she suffered her most severe decline. As a result, the often illiterate rural population, unable to develop its holdings, fell into extreme poverty and sank into apathy. But, as has frequently been stated, in the course of the nineteenth century Denmark underwent exceptional development.

> The backward little Scandinavian kingdom of 1800, with its countryside only just emerging from feudalism and its culture confined to a small circle of aristocrats and urban intellectuals, developed into the co-operative commonwealth of today, the pioneer in many fields of progress . . . the self-relying democracy whose rural civilization and genuine folk culture are rivalled by few, if any, of the bigger nations.[10]

During the eighteenth century, Denmark had enjoyed a long period of peace under an absolute monarchy ruling over the kingdom of Denmark–Norway–Slesvig Holstein, and also governing Iceland, Greenland, the Faroe Islands, and the Virgin Islands in the West Indies, not to mention some trading stations in Guinea and India.[11] A small class of wealthy Danish merchants, in co-operation with the Norwegians, conducted a world-wide trade and the Danish–Norwegian fleet ranked as the second largest after the English. The Danish government also controlled the Sound and levied a toll on all foreign ships passing through the Straits and the Danish Baelts while sailing in and out of the Baltic Sea.[12]

In 1801, this situation began to change for the worse. Although the government managed to refrain from becoming entangled in the European wars following the French Revolution, England wanted to compel neutral Denmark to side with her and provoked a conflict by sending her fleet into the Sound. In the ensuing battle (on 2 April 1801), just off Copenhagen, Nelson forced the Danes to surrender.

During the following years, the government's policy vacillated between alliance with Napoleon and sympathy for England. Following Napoleon's triumph in the Treaty of Tilsit in July 1807, England became very aggressive and demanded that the entire Danish–Norwegian navy be handed over 'in pawn for the duration of the present situation'.[13] As the Danes, quite understandably, gave evasive answers, the English again sent their fleet into the Sound. This time, avoiding another naval battle, they landed a considerable force, outnumbering the weak Danish army, a few miles south of Copenhagen, under the command of General Wellesley, later Duke of Wellington. They then simply demanded the surrender of the whole fleet anchored in the harbour. On 1 September 1807, in reaction to the Danes' hesitation, the English started bombarding Copenhagen and continued for four days almost without interruption. Large parts of the city were destroyed, hundreds of defenders and civilians killed, and thousands of the approximately 100,000 inhabitants wounded. Admitting defeat, the Danes had to hand over their entire fleet, dockyards and naval storehouses. Nevertheless, they immediately started building new gunboats. They also kept some ships which had not been in port at the time. Openly siding with Napoleon, Denmark now became involved in The Seven Years War with England, which ended in an even greater disaster in 1814.

During the war, their flourishing maritime trade was ruined and their tiny far-away tropical colonies were cut off. Even worse, the union with Norway was dissolved. In 1814, a Norwegian constitution was proclaimed in the twin kingdom, and then Norway had to conclude a federative arrangement with Bernadotte who ascended the Swedish throne and wanted to swallow her up. With the separation of the two countries, the Danish–Norwegian merchant navy was also split. In 1813, the Danish government went bankrupt. The remaining overseas possessions yielded little.

By backing Napoleon the country had sacrificed her international renown. In 1814 Denmark was in social dissolution, terribly maimed, without political authority among the nations, and economically ruined.[14]

Slowly, Denmark's merchant fleet grew again and toward the middle of the century had returned to its original strength. Progress was also made in agriculture. But there was much unrest in the country, and the people, conscious of the rise of liberal forces in Europe, started to demand the abolition of the absolute monarchy. In the years between 1831 and 1834, popular, so-called Advisory Councils became established in the provinces and in 1848 the growing influence of the Liberal Party led to the formation of the Constituent Assembly which prepared Denmark's constitution. On 5 June 1849, Denmark became a democracy and the new parliamentary government was installed 'without a shot fired'.[15] The date of the proclamation of the constitution has been celebrated as Denmark's national festival ever since.

At the same time, however, shots were fired in the south of the country. The two duchies of Slesvig and Holstein had been connected, as dominions, to the Danish crown. Now, with mounting national consciousness, German influence was growing and became predominant in Holstein and southern Slesvig, where the population demonstrated its alliance with Germany by using the German language. Since the Congress of Vienna in 1815, Holstein had also formally adhered to the German Confederation. In the revolutionary year of 1848, revolt against Danish domination broke out in Holstein, and demand for separation from Denmark included the claim that Schleswig join it and stay in the union of the duchies. When the two Estates turned to the German Federation for help, the Prussian army entered Denmark and proceeding to the north, threatened to conquer even Danish Jutland. The war lasted for two years, and eventually the Danes prevailed. Then England's Palmerston intervened, and in 1852 the Treaty of London was concluded, with the five main European powers, together with Sweden and Norway, acting as guarantors. The treaty reaffirmed the traditional rights of the Danish crown (whose succession was also regulated at this time) in order to maintain 'the integrity of the Danish Monarchy as connected with the general interests of the balance of power in Europe'.[16] The Diet at Frankfurt am Main, representing the German Confederation, did not accept the treaty. This enabled Bismarck to exploit the unsettled conflict in order to pursue his plans for the unification of Germany under Prussia's leadership. So in 1864 he attacked Denmark. The easily defeated Danes were forced to renounce the king's right over Schleswig-Holstein. This loss of one third of the kingdom's territory with its population of one million of the country's two and a half million inhabitants was regarded as a national catastrophe. After Prussia defeated Austria in 1866 and constituted the new separate German Federation, she incorporated the two duchies. It was, however, conceded that northern Schleswig could be returned to Denmark on the grounds of a plebiscite. This proviso was enacted by the Treaty of Versailles, and in 1920, about 75 per cent of the population voted in favour of Denmark and restored the province to her.

This, then, was the background against which Grundtvig grew into such an oustanding personality, initiating educational, social and religous reforms. His spiritual essence was basically composed of three elements: Nordic mythology and tradition, Christianity, and the significance of poetry and history. In different periods of his life one or other of these seemingly antipodal conceptions became predominant, but eventually Grundtvig combined them in his specific philosophy of life, on the basis of which he aimed to build what he called 'the people's rebirth'.

During the early years of the nineteenth century, he worked as a tutor to a family on a rural estate, and developed the German cultural influences to which he had been exposed during his study years. An ardent reader, he immersed himself in the works of the Romantic and Idealistic schools. Notwithstanding his tendency to become over-emotional, his sense of rational reality was never dimmed, and he learned to give literary expression to his spiritual exaltation. At the time, poetry became the main vehicle for his expression of man's inner life, including his own, and what he conceived to be universal truth. Such truth he found in ancient Nordic mythology. Initially he devoured it in romantic fashion, but later studied it in depth. It was the calamitous situation after the unfortunate clash with the English navy in 1807 and the ensuing war that aroused his patriotic feelings and stimulated him to lift the people's spirits by confronting them with the heroism of Nordic poetical mythology, thus making them conscious of their great heritage. 'A people reveals itself in its gods,' he wrote. 'The Greek gods rank highest in formal beauty but in physical and spiritual strength they cannot compare with those of the North.'[17] By and by, his approach became less intuitional and more rational. In 1807 his dissertation on the Norse cults was published and in 1808, the year he moved to Copenhagen, his poetic *The Mythology of the North* appeared, in which he showed that the Eddas were drawn from different sources. Explaining his intentions, he wrote: 'The myth is a symbol of the eternal which lives in man. . . . Therefore, if we wish to learn how to understand ourselves, we must go to the myths of our ancestors.' Eventually, he completely cast away his romantic concept of the Nordic myth and called his former romantic enthusiasm 'nonsense'.[18] This new conception had its roots in spiritual stirrings of two kinds. One was his growing sense of the importance of universal and national history, to which we shall return later. The other was the increasing predominance of his religious faith.

In his early period of Romanticism, he tried to find common ground for his infatuation with the pagan Nordic myth and his basic belief in Christianity as the true way to redemption, which seemed to be irreconcilable. He wanted to show that both were derived from one eternal source of life (called the father of all). He articulated what has become an often-quoted formula: 'Mighty Odin, pure Christ, your contest is abolished. You are both sons of the All-Father.'[19] However, as well as moderating his romantic approach to the myths, he struggled hard to confirm his inner faith and to establish his place as a priest in the state Church. In spite of the fact that his probational sermon (published in 1810), in which he attacked the clergy, was censured by the Consistory, he was ordained in 1811. From then until 1815, he served as a priest, first as curate to his father and, after his father's death, as a vicar in Copenhagen.[20] But he steadily aroused the wrath of the official Church, whose prevailing rationalism and lack of religious freedom he attacked. Eventually he was reprimanded and stopped from serving even in a provincial town. However, the ban was lifted three years later and in 1822 he was able to return to Copenhagen as a minister. At that time he was joined by other groups also demanding reforms within the Church (later known as 'Grundtvigians'). Nevertheless, in 1826 he resigned from the pulpit and was again placed under censorship which lasted for another twelve years. But from 1839 until the end of his life, he again worked as a vicar. Grundtvig opposed sectarianism and directed all his efforts toward reform *within* the state Church. Eventually, towards the middle of the century, he succeeded in his endeavours, after the structure of the Church — now renamed the National Church — had been defined by the constitution. The reforms which he initiated secured greater individual freedom.[21] In 1853, on Grundtvig's seventieth birthday, when King Christian IX appointed him honorary Bishop, his reform work was acknowledged.

Grundtvig's own religious faith emerged from a great spiritual crisis which he suffered at the end of 1810. He then cast away all his romantic and high-flying aspirations and humbly longed to be redeemed by faith. It was this faith that inspired the hymns which made him popular with all believers. He found the basis for his new religious life in the Bible. In a poem, he described his search for God and where he found Him:

> Found Him in the songs of the poet,
> Found Him in the word of the prophet,
> Found Him in the myth of the North,
> Found Him in the rolling of the ages,
> Yet then, clearest and surest,
> Found him in the Book of books.[22]

Armed with this faith, he fought rationalistic as well as romantic disbelief.

While living in Copenhagen and dedicating himself mainly to writing, Grundtvig was witness to the disastrous events of 1814. As had been the case in 1807, he reacted to the country's great crisis with a determination to lift the people out of their defeatism.[23] As a preacher, he called his congregation to repent. The real danger lay not in the external enemies, but in the unbelief and godlessness of the people.[24] While in 1807 he had reminded the Danes of their great past by spreading the Nordic myths, he now turned to history, studying and publishing the old Scandinavian chronicles, which he translated from Latin. 'Translating the Chronicles into Danish, he became intrinsically Danish himself, and learned to speak simply about higher things.'[25] This simplicity also found expression in his patriotic poetry in which he showed the people their new and difficult position in a positive, somehow ironic fashion. In one poem he praised the simple Danish life:

> Far more of those metals so white and so red
> Find others by digging and selling.
> We Danes, though, can point to every day's bread
> In even the lowest dwelling,
> Can boast that in riches our progress is such
> That few have too little, still fewer too much.[26]

His striving for religious freedom merged with his patriotism. He stated that, unlike the Latin peoples who had adopted Roman culture along with Christianity, the Norse peoples had become Christians without abandoning their folk characteristics, and had conserved their original language and indigenous sagas.[27] The individual nation's history must serve as the source from which its constitution and laws had to be drawn.[28] But Grundtvig saw the Danish cause in the wider context of the North as a whole and subsequently of humanity:

> When we regard the world of the spirit with Nordic eyes in the light of Christianity, then we get an idea of a universal historical development, art, and science which embraces all human life . . . and must necessarily lead to the most perfect explanation of life which is possible on earth.[29]

It was 'life on earth' that became the main object of Grundtvig's endeavours. His human vision was a realistic one. A human being had first to acknowledge that he was a man and only then could he become a Christian. His formula 'first man then Christian' meant that man's responsibility was first and foremost to this life on earth.[30] He thus negated the romantic, monistic attitude toward life which did not distinguish between good and bad, light and darkness, truth and falsehood, but was based on a dim wholeness of feeling and a cult of death. On the other hand, he also dissociated himself from the pietistic trend of Christian pilgrimage which denied the value of earthly life and saw it only as a time of probation and preparation for the eventual heavenly life.[31]

According to Grundtvig, the Jews' interpretation of man, based on their myth of the Creation and the Fall, was the deepest and most universal. Thus, in his philosophy of life he combined 'Mosaic-Christian' understanding with a 'Greek-Nordic humanism'.[32] His admiration of the Bible was also aroused by its poetry, which he called 'the most poetical nation's poetry'. He saw in poetry the highest human expression, 'an image of the eternal'.[33]

Grundtvig's 'enlightenment of life' comprised his strong historic consciousness. Human existence could be conceived only in history: 'Only in history does man reveal his reality and true form.'[34] He saw two forms of history. First, the universal one that he wished to base on the Bible, starting with the Creation, but Christ was seen as the central figure, the connecting point of the ages.[35] The other aspect was that of human experience revealed in the history of nations. At the beginning, the history of a people lies concealed in its myth. But eventually the experience of a nation's life, as presented in its history, provides each individual with enlightenment. History is the memory of mankind; without living memory, man is nothing. Grundtvig believed in a vital force, a uniting factor acting in history, which he called 'spirit', something that may manifest itself in a whole nation at decisive moments in its history.[36]

In line with this view of history, Grundtvig rejected any form of national animosity. Each nation or 'folk' developed its own 'spirit'. His cultural-religious opinions excluded any notion of racism, or anti-semitism. Notwithstanding his universal approach, Grundtvig was convinced that the Danish people were chosen by God as a 'divine experiment', and he spoke of Denmark as 'the Palestine of history'.[37] 'The Danish cause is one of all the North, of humanity, of Christianity.' Denmark had a mission in which living Christianity and a new 'historical culture' would be combined. One of his biographers remarked:

> The combination of the religious and the patriotic trends in Grundtvig's thought sometimes gives to his writing a curious apocalyptic tone like that of some ancient Hebrew seer . . . . At times his mystic visions and prophesies appear to modern eyes to verge on the fantastic; but often they seem to spring from some deep source of spiritual insight which justifies his title of 'Prophet of the North'.[38]

Between 1829 and 1831 Grundtvig visited England three times and once again in 1843. The first visits were made possible by a special grant which he received from King Frederik VI[39] to enable him to study original Anglo-Saxon manuscripts held in several English archives. These visits had a decisive affect on Grundtvig's thinking and on his later public and educational activities that were to be so influential. On one occasion, when discussing England and Denmark, he was asked: 'But what do you *do*?' It came as a shock to him that he had thought, written and spoken but had not *acted*.[40] 'I felt', he wrote later, 'that the obstinate Englishman was actually right: the most important thing about a man is that he himself does something which shows what he is capable of', and he summed up the English conduct that had impressed him so much: 'The free-living activity, the masterly grip of the beneficial, and the clear vision of the actual and lasting glorious, that was what I really admired in England.'[41] He realized that the revival of his people he envisioned could not be initiated merely by preaching sermons and writing poetry and history. In 1832, in a letter to a friend, he wrote:

> Only now did I see, that we who haughtily scorned the present with its low prosaic views of all human conditions stood just as much in the way of a better future as the idolaters of the present . . . . Then I made it my task to consider the present time as minutely and as impartially as possible, and actively bind myself to everything in it that prophesied a better and happier future.[42]

In the same letter he pointed out another radical change he underwent in England. He became what he called un-German and very much pro-English. He felt that a great affinity existed between the Northern and the English peoples, who were akin in their language, mythology, history and way of life. He saw similarities in their spiritual outlook, but also envisaged the development of much closer political and economic ties between Denmark and the United Kingdom, a view that proved to be correct.

What were the tasks that Grundtvig undertook from the 1830s? After some hesitation he joined the movement toward democratization of the regime and eventually entered parliament. At the same time, his struggle for the reformation of the Church became effective. However, his main contribution to the changes in the outlook and behaviour of the Danish people was the ground he laid for the realization of his idea of the Folk High School.

Originally, the Advisory Councils of the provinces had been mainly under the influence of the aristocratic owners of big estates. The smallholders, though comprising the majority of the rural population, were only beginning to improve their situation and lacked political influence. They still suffered from poor primary education which had been nominally introduced in 1739, but in spite of its becoming compulsory in 1814, the situation had not improved much, mainly because of lack of money and suitable teachers.[43] As early as 1807, after Denmark's decline and in the general mood of defeatism, Grundtvig had conceived the idea of a popular high school as a new system of education. But it was not until 1831–2, under the influence of his English experience, that he envisioned the scheme of what he called the Folk High School. Two motifs mingled in his conception: his national consciousness and his perception of enlightenment. Since nationalist German aspirations were making themselves felt in Holstein and were spreading to southern Slesvig, strengthening the Danish spirit appeared to be obligatory. According to Grundtvig's views, this should be done by the right kind of 'enlightenment of life' to let people understand what it meant to be a human being: a link in the nation but also a citizen of the world.[44]

'Understanding,' he concluded 'comes only by experience; therefore, it is only by consideration of the human race and one's own experience that one can gain understanding of human life.'[45] Thus, he did not want to teach small children but youngsters, who, after finishing primary school, had already gained some experience working in agriculture or in trade. People under the age of eighteen were not to be accepted into the school. All his life Grundtvig objected to the classical education provided by the Latin school and the university. In his eyes, this education of a privileged minority was alien to the people and sterile. Moreover, he abhorred 'things Roman' and considered Rome a 'robber state', whose people stole the Hellenic culture.[46] Grundtvig saw in his vision of the Folk High School a counterpart and contrast to the academic institutions. It should provide 'education and competence for life, ordinary human, civic life' for the present.[47] He combined his humane philosophy with this idea of 'enlightenment of life' and wanted the school to make its pupils conscious of what he considered the true condition of man as expressed in the 'Mosaic myth' of the Creation and the Fall. With this double aim, the school would also prepare its pupils to meet the Gospel, which otherwise would remain 'remote, indifferent, and inimical to human life'.[48] Thus he intended to put into practice his fundamental principle of 'first man, then Christian'.

Grundtvig's fundamentals as well as his pedagogical approach found their expression in the structure and teaching practice of the school he conceived and some of his followers developed. In contrast to an academic education, he asked for the 'living world'. He considered 'everything which begins with letters and ends with knowledge gained from books a school of death . . . book learning is dead if it is not combined with a corresponding life from the teacher'.[49] The fruitfulness of the instruction depended on the 'interplay' between teacher and pupil. The teacher, however, must realize that he cannot create life but only 'arouse, nourish, and enlighten' that life which already exists in the young.[50] Lectures had to turn into conversations between the teacher and pupils and among the pupils themselves. Such discussions and the meeting of people of different kinds and from different places would widen their horizons and open their eyes for the common good. This would counteract 'boyish conceitedness and wilfulness, all manner of vanity . . . and the greed for a so-called secure means of livelihood'.[51]

When the school developed, its structure and rules were shaped according to Grundtvig's principles. Attendance was voluntary. The students formed a council and with its assistance the teachers and the director planned and developed the curriculum. School rules were fixed the same way. No discipline was imposed from above, nor was it needed, and no examinations were held. Grundtvig placed great emphasis on the vitalization of the Danish language. At the time, the scholarly language was Latin and in educated circles much German and French were spoken. The majority of the population spoke little of any language. Grundtvig wanted his students to develop a plain Danish manner of speaking which would engender plain Danish thinking and would also serve to bridge all gaps and unite the people.[52] To foster and strengthen a feeling for the language, poetry was not only taught but read, declaimed and sung. In addition, identification with folk culture was complemented by study of the Nordic myths and national history as part of the history of the world. Some of Grundtvig's books on these subjects became standard works in the Folk High School. At the start, he was not interested in mathematics and the sciences, but this changed in the course of time and under the influence of some of his colleagues.

Much time elapsed from the beginning of the 1830s when Grundtvig conceived the idea of the Folk High School with the aim of educating the rural population so that it could take an active part in shaping Denmark's future, until he saw his plan realized. The first school began functioning in 1844, and it was certainly not by chance that it was set up in the disputed area of northern Slesvig, where the need to strengthen the Danish spirit and enhance the Danish language was strongly felt. The schools did not become government institutions, but received some financial aid, even though there was much opposition to them in educational officialdom and amongst the clergy. They were founded and run by individuals, followers of Grundtvig, and adopted by rural communities in many of which they stimulated new cultural centres where diverse activities and free discussions took place.

> To ensure the continuance of this work, special meeting-houses were built . . . . With such meeting-houses as centres of interest and endeavour, people very often live a rich and full life, a life representing much of what is best in the Danish character.[53]

By the 1920s, there were about a thousand of such 'lecture associations', each with around one hundred members. The lecturer, it was said,

> voices to the best of his ability all the emotions that have flowed through the life of the people during the last hundred years. Many of these lectures are, of course, rather poor in quality, but the effect of 'the living word' is everywhere becoming evident; and those lectures which combine intelligence with feeling exercise a great influence on the minds of the people.[54]

The years following 1864 were a period of conflict between the conservative and financial forces and their democratic opponents. But they were also the years when the peasants came more and more into their own and rose to political power. In 1870, a large party of the left was formed and among its different sections it was the Grundtvigian that led this parliamentary opposition. 'In large numbers the pupils of the high schools became the left's leaders in the districts and in parliament', where in 1903 about 35 per cent of its members were former high-school pupils.[55] It was the catastrophe of 1864 that put the spirit of the Danish people to its most severe test, and then it became obvious that a new national consciousness had grown out of the seed that Grundtvig had planted, engendering the decisive changes in the country's educational, social and political structure, including reform of the Church. One has to bear in mind, however, that at the time Denmark was a mainly agricultural country and, therefore, the development of true democracy depended on the emergence of the peasantry as a self-conscious, constructive, political power. Its creativity showed itself in the formation of the co-operative movement that reorganized Danish agriculture. Later industrial modernization changed the social and political equilibrium, but the specific spirit of Danish democracy prevailed:

> The freedom from internal social conflicts enjoyed by the Danish country population has meant that intellectual and spiritual pursuits have not been the privilege of particular groups but the common treasure of all. Further, the strong spiritual currents . . . have done much to establish the plain, democratic character of the men and women, and to check influences tending to divisions.[56]

Comparing Danish nationalism of the nineteenth century with its German counterpart, it is impossible within the scope of this paper to give an exhaustive account of the complicated evolvement of the latter, its causes and effects. However, we shall try to show some of its basic elements which can be found in Ernst Moritz Arndt's writings and poetry and in Johann Gottlieb Fichte's famous *Addresses to the German Nation*. These two contemporaries of Grundtvig (Arndt 1769–1860, Fichte 1762–1814) developed their ideas under the impact of the same revolutionary historical events and intellectual movements which shaped the young Grundtvig's outlook. As with Grundtvig, the fateful experience of the Napoleonic Wars led them to interpret the implications of the catastrophe that had befallen their country and to work out how to overcome it.

As the son of a farmer on the island of Rügen, E.M. Arndt was born a Swede. Germany became his fatherland by choice. He studied in Germany, explored the country on foot, and taught modern history, first at the University of Greifswald and later in Bonn. All his writings — books, articles, pamphlets and poems — were in German, even the few relating to Sweden, to where he returned on several occasions, but never for long. The decisive years during which he conceived and disseminated his ideas on German nationalism were the crisis years at the beginning of the nineteenth century. His main opus, *Geist der Zeit* (Spirit of the Time) appeared in four volumes (1806, 1809, 1813, 1818). Of the first three volumes it was said:

> It is a political book, and this political book had the greatest impact on its time; as far as the modern history of national consciousness is concerned, its significance is

about the same as that which today is claimed by general opinion for Fichte's *Addresses.*[57]

The book's impact was so strong that in 1812 Freiherr vom Stein, who was preparing Prussia's rise against Napoleon in Peterburg, asked Arndt to join him and put him in charge of what today would be called public propaganda. Arndt's two main pamphlets, *Kurzer Katechismus für deutsche Soldaten* (Short Catechism for German Soldiers) (1812) and *Was bedeutet Landsturm und Landwehr?* (What is the Meaning of General Levy and Defence Corps?) (1813), were circulated in tens of thousands of copies and reprinted in newspapers. The latter especially became very popular and saw no less than eleven editions between 1813 and 1815.[58] To these have to be added the patriotic poems Arndt published at this time. From 1814 on, he dealt mainly with the problems of the future political structure of Germany and, after the disappointing results of the Congress of Vienna and of Napoleon's final defeat, in 1818 he published the fourth volume of *Geist der Zeit*, full of criticism of the prevailing situation in Germany. In the wake of the harsh reactionary trend of the Prussian regime, Arndt, who had taken up his professorship in Bonn in 1818, was suspended in 1820, after all his papers, letters, etc. had been confiscated. It was twenty years before he was rehabilitated and, at the age of seventy, reinstalled in Bonn. He participated in the political discussions of the 1840s and at the meeting of the National Assembly of Frankfurt in 1848 became honorary senior member, and also took part in the legation that unsuccessfully offered the imperial crown of Germany to the Prussian king, Friedrich Wilhelm IV.[59]

The country Arndt claimed as his fatherland was divided into 1,800 sovereign entities, ranging from Prussia, the biggest and most powerful, to tiny sectors comprising a few villages. The formal overall rule of the Habsburg monarchy did not inspire a sense of German unity. Thus, the idea of German identity took the form of the idealistic concept of *Volk*. The concrete substance of this *Volk* was the economically, socially and politically divided population of the diverse regions of Germany that differed also in their cultural and religious traditions. German culture, however, as embodied in philosophy, literature and music, had developed in a unique and significant way.

German patriots, longing for national unity and independent statehood as exemplified in most of the other European countries, embraced two spiritual elements: the myth of the seemingly glorious nature of the original German tribes and the German language as the one existing, unifying element. From these two elements they created the romantic image of the ideal German personality, derived from a German *Ur-Volk*, whose superior, pure racial characteristics were inherent in the present-day Germans, together with the purity of the German language. The one way of expressing love for this immanent national reality was by praising the beauty of the German land as the 'fatherland'. Since social and political realities militated against any positive expression of such feelings, they manifested themselves in aggression. Fighting against alien influences was postulated as a holy duty and directed mainly against French culture and, under the impact of the Napoleonic oppression, against the oppressor. Hate was now the carrier of the spirit of the *Volk* and death in battle served as proof of love of the fatherland and freedom.

It was E.M. Arndt who disseminated these ideas most radically. Their most concentrated expression is to be found in his pamphlets and poems of 1812–13. Otherwise his ideas are repeated over and again throughout his voluminous writings. Here we can only indicate some of the basic motifs. His Germanism had already a clear racial meaning:

> Germans are not bastardized by alien peoples, they have not become a mixed breed [*Mischling* in the original]. More than many other nations they have retained their original purity . . . . Every *Volk* will only become the best and noblest and create the best and noblest by always choosing the strongest and most beautiful of its race to unite in producing offspring.

He also indicated that legislators should be conscious of 'pure and equal blood'.[60] The language of the Germans, being an *Ur-Volk*, was an original, undefiled *Ursprache*. The language provided the legitimation for German national aspirations; only in a powerful Germany, full of glory, would it be possible to preserve its purity.[61] In a famous poem, *The German's Fatherland* (1813), he asks, at the beginning of each of the many verses, 'What is the German's fatherland?' and proceeds to list all the regions inside and outside Germany where German is spoken, always concluding: 'O no! no, no, his fatherland must be bigger.' Eventually he comes to the conclusion that everywhere the German language is spoken the Germans can call that land their own. He then goes on to praise all the wonderful characteristics which he attributes to the image of the German.[62]

According to Arndt, faith in the fatherland is the highest religion. One has to love it more than all rulers and princes, more than father and mother, wife and children. He even identifies this religion with redemption through Christ: '. . . and after you have completed the revenge and the liberation, under green oak trees you shall sacrifice the joyful offering to the protecting God'.[63] God is the special protector of the Germans. Their enemies, especially the French and Napoleon himself, belong to Satan. For him hate of everything French was essential. 'I don't want hate of the French only for this war, I want it for a long time, I want it for ever.' This hate would secure Germany's borders. It would glow as the religion of the German people, as a holy frenzy in all their hearts.[64]

One of the most famous poems with which Arndt inspired the Germans in the crucial years of 1812 and 1813 was *Vaterlandslied* (Song of the Fatherland).[65] It spread throughout Germany and later served as inspiration to the *Burschenschaften* (student fraternities, some of which became extremely nationalistic). The following is the translation of three of its verses — the first, third and sixth, the last — which express almost all the main elements of Arndt's teaching.

> The God that let the iron grow
> He did not want the slaves,
> Therefore he gave sword, spear and lance
> To man in his right hand,
> Therefore he gave him daring courage,
> The scorn of his free word,
> Thus to withstand with all his blood
> The struggle until death.
>
> O Germany, holy fatherland!
> O German love and trueness!
> You country high and beautiful!
> We swear to you again:
> The ban be laid on hooligan and slave!
> Raven and crow may feed on him![66]
> But we go into Arminius's battle
> And want to have revenge.
>
> Let fly whatever has to fly,
> The standards and the flags!
> Today we will, man for man,
> Call for the hero's death:
> Up! fly ahead of daring lines
> You proud victorious banner!
> We shall here win or die
> The free man's dulcet death.

In his late writings (1853), Arndt (then an old man whose dearly loved son had been drowned in the Rhine, which he called

'Germany's stream not Germany's border') preached the Christian faith and asked for humility.[67] Still, the aggression which before had been directed against the French was now turned against an internal enemy: the Jews. Perhaps nowhere is the historical sequence, from the exalted German nationalism of the early nineteenth century to the anti-semitism that evolved at its end, so clear as in Arndt's development. The Jews are not mentioned in his early writings. In 1848 he wrote:

> Jews and Jew-collaborators [*Judengenossen*], baptized or non-baptized [!], relentlessly work . . on the decay [*Zersetzung*] and the dissolution of what seemed until now to us Germans to hold our humanity, and the most holy: [work] on the dissolution and destruction of all love for the fatherland and fear of God.[68]

Kurt Lenk states that it is here that the word 'decay', related expressly to the Jews, entered the language of the conservative parties of Prussia-Germany, and concludes: 'The projection onto the internal enemy is as total as onto the external one.'[69]

Johann Gottlieb Fichte was born the son of an artisan in a small place in the duchy of Saxony. A benevolent nobleman, struck by the boy's gifts of oratory, enabled him to become a student.[70] In his extensive introduction to Fichte's *Addresses to the German Nation*, George Armstrong Kelly characterizes him as a 'son of the people' and as 'radical and utopian in temper'.[71] After graduating from the university of Jena he, like Grundtvig, worked as a private tutor in noble or upper-class households. Coincidentally, he got to Königsberg and attended Kant's lectures. 'Fichte's deep respect for the mind as an instrument of logical inquiry — his Kantianism — prevented him from being a true Romantic.'[72] Kant helped him to publish his first philosophical treatise, *A Critique of all Revelation* (1791), which established his reputation, and in 1793 he assumed the chair of philosophy in Jena. Deeply impressed by the French Revolution, his 'Jacobinism' brought him under attack, and in 1798 he had to resign from the university. With the help of the Schlegel brothers he was invited to Berlin and thus became linked to the Prussian kingdom. 'One may speculate that Fichte's growing patriotism found its roots in this act of asylum.'[73] However, owing to the prevailing conditions of war and French occupation, he only assumed the chair of philosophy at Wilhelm von Humboldt University in 1810, serving also as its first rector. He died a premature death

in a typhus epidemic in 1814. While he was without fixed employment, he nevertheless gained recognition as a writer and orator. His
Addresses to the German Nation were delivered in the winter of 1807–8
before a small audience in one of the rooms of the recently built
university. It was not until much later and especially after the first
world war that his appeal to the German people became an authentic
expression of German nationalism. In the introduction to one of the
editions of the *Reden*, the renowned philosopher Rudolf Eucken
justified the reprinting of Fichte's *Addresses* and explained their
lasting merit and significance. He was not uncritical and also warned
against 'infertile racial arrogance'. But — like Fichte — he was
convinced that only the German nation, among all the nations of the
world, embodied the faculty to realize an original and self-sustaining
way of life and that its creativity, emanating from the depth of its soul,
expressed the wholeness and wholehearted dedication of the nation's
being.[74]

In 1804 Fichte was still a cosmopolitan and in his eyes Europe was
the fatherland of every civilized European. However, the catastrophe
that hit Prussia and Germany in 1806 'caused his thought to take a
remarkable turn'.[75] He now concluded that the catastrophe had
occurred because of the people's and the government's corruption
through egotism, 'which is the root of all corruption'.[76] In his first
address, he stated that if a generation lost its former self and world, a
new self and world should be created. 'Now for my part I maintain
that there is such a [new] world, and it is the aim of these addresses to
show you its existence and . . . to indicate the means of creating it.'[77]
He did not cast away the moral principles that had been at the centre
of his idealistic philosophy, but merged them with his new patriotic
assumptions. With almost religious fever he postulated the German
nation as the incarnation of humanity at its purest and most
wholesome: 'Only the German — i.e. the original man not strangled
by arbitrary rules — has a true *Volk*, while the foreigner has none.'[78]
Thus the aggression against everything foreign, and first and
foremost everything French, was transferred to and projected into the
moral realm.

The Germans retained their original character because they
conserved their primary language (*Ursprache*). It remained a living
language and the essential expression of the *Volk*'s soul, injecting its
spiritual culture (*Geistesbildung*) into life; otherwise spiritual culture
and life would follow separate routes.[79] The developing *Ursprache*
emanated from life and influenced life, while the language of those

who adopted a foreign language (i.e. Latin as adopted by the French) became dead and was used only by small groups of educated people totally divorced from the repressed and exploited masses. This living language, 'flowing from the source of all spiritual life, from God', enabled the German *Volk* to create something new.[80] This creation of a new mankind was the goal of Fichte's education of the German nation as outlined and explained in his discourses.

The most advanced development of mankind hitherto — according to Fichte — had come to nothing. Now a new age had to be started and a completely different mankind created. This would be achieved through education, with the primary aim of instilling a 'pure morality' (*reine Sittlichkeit*). This primary morality was independent, self-sustaining and unadulterated. The new education had to be implemented according to fixed rules, and its product, the pupil, would emerge as an 'unchangeable work of art'.[81] The rules that would infallibly determine the pupil's way of life consisted of two main elements: coercion of the will and clearness of perception. Fichte declared that the old style of education, aimed at directing man's free will toward the performance of good, had failed. Therefore, the new education must completely destroy freedom of will and render decision the outcome of stern necessity, giving the will no chance of effecting the opposite: 'For him [the pupil] freedom of the will is destroyed and swallowed up in necessity,'[82] i.e. the necessity of virtue. The pupil would attain the clear perception of necessity through learning, i.e. '*Bildung*'. He would love learning and freely develop his own ability to perceive and acknowledge the general and infallible laws of life and the spirit.[83] In order to achieve this, children would have to live, from their early years, in special institutions, where they would form their own community, completely isolated from the surrounding society and even separated from their families. This community would have its own specific structure.[84] Reared in this way, as adults they would build the new Germany. This new national education (*Nationalerziehung*) must be the most urgent concern of any German who loved the fatherland while, at the same time, it would lead to the improvement and regeneration of all mankind.[85] Consequently, national education had to be the foremost duty of the state, especially under the prevailing conditions, with military and political power in ruins. The state alone was able to introduce the new national education, encompassing the whole population — something private, well-intentioned individuals could never do.[86]

How was all this to be achieved? To this question Fichte answered: 'We must here and now become what we have to be anyway — Germans.' And he added: 'We must — in a word — obtain character; for to have character and to be German [*Charakter haben und deutsch sein*] without doubt means the same.'[87]

Three times — in 1807, 1814 and 1864 — the Danes suffered defeat. The recovery in 1864, according to the slogan 'to win inwardly', included the reclamation of wasteland, heath and moorland which were turned into forests, fields and farms, thus making up for areas the country had lost. Grundtvig is hailed as the one who, by having faith in the people's strength, helped them to achieve their potential. The Danes' nationality became firmly rooted in the state's democratic structure in spite of the fact that their parliament was constituted while the country was at war with Prussia. In contrast to the basically positive and self-composed attitude of the Danes as manifested in Grundtvig, Arndt's and Fichte's disposition was essentially negative. For Arndt the world was ruled by war, and there were only two alternatives: freedom through victory or slavery after defeat. Hate and heroism became the life-saving elements. Defeat should never be accepted. In a poem written in 1803 called *Song of the Free*, he describes a young widow bringing her baby son to his soldier father's grave, praying that the gods might grant the son also such a heroic death and exclaiming that the men would be accepted by the fatherland if victorious, but not if defeated.[88] In his old age, he changed his tone and warned against too much enthusiasm for war,[89] but this warning went unheeded by the German nationalists. During the second world war, the death announcements of those who had fallen in battle appeared under the headline: 'In Stolzer Trauer' (In Proud Mourning).

Fichte said that he despaired of the German people in their present situation, as of mankind as a whole. In a mental *salto mortale*, he turned his despair into a utopian vision of a new mankind the Germans would build. Little did he know or imagine that his desire to arouse the people from their defeatism would be used to justify the Germans' hubris and their ambition to conquer the world. No less dangerous were his pedagogic assumptions. Fichte was not the only one who tried to rectify human nature and attain lofty goals by coercing the human will. Grundtvig's perception was the exact opposite: nothing could be changed completely. On the contrary, one had to start with the normal human condition of family ties and first experiences of life and only then try to develop in the young their inherent potential. Thus, in a completely free manner, real human intercourse would grow and true responsibility of the individual for himself and for the community would develop. The prevailing reality served as a starting-point and its improvement would be achieved through 'enlightenment of life'. Young adults entering this process of learning must be tutored by private individuals who would foster the 'interplay' between themselves and their pupils.

In accordance with the romanticism of the age, language and myth played an important role in the intellectual concepts of Grundtvig as well as of Arndt and Fichte. For the two Germans, their language was the main, indeed the only authentic proof of German nationality. Its derivation from the *Ursprache*, in combination with the theory of the *Urvolk*, guaranteed the genuineness of the German *Volk*. Grundtvig had no need to prove the existence of the Danish people, since they had been unified for centuries. For him, language together with myth and history were vehicles to arouse national consciousness and to inspire the Danes to work for their country's well-being. When Grundtvig became 'un-German', he said that he 'gave up the German desire to shape the whole world according to my concept'.[90] In 1838 he added that he would not like to be alive

> when the whole of so-called Germany . . . became an Empire or Republic in more than name; for even the tyranny France practised under Napoleon in Europe would be a mere bagatelle compared with that of a Germany under its god of war . . . and we poor Danes, who have difficulty enough defending our own characteristics against a Germany of small states, would easily be completely swallowed up by a united one.[91]

To a great extent thanks to Grundtvig, the Danes were not swallowed up.

Notes

1. See Leni Yahil, *The Holocaust: The Fate of European Jewry, 1932–1945*, translated by Ina Friedman and Haya Galai (New York 1990), chaps 19,20.

2. Idem, *The Rescue of Danish Jewry: Test of a Democracy*, translated from the Hebrew by Morris Gradel (Philadelphia 1969), passim.

3. S.H. Nissen and H. Poulsen, *Paa Dansk Frihedsgrund* (Copenhagen 1963), 35,76, quoted in Yahil, ibid., 34f.

4. P.G. Lindhardt, *Grundtvig: An Introduction* (London 1951), 127.

5. Ibid., 98.

6. Kaj Thaning, *N.F.S. Grundtvig*, translated from the Danish by David Hohnen, *Det Danske Selskap* (Odense 1972), 9.

7. Grundtvig was a member of the Folketing in 1849 and between 1853 and 1855 and a member of the Landsting (Upper House) in 1866.

8. Thaning, *N.F.S. Grundtvig*, 161.

9. Nöelle Davies, *Education for Life: A Danish Pioneer* (London 1931), 21; bibliography 201–3.

10. Ibid., 13.

11. Palle Lauring, *A History of the Kingdom of Denmark*, translated from the Danish by David Hohnen (Copenhagen 1960), 205. Before the slave trade was prohibited this was a major source of income.

12. The toll had been introduced more than 400 years before when Denmark's reign had been extended to the opposite coast of the Sound; it was soon abolished.

13. Lauring, *A History*, 193f. The treaty contained a secret article against the English navy, whose blockade the Danes were supposed to join.

14. Lindhardt, *Grundtvig*, 7.

15. William Shirer, *The Challenge of Scandinavia: Norway, Sweden, Denmark, and Finland in Our Time* (London 1956), 218.

16. David Thomson, *Europe since Napoleon*, rev. ed. (London 1974), 242.

17. A.H. Hollman, 'The Folk High School' in *Democracy in Demark*, translated into English by Alice G. Brandeis (Washington DC 1936), 7.

18. Lindhardt, 16, 19.

19. P.G. Lindhardt, *Grundtvig* (Copenhagen 1964 [in Danish]), 22; Lindhardt, 16; Thaning, 24; Hollman, 7.

20. Hollman, 9.

21. Ibid., 10; Davies, *Education*, 40.

22. Lindhardt, 20.

23. Davies, 32.

24. Lindhardt, 26f.

25. Ibid., 27.

26. Ibid.

27. Hollman, 16, 27.

28. Thaning, 81.

29. Lindhardt, 98f.

30. Ibid., 92f.

31. Lindhardt (Danish), 10.

32. Thaning, 74f.; Lindhardt, 105.

33. Thaning, 37.

34. Quoted in Lindhardt, 21.

35. Ibid. 25.

36. Thaning, 91f.

37. Lindhardt, 95, 97; Davies, *Education*, 31.

38. Davies, ibid.

39. On several occasions Grundtvig had personal contact with the Royal House and was financially supported by the King or Queen, or both.

40. Lindhardt (Danish), 69f.; Davies, 34; Lindhardt, 60f.quotes Grundtvig: 'I shall never forget it, even if I live to be a hundred.'

41. Lindhardt, ibid.

42. Ibid., 62.

43. Davies, 15; Thaning, 86; Lindhardt, 103.

44. Lindhardt, 104–6.

45. Ibid., 105.

46. Hollman, 'The Folk High School', 26.

47. Thaning, 85f.

48. Lindhardt, 110f.

49. Ibid., 108.

50. Thaning, 95.

51. Ibid., 96.

52. Ibid., 98.

53. Thaning, 162; Hoger Begtrup, Hans Lund, and Peter Manniche, *The Folk High School of Denmark and the Development of a Farming Community* (London and Copenhagen 1926), 60.

54. Begtrup et al., 91.

55. Ibid., 29.

56. Ibid., 21.

57. Wolfgang von Eichborn, *Ernst Moritz Arndt und das deutsche Nationalbewusstsein* (PhD thesis, Heidelberg 1932), 51. This is not a PhD thesis as we are used to today, rather a treatise written at the time when Arndt was hailed as a forerunner of National Socialism. I used it mainly for biographical facts, bibliography and quotations.

58. Ibid., 56–9, 67.

59. Extensive biography together with a description and evaluation of his ideas in the Introduction of Ernst Müsebeck (ed.) to Ernst Moritz Arndt, *Staat und Vaterland: Eine Auswahl aus seinen Schriften* (Munich 1921), IX–LXXXVI, scientifically more sound but also in a rather nationalistic sense.

60. Hans Kohn, *The Mind of Germany: The Education of a Nation* (London 1963), 76; Kurt Lenk, *Volk und Staat: Strukturwandel politischer Ideen im 19. und 20. Jahrhundert* (Stuttgart, Berlin and Köln 1971), 91.

61. Lenk, ibid., 89.

62. Kohn, *The Mind*, 78; Ernst Moritz Arndt, *Gedichte: Vollständige Sammlung* (Berlin 1860), 233–5.

63. Eichborn, *E.M. Arndt*, 62f.

64. Lenk, *Volk und Staat*, 90.

65. Arndt, *Gedichte*, 212f.

66. The reference is to those in Germany who came to terms with Napoleon. In his writings he calls for insurgence against these German rulers and wants the people to volunteer for the *Freikorps*.

67. 'Jesusgebet', ibid., 583.

68. Arndt, *Reden und Glossen* (1948) quoted Lenk, *Volk und Staat*, 92.

69. Lenk, ibid., 92.

70. Frederik Hertz, *Nationality in History and Politics: A Study of the Psychology and Sociology of National Sentiment and Character* (London 1944), 326f.

71. Johann Gottlieb Fichte, *Addresses to the German Nation*, edited with an Introduction by George Armstrong Kelly (New York and Evenston 1968), VIIf. (henceforth *Addresses*).

72. Ibid., IX.

73. Ibid., XIII.

74. Johann Gottlieb Fichte, *Reden an die deutsche Nation*, eingeleitet von Rudolf Eucken (Leipzig 1925), XIVf. (henceforth *Reden*). Lenk, *Volk und Staat*, his analysis of Fichte's national ideas, 74–84.

75. Hertz, *Nationality*, 339.

76. *Reden*, 9; *Addresses*, 7. I used the German original and the English translation simultaneously, and on several occasions preferred my own translation.

77. *Addresses*, 2.

78. Hertz, *Nationality*, 342.

79. Ibid., 341; George L. Mosse, *The Crisis of German Ideology: Intellectual Origins of the Third Reich* (New York 1971), 4; *Reden*, 71–5; *Addresses*, 58–63.

80. *Reden*, 58ff., quote p. 75; *Addresses*, 47ff.

81. *Reden*, 38, 49; *Addresses*, 31, 40.

82. *Reden*, 21; *Addresses*, quote p.17.

83. *Reden*, 26; *Addresses*, 21.

84. *Reden*, 32–5; *Addresses*, 26–8.

85. *Reden*, 187; *Addresses*, 160.

86. *Reden*, 191–5; *Addresses*, 163–6.

87. *Reden*, 209; *Addresses*, 177. Lenk is certainly right when he indicates that this was the first time that the slogan 'und so soll am deutschen Wesen künftig noch die Welt genesen' became emphatically expressed. *Volk und Staat*, 75.

88. Arndt, *Gedichte*, 60–2.

89. 'An die Jünglinge die Krieg schreien' (1843), ibid., 513f.

90. Lindhardt, *Grundtvig* (Danish), 84.

91. Lindhardt, *Grundtvig*, 58.

Leni Yahil

is Professor Emeritus of Haifa University. She is the author of numerous articles on the Holocaust, modern Jewish history and historiography, and of *The Rescue of Danish Jewry: Test of a Democracy* (1969) and *The Holocaust: The Fate of European Jewry* (1990).

Stanley G. Payne

Nationalism, Regionalism and Micronationalism in Spain

In most of Southern Europe, the epoch of modernization has been accompanied by intense nationalism. This has assumed such specific and sometimes extreme forms that it has given rise to several neologisms, ranging from Italian 'irredentism' to the Greek 'Megali idea' and what Myron Weiner has termed the 'Macedonian syndrome'. Such features are familiar enough from any reading of Italian or Balkan history. When, however, we turn to the other peninsula of Southern Europe, familiar signs of this nature largely disappear. Spain and Portugal were 'old' imperial powers of the first era of European expansion, which in fact they pioneered, but their modern history has largely seemed to be characterized by frustrated modernization and intense, imploding domestic conflict. Untroubled from without after the defeat of Napoleon's invasion, they have remained apart from the great wars of this century (with the sole exception of Portuguese participation in the last two years of the first world war).

It is probably fair to say that in no other European country has nationalism been weaker than in Spain prior to 1936, and in very few so weak. Some of the basic reasons for this are obvious enough:

1. Spain has been independent since approximately the eleventh century and achieved the first true world Empire in human history, long maintaining the status of an established power.

2. The traditional Spanish monarchy was confederal in structure and never created fully centralized institutions.

3. Culture and tradition in Spain were identified with religion in a manner that was more exclusive than in most other Christian lands, creating a climate of national Catholicism that would resist secularization until the 1960s.

4. During the past 200 years no genuine foreign threat to Spanish security emerged after the defeat of Napoleon.

5. Similarly, due to its geographic location and limited external ambitions, the country has avoided involvement in the major wars of the twentieth century.

6. Classical liberalism dominated Spanish political life for more than a century prior to the Civil War of 1936, discouraging military and aggressive ambitions.

7. Prior to the first world war, the pace of economic and social modernization in Spain was slow. This made it possible to sustain an early nineteenth-century model of élitist liberalism without serious pressure from below until the 1930s. Similarly, cultural life was dominated by the values and attitudes either of nineteenth-century liberalism or of traditional Catholicism, discouraging the introduction or diffusion of new doctrines or philosophies except in the working-class subculture. Thus in Spain expressions of both the early twentieth-century new right and of generic fascism were at first weaker than elsewhere.

This is not to say that there has not been a sort of national ideology in Spain. Virtually throughout Spanish history there has been an idea or a set of attitudes that can be called the 'Spanish ideology', even though the term is not commonly in use among historians. What I have referred to elsewhere as the 'Spanish ideology'[1] refers first of all to the opinions originally established (perhaps by Mozarab clergy from the South) in the kingdom of Asturias-Leon during the ninth century. According to this, the kingdom (which would be the original nucleus of the eventual Spanish monarchy) was charged with a primordial mission to fight for Christendom, expanding its own frontiers and rescuing land lost to the Muslims. At first the Spanish ideology was a fundamentally minoritarian current that did not triumph completely until the end of the fifteenth century, reaching a climax in the reigns of the Catholic monarchs and Philip II only to fall into decay in the latter part of the seventeenth century. Yet it never entirely succumbed to the Enlightenment and rationalist liberalism, reappearing time and again in moments of crisis. During the nineteenth century it was reflected in the doctrines of Apostolicism, Carlism and Integrism, and flourished once more in the doctrines of the radical right of the 1930s and the Franco regime, only to perish — presumably definitively — in the secularism of the 1960s and 1970s.[2] Yet the Spanish ideology was not a doctrine of modern nationalism, representing simply the Spanish form of national messianism (e.g. Poland as 'the Christ Among the Nations', Moscow as the 'Third Rome', and many other examples that might be cited). Rather, it served as the ideological and functional equivalent of a kind of nationalism in the pre-modern and pre-nationalist era. Its only political content consisted normally of a kind of monarchist traditionalism.

Indeed, during the nineteenth century the only political group that expressed anything approaching a kind of nationalism was that of the Carlist traditionalists. Though always defeated, in the end, they waged three civil wars on the thesis of a unique Spanish identity based on traditional values and institutions. The effect of this was not to promote a true nationalism, but to guarantee that Spanish liberalism would compromise more broadly with Catholicism than was the case in most other Catholic countries during the period, and also to help preserve a portion of the institutional autonomy of Navarre and the Basque provinces (the strongholds of Carlism).

During the first quarter of the twentieth century, Spanish affairs were heavily influenced by the diffuse Regenerationist movement, which developed in response to the military and imperial débâcle of 1898 and the slow pace of modernization. Both of the major political parties, as well as the republican and socialist movements, gave voice to Regenerationism, and all the principal leaders of the period professed to be Regenerationists. This was obviously not a unified movement, but rather consisted of a related set of goals and attitudes. The main concern of Regenerationism was practical progress and modernization, but its reformers were also concerned about the character of civil society and the latter's inability to focus coherently on common Spanish interests. Though the Regenerationists often did not agree among themselves, they found Spain's place in the world and sometimes even the question of Spanish identity problematic. There was a general tendency to agree that Spanish interests were poorly represented and that the entire society needed stronger leadership, sometimes with the implication of a more authoritarian style. Most Regenerationists were not overt nationalists compared with those elsewhere, but they bore the elements of a sort of proto-nationalism. Spain's few colonial possessions were expanded with the establishment of a Protectorate over the northern 5 per cent of Morocco in 1913, yet this event can scarcely be compared with the expansionist enterprises of other European states, having been prompted in large measure by mere embarrassment over France obtaining all the rest of Morocco while Spain did nothing. The only overt nationalists in Spain during these years, aside from an occasional journalist or secondary political figure, were to be found among the military, yet the latter rarely received any encouragement from the dominant political forces. As an editorial in *El Heraldo Militar* on 23 November 1908 proclaimed, under the headline, 'Worse Than Anywhere':

> Wherever we look, we find more virility than we do in the people here . . . .Turkey, Persia, China, the Balkan states — everywhere we find life and energy . . . even in Russia! In Spain there is nothing but apathy and submission . . . .How sad it is to think of the plight of Spain!

At that time, one form of nationalism was taking root in Spain, in the form of regional micronationalism in Catalonia and part of the Basque provinces. Regional micronationalism was a centrifugal protest against the manifold frustrations attending the process of modernization, and in part was a reaction against the relative failure of nineteenth-century liberalism in Spain. Distinct regional cultures and even separate languages had long been spoken in parts of France, for example, but the force of modernization, combined with a centripetal French nationalism, had largely overcome their divisive effects during the course of the nineteenth century. The Spanish problem lay in the fact that the 'short-circuiting' of modernization in the seventeenth century and the relatively slow pace of development in the two centuries following made an equivalent outcome in Spain impossible. The modern Catalan élite had played a major role in the development of political liberalism and what there was of economic industrialization during the nineteenth century, and had tended to view Catalonia not as the antagonist but to some degree the leader of a freer, more modern and prosperous Spain. Barcelona had been by far the most modern city in the peninsula throughout this period, and harboured more 'advanced' federalistic and/or anarchist ideologues than might normally be found elsewhere, but neither Proudhonian republicans nor revolutionary anarchists sought a special regime for Catalonia. Political feeling became more ethnocentric and inward-looking only after the débâcle of 1898 and after the crisis of liberalism became evident. Even then, the main Catalanist nationalist party, the bourgeois Lliga, never sought separatism but rather a more discrete and distinctive place for a self-governing Catalonia within a more reformist and progressive Spain. The Lliga's leaders ran their 1916 electoral campaign under the slogan 'Per l'Espanya Gran' (For a Great Spain). In the aftermath of the first world war, however, Catalan nationalism split in two between the reformist bourgeois liberalism of the increasingly conservative Lliga and the emergence of a more radical and republican petit-bourgeois Catalanism. Both in turn were outflanked by the explosion of violent anarchist-led class struggle between 1919 and 1923, so that some Lliga leaders finally accepted a temporary Spanish military dictatorship in the latter year with relief.[3]

The Primo de Rivera dictatorship, representing at least a part of the army, created the first nationalist government in Spanish history. It stood for a kind of authoritarian exaggeration of Regenerationism, on the one hand fomenting industrialization and expanded public works, on the other attempting a more ambitious foreign policy with scant success and seeking with equal futility some form of authoritarian political alternative. Despite the political failure of his regime, Primo de Rivera did succeed in first suggesting the ingredients of an alternative authoritarian nationalist system that would feature authoritarian centralism with a state political organization, a developmental and corporative economic policy, resting on modern rightist doctrines, and nationalism in culture and ideology, closely identified with the religious establishment.[4] Though he was unable to organize these approaches into a viable system, his temporary dictatorship did suggest the lines of development such an alternative might pursue in the future.

The Republic that was inaugurated in 1931 constituted the final expression of the post-first world war movement toward democracy, occurring anachronistically after the onset of the Depression when the movement in most Southern and Eastern European countries was toward rightist authoritarianism. The Republic was certainly not nationalist, virtually writing the Covenant of the League of Nations into its constitution and officially renouncing war as a normal instrument of policy. Through its de facto permanent representative in Geneva, the noted polyglot and moderate liberal Salvador de Madariaga, Spanish diplomacy played a not undistinguished role during the five years of the Republic, always on the side of the peaceful resolution of disputes and of the rights of smaller and weaker countries. Republican policy showed little interest in making an irredentist cause out of Gibraltar. It maintained the Spanish position in Morocco and even slightly expanded Spanish territory in the region through the occupation of Ifni, a small, relatively uninhabited enclave on the south-west coast of Morocco that had been ceded decades earlier but never effectively occupied. In general, the only nationalism shown by the Republic was cultural, particularly in promoting pan-Hispanism and granting full rights of co-citizens to all

Latin Americans and Portuguese residing in Spain who wished to claim it. The only foreign policy ambition of the Republic was to create a kind of bloc of neutrals as potential leverage on the great powers, but this proved too militant a proposal for some of the erstwhile partners and never came to fruition.

In domestic affairs, the Republican politicans were eager to avoid the mistakes of the abortive Federal Republic of 1873–4, while recognizing that a democratic regime could not be solidified without giving satisfaction to Catalan autonomists. The Republican constitution thus proclaimed an 'integral state', rejecting federalism, but provided means for transferring relative autonomy to special regions. This produced the Catalan Autonomy Statute of September 1932 that at first seemed to satisfy the nationalist demands of the Catalanist parties. This also exercised considerable 'demonstration effect' on other regions, and efforts soon got under way to prepare autonomy proposals elsewhere.

By far the most difficult other case was that of Basque nationalism. It is clear that there has been a Basque culture and language for many centuries, but the concept of the 'Basque nation' was a creation of the 1890s. The political history of the Basque region was a history of clans, tribes, lineages, seigneurial domains, and eventually of partially self-governing individual provinces owing allegiance to the crown of Castile/Spain, but never at any time prior to the twentieth century did it concern a joint and distinct political unit. The mythologization of Basque history and institutions, however, has a long history of its own, beginning no later than the sixteenth century. It was then that the myth of supposed historical Basque sociopolitical egalitarianism was created, primarily to help open the existing power structure to a new economic élite.[5]

The Basque provinces lost less to the partial centralization of the Spanish state than did the lands of the Aragonese crown (Aragon, Catalonia, Valencia) because they had less to lose. Unlike the latter, they never formed a completely organized political unit during the Middle Ages, nor had they avoided being caught on the losing side in the Succession War. With a less elaborate system, the Basque provinces were able to retain their legal exemptions and individual provincial assemblies into the nineteenth century, while Navarre retained its own more complete traditional legal and administrative system as well. Thus, while Barcelona province was becoming the most liberal and modern part of Spain, the Basque provinces and Navarre remained the most traditionalist, and provided the principal base for Carlism. After the defeat of the latter, even Basque liberals remained 'foralist', that is, concerned to protect certain separate provincial rights and exemptions. Neither Carlism nor foralism represented nationalism, however.

Though there is no agreement as to the precise causes of modern nationalism, and certainly no fully satisfying overarching theory, one may posit two fundamental incentives that account for the majority of nationalisms: foreign oppression, menace or military defeat on the one hand, and/or the beginning of cultural and economic modernization which threaten the traditional values or way of life on the other. These factors were more immediate in the Basque than the Catalan case, for by the late nineteenth century the Basques had lost three Carlist civil wars, were living under a much more centralized Spanish system than at any previous time, and were in the process of a fairly rapid process of industrialization, at least in the key province of Vizcaya. Though a kind of Basque cultural revival — similar to what had occurred a generation or more earlier in Catalonia and elsewhere — was already under way, the specific doctrine of a political nationalism and an independent state was created by Sabino de Arana y Goira in the 1890s, for the very first time in the long history of the Basque provinces. These circumstances exactly fitted the interpretation developed by Anthony Smith in his *Theories of Nationalism* (1971), according to which nationalism is originally born of the intersection between traditionalism and modernization, and from the need of intellectuals to rationalize an adjustment to modernity while retaining as much as possible of the traditional.[6] The ethos and doctrine of the two micronationalisms differed very considerably during the first years of the Basque movement, which was more drastic and sectarian in almost every respect. Arana publicly denounced what he termed the 'Catalanist error' of seeking autonomy and co-operation within the Spanish framework, insisting that the Basque movement demanded total separation. It was also at one and the same time racist (positing a distinct and superior Basque race), reactionary, segregationist, intolerant, ultra-clerical and in its own way quite radical. It was also much weaker than the Catalanist movement for many years, since for long the conservative and relatively pious Basques were not attracted to so novel and radical an alternative. In the process of its slow gestation into a mass movement — only completed in 1931 — it lost many of its extremist overtones, abandoning racism, extreme separatism and reactionary clericalism to emerge under the Republic as a micronationalist movement of a sort of Christian democracy. As the Basque movement moderated, conversely, much of political Catalanism became more radical, republican and anti-clerical.

The prospect of regional autonomy, which became reality for Catalonia in 1932, was only one of a number of rapid, sometimes drastic changes under the Republic that soon elicited a powerful reaction. This reaction developed the first and only significant Spanish nationalist force, responding to the threat of federalization, secularization and ultimately of collectivist revolution. The nationalist reaction assumed four different forms under the Republic: moderate but semi-authoritarian Catholic corporatism, the revival of Carlist neo-traditionalism, creation of a new radical right authoritarianism, and the generic fascist nationalism of the Falange. Of these only the first achieved broad popular mobilization, the Catholic CEDA becoming the largest single political party during the last three years of the Republic. The most serious theorizing was accomplished by the right radicals of the journal *Acción Española*, who developed a new theory of authoritarian monarchism (in considerable measure from *Action Française*) and also a doctrine of cultural and religious values (which largely represented an updating of Carlism).[7]

These were the forces that Franco brought together behind his new military regime to win the revolutionary/counter-revolutionary Civil War of 1936–9. The particular doctrines that primarily served his new nationalist regime were those of the *Acción Española* monarchists and the Falangists, just as in the early years his regime represented a mixture of fascistic politics and cultural-religious neo-traditionalism. The nationalist banner of the new dictatorship had been sparked by the reaction to the latent leftist revolution, yet it soon came to stand for a future project of its own, as Franco vowed to reunify the erstwhile nation, modernize its economy and regain its imperial or international status.

The outcome of the second world war made the last design impossible, but even after Franco's nationalism was limited to authoritarian centralism, cultural and religious neo-traditionalism, and economic modernization, it soon found itself an anachronism in contemporary Western Europe. Moreover, it constituted an anachronism in which the very goal of economic development tended to undercut first the framework of cultural and religious traditionalism and ultimately authoritarian centralism itself. By the time that Franco died, Spanish society closely approximated the social and cultural values of the rest of Western Europe, and the temporary nationalist temper of Francoism had vanished even more completely than was the case with Italian nationalism, itself moribund.

The experience of the civil war had temporarily discredited and dampened the spirit of micronationalism in Catalonia and the Basque provinces, as Basques and Catalanists had ended fighting among themselves, and, in the case of Catalonia, often in conflict with the autonomist republican state itself. A window of opportunity for a common Spanish community to overcome centrifugalism was widest in the 1940s and 1950s, but the heavy-handed dictatorship was completely incapable of taking advantage of it. In the long run, the extension of the political dictatorship all the way to 1975 had the counterproductive effect of reawakening intense nationalist feeling in the most distinctive regions, and indeed of sparking a more intense nationalist identity in the Basque provinces than had ever existed before the Civil War.

This set in motion the third cycle of the development of micronationalism in the peninsula, the comparative chronology being approximately as follows:

Cultural development	1875–95	1924–30	1955–75
Political growth	1895–1917	1931–6	1975–9
Political breakthrough	1917–19	1932/6–7	1979–
Decline	1919–23	1937–55	

Each cycle has begun with a period of cultural development, first under the restored monarchy after 1875, secondly under the rather permissive Primo de Rivera regime, and thirdly during the more relaxed and tolerant atmosphere of the second half of the Franco dictatorship. Three different phases of political growth then followed, the last two being briefer and more intense than the first comparatively slow phase of political development. This has been followed by three phases of political breakthrough, the first proving abortive at the end of the first world war, the second achieving temporary autonomy between 1932 and 1936, the third being generally successful and resulting in the broadest decentralization seen in Spain since the Old Regime.

Spanish nationalism, discredited by Francoism, is weaker than ever and has for all practical purposes disappeared, as the socialist government of the 1980s welcomes mass buy-outs of Spanish firms by foreign investors and industrialists. Catalanism has generally proven discreet under the democratic monarchy, although the granting of

autonomy to the two special regions has had a powerful demonstration effect on the rest of the country, producing de facto
federalization by 1982, and momentarily spawning such grotesque
political organizations as the Partido Cantonalista de Cartagena
(presumably nostalgic for the cantonalist chaos of the First
Republic), the Partido Racial Democrático de Andalucia (to protect
the otherwise non-existent 'Andalusian race'), or the terrorist
MPAIAC (Movement for the Self-determination and Independence
of the Canary Archipelago, briefly recognized by the Organization of
African States, capping the grotesque with the absurd). Most of these
more extreme manifestations have happily died away with the
passage of time. Though federalization complicates Spanish life and
adds considerably to political and administrative expenses, the only
truly serious problem has been the Basque country, now known by
the nationalist neologism of Euskadi (long spelled Euzkadi, before it
was decided to change a consonant in this somewhat artificial
nomenclature).

This is rather paradoxical in view of the long-standing
conservatism of Basque society, which had long made it impossible
for nationalists to mobilize a majority in the three provinces.
Nationalism had been a prototypically middle-class movement, with
both the financial and industrial bourgeoisie on the one hand and
organized labour on the other identifying with Spanish rather than
regional parties and interests.[8] A more radical leftist nationalism was
unknown prior to the emergence of the militant Euskadi Ta
Azkatasuna (ETA — Basque Homeland and Liberty) in the 1960s.

The extreme radicalization of Basque nationalism under
democracy compared with the restraint shown by the Catalanists —
seemingly a reversal of predominant traits in the history of the two
movements — has baffled many contemporary observers. No simple
theory or interpretation can explain the former any more than any
single theory has served to explain contemporary terrorism in
general, but certain factors and influences can at least be pointed out.
The revival of Basque nationalism coincided with a kind of 'future
shock', particularly in the province of Guipuzcoa, which had retained
the heaviest concentration of Basque speakers. The great economic
expansion of the 1960s rapidly completed the full-scale industrialization and urbanization of the province, uprooting much of the
remaining traditional rural population and carpeting through
various rural and suburban regions with new construction.
Thousands of traditional *baserris* (rural homesteads), many of them

in the same families for centuries, disappeared. This sudden extension of industrialization and urbanization, displacing much of the rural and small town population, was accompanied by an almost equally rapid secularization of what had been in some ways the most traditional and devout Catholic society of the peninsula. Secularization was paralleled by manifold social, cultural, psychological and political changes. In this atmosphere, some young militants moved directly from Catholic youth organizations to nationalist cells, and transferred the traditional fervour of Basque Catholicism and Carlism to a new and secular messianic politics. This in turn made the Basque provinces the region which suffered the most intense repression during the final decade of the Franco regime, creating a persecution complex which only redoubled fanaticism and for the first time gave credence to the nationalist position in the minds of tens of thousands of formerly sceptical or indifferent fellow countrymen. Moreover, it was clear that the proportionate taxes paid by the Basque economy had not generated an equivalent investment in regional services by the Spanish government, while the beginning of democratization coincided with a notable downturn in the Basque industrial economy, the older sectors of which soon became the greatest proportionate 'rustbelt' in Spain. Negotiations for autonomy did not at first proceed as rapidly and smoothly as in the case of Catalonia, for reasons mainly to do with the Basques themselves, but all this created an atmosphere of mounting resentment based on feelings of discrimination and even oppression.[9]

The experience of micronationalism in Spain has belied the theories of prominent social scientists such as Karl Deutsch concerning the future of nationalist sentiment in advanced industrial societies, and in fact seems more akin to Eastern Europe than to anything in the West (save Ulster). The chief reasons for this have obviously stemmed from the lagging and frustrated modernization of Spain during the nineteenth and twentieth centuries. Even after relative economic modernization had been achieved in the final years of the Franco regime, political development lagged well behind economic and technological expansion. Beyond that, however, the theory which held that nationalism would inevitably wither in the face of modernization requires serious modification, for nationality and nationalism must be seen as major forms of modern secular identity, long able to survive and even to grow in appropriately varied circumstances. Nationalism may disappear for a generation or two in nations to whom extreme nationalism has brought disaster, and may long wither in prosperous and satisfied countries feeling no sense of oppressor or oppression. Conversely, the future of nationalism seems depressingly bright in Eastern Europe and, though the worst may now be over in democratic Spain, the final round has not yet been fought.

Notes

1. I have discussed this in my *Spanish Catholicism* (Madison 1980), particularly in chapters 1 and 2.

2. The work of Juan Saiz Barberá, *El espiritualismo español y destino providencial de España en la historia universal* (Seville 1977), is the last major statement of the traditional Spanish ideology, published two years after the death of Franco.

3. For a general introduction, see Jaume Rossinyol, *Le Problème national catalan* (Paris 1974); Maximiano García Venero, *Historia del nacionalismo catalán* (Madrid 1967), 2 vols; J.M. Problet, *Història bàsica del catalanisme* (Barcelona 1975); Félix Cucurull, *Panoràmica del nacionalisme català* (Paris 1975); Albert Balcells, *Historia contemporánea de Cataluña* (Barcelona 1983); and Josep Termes, 'De la revolució de setembre a la fin de la guerra civil, 1868–1939', *Història de Catalunya*, VI (Barcelona 1987).

4. The best study is Shlomo Ben-Ami, *Fascism from Above: The Dictatorship of Primo de Rivera in Spain, 1923–1930* (Oxford 1983).

5. See Alfonso de Otazu y Llana, *El 'igualitarismo vasco': mito y realidad* (San Sebastian 1986), and Juan Aranzadi, *Milenarismo vasco* (Madrid 1982).

6. Though it may be noted that the Basque case does not fit every aspect of Smith's refinement of the theory, which in the process becomes overly determined.

7. The chief expression of this was Ramiro de Maeztu's *Defensa de Hispanidad* (Madrid 1934).

8. The Basque bourgeoisie, in fact, has made major contributions to all-Spanish rightist nationalism in the twentieth century, in five distinct phases:

    1) The Liga de Acción Monárquica, the political organization of the Basque new right, played an important role in the attempt to create an all-Spanish new right in the years immediately after the first world war.

    2) The Basque bourgeoisie collaborated fairly closely with the nationalistic new dictatorship of Primo de Rivera during the rest of the 1920s.

    3) Representatives of the Bilbao bourgeoisie contributed more than any other single group in the first efforts to stimulate a fascist movement in Spain between 1931 and 1933.

    4) They played an important role in the attempt to form a nationalistic all-Spanish radical right around José Calvo Sotelo between 1934 and 1936.

    5) The Basque right enjoyed disproportionate representation under the Franco regime. For example, in 1960, when the Basque provinces and Navarre contained 5.8 per cent of the population of Spain, they had 9.5 per cent of the Cortes seats, 8 per cent of all the military ministers of

Franco, 12.9 per cent of the titles of nobility granted by the General-issimo, and approximately 15 per cent of all the cabinet ministers in the regime to that point, according to Luis C. Núñez, *Clases sociales en Euskadi* (San Sebastian 1977), 76–7.

9. There is extensive literature on ETA, Spanish Basque terrorism and contemporary Basque politics. A cogent analytical introduction to the problem may be found in Peter Waldmann, 'Sozio-ökonomischer Wandel, zentralistische Unter-drückung und Protestgewalt im Baskenland' in *Die geheime Dynamik autoritärer Diktaturen* (Munich 1982) ed. P. Waldmann et al., 199–286. Joseba Zulaika, *Basque Violence: Metaphor and Sacrament* (Reno 1988), presents a suggestive approach through cultural anthropology. The most succinct and accurate summary of the history of ETA is John Sullivan, *ETA and Basque Nationalism* (London 1988). Juan J. Linz et al., *Conflicto en Euskadi* (Madrid 1986), is the most comprehensive single study of contemporary Basque politics and society.

Stanley G. Payne
is Hilldale Professor of History at the
University of Wisconsin-Madison. His latest
book is *The Franco Regime, 1936–1975*
(1988) and he is currently preparing a history
of the Second Republic in Spain.

Shlomo Ben-Ami

Basque Nationalism between Archaism and Modernity

A small people centred in the northern corner of the Iberian peninsula, the Basques claim their language is the oldest in Europe,[1] and proudly assert that it took the overwhelming might of the Roman Empire more than two centuries to conquer them. Nor were the Muslims and Charlemagne, at the peak of their power, more successful in this respect.[2] The geographic isolation of Euskadi, as the Basque country is commonly known, helped develop among its people a strong attachment to millenarian social and family structures as well as a xenophobic mind deeply suspicious of foreign cultural influences.[3] But, in spite of the nationalists' fanatic emphasis on their homeland's historical, ethnic and linguistic distinctiveness, the link of the Basque country with the rest of Spain was never seriously questioned. Of the four Basque provinces, three — Vizcaya, Guipuzcoa and Alava — were integrated into the Castilian Kingdom in the thirteenth and fourteenth centuries, and that only after the Castilian kings had recognized their regional *fueros* (the Spanish word for rights or laws) in matters of jurisdiction, administration and financial management.[4]

Strongly conservative and fanatically Catholic, the agrarian-based Basque society was consistent with the overall physiognomy of the Spain of the old regime. However, the invasion of the country by the legacy of the French *philosophes* late in the eighteenth century and by European liberalism in the first half of the nineteenth century threatened to undermine the cohesion and homogeneity of Basque society. The Carlist rebellions, the power base and social support of which was centred in the Basque provinces, especially in highly devout and Catholic Navarre, were essentially the violent protest of primitive peasant communities against the sins of liberalism and the corruption of urban society. Consequently, unlike Catalonia, where nineteenth-century nationalism was a cause advocated in an advanced industrial and secular society scornful of the 'parasitic' and 'oligarchic' centre — Castile and its capital Madrid — Basquism started as the anti-modernist rebellion, a kind of Spanish *Vendée*, of archaic, immobile communities that refused to succumb to the liberal sin. Yet, liberalism, distorted and perverted as it might be, won the day. Consequently, the liberal monarchist constitution of 1876 wiped out the *fueros* altogether.[5]

By the end of the century, Basque society had undergone important, even dramatic, structural changes that were to have far-reaching consequences for the future of Basque nationalism. Heavy industry and mining developed considerably, urban middle and working classes emerged with the changing patterns of the economy, and internal migration started to alter the until then purely Basque physiognomy of the population.[6]

The emergence of modern Basque society was inevitably influenced by the modernization of the economy — initial Basque industrial- ization occurred with a rapidity probably unequalled in the European experience — and by the concomitant strains on the Basque social fabric.[7] The whole ideological and political framework of Basque society was transformed during the process of modernization. Thus, for example, socialism altered and disrupted the old balance between the traditional forces of Euskadi such as conservative nationalism and liberalism. It was in Vizcaya that the Spanish Socialist Party (PSOE), the first mass party in contemporary Basque politics, emerged. It was also here that modern Basque nationalism was born as a reaction by traditional Basque society to the challenge of socialism and to the collapse of the old social and cultural order.[8] Significantly, the social sectors which turned to nationalism were precisely those which formed part of the traditional pre-industrial Vizcayan society, and were now alarmed by the corruption of Basque values by industrialization. Their defensive reaction was to resort to a brand of nationalism derived from a mythical ideology based on rural symbols. Indeed, modern Basque nationalism can be explained as a response by traditional society to the tortuous road leading from tradition to modernity.[9] In the process, the old Catholic-integrist and 'foralist' tradition — always respectful to the historical unity of Spain — gave way to a secessionist and anti-Spanish brand of Basque nationalism. In the two other Basque provinces — Alava and Guipuzcoa — the process of politicization was less polarized than in industrialized Vizcaya. Far slower to join the industrial age, these provinces managed to maintain the stability of the traditional order well into the 1950s, and when the social fabric was finally transformed, it was done without traumatic upheavals and ruptures. It was not until the Second Republic that Basque nationalism started to play a decisive role in the politics of Guipuzcoa, and in Alava not even then.[10]

The inevitable conclusion is that the degree of economic and social modernization, and the Basque commitment to nationalism, were never homogeneous. Essentially, the Basque country was and continues to be a pluralistic society where a variety of political options vie for hegemony; nationalism had never been the sole and exclusive master of the situation. From the start of industrialization, socialism was always at least as strong. The socialists rejected Basque nationalism for its ultra-religious and traditionalist tenets and for its xenophobic attitude that excluded the immigrant proletariat from the Basque order of things.[11] One may argue that rather than a coherent Basque country and society, what one should speak of is various Basque countries with a remarkable degree of political pluralism ranging from 'españolista' socialism through Carlism and integrism to an incoherent nationalism divided between a possibilist and a radical wing.

Modernization undermined the traditional homogeneity of Basque society but never to the point of totally destroying its archaic, pre-industrial legacies, that are the very essence of traditional Basquism. Moreover, the emergence of the modern industrial Leviathan strengthened, if anything, the commitment to the particularistic old traditions, lest they be violated by the 'corrupting' and 'disintegrating' influences of urbanization. Eventually, modern Basque society developed a balanced equilibrium between modernity and tradition, a unique kind of co-existence between industrialization and mass urban society on the one hand, and a patriarchal mentality, puritanism and a tendency for populist mythology on the other. This symbiosis between tradition and modernity fostered the creation of a deep religious, even integrist, sentiment that the Basque Church managed to identify with a spirit of religious communal life. It was this very sentiment, in its version of intolerant crusade, which would later underscore ETA's brand of fanatic terrorism. Economic development in the Basque country was not then accompanied by an equally profound cultural revolution. The Basques — or perhaps the central state was to blame — had never been either willing or able to create an important secular Basque university. The Jesuit Deusto university in Bilbao, and the Opus Dei university in Pamplona have always been the major centres of higher learning in the Basque country.[12] Clearly, the dramatic secularization of life in no way undermined the centrality of religious culture in Euskadi; nor did it destroy the style and culture of local life which remained essential for nurturing the nationalist fire.[13] It would be wrong to refer to the persistence of the pre-industrial spirit in Euskadi as a merely folkloristic residue; it is a deep conviction, a kind of active defence against the excesses of modern civilization. Populist mystique succeeded in turning the attachment to Basque traditional values into the hegemonic ideal in Euskadi, the major test of 'belonging' to the Basque nation. Only in this manner can the widespread legitimacy that was later to be acquired by Basque terrorism in defence of that very mystique be understood.[14]

The founder of modern Basque nationalism, Sabino de Arana y Goiri was a genuine embodiment of the balance between modernity and archaism that consistently characterized Basque nationalism.[15] Significantly, he was not a peasant but an upper middle-class Vizcayan intellectual whose family, though of Carlist political background, had strong links with the newly emerging Basque business community. For him, the lesson to be learned from the Catalan experience was that nationalist exclusivism was the indispensable pre-condition for Basque material and cultural development. Absolutely ignorant of the Basque historical, linguistic and cultural legacy — a not uncommon phenomenon among nationalist leaders in other places — he set out to study it.[16] Sabino de Arana's nationalism was, however, emphatically xenophobic, ultra-Catholic and violently anti-Liberal. According to Arana, Euskadi had to be independent, because 'dependent on Spain, she cannot address herself to God, she can never be truly Catholic'.[17]

Basque nationalism, as elaborated by Sabino de Arana and propagated later by the Nationalist Basque Party (PNV), advanced the thesis of an independent republican confederation of the seven Basque provinces, four on Spanish soil and three across the French border, each of which would enjoy full internal autonomy. A radical emphasis, always alien to Catalan nationalism, was reflected in the demand that Spanish immigration should be restricted in order to preserve the Basque *pureza de sangre*.[18] Arana's major concern was that of preventing the degeneration and possible extinction of the Basque race by the invasion of 'foreigners', that is Spanish immigrants who moved to the Basque country in search of the job opportunities opened by the region's rapid industrialization. These 'foreigners' were, according to Arana, a mass of degenerate, immoral, godless and subversive socialists. Basque independence was then to be conceived as a *cordon sanitaire* against these disintegrating influences; and the intensification of Basque culture and language was a means of separating the 'true' Basques from the 'Spanish' immigrants.[19]

The Basque autonomous entity that Sabino de Arana dreamt of would also, as a matter of course, be completely subordinated to the tenets of Catholicism and even to the institutional authority of the Church. Indeed, it was thanks to Sabino's religious integrism that the Basque Church became a staunch supporter of Basque nationalism.[20] In Sabino's philosophy, the Christianization of the Basque people was an integral part of, indeed, a condition for, its liberation. The whole world of symbols and rhetoric of Basque nationalism rested on, and was inspired by, the Christian mystique of service and salvation. Sabino himself was portrayed by his followers through metaphors taken from Christian imagery: he was the Martyr, the Father, the Master. It was even claimed that just like the Jews, the Basques also suffered for committing deicide: they lost their *patria*.[21]

However, the archaic and millenarian roots and features of Basque nationalism, as well as its aspiration to racial purity, were not exactly a recipe for quick expansion of the nationalist gospel in a modern society. Nor could the archaic roots of the Basque language and the general ignorance of the Basque cultural heritage be instrumental in fostering the cause of Basquism. Basque literature lacked the vitality and glamour of the Catalan *renaixanca*, the cultural renaissance of *fin de siècle* in Catalonia.[22] Basque literature remained the archaic, 'savage' and primitive concern of dedicated, narrow parochial minds; and the falsification of history alienated many Basque intellectuals from nationalism. The three greatest prose writers of Spain in the present century — Unamuno, Ramiro de Maeztu and Pio Baroja — were Basque, but they hardly wrote a word in Sabino de Arana's language. They preferred that of Cervantes.[23] For Unamuno, the Basque tongue — *euskera* — was nothing but a rural and agonizing language.[24]

Nonetheless, the PNV founded in 1895 by Sabino de Arana was, unlike most Spanish parties, much more than just an electoral machine. It was the integrative expression of the Basque soul, the guardian and revealer of Basque culture and tradition. The party, therefore, attracted a great number of people who wanted to counter the threats of liberalism, socialism and the moral degeneration fostered by industrialization and the concomitant 'Spanish invasion'. The PNV integrated Arana's mythical concept about a pre-industrial Basque egalitarian Arcadia[25] that was now being destroyed by mass immigration, emphasizing in its propaganda the virtues of traditional rural life, and the superiority of the Basque race as compared with the 'violent', 'dishonest' and 'immoral' immigrant.[26] The PNV's propaganda, however, was thoroughly ambiguous, not to say cynical. The social problems that resulted from the rapid process of industrialization were blamed on the 'Spanish' workers, whereas industrialization as such, notwithstanding the frequent nostalgia for the rural past, was never condemned. On the contrary, the high level of economic development of Euskadi was conveniently presented as additional proof of Basque superiority.[27]

It would, therefore, be incorrect to insist on the reactionary aspects of Basque nationalism; its attitude to modernity was thoroughly ambiguous. When it came to power in the autonomous government of October 1936, the PNV was a far more liberal and flexible party than that conceived by Sabino de Arana.[28] The incorporation of Social-Catholic sectors into the party in the first decade of the present century helped turn it into a fairly moderate Christian-Democratic movement, committed, it is true, to the most fundamental tenets of Sabino de Arana's philosophy: a radical and purist conception of the Basque ethnic legacy and nationalism.[29]

The political mission of the PNV remained that of achieving the widest possible degree of self-government, and of defining Euskadi's links with 'Spain' as an association between two sovereign peoples. There was always, however, a kind of calculated ambiguity in the political strategy of the PNV, an ambiguity which the radical nationalists of the 1960s would challenge most successfully. The PNV defended Basque sovereignty and nationhood, but it never said this should entail fully-fledged independence and a national state. In fact, this pragmatic attitude was advocated as early as 1902 by Sabino de Arana himself when he advanced the idea of autonomy as being more realistic than that of independence.[30]

The PNV's calculated ambiguity resulted in a split among Basque nationalists without calming Spanish fears of a possible nationalist flare-up in the north. The PNV's brand of nationalism was challenged within Basque society itself not only by the 'godless' socialists, but also by the staunchly Catholic *fuerista* tradition that was solidly backed by Basque conservatives — especially Carlists and traditionalists — who viewed the *fueros*, a formula of self-rule within the unquestionable unity of Spain, as an outlet still valid for Basque national aspirations. The *fueros* were conceived as a means of reconciling Basque rights with Spain's historical unity, rather than as a principle of Basque sovereignty[31] which was exactly why modern Basque nationalists could not accept it. 'Spanish' society rejected out of hand as false and dangerous the historical revisionism upon which the whole political philosophy of the PNV rested. Contrary to what Basque nationalists liked to say, the Basque country had always been linked to Spain, and in spite of the surprising persistence of its archaic language, Spanish had always been the predominant language of Basque society and culture. Even the famous *fueros*, the old statutes of self-rule, had been written in Spanish, not in *euskera*.[32]

Flanked by the *fuerista*, conservative challenge on the one hand and the socialist threat on the other, Basque nationalism shed, throughout the first half of this century, the appearance of a narrow, failing movement. Whereas in Catalonia, lower middle-class Catalanism gained strength, among other things, by relying heavily on working-class support, the PNV failed to gain any substantial foothold among the urban workers, and, like the *Lliga Regionalista* — the party of middle and upper middle-class Catalan nationalism — it rested on a fairly narrow social base.

But the prospects of Basque nationalism were always linked to its encounter with the challenge of development and modernity. This was once again corroborated by the experience of the 1920s and 1930s. Basque nationalism, though justly considered by Unamuno as 'absurd racial virginity', gathered substantial momentum during the dictatorship of Primo de Rivera (1923–30). Nationalist consciousness expanded as a result of the successful cultural campaigns carried out by the Society for Basque Studies and the Academy of the Basque Language. A major incentive was also given to the nationalist movement by the progressive integration of Basque society as a result of the expansion in the 1920s — an age of economic boom and prosperity — of modern means of mass communication such as the radio, the telephone and the press. The new railways, the expanding road network, the private car and the public bus, as well as new phenomena of mass culture, such as soccer, helped create a more cohesive Basque society.[33] Moreover, by destroying the party structure of the monarchist right,[34] Primo's dictatorship created the conditions for the emergence of the PNV as the predominant expression of Basque right-wing politics in the Basque country. The

PNV of the Second Republic was a populist Catholic party that strove to create an egalitarian Basque society based on an ethnically pure Basque community. Although it was clearly no longer the same party created by Sabino de Arana, it nevertheless maintained xenophobic and even racist residues. Rather than to Liberal democracy, the PNV professed a strong attachment to Christian, organic democracy where the family and the municipality, not the autonomous individual, would become the spinal cord of the future Basque society.[35]

Paradoxically, however, the PNV's leader, José Antonio de Aguirre, led the movement toward a close collaboration with the liberal Republic, in spite of the latter's commitment to anticlericalism. He knew that a nationalist clerical regime would nip in the bud any centrifugal trend. A dictatorship, he rightly feared, would immediately resort to brutal repression to curb the 'disintegration' of the *patria*.[36] This dramatic change of tactics by Basque nationalism was tantamount to a recognition that only a tolerant, democratic and pluralistic regime would ever accept the idea of Basque autonomy. Autonomy was a concomitant of democracy, while serving as a standing temptation for repression by a dictatorship. The 'catastrophic' right would, at best, accept the folkloristic distinctiveness of the various Spanish regions. It would never recognize the legitimacy of their national aspirations.

Nor was the secular Republic that generous in conceding autonomy to the Basque ultramontane enclave in northern Spain. The story of the failure of Basque autonomism under the Republic started with the elaboration by a Basque commission of a statute of autonomy for the region. It called for the creation of a 'Basque state . . . autonomous within the totality of the Spanish state', with the latter retaining competence over foreign relations, currency, penal and mercantile law, the armed forces, and suffrage in national elections. The four constituent provinces would themselves be autonomous within the Basque state and would be entitled to leave it at will.[37] The major difference, and the crucial one indeed, between this project and the Catalan statute lay in the provision that Church–State relations were to be within the competence of the autonomous region, which would, moreover, be empowered to make its own Concordat with the Holy See. This provision, however, failed to pave the way for the incorporation of traditionalist Navarre into the Basque Nationalist movement. It only succeeded in enhancing the government's unwillingness to grant autonomy to the Basque reactionaries, who now threatened the democratic Republic with the establishment of what the socialist Prieto called a 'Vaticanist Gibraltar'.[38]

The removal, under governmental pressure, of the religious clauses from the autonomy statute only contributed to the splitting of the Basques without really advancing the cause of autonomy. It intensified Navarre's alienation from the Basque cause. Its case for local liberties was definitely overshadowed by its commitment to Spain's religious unity. Overwhelmingly rural and fanatically traditionalist, Navarre refused to flirt with a Basque nationalist movement that might degenerate into a republican secessionist adventure.

As the Civil War loomed on the horizon, the impracticability, indeed the senselessness, of a united Basque state became more evident than ever. The Basque nationalists accentuated their rapprochement with the republican left and its socialist allies as the most solid alternative available for the cause of autonomy. This move was most obviously discernible in Guipuzcoa and Vizcaya — the urban provinces of the Basque country. Rural Navarre and Alava joined the nationalist cause. They would not sacrifice deeply entrenched traditionalist values for the sake of autonomy under the auspices of a 'masonic', 'bolshevik' Republic.[39] In October 1936, when Franco's crusade was well under way, a new autonomy statute set up the Autonomous Government of Euskadi. Very soon though, Guipuzcoa, or most of it, fell to the nationalists, so that autonomy was basically confined to the highly developed region of Vizcaya. The Spanish Civil War was actually also a war between the Basques.[40]

Franco's victory in the Civil War marked the complete defeat of Basque and Catalan nationalism. Not surprisingly, only loyalist Navarre enjoyed a special status under Franco, especially in matters of taxation and tariffs. Otherwise, any manifestation of Catalan and Basque particularism was crushed mercilessly. The use of the vernacular was banned; even its use in telephone conversations was strictly prohibited. Those organizations pleading for autonomy, and which had survived the Civil War, now either went underground or moved to a frustrating exile.

Basque nationalism, which after its defeat in the Civil War had entered a lethargic stage in conditions of decline and despair, was once again saved from oblivion by industrialization. The 'second wave' of modernization, that is the famous economic miracle of the last twenty years of Francoism, just like the industrialization of the Basque provinces in the 1890s, was to have a direct impact on the awakening and renewed expansion of Basque nationalism. The whole of Spanish society reached a turning-point during the late 1950s and 1960s. A dramatic economic miracle and the emergence in Spain of a consumer society helped, gradually but consistently, to erode the oppressive characteristics of Francoism. Catalonia and the Basque country were the two major poles of development during the Francoist economic boom. In the Basque country, industrialization reached traditional rural provinces such as Alava that soon became the most developed and urbanized of all the Basque provinces. By the mid-1970s, its income *per capita* was the highest in Spain.[41] Fundamentally authoritarian and police-minded, the regime was driven, nevertheless, to the conclusion that a certain relaxation of political and cultural restrictions was inevitable if development and open borders were to be maintained.[42]

Rapid economic development had in a sense accentuated the difference between the periphery and the centre. The hard-working Basques and the highly industrialized Catalan society began to resent that their profits were being channelled by centralistic priorities to the stagnant areas of Spain. Basque Marxist extremists and the middle class would have agreed with Jean Paul Sartre's observation that, in spite of their high degree of development, the Basque provinces were ruled by Spain as a colony. Subjected to foreign economic domination and deprived of their inherent right to self-determination, the Basques were not substantially different from the Palestinians, Welsh or Bretons; thus runs the argument.[43] Indeed, there can hardly be any doubt that, as a reaction to what the Basques viewed as Madrid's vendetta against their economic interests, Basque cultural and political nationalism gathered meaningful momentum during the last years of Francoism.

Francoist repression could only do away with the external manifestations of Basquism and Catalanism, it could never uproot nationalist aspirations. On the contrary, nationalism remained alive, though dormant, for decades. As soon as governmental repression showed signs of relative relaxation, it erupted again with renewed vigour; the policy of neglecting regional nationalism proved to be fallacious in the long run. Basque traditional identity might have been somewhat eroded by the spectacular industrialization of the 1960s and by the emergence of a consumer society bent on modern bourgeois values. Yet, unquestionably, Franco's belief that development and *panem et circensem* would eradicate regional nationalism proved to be illusory. The vertiginous modernization of the Basque and Catalan provinces did not do away with their sense of identity; and it certainly sharpened their sense of superiority in relation to the 'parasitic' centre.

Of all the nationalist groups that emerged in Spain in the early 1960s to back nationalist claims, it was ETA (Euskadi Ta Azkatasuna — Basque Homeland and Liberty) that gained most notoriety. ETA was a Basque nationalist revolutionary organization which in 1959 split from the PNV in protest against the latter's excessive conservatism. From its headquarters beyond the Pyrenees, ETA conducted an unrestrained and highly efficient campaign of terror against the Spanish state throughout the 1960s and 1970s, climaxing in the murder in 1973 of Premier Carrero Blanco.[44] Fully-fledged independence under the auspices of a Marxist, Castroist regime rather than a vague autonomy was, and remains to this day, ETA's major aspiration. This is to be achieved not through negotiations with Madrid but through the revolutionary élan of the masses, guided by a highly motivated minority, namely ETA.

The origins of ETA can be traced back to the early 1950s when a group of students at the University of Bilbao formed *Ekin* ('to do'), a Basque movement of 'action' opposed to the conservative strategy of the PNV. The group's leader, Txillardegi, claimed that the PNV's response to the threats affecting the Basque nation was totally inadequate. He maintained that the salvation of the Basque language and its promotion were central to any nationalist policy.[45] Indeed, *Ekin* concentrated its activities on culture and the distribution of educational material based on social-Catholic teaching.[46] But *Ekin* was more than that. It also called for more active resistance to Spanish oppression, defended a strategy of national liberation through armed struggle, and rejected the PNV's exclusive concentration on cultural projects.[47] ETA was created officially on San Ignacio de Loyola day, 31 July 1959. The day was not accidental; San Ignacio de Loyola, founder of the Jesuit order, thus became the inspiration of a military order of devout nationalists deeply imbued with religious values. Indeed, Catholic and ecclesiastical organizations provided a congenial recruiting ground for ETA.[48] The Church was the main shelter of Basque culture; the rural clergy was always a bastion of Basque sentiments. Most of the periodicals written in *euskera*, the Basque language, were published under Church auspices[49] and most of the Basque schools founded during the Franco dictatorship were created at the exclusive initiative of the Church. It was this resurrection of Basque language and culture which created the conditions for the growth of ETA.

In the Basque country, religion, millenarian traditions and nationalism had gone hand in hand since Sabino de Arana's days. Francoist repression of both only strengthened the alliance and turned the Basque Church into a staunch defender of the 'ethnic, linguistic and social characteristics given to the Basques by God', as it was put by a manifesto of protest signed by hundreds of Basque priests on 30 May 1960. It is noteworthy that both Catalanism and Basquism in the 1960s found a strong ally in the Church. Imbued with a renovating spirit by Pope John XXIII's policies, and eager to detach themselves from an increasingly anachronistic dictatorship, the Basque and Catalan Churches turned into the spearhead of social and national protest. Pope John XXIII's defence of *nationes minores* in his 1963 encyclical *Pacem in Terris* certainly contributed to an alleviation of the Catalan and Basque lot.[50] Their nationalist aspirations, however, fell far short of redemption. The Basque Church managed to maintain its leadership in Euskadi thanks also to its commitment to become the shelter of the persecuted Basque culture. In the 1960s, about 75 per cent of the writers who used *euskera* were priests, and the whole movement of *ikastolas* (Basque schools) was run by the Church.[51]

Surprising as it may seem, ETA did not start as a Marxist-Leninist movement committed to the armed struggle, but rather as a nationalist-conservative offspring of the Basque Youth of Catholic Action. Young priests and religious youth moved away from what they saw as the paralysing conformity of Basque nationalism, and advocated a more radical strategy. Many of the leaders of ETA, and indeed other Basque nationalist leaders, received a religious education, and some of them were even ordained as priests. The Basque freedom fighter was expected to be at the same time a *jeldike* and a *gudari*, that is 'half monk and half soldier'.[52] ETA was instrumental in the secularization of the Basque religious world. The Basque Church and its priests provided ETA with the necessary infrastructure for its war against the Spanish state. Indeed, before ETA started its bloody campaign of violence and murder in 1965, it asked for the Church's blessing.[53] Significantly, the Basque Church was consistently, even after Franco's death, reluctant to condemn ETA, to which it always referred as 'a movement of national liberation', whose heroes and fallen were glorified as the 'martyrs' of a sacred cause.[54] Basque terrorism, like that of the French Revolution, thus acquired a kind of divine sanction that resulted in the 'religious' exaltation of the nation.[55] The symbiotic link between religion and nationalism turned the Basque idea into a kind of 'political theology',[56] and Euskadi into a country where religious violence was secularized and nationalist terrorism sanctified. Not unlike other national wars of liberation, the Basque war against 'Spain' was conceived as a religious crusade.[57] It was this strong alliance between nationalism and religion in the Basque country that prevented the Basque Church from playing the same kind of progressive role played by the Spanish Church in facilitating the transition to democracy in the late 1970s. ETA's greatest success was undoubtedly that of linking Basque consciousness, indeed the whole idea of being a Basque, with a rejection of 'Spanish oppression' and its agents in the region.

It was at its first General Assembly in May 1962, conspicuously celebrated in a monastery in southern France, that ETA started to define its principles. Its Declaration of Principles[58] called for the independence of the French and Spanish Basque countries and their reunification in a democratic state that would guarantee religious freedom. *Euskera* would as a matter of course be the official language of the new state where, it was promised, the immigrants would not be discriminated against 'so long as they did not act against the Basque national interest'. The socialist colouring of the new organization was given by the clause calling for the nationalization of the basic industries in the Basque country. In fact, the gradual acceptance by ETA of the 'Spanish' immigrants as 'potentially Basque', and its progressive solidarity with their social aspirations gradually strengthened ETA's socialist credentials. But the question of the immigrants was more complicated than that. The total and un-equivocal acceptance of the immigrants into the Basque nation could have separated ETA from its most genuine nationalist roots, and would have brought it closer to an alliance with the 'Spanish' left. Therefore, those elements in ETA which adopted this kind of line ended up accepting the idea of a bilingual Basque independent state. As a modern movement different from the 'lethargic' and conserv-ative PNV, ETA had no other choice but to develop a more open attitude towards the immigrants, even at the price of being accused of 'españolismo'.[59]

ETA adopted socialist and revolutionary positions under the impact of the anti-colonial wars in Algeria and Cuba. These kinds of wars of liberation seemed to reconcile socialism with nationalism, exactly the dilemma faced by ETA. ETA learnt from the wars of the

Third World that Euskadi was also an exploited colony and that guerrilla warfare — that is the models of Algeria, Vietnam and Cuba — were the appropriate means to get rid of the occupying, foreign force. This analogy, however, was not accepted by everybody in ETA. There were those who refused to accept that Euskadi, one of the most developed regions of Spain, was comparable to a Third World society. They preferred to adopt a socialist strategy based on an alliance with the 'Spanish' working class and its children. Within ETA, a division was being created between those who, on the one hand, wanted a Marxist strategy based on the working class, including immigrants, and on the other, a coalition made up of those who defended a Third World kind of guerrilla strategy and others, like Txillardegi, who traditionally rejected all that was Spanish, including the oppressed Spanish proletariat. The guerrilla strategy was the basis of Federico Krutwig's book, *Vasconia*,[60] a book that proposed a whole theory based on the experience of anti-colonial movements. Krutwig's major contribution to ETA's strategy was his theory about the 'spiral' action–repression–action, and his conviction that the Basque movement of liberation should develop a parallel system of administration in order to get rid of the administration of the colonial power, and force it to negotiate Basque independence.[61] Indeed, the most important effect of ETA's guerrilla strategy was that of creating heroes and martyrs — for example, those involved in the Burgos trial[62] — capable of mobilizing the masses.

In spite of its Marxist ideology, ETA gave neither a theoretical nor practical role to the proletariat in its strategy.[63] Even the capitalist class — so central in any Marxist strategy — was curiously absent from ETA's formulations. A movement based on the 'people' could not afford the luxury of attacking a social class whose members belonged to that very 'people'. The name of the enemy was 'Spain' and later 'imperialism', not a particular social class. When a more precise categorization was needed, the enemy was the 'oligarchy', a small group of Basque capitalists, which had supposedly betrayed Euskadi in order to obtain benefits from its participation in the Spanish economy. The lack of any analysis in terms of social classes allowed ETA to include in, or exclude from, the 'Basque working people' any social group, the sole criterion being its attitude to Basque nationalism, not its social affinities or aspirations. The emphasis that ETA put on the role of the armed élite had an immediate consequence: it eroded the concept of class. Therefore, the nature of socialism to which ETA claimed to be attached was never sufficiently clear. Neither the first leaders of ETA nor the activists of Herri Batasuna, a kind of Basque Sinn Fein, a political branch of the terrorist organization, ever showed any special interest in spelling out their proposals on how the social and economic structure of the Basque country was to be changed. Socialism was conceived in very vague terms as a more just society. Idealism and self-sacrifice, rather than a clearly defined socio-political programme, were the main values.

The dilemmas and contradictions of ETA did not end there. The absurdity of ETA's idea of considering Euskadi as an exploited colony was also reflected in its failure to create a real guerrilla army that would liberate Euskadi from the 'imperialist' forces. The sporadic acts of terrorism and violence perpetrated by ETA had in reality very little to do with the strategy proposed by Krutwig; they were essentially nothing but a series of daring actions carried out by minority groups, admittedly backed by popular sympathy. According to Krutwig, the Basque theoretician of the armed struggle, the major object of the violent actions of an armed avant-garde was that of radicalizing the population and enhancing its commitment to the nationalist cause. Consequently, Krutwig believed that the distinction between mass struggle and élite revolutionary violence would fade away the moment the avant-garde became part of the popular army. During the last years of Franco's dictatorship, the leaders of ETA pretended to settle their ideological contradictions by claiming that the mass struggle was their aspiration but, given the conditions of illegality under which they were forced to operate, the exclusive reliance on an armed avant-garde was still needed, and indeed inevitable. The most coherent posture was adopted in 1975 by *ETA militar*, one of the groups that split from the organization, when it decided to abandon the idea of mass struggle and concentrate exclusively on élite armed struggle. But the contradiction never really disappeared; ETA never managed to combine the two forms of struggle as stipulated in its own theory.

Whatever the contradictions and inconsistencies of ETA might be, its significance for the development of the Basque question cannot be underestimated. The emergence of ETA signalled a momentous turning-point in both the tactics and the strategy of Basque nationalism. By defining itself as a 'Basque socialist movement of national liberation', ETA broke away from the PNV's conservative tradition of pragmatic accommodation with 'Spanish' governments. With the birth of ETA, the whole character of the Basque nationalist movement was radically transformed. Nationalism that had so far been conceived as some kind of abstract phenomenon unrelated to social realities was now embodied in a Marxist group claiming that national liberation could not be achieved without the salvation of the oppressed classes. The old traditional barrier between socialism and nationalism was thus broken, and the social distance between Basque natives and immigrant workers was supposedly narrowed. The new social emphasis of ETA brought the PNV monopoly of the nationalist movement to an end, and by developing a new concept of national emancipation that would also include the humblest strata of society, it helped create the conditions for their integration into a wide protest against the social and political order.

Entirely indifferent to the nature of the Spanish state or to the kind of regime that should prevail in it, ETA was not created to fight the Franco dictatorship and restore democracy in Spain, as some observers and European romantics liked to think, but to bring about an independent, socialist Basque state. This is the reason why ETA continues to fight the young Spanish democracy as violently and relentlessly as it did Franco's military dictatorship. Suffice it to say that from Franco's death in November 1975 to December 1986 ETA claimed responsibility for the death of 421 people, the victims of its indiscriminate orgy of terrorism. Moreover, the radicalizing effect that the dialectics of ETA's strategy had on Basque politics was precisely that of increasing the support for the nationalist option in Basque society. Consequently, whereas in the first democratic elections of June 1977 35 per cent of the votes went to nationalist parties, ten years later, in the elections of June 1987, the proportion of the nationalist vote more than doubled to 67.8 per cent. Terrorism and nationalist hegemony were the salient characteristics of Basque politics during the democratic phase begun in 1975.

Juan Linz is right in asserting that in spite of the unquestionable hegemony of nationalism, Basque politics and society continue to be essentially pluralistic.[64] Not only does the Basque panorama offer a variety of nationalist options and groups, but also the tension between nationalism and 'Spanishness' is now more radical and acute than in the past. After the democratization of the Spanish political system in 1975, the consciousness of Basque identity became more pronounced than ever before; now this identity affected, for the first time in Euskadi's history, the majority of Basque society. This expansion of Basque identity was reflected not only in electoral results, but also in the dramatic increase in the number of matriculations in Basque schools, in the publication of books written in *euskera*, in the identification of the masses with Basque symbols, such as the *ikurriña*, or with Basque sport teams, and in the fashionable and widespread conversion of names and places from Spanish into *euskera*. It seemed as though the traditional split of the Basque conscience around the very idea of nationality that had characterized the politics and defined cultural life in the Basque country until the Civil War, was now fading away in favour of a more coherent commitment to a Basque identity. In the past, the issue seemed to have been whether a Basque identity existed at all. The intellectual and political debate after 1975 took that identity for granted; it only confronted two different conceptions of it, an exclusively Basquist vision on the one hand, and an eclectic and historicist concept on the other. The former entails a totalitarian and messianic attitude; the latter envisages a more democratic and flexible solution to the Basque problem.[65]

But even if one accepts the argument that nationalism in Euskadi is a minority phenomenon, in the last analysis what really matters is the magnitude of the political challenge it presents to the central government. Francoism and its democratic progeny could not find any consolation in an academic exposé that would prove that Basque nationalism was an artificial invention popularized by the dialectic of guns and bombs. Governments can hardly be expected to respond to academic anxieties. They might be doomed, however, if they fail to tackle pressing, vital political challenges. The vicious circle of mounting terrorism and indiscriminate police retaliation, and the consequent radicalization of the population in the Basque country developed into just such an issue in the twilight of the Caudillo's life. The evolution of the Basque problem is indeed a lesson in the radicalizing effects of violence. ETA's most spectacular action was the assassination on 20 December 1973 of Franco's prime minister and potential successor, Admiral Carrero Blanco. ETA maintained that rather than a counter *coup d'état* by the army and the right, Carrero's death would accelerate the end of the regime. The terrorists were right.[66] A dictatorship such as Francoism can always, of course, resort to brutal repression in order to remove political challenges from the agenda. Such a luxury is not granted to a democracy; its *raison d'être* and, indeed, its very survival depend on its capacity to resolve problems through dialogue and compromise. It should not be surprising then, that, out of an instinct for self-preservation, the democratic regime established in Spain after the agonizing death of the Caudillo approached the Basques and the Catalans with a view to granting them autonomy. The new regime immediately understood that unless rampant terrorism and nationalist agitation were curbed, the young and fragile democracy would be imperilled. Once again, a democratic regime in Spain had paved the way for the fulfilment of regional-nationalist aspirations.[67]

The pressing political problem from the point of view of the government was, in any event, that of elaborating a constitutional framework within which autonomies that would not disrupt the unity of the state could be conceded. The government could not afford to make concessions to radical nationalists lest this provoked a military coup. This fear certainly limited the nature of the Statute. The PNV in the Basque country might have easily reconciled itself to a moderate statute of autonomy but for the pressure of ETA. This pressure resulted in the PNV abstaining in the national referendum that approved, on 6 December 1978, Spain's democratic constitution. The high rate of abstention in the Basque country (46.5 per cent) was tantamount to a spectacular victory for ETA tactics. It was also, however, the reflection of the PNV's hypocritical attitude. The PNV knew the constitution would be approved without its votes and it had every intention of operating within the framework of that constitution and exploiting its benefits. The truth was that the PNV tacitly supported a constitution that did not recognize the Basque people's right of self-determination. But the main problem now created for the government was that of the very survival of democracy. Hard-liners and fanatics lost no time in demanding an outright return to dictatorial methods. *It had become clear throughout 1978–9 that either the government would eradicate ETA, or ETA would do away with democracy.*

In July 1979, Prime Minister Suarez was able to conclude negotiations with moderate autonomist leaders on a statute of autonomy, which in October was submitted for approval, by means of a referendum, to the Basques and the Catalans. Basically, the new Statute rested on the same principles upon which autonomy had been granted in the 1930s. The PNV's leader, Xavier Arzallus, admitted, however, that the present Statute was even better than that of 1936.[68] It established a regional parliament with control over local administration, police, social services, education, internal commercial regulations, taxes, and courts. The regional government would finance its activities through local taxes and the budget that would be granted by the central government, the amount of which would have to be decided every year by negotiations. Elected by universal and secret ballot for a four-year term, the regional parliament would elect the region's president as the chief executive. The autonomous government would be responsible for its actions before the regional parliament. The latter would be entitled to discuss and pass any laws 'that do not infringe upon the general interest of the state', so long as they would be consistent with the national constitution. The Supreme Court in Madrid would have ultimate authority to pass judgment on whatever constitutional conflicts might arise between the regional and central powers.[69]

The Catalans overwhelmingly approved their Statute in a referendum in October 1979. In the Basque country, however, at the urging of ETA, about 40 per cent of the electorate abstained.[70] Nevertheless, the referendum was a severe blow to ETA and to its political branch, Herri Batasuna. A democratic way to solve the Basque problem had finally been legitimized by the popular vote. Moreover, the PNV and the political-military branch of ETA supported the Statute, thus splitting the nationalist vote. The political-military branch of ETA shrewdly claimed that autonomy should be used as a first step towards full self-determination and eventual secession from Spain. The challenge of autonomy indeed revealed an internal rift within the Basque separatist movement. What the radical nationalists were now forced to admit was that the approval of the Statute was tantamount to a rejection by the Basque people of the notion that Navarre and the French Basque country were part of the Basque homeland.[71]

The PNV's half-hearted support for the Statute and its ambiguous attitude to the Spanish constitution presented a serious challenge to the Spanish authorities. The Basque nationalists as a whole — including the PNV — were ready to operate within a constitutional framework that could secure them a degree of self-government, but at the same time, in order to achieve more political advantages, they did not hesitate to deny full and clear-cut legitimacy to the system. All Basque nationalists, radical as well as moderate, viewed the 'external universe', Spain, as a hostile world by definition, contact with which was to be allowed only in as far as it advanced the interests of the Basque nation.[72] Moreover, after the 'second wave' of industrialization, that of the 1960s, the PNV started to flirt again with the xenophobic rhetoric so popular among Basque nationalists at the turn of the century. The Francoist economic boom helped revive the latent racism of the PNV; some of its ideologues dismissed the new

Spanish immigrants as a mass of degenerate 'Koreans' who were totally indifferent to the traditional values of Basque society.[73] But the gravest consequence of the PNV's calculated ambiguity as to the final objects of nationalism was that it granted legitimacy to those, like ETA, who confronted the system with guns and dynamite in the name of an independent revolutionary Basque state.

ETA's attitude toward the Statute left no room for ambiguities. The Statute, it claimed, left the Basques subservient to the Spanish constitution with no prospect of genuine self-determination. This was not even full autonomy, the maximalists said; at most it was administrative decentralization. An arrangement that fell so short of the full independence ETA had been murderously seeking for two decades, the Statute was branded 'illegal' by Miguel Castells, the leader of Herri Batasuna. 'The state of war against Spain continues,' he warned.[74]

ETA obviously made every effort to undermine the project of autonomy. It realized that a viable compromise would isolate it and doom its aspirations for a Marxist independent state. In the Basque country, the years of democracy and autonomy were years of virtual warfare between ETA and the Spanish authorities. The only political solution to the conflict that ETA and its political branch, Herri Batasuna, were ready to contemplate was that represented by what they called the *alternativa Kas*,[75] namely the recognition of Basque self-determination, the incorporation of Navarre into the independent Basque state, the complete legalization of all political parties, a withdrawal of the Spanish police and the Civil Guard from the Basque country, and a variety of social benefits to be granted to the Basque working class. While falling short of forcing the government to negotiate on ETA's terms, the campaign of terrorism nevertheless helped to erode the credibility of the autonomous institutions, increase Basque national consciousness, and expand the social base of Herri Batasuna, a party that since its foundation had not ceased to conduct mass mobilizations in support of nationalist causes and their symbols. Indeed, in the elections of June 1987, Herri Batasuna won a spectacular 20 per cent of the votes in the Basque country.[76]

ETA's strategy against the young and initially precarious Spanish democracy was not, however, intended to destroy the system altogether. The aim was to provoke a continuous state of instability that could benefit the Basque cause without producing the total collapse of the Spanish state and a consequent return to indiscriminate repression. More sensitive and logical than some may think, ETA was loyal to Clausewitz's maxim that a victory is better defined if it is limited. Another Clausewitzian principle — the definition of the enemy's centre of gravity — led ETA not to aspire to, or aim at, the destruction of the Spanish state or its newly won democracy, but to *break the national will to maintain Spanish unity*.[77]

The Spanish left could not really understand, let alone sympathize with, the Basque campaign of terrorism against a widely legitimate democracy; it rejected ETA's refusal to collaborate in a common historical project: the irreversible consolidation of democracy in Spain. During the Francoist era, both socialists and communists viewed ETA as one of the important forces fighting to demolish the citadels of Franco's dictatorship. Now they were forced to realize that as far as ETA was concerned, the enemy was 'Spain'; Franco, Suarez or Felipe Gonzalez were nothing but the political embodiment of that enemy. It took the Spanish left some effort to start condemning ETA terrorism because of its gratitude for that organization's record in the war of attrition against what proved to be only circumstantially the common enemy: Franco.[78]

Indeed, one of the most interesting consequences of ETA's violent tactics after Franco's death was its alienation from the other democratic forces in Spain. The latter expected ETA to sustain the democratic process, as the best way to satisfy the legitimate aspirations of the Basque nation, rather than undermine it by terrorism. ETA's terrorism reached higher levels of intensity during democracy that it had ever reached during the Franco regime. For example, six people were killed by ETA in 1975, the year of Franco's death; in 1976 the toll was fifteen and in 1978 sixty-four.[79] Just like dictatorship, democracy failed to do away with the fatalistic spiral of terrorism and repression. Moreover, it now looked as though the culture of terror and violence had spread beyond the armed élite of ETA activists and affected wider sectors of Basque society.[80] Not only did the Spanish police resort frequently to indiscriminate repression of the Basque population, but also ultra-rightist squadrons, some of them supported by democratic governments, emerged to murder ETA members and sympathizers. The rejection of, and hatred towards, the Spanish police in the Basque country became an overwhelmingly widespread phenomenon.[81] But Krutwig's prediction fell short of materializing. The spiral of violence and repression never did produce the longed-for popular rising that he had predicted. The democratic forces nevertheless feared that the radicalizing effect of terrorism, state repression and uncontrolled ultra-rightist murders would jeopardize the chances of the young Spanish democracy surviving. These fears were indeed vindicated when, on 23 February 1981, Spain's potential Pinochet, General Milans del Bosch staged an abortive *coup d'état*. The 'crisis of authority' reflected in the government's inability to crush the Basque threat to Spain's 'unbreakable unity' was one of the major motives behind this military challenge to Spain's young democracy. The typical extremist sport of defending the community against invented phantoms almost ended in catastrophe.[82]

Democracy was seriously imperilled, as the hope of democratic governments that elections and the promise of a Statute of Autonomy would bring peace to the Basque country was totally frustrated.

In conclusion, what is the secret of Basque nationalism and of its remarkable persistence as an archaic remnant in a modern society in spite of its isolation from the rest of Spanish society and its total lack of any kind of international support? Clearly, notwithstanding its archaic and millenarian features, modern Basque nationalism had its most direct roots in the changes brought about by industrialization; it was a response of Basque traditional society to modernity and its concomitant social and economic divisions. After all, it hardly needs to be proved that the Basque cultural singularity — 'differential factor' as the Catalans would have put it — did not generate any kind of noteworthy nationalist movement before the 'first wave' of industrialization in the Basque country at the turn of the century. Moreover, the vital forces of Basque society, entrepreneurs, merchants and industrialists, rejected the culture of the *fueros* and anything that might lead to separation from Spain. Their whole economic prosperity depended on uninterrupted access to Spanish markets; Spain, not the Basque country, was the key to their well-being. Basque nationalism was not, therefore, the case of a middle class in an underdeveloped region that aspired to reach independence as a vehicle for economic development. It is noteworthy, however, that the breakdown of the system of the *fueros* in the 1870s was nevertheless instrumental in the emergence of modern Basque nationalism. Those Basques who under the *fueros* system found no contradiction between their Spanishness and their Basque condition, now developed a sentiment of communal distinctiveness. They challenged the centralist Spanish state for its 'incapacity to imbue the

Basques with a liberal-democratic brand of Spanish nationalism. The old Spanish patriotism of the Basques was seriously eroded the moment the old regime that sustained it disappeared.'[83]

The emergence of Basque nationalism coincided with the arrival of 'Spanish' immigration in the 1880s. Essentially it was a defence of Basque traditional society against the threat of degeneration represented by the *maketos*, as the Spanish immigrants were commonly and derogatively known. It was, therefore, no surprise that Bilbao, the first Basque city to experience rapid and intensive industrialization, should have been the cradle of Basque nationalism; its spread to other parts of Euskadi was simultaneous with industrialization, the arrival of the *maketos* and the emergence of socialism. Indeed, Basque nationalism proved to be an excellent vehicle for the mobilization and expression of conservative opinion, essentially the Basque middle and lower-middle class.[84] Not until the Second Republic, when an alliance between these conservative nationalists and the 'godless' Republic became essential for the achievement of self-rule for Euskadi, did the conservative coalition of Carlists and nationalists break down. It was the refusal of the Spanish right in the 1930s to concede autonomy to the Basques that forced the conservative PNV into an alliance with its traditional enemies, the socialists and the republicans, and opened a new avenue for Basque nationalism, that would lead it after the 1950s into a more profound sympathy with leftist and revolutionary ideas. ETA's flirtation with Marxism and revolution had been anticipated by the PNV's cynical alliance with the 'godless' Republic in order to achieve a degree of self-rule for Euskadi. But the PNV's strategy was thwarted by Franco's victory. The defeat of the Republic in the Civil War left nationalism practically paralysed, a folkloristic movement of the nostalgic and the dreamers.

What finally resurrected Basque nationalism and saved it from oblivion was the spectacular recovery of the Spanish economy after the late 1950s and the consequent invasion of Euskadi by new waves of *maketos*. The new dilemmas faced by Basque nationalism in the wake of the most dramatic process of industrialization ever to have taken place in Spain, and as a consequence of the need to fight a most repressive dictatorship in order to save nationalism from extinction, ended up exposing the inadequacy of the PNV's conservative tactics. The PNV was simply unable to exploit the new conditions. The new generations of nationalist sympathizers found ETA to be a more appropriate vehicle for the expression of their grievances and youthful nationalist energies.

The extraordinary capacity of ETA to survive repression, now a combined strategy of the French and Spanish authorities, can only be explained by the remarkably strong sense of ethnic solidarity existing in the Basque country. Industrialization did not eradicate the powerful Basque myth of cultural distinctiveness and uniqueness and the Basques' nostalgia for their mythical golden past. But the PNV failed in its commitment to redeem the Basque nation. The deficiencies of Basque conservative nationalism had therefore to be corrected by the young generation that in 1959 created ETA and embarked upon a long and painful march toward revolution and independence, both highly elusive goals. ETA's flirtation with social revolution also meant that its theoreticians understood that industrial development and its social consequences inevitably reduced the traditional Basque nationalist emphasis on the aspiration to return to the mythical, egalitarian, idyllic Arcadia of the archaic and pre-industrial Basque society. ETA had to absorb and integrate all the consequences of industrialization if it wanted to maintain its coherence and respond in a consistent way to the imperatives of a highly urbanized and mixed Basque society. Of course, ETA's theoreticians did not fail to claim that as much as industrialization might have been a deviation from the traditional Basque way of life, it nevertheless was yet more proof of Basque superiority over backward Spain. Independent Euskadi would then be a synthesis of the glories of the archaic past with the best legacies that modernity could offer. Whatever the nature of the future Basque state, the young men who responded to the call of independence for Euskadi accepted the inevitable price of blood and martyrdom that had to be paid in the long march toward their absurd, and therefore unattainable, goals.

Unattainable goals they may be, but ETA continues to be loyal to them. Not even the transition to parliamentary democracy and the concession of autonomy to the Basque country were able to reduce the puissance of radical nationalism. Although it is true that ETA continues to be as far away as ever from the realization of its wild aspirations, it is also noteworthy that its social base has been reduced only slightly, as is shown by the electoral results of the PNV and Herri Batasuna. The constant manifestations by the Spanish authorities that the problem of ETA or Basque terrorism is on the verge of solution are continuously being denied by reality. The probable, albeit hardly promising, perspective for the Basque country is that a limited degree of armed struggle will persist and will continue to fire the dreams of an independent state. A precarious balance between

Euskadi's aspirations and Spain's 'unbreakable unity' will have to be maintained for lack of any other viable solution. Self-determination, as some other cases of frustrated nationalisms may corroborate, is a relative value. Its limited application in the Basque country will never satisfy everybody.

Notes

1. Cf. Antonio Tovar, *The Basque Language* (Philadelphia 1957).
2. For the early history of the Basques, see Maximiano García Venero, *Historia del nacionalismo vasco* (Madrid, 3rd edn 1969), 21–43. For a general history of the Basques and their nationalist movement, see Stanley Payne, *El nacionalismo vasco: de sus origenes a la ETA* (Barcelona 1974).
3. Antonio de Trueba, *Bosquejo de la organizacion social de Vizcaya* (Bilbao 1870); Luis Chalbaud y Errazquin, *La familia como forma típica y trascendental de la constitución social vasca* (Bilbao 1919).
4. García Venero, op. cit., 69–94.
5. For the history of Carlism throughout the nineteenth century, see Ramón Oyarzun, *La historia del Carlismo* (Madrid 1969); Edgar Holt, *The Carlist Wars in Spain* (London 1967).
6. An excellent analysis of these processes of socio-economic change in the Basque country can be found in Juan Pablo Fusi, *Política obrera en el País Vasco 1880–1923* (Madrid 1975). A comprehensive account can also be found in Emiliano Fernández de Pinedo, *Crecimiento económico y transformaciones sociales en el País Vasco* (Madrid 1974).
7. See M. González Portilla, *La formación de la sociedad capitalista en el País Vasco (1876–1913)* (San Sebastian 1981).
8. A very detailed and meticulous description of the origins and early development of modern Basque nationalism with an emphasis on the PNV can be found in J.J. Sorozabal, *El primer nacionalismo vasco (industrialización y conciencia nacional)* (Madrid 1975); and in Koldo San Sebastián, *Historia del Partido Nacionalista Vasco* (San Sebastian 1984). For the impact of the appearance of socialism, see J. M. Eguiguren, *El PSOE en el País Vasco* (San Sebastian 1984). The increase in the number and intensity of labour disputes was directly related to industrialization and the emergence of socialist unions, see J. Olábarri Cortázar, *Relaciones laborales en Vizcaya, 1890–1936* (Durango 1978).
9. Cf. Marianne Heiberg, *The Making of the Basque Nation* (Cambridge 1989), 45–69.
10. Fernando García de Cortazar and Juan Pablo Fusi, *Política, nacionalidad e iglesia en el País Vasco* (San Sebastian 1988), 14–15.
11. For a socialist criticism of Basque nationalism, see F. Carretero, *Crítica del nacionalismo vasco* (Bilbao 1932).
12. Cf. José Estornes Lasa, *Los vascos y la Universidad (Antecedentes y realizaciones)*, vol. II, (San Sebastian 1970), 265.

13. See a historical analysis combined with anthropological research that points at this unique equilibrium between archaism, modernity, and ethnic nationalism in Basque society, Marianne Heiberg, *The Making of the Basque Nation*. See also some especially lucid observations in José Luis Aranguren, 'El terrorismo como secularización de la violencia religiosa' in Fernando Reinares-Nestares (ed.), *Terrorismo y sociedad democrática* (Madrid 1982), 75.

14. José Enrique Rodríguez-Ibáñez, 'Fragmentos sobre el terrorismo' in Reinares (ed.), *Terrorismo y sociedad*, 54–5.

15. The profound common roots of millenarism and nationalism in the Basque country have been splendidly explained in Juan Aranzadi, *Milenarismo vasco (Edad de oro, etnia y nativismo)* (Madrid 1981).

16. Ceferino de Jemein, *Biografía de Arana Goiri'tar e historia gráfica del nacionalismo* (Bilbao 1935); García Venero, op. cit., 239–310.

17. Quoted in Javier Corcuera, 'La difícil definición del "problema vasco" ' in Fernando Reinares (ed.), *Violencia y política en Euskadi* (Bilbao 1984), 41.

18. For an analysis of Arana's brand of racism, see Stanley Payne, op. cit., 91–2.

19. For Sabino's ideology and his elaboration of modern Basque nationalism, see Sabino Arana Goiri, *Obras completas* (Buenos Aires 1965), and a monographical study: Jean-Claude Larronde, *El nacionalismo vasco: su origen y su ideología en la obra de Sabino Arana Goiri* (San Sebastian 1977). The major ideologist of Basque racism was a close collaborator of Sabino Arana: Engracio de Aranzadi, *La nación vasca* (Bilbao 1918).

20. De Cortázar and Fusi, op. cit., 64–6.

21. Ibid., 67.

22. See Rafael Tasis, *La renaixença catalana* (Barcelona 1967).

23. García Venero, op.cit., 423–46.

24. For the ironic attitude of Unamuno towards Basque nationalism, see Miguel de Unamuno, *Paz en la guerra* (Madrid 1923); and *Recuerdos e intimidades* (Madrid 1975).

25. Cf. Alfonso Otazu, *El igualitarismo vasco: mito y realidad* (San Sebastian 1973).

26. John Sullivan, *El nacionalismo vasco radical 1959–1986* (Madrid 1986), 17.

27. Ibid., 17–18.

28. For this evolution of the PNV, see J.L. Granja, *Nacionalismo y II República en el País Vasco* (Madrid 1986), and Juan Pablo Fusi, *El problema vasco en la II República* (Madrid 1979).

29. Javier Tusell, *Historia de la Democracia Cristiana en España* (Madrid 1974), vol.II, 13–119 defines the PNV as a Christian Democratic party.

30. Jean Claude Larronde, *El nacionalismo vasco*, 343–60.

31. The best exposé of the 'foralista' thesis can be found in E. Echave-Sutaeta, *El partido carlista y los fueros* (Pamplona 1914). For the tensions between the Carlist tradition of the *fueros* and Basque nationalism, see Javier Real Cuesta, *El carlismo vasco 1876–1900* (Madrid 1875). Victor Pradera, the main ideologist of Basque traditionalism (Carlism), was also the major enemy of Basque nationalism. See his *Obras completas* (Madrid 1945).

32. De Cortázar and Fusi, op. cit., 25.

33. For the socio-economic processes of the 1920s see Shlomo Ben-Ami, *Fascism from Above: The Dictatorship of Primo de Rivera in Spain* (Oxford 1983), 240–318. For a special emphasis on the Basque country and the impact of 'development' on Basque nationalism, see Payne, op. cit., 120–36.

34. Shlomo Ben-Ami, *The Origins of the Second Republic in Spain* (Oxford 1978), 154–68.

35. Cf. Tusell, op. cit., 13–119.

36. For Aguirre's account, see his *Entre la libertad y la revolución 1930–1935* (Bilbao 1935), and his memoirs: José Antonio de Aguirrre, *De Guernica a Nueva York pasando por Berlin* (Buenos Aires 1943).

37. For the Basques under the Republic, see Martin Blinkhorn, *Carlism and Crisis in Spain 1931–1939* (Cambridge 1975). A concise and illuminating study of the Basque problem under the Second Republic is Juan Pablo Fusi, *El problema vasco en la II República*.

38. Blinkhorn, op. cit., 41–67. The full text of the Statute is in García Venero, op. cit., 639–58.

39. For the rift between the Basques and Navarrese, see Blinkhorn, ' "The Basque Ulster": Navarre and the Basque Autonomy Question Under the Spanish Second Republic' in *Historical Journal*, 17 (1974), 595–613. See also García Venero, op. cit., 507–56.

40. For the Basques in the Civil War, see Carmelo Garaitaonaindia and José Luis de la Granja (eds), *La guerra civil en el País Vasco. 50 años después* (Bilbao 1987).

41. See Milagros García Crespo, Roberto Velasco and Arantza Mendizábal, *La economía vasca durante el franquismo. Crecimiento y crisis de la economía vasca: 1936–1980* (Bilbao 1981).

42. Raymond Carr and Juan Pablo Fusi, *España, de la dictadura a la democracia* (Barcelona 1979).

43. See Sartre's introduction to Giselle Halimi, *Le procès de Burgos* (Paris 1971).

44. Julen Aguirre, *Operación Ogro ¿ Cómo y por qué ejecutamos a Carrero Blanco?* (Hendaya 1974).

45. Eugenio Ibarzabal, *50 años del nacionalismo vasco* (San Sebastian 1978). Quotes Txillardegi.

46. Ibid.

47. See the account of one of the founders of Ekin. Julen Madariaga, *Lutte revolucionnaire en Euskadi. Etat de guerre larvée. Documentos Y*, vol.IX, 385–95.

48. Sullivan, *El nacionalismo vasco*, 43.

49. One should not exaggerate, however, the popularity of the Basque language in Euskadi, or its validity as a means of cultural diffusion. Many of those who spoke it could not read it, see Luis C. Nuñez, *Opresión y defensa del euskera* (San Sebastian 1977).

50. For the Church and the national question, see José Chao Rego, *La iglesia en el franquismo* (Madrid 1976); Fernando Gutierrez, *Curas represaliados en el franquismo* (Madrid 1977); Rossinyol, *Le problème national catalan* (Paris 1974), 422–3.

51. De Cortázar and Fusi, op. cit., 102–3.

52. José Luis Aranguren, 'El terrorismo como secularización de la violencia religiosa' in Reinares (ed.), *Terrorismo y sociedad democrática*, 75–6.

53. Cf. G. Morán, *Testamento vasco* (Madrid 1988), 160; and his *Los españoles que dejaron de serlo* (Barcelona 1982), 32.

54. See a most revealing quotation from a homily at the funeral of an ETA militant who fell in action, in de Cortázar and Fusi, op. cit., 113.

55. José Luis Aranguren, 'El terrorismo como secularización de la violencia religiosa' in Reinares (ed.), *Terrorismo y sociedad democrática*, 76. See also Aranguren's book, *España: una meditación política* (Barcelona 1983), 71ff. For the role of religion and millenarism in the violence in Euskadi, see also Juan Aranzadi,

'Milenarismo vasco y antisemitismo democrático' in *El Viejo Topo*, 30 (1979).

56. For a discussion of the meaning of 'political theology' as a mental and ideological structure that sanctifies political concepts and politicizes religious dogmas, see Uriel Tal, *Structures of German 'Political Theology' in the Nazi Era* (Second Annual Lecture of the Jacob M. and Shoshana Schreiber Chair of Contemporary Jewish History, University of Tel-Aviv, 16 May 1979). For the sanctification of politics and nationalism in Euskadi, see Juan Aranzadi, 'El mito de la edad de oro vasca', in *Tiempo de Historia*, 59 (October 1979).

57. Aranguren, 'El terrorismo como secularización de la violencia religiosa', in Reinares (ed.), *Terrorismo*, 77–8.

58. Cf. Francisco Letamendia (Ortiz), *Historia de Euskadi: el nacionalismo vasco y ETA* (Ruedo Ibérico 1978), 300.

59. Sullivan, *El nacionalismo vasco radical*, 47–51. See also Hollyman, 'Basque Revolutionary Separatism: ETA', in Paul Preston (ed.), *Spain in Crisis: The Evolution and Decline of the Franco Regime* (Sussex 1976), 212–33.

60. Fernando Sarrailh de Ihartza (Federico Krutwig), *Vasconia* (Buenos Aires 1962).

61. Sullivan, *El nacionalismo vasco radical*, 47–71.

62. Cf. Juan María Bandrés, *Burgos, juicio a un pueblo* (San Sebastian 1978); Federico de Arteaga, *ETA y el proceso de Burgos* (Madrid 1971).

63. The bibliography on ETA is fairly extensive; see select examples: Gurutz Jauregui Bereciartu, *Ideología y estrategia política de ETA. Análisis de su evolución entre 1959–1968* (Madrid 1981); José Mari Garmendia, *Historia de ETA* (San Sebastian 1980); Angel Amigo, *Pertur, ETA 71–76* (San Sebastian 1978); Luciano Rincón, *ETA (1974–1984)* (Barcelona 1985); Robert Clark, *The Basque Insurgents, ETA, 1952–1980* (Wisconsin 1984). A compact account can be found in Francisco Letamendia (Ortiz), *Historia de Euskadi: el nacionalismo vasco y ETA*, 297–417.

64. Juan Linz, *Conflicto en Euskadi* (Madrid 1986).

65. Cf. Julio Caro Baroja, *El laberinto vasco* (San Sebastian 1984); Manu Escudero, *Euskadi: dos comunidades* (San Sebastian 1978); F. Savater, *Contra las patrias* (Barcelona 1984).

66. For a discussion of the meaning of Carrero's assassination, see Paul Preston, 'The Assassination of Carrero Blanco and its Aftermath' in *Iberian Studies*, vol. III, 1, 1974.

67. If proof was needed of the strength of autonomist feelings, the democratic elections of June 1977 provided it. See *Informaciones*, 14 January 1978: PNV = 286, 540 votes; Euskadiko Eskerra = 58,377; Pacte Democratic Per Catalunya = 498,744; Esquerra de Catalunya = 134,953.

68. Sullivan, *El nacionalismo vasco radical*, 284.

69. For current accounts on the elaboration of the Statutes, see *Cambio 16*, 15, 22, 29 July 1979; and Virginia and Carlos Tamayo Salaberria, *Fuentes documentales y normativas del Estatuto de Guernica* (Alava 1981).

70. For the plebiscites, see *Time, Newsweek*, 5 November 1979.

71. Sullivan, *El nacionalismo vasco radical*, 285.

72. Ana Miranda, 'El acuerdo interno del pueblo vasco: la única vía de pacificación de Euskadi' in Reinares (ed.), *Violencia y política en Euskadi*, 231–2.

73. G. Morán, *Los Españoles que dejaron de serlo*, 261.

74. *Time, Newsweek*, 5 November 1979,.

75. Koordinadora Abertzale Socialista. Cf. Natxo Arregui, *Memorias del Kas 1975–1978* (San Sebastian 1981).

76. For electoral behaviour in Euskadi in all the elections that took place from 1977

to 1980, see Luis Nuñez, *Euskadi Sur Electoral* (San Sebastian 1980). The daily press is a valid source for the results of later elections.

77. Miguel Angel Aguilar, 'La estrategia del desistimiento. Algunas observaciones sobre el caso español', in Reinares (ed.), *Terrorismo y sociedad democrática*, 150.

78. Miguel Angel Aguilar, 'La estrategia del desistimiento', 146–9.

79. Sullivan, *El nacionalismo vasco radical*, 236.

80. See, for example, Equipo de Investigacion Social IKERGINTZA, *Juventud vasca y violencia* (Vitoria 1982).

81. See Ladanzuri, *Que se vavan ya* (Hendaya 1978), and José Miguel de Barandiaran, 'Mitología vasca' in *Obras completas* (Bilbao 1972), 395–450.

82. Cf. José Oneto, *La noche de Tejero* (Barcelona 1981).

83. Cf. Aranzadi, *Milenarismo vasco*, 21.

84. Beltza (Emilio López Adán), *Del Carlismo al nacionalismo burgués* (San Sebastian 1978).

Shlomo Ben-Ami
is Professor of Modern History at Tel-Aviv University and Israel's ambassador to Spain. He is the author of *The Origins of the Second Republic in Spain* (Oxford 1978) and *Fascism from Above. The Dictatorship of Primo de Rivera in Spain* (Oxford 1983). He is currently preparing a study on Spain and the West.

Bernard Lewis

Watan

In the twelfth book of the *Iliad*, the Trojan hero Hector, dismissing the fears of Polydamas that inauspicious omens may presage a bad result in the impending battle, robustly assures him: 'One omen is best, to fight for one's country.'[1] Hector was mistaken about the omen, since he himself was killed and Troy was doomed, but the duty to fight was not affected. Centuries later, the Roman poet Horace, in his *Odes*, goes a step further, and asserts that 'it is sweet and becoming to die for one's country'.[2] The Greek *patris* and the Latin *patria*, translated as country in the foregoing citations, are obviously related, and both derive from words meaning father. Both convey the meaning of paternal and ancestral home. In ancient Greek and Roman civilization, this usually meant a city — the normal unit of political identity, loyalty, and authority. A Greek or Roman was not merely a city-dweller; he was a citizen, in Greek *polites*, in Latin *civis*, with the right to share in the formation and conduct of the government of his city, and a corresponding duty to fight and if necessary to die in its cause.

In the Roman Empire, the unit of identity became larger, and could extend from a city to a whole province or even to what we would nowadays call a country. The level of civic responsibility and political participation was sharply reduced, but the duty to fight for one's *patria*, however redefined, remained.[3]

It continued into medieval and early modern Europe, where, despite the definition of identity by the churches and the claims to allegiance of feudal kings and lords, the sense of country, as the ultimate identity and loyalty, remained strong and became stronger. The Byzantine *Autocrator* and the Holy Roman *Kaiser* put forward their competing claims to be head of all of Christendom, but in most Christian lands rule was exercised by kings who defined their sovereignty in terms of territory — kings of England and of Scotland, of Denmark and of Sweden, of Poland, Hungary and Bohemia, and later, because of an Arab hiatus, of Portugal and Spain. The same process may be seen in the work of the historians of medieval Europe, who proceeded, fairly rapidly, from the history of kings and tribes and peoples to the history of kingdoms and countries. By the sixteenth century, Joachim du Bellay celebrates his country as 'France, mère des arts, des armes et des loix', and Shakespeare, in one of several passages, expresses his love for

> This blessed plot, this earth, this realm, this England,
> This nurse, this teeming womb of royal kings.

The Greek *patriotes* and the late Latin *patriota*, which originally meant no more than compatriot or fellow countryman, in their later European versions acquire a new sense, of one devoted to the service and cause of his country, and a new word, patriotism, denotes the sentiments and beliefs of the patriot.

The Arabic word *watan*, which, with slight changes of pronunciation is also used in Persian, Turkish and other Islamic languages which draw on Arabic for their conceptual vocabulary, had a somewhat different evolution. The Arabic verb *watana* means to reside or sojourn in a place; it also means to choose a place of residence or to settle in it. The noun *watan* has none of the paternal or ancestral connotations of *patris* or *patria*, but simply means one's place of residence, which may be adopted or temporary. Normally a *watan* is a town, but it may also be a village or, more extensively, the province in which one's town or village of *watan* is situated. The plural form *awtān* appears commonly in the sense of provinces. The fourteenth-century author Juzjānī distinguishes between the *watan* proper, 'a man's birthplace and the place where he lives' and the *watan* of sojourn, where a man spends at least fifteen days but does not establish permanent residence.[4] This is obviously very far from the classical and modern connotations of *patris*, *patria* and their equivalents in European languages.

Despite this lack of political content, the word *watan* — in the simple meaning of home or homeland — could have many sentimental associations, and there are many allusions in classical Arabic and other Islamic literatures, in both prose and verse, to the love and devotion which people felt for their birthplace or homeland.[5] Even the nomadic bedouin felt a kind of association, an emotional involvement, with the pasturages through which they roved at different times of the year. One of the basic themes of ancient Arabian poetry is the nostalgic sentiment evoked in the poet by the traces of an abandoned camp, where he and his tribe had halted at some time in the past. The great ninth-century essayist Jāhiz even devoted a whole essay to the subject of love of one's *watan*, [6] and a late and therefore certainly spurious hadith even attributes to the Prophet the dictum that 'love of one's *watan* is part of the faith'. The thirteenth-century Syrian geographer Ibn Shaddād begins his geographical work with his native city of Aleppo, and defends his choice with a series of quotations from poetry and tradition, exalting the love of *watan*.[7] A fifteenth-century central Asian Turkish poet, 'Alī Shīr Navā' ī, even speaks of fighting for one's *watan*, but significantly links it with family:

For family and *watan*, as long as he has life
A man will fight as long as he can.[8]

Another central Asian text of the same period tells how a pious Sufi sheikh was asked: 'How can love of *watan* be part of the faith, since the infidels also love their *watan*? What therefore is the meaning of this hadith?' To this the sheikh replied that when someone passes from the world of contemplation to the world of darkness, he then loves the previous world, and such loving is part of the faith.[9]

The *watan* was thus a focus of sentiment, of affection, of nostalgia, but not of loyalty, and only to a limited extent of identity. The great Arab historian Ibn Khaldūn relates that on a certain occasion the caliph 'Umar said to the Arabs: 'Learn your genealogies, and don't be like the Nabataeans of Mesopotamia who, if asked about their origin, reply: "I come from such and such a village".'[10] There may be some question about the authenticity of the quotation and its attribution, but there can be no doubt about the authenticity of the sentiment, which is echoed and re-echoed throughout the centuries. It is attested in the titulature of Muslim monarchs, who defined their sovereignty, in inscriptions, documents and coins, always in religious terms, rarely in ethnic terms, never in territorial terms. European monarchs might call themselves the King of England, the King of France, or the King of Spain, but in the lands of Islam, territorial titles were used to belittle a rival, not to aggrandize oneself. In the conflicts and also in the correspondence between competing Muslim great powers in the sixteenth and seventeenth centuries, the Sultan of

Turkey and the Shah of Persia called each other by these titles, but never themselves.[11] Each was concerned to reduce his rival to the level of a local potentate. Each in his own titulature was the Supreme Lord of the Muslims. This same perception of identity and authority may be seen in the work of pre-modern Muslim historians, who write the history of Islam, of caliphs and sultans and dynasties, and sometimes also local history, but not the history of countries or nations.

The use of the word *watan* (Turkish *vatan*) in a political sense, equivalent to the French *patrie*, the English country, or the German *Vaterland*, dates from the late eighteenth century, and is clearly due to European influence and example.[12] The earliest occurrence that I have been able to trace of the use of the word *watan* in this sense is in a Turkish document — a report by Morali Esseyyid Ali Efendi, who served as Ottoman ambassador in Paris under the *Directoire*. In a description of the hospitals and homes provided by the French authorities for pensioned and disabled soldiers, he speaks of these soldiers as having striven 'in the cause of the republic and out of zeal for the *watan* [*Cumhur uğurunda ve vatan gayretinde*]'.[13] Both words, *cumhur* and *vatan*, were old, with roots in classical Arabic. *Cumhur* had already acquired a political connotation at an earlier date, throughout Ottoman acquaintance with Venice and other European republics.[14] Patriotism was a new discovery, from the French Revolution. The phrase was almost certainly translated by Ali Efendi's interpreter from a document made available to him in French, and one may wonder how much meaning it conveyed to him. Later in the same report he speaks frequently of the French Republic, and occasionally of the French state (*devlet*) and nation (*millet*), terms which would have been more familiar, rather than of *vatan*.

Nevertheless, the new meaning of the word gradually became increasingly familiar. The earliest references in the nineteenth century are mostly in translated texts or descriptions of European events, but by the 1830s the word had entered Ottoman official usage. A report published by the Board of Public Works in 1838,[15] speaking of the need for better and more extensive education, observes that 'without science, the people cannot know the meaning of love for the state and *vatan*'. In the following year, *vatan* even appears in an Ottoman official document, no less than the great reform decree of 1839, known as the Edict of the Rosebower, *Gülhane*. In this the Sultan, speaking of military matters, observes that 'it is the inescapable duty of all the people to provide soldiers for the defence of the fatherland [*vatan*]'.[16] In 1840, a Turkish diplomat called Mustafa Sami lists the praiseworthy qualities of the people of Paris as modesty, composure, love of country (*vatan*) and nation (*millet*) and the safeguarding of the law.[17] By the mid-century, the association of country (*vatan*), with state (*devlet*) and nation (*millet*), as something not only to be loved but also to be served and if necessary fought for, has become commonplace. A striking example of this association of ideas occurs in a letter which the Turkish poet and journalist Şinasi wrote to his mother from Paris in 1851: 'I want to devote (or sacrifice) myself to the cause of my religion, state, country (*vatan*) and nation (*millet*)'.[18]

The events of the Crimean War, 1854–6, in many ways favoured the development of the new patriotic sense of identity, loyalty and duty. Since the beginning of the sixteenth century, almost all the many wars of the Ottoman Empire, apart from a few with the Persian Shiite heretics, were against the Christian powers, and the Ottomans had become accustomed to seeing each of these wars as a *jihād*. In their perception, even in their language of warfare, their cause was Islam, their enemy the infidels; their fighters were Gazis, their dead were martyrs. In their early wars in the Balkan peninsula, the Ottomans sometimes made use of local Christian auxiliaries and mercenaries. In their later wars, notably in the Napoleonic period, they found themselves involved in larger European struggles, with Christian powers supporting as well as opposing them. But these had little effect on Ottoman perceptions, and as late as the early nineteenth century, those Christian powers who joined them against their Christian enemies were not allies but rather loosely associated co-belligerents. The Crimean War was a new and unprecedented experience. For the first time, the Ottoman Empire fought against its old enemy, Russia, with two major West European powers as allies — this time not as remote and barely visible associates, but as comrades in arms, with armies on Ottoman soil and fleets in Ottoman waters, fighting side by side against the common enemy. The rapid and forced development resulting from involvement in a major war brought many changes to Turkey, among them the telegraph, the daily newspaper and a wide range of new ideas. The patriotism of the British and the French, and their lack of concern at fighting with Muslim allies against a Christian enemy, can hardly have escaped Turkish notice. The term *vatan* begins to appear frequently in Turkish newspapers, and a poet of the time, Halis Efendi, published what was probably the first patriotic poem.[19] Before long, there were many others, and some of them sounded a different note.

The adoption of this new patriotic ideology was by no means

unresisted. No less a person than the great jurist and historian Cevdet Paşa made a powerful protest against it. During the Grand Vizirate of Fuad Paşa, a special commission was appointed to consider the incorporation of non-Muslim subjects of the Ottoman state into the armed forces, from which hitherto they had been excluded. Cevdet Paşa was consulted on this proposal, and objected in the strongest terms. The non-Muslim subjects of the Ottoman state, he said, were of many different varieties — 'Orthodox, Catholic, Armenian, Jacobite, Protestant . . . Melkite, Maronite, Syriac, Chaldee, and many others . . . '. They would all need their different priests, as the Jews would need their rabbis, and while Muslims fasted during Ramadan, the others would also observe their various fasts. Such a mixed body would be unmanageable. In times of strain and stress, military commanders use their eloquence to call on their men for greater endurance and sacrifice. For Muslims, the most effective call is to holy war or martyrdom in the cause of the true faith. These are words familiar to them from childhood, inculcated in them at school. The vigour and endurance of Muslim soldiers in battle, greater than that of other religions, are due to such religious sentiments.

But in time of need, how could the colonel of a mixed battalion stir the zeal of his soldiers? In Europe, indeed, zeal for country has taken the place of zeal for religion, but this arose after the decline of their feudal age. Their children hear the word *vatan* when they are still small, and so, years later, the call of patriotism is effective with their soldiers. But among us, if we say the word '*vatan*', all that will come to the minds of our soldiers is their village squares. If we were to adopt the term *vatan* now, and if, in the course of time, it were to establish itself in men's minds and acquire the power that it has in Europe, even then it would not be as potent as religious zeal, nor could it take its place. But even that would take a long time, and until that time our armies would be left without spirit. In a tight spot, would Private Hasan obey the order of Captain Christo, who sends him to his death? In India the English may promote non-Christian soldiers to the level of sergeant but no higher, and no one interferes or objects. But among us, if we accept Christians as soldiers, it will be necessary to give them the ranks to which they are legally entitled in the same way as Muslims. If they are not given these ranks, the so-called friendly states will offer friendly advice by way of protecting them, and our military organization, hitherto exempt from interference by foreigners, will be exposed to foreign interventions.

And that is not all.

During military operations, Muslim soldiers have an extraordinary capacity to endure the fatigues of battle. As soon as they smell powder, they want no more than ammunition and dry biscuit. But Christians cannot endure such hardships. It will

be necessary to give them regular pay at the beginning of every month and to secure
and provide food and drink regularly every day. And if we don't, we shall again be
the target of foreign objections.[20]

Cevdet Paşa's dire forebodings were by no means groundless, and a
far more serious problem arose when first the Christian and later even
some of the non-Turkish Muslim subjects of the Empire began to see
their *watan* not as the Ottoman realm but as their own ethnic
homeland.

Among Ottoman Turkish Muslims, their *vatan* was the Ottoman
Turkish Empire, embracing most of the heartlands of Islam in the
Middle East. Its former rulers included Arab caliphs as well as
Turkish sultans; among its great men, in whom they took pride, there
were also Arab poets and Persian philosophers, who lived and died
long before the Ottoman state was founded. Its present sovereignty
was embodied in the Ottoman sultanate, the last and legitimate
successor of the great Islamic realms of the past. Patriotic loyalty was
owed to the *vatan* and payable to the Ottoman Sultan.

But other ideas were current, and some of them made their first
appearance in the Arabic-speaking provinces of the Empire. One of
the first writers to express patriotic sentiments in Arabic was the
Egyptian sheikh Rifā'a Rāf'i al-Tahtāwī. Between 1826 and 1831 he
had lived in Paris, as religious preceptor to an Egyptian student
mission, and his writings make clear how deeply he was affected by
what he saw. In 1855 he published an Egyptian patriotic ode, *Qasīda
wataniyya Misriyya*, in praise of the new ruler of Egypt, Sa' īd Pasha.
The Pasha, in fulfilment of his duty to his suzerain the Ottoman
Sultan, sent a contingent of Egyptian troops to join the Turks in the
Crimean War, and Sheikh Rifā'a published a collection of 'Egyptian
Patriotic Verses' in their praise. He later produced further patriotic
poems, to celebrate the accession of Ismā'īl Pasha in 1863, and
another group of poems to honour the return of the battalion of black
troops whom the Pasha had sent to Mexico, as part of Napoleon III's
expeditionary force.[21]

Sheikh Rifā'a's poems and the various prose works in which he
tried to inculcate patriotic sentiments in his readers enjoyed the
support of the dynastic rulers of Egypt, and were part of their
campaign to establish that country as a separate entity, with its own
ruling dynasty and a large measure of autonomy under the loosest of
Ottoman suzerainty. Sheikh Rifā'a's patriotism is not Ottoman, since
it shows little interest in the larger Ottoman *watan*. It is not Muslim,

since it takes pride in the glories of both pagan and Christian Egypt before the advent of Islam. It is not Arab, since it is not concerned with other Arabic-speaking countries — the idea of a greater Arab political fatherland did not arise until sometime later. Sheikh Rifāʿa wrote extensively on ancient Egypt — something of a novelty in Arabic historiography. Until his time, histories of Egypt began with the Arab conquest. His was the first to end with that event. This idea of a country and its people, maintaining a living, continuing identity through several changes of language, religion and civilization, was new and unknown in the Muslim world. Some time was to pass before Sheikh Rifāʿa's Egyptian patriotism found imitators in other Muslim countries.

Sheikh Rifāʿa's patriotism, as we saw, was encouraged and indeed sponsored by the rulers of Egypt, who appreciated the help it could give to the realization of their dynastic and separatist purposes. In the neighbouring Syrian lands, still under more direct Ottoman rule, the first patriots adopted another and more radical component of European patriotism — the idea of freedom. The great Lebanese Christian scholar and writer, Butrus al-Bustānī, made the point explicitly in 1860: 'It is for the sons of the *watan* to claim their *watan*'s protection of their most precious rights, namely, their life, honour and property, including freedom of their civic, cultural and religious rights.'[22] Significantly, it is not, according to al-Bustānī, to the ruler that the patriot devotes himself in return, but rather to his country's welfare.

Such ideas became commonplace in the writings of the Young Ottomans, the first important Ottoman opposition group, and particularly in the journals published by them in exile. An article published in 1873 by the leader and most distinguished writer of the group, Namik Kemal, explains what *vatan* means for them:

> The *vatan* does not consist of imaginary lines drawn on a map by the sword of a conqueror or the pen of a scribe. It is a sacred idea, sprung from the union of many lofty sentiments, such as nation, freedom, welfare, brotherhood, property, sovereignty, respect for ancestors, love of family, memory of youth . . . [23]

During the century and a half that have passed since the first patriotic writings of Namik Kemal in Turkey and Sheikh Rifāʿa in Egypt, the idea of country — of the national territory as the basis of identity and the focus of loyalty — has had a chequered history in the Middle East. It has in particular had to compete with two very powerful rivals. One was the old, deep-rooted and now renascent religious and communal loyalty to Islam; the second was another importation from Europe, the idea of the ethnic nation, defined by language, culture, and real or imagined descent. The one retained, the other rapidly acquired a powerful hold on the sentiments and loyalties of Middle Easterners, many of whom found it difficult to accept the idea of kinship and common identity with their pagan forbears and their infidel neighbours. In many countries nationalism, which corresponded more accurately to the ethnic confusion of the Middle East, was both more intelligible and more appealing than territorial patriotism, and even where the language of patriotism is used in public discourse, it often masks a deeper commitment to communal and ethnic loyalties. In Egypt there has been continuing tension — sometimes conflict, sometimes interaction — between Egyptianism, Arabism and Islam.

In Turkey, the patriotic idea has by now virtually supplanted all others. Despite a continuing commitment to Islam and even a return to inter-Islamic organizations, and notwithstanding a growing interest in the affairs of their Turkic kinsfolk in the Soviet Union, the people of Turkey remain, first and foremost, Turkish patriots, defining their primary identity and loyalty on the basis of the country called Turkey, which was created by the Turkish Republic from the ruins of the multinational, dynastic Ottoman Empire. In Iran, the idea of country, assiduously fostered by the late Shah, has had a setback with the establishment of an Islamic Republic that explicitly rejects the Shah's notion of a common identity between Islamic and pre-Islamic Iran. But even in Iran, the rejection of patriotic notions may not be as complete as would at first appear. When, after the fall of the monarchy, the Sultan of Oman requested the return of three small Arabian islands which had been seized by the Shah, the Republic refused. More strikingly, the constitution of the Islamic Republic lays down that the president must be an Iranian by birth and origin — rather more than is required in the American system, where birth is sufficient. The long war with Iraq gave encouragement and provided expression for patriotic loyalties.

In the Arab lands, the situation is more complex. Of these, only Egypt, a country sharply defined by both geography and history, can claim and demonstrate a continuing national identity, in the same country, from remote antiquity to the present day. The other Arab countries vary widely, from venerable monarchies like Morocco, through old established Ottoman autonomies like Kuwait and Lebanon, to artificial imperial creations like Libya and Jordan. And yet even the most artificial of these have shown a remarkable persistence — a determination to survive as separate entities, despite all the appeals and occasional actions of the pan-Arabists. By now it is becoming increasingly clear that pan-Arabism, for the time being at least, has ceased to be a realistic political objective and has taken its place as a noble ideal. Its enactment in so many constitutions of Arab states, along with other noble ideals, is an indication of this change. In the Arab world as in most other regions, a citizen owes his first loyalty to his country. The question that remains to be determined is whether the primary claim on that loyalty will be obedience to the country's rulers or service to its people.

Notes

1. Homer, *Iliad*, xii, 243.

2. Horace, *Odes*, ii, 13.

3. On the kind of political benefits a Roman politician conferred on his home province, see Sir Ronald Syme, *Roman Papers*, II (New York 1979), 620–2. My thanks are due to Professor Z. Yavetz for drawing my attention to this paper.

4. Al-Juzjānī, *Al-Ta'rīfāt* (Istanbul 1327), 171.

5. For examples see Gustave E. Grunebaum, 'The Response to Nature in Arabic Poetry' in *Journal of Near Eastern Studies*, iv/3, 1945, 144–6.

6. Al-Jāhiz, 'Al-Hanīn ilā'l-Awtān' in *Rasā'il al-Jāhiz*, ed. 'Abd al-Salām Hārūn, ii (Cairo 1965), 379–412; German translation in O. Rescher, *Excerpte und Übersetzungen aus den Schriften des Philologen und Dogmatiken Gâhiz aus Basra*, i (Stuttgart 1931), 488–97. Jahiz's final example of love of country is the practice which he ascribes to 'the sons of Aaron and the house of David' during the Babylonian captivity. It was their custom, he says, when any one of them died anywhere in Babylonia, to give his body temporary burial, and after an interval to remove his remains and give them final burial in Jerusalem.

7. 'Izz al-Dīn Abū 'Abdallah Ibn Shaddād, *Al-A'lāq al Khatīra fī dhikr umarā' al-Shām wa'l-Jazīra*, ed. D. Sourdel, i/I (Damascus 1953), 2–4.

8. Ali Sher Navoy, *Khamsa* (Tashkent 1960), 750.

9. Darwīsh Tawakkul b. Ismā'īl b. Bazzāz, *Safwat al-Safā*, ms. British Museum, Add. 18548, fol. 202a and Or. 7576, fols. 38a-b.

10. Ibn Khaldūn, *Al-Muqaddima*, ed. Etienne Quatremère, i (Paris 1858), 237; English translation by Charles Issawi, *An Arab Philosophy of History* (London 1950), 106 and F. Rosenthal, *The Muqaddimah*, i (New York 1956), 266.

11. Bernard Lewis, *The Political Language of Islam* (Chicago 1988), 55ff.; Hasan al-Bāsha, *Al-Alqāb al-Islamiyya fī'l-Ta'rīkh wa'l-Wathā'iq wa'l-Athar* (Cairo 1957).

12. The seventeenth-century lexicographer Francis Mesgnien-Meninski, in his great Turkish–Persian–Arabic Thesaurus, defines *watan* in accordance with the classical lexica, and gives many examples of its use, none of them political.

Interestingly, he cites the above-mentioned saying attributed to the Prophet, and cautiously translates it: 'Amor patriae est de fide, *aut* ex fide. L'amor della patria é cosa di fede, ò di religione.' Meninski, *Thesaurus*, s.v.

13. 'Ali Efendinin Sefaretnamesi. . .', ed. Ahmed Refik in *Tarih-i Osmani Encümeni Mecmuasi* (1329), 1459.

14. On *Cumhur* as Republic, see 'Djumhūriyya' in *Encyclopaedia of Islam*, 2nd edn.

15. Report published in Ottoman official journal of 21 Dhu'l-Qa'da – 1254–1839, reprinted in Mahmud Cevad, *Maarif-i Umumiye Nezareti Tarihçe-i Teşkilât ve Icraati* (Istanbul 1922), 6–10; English translation in Niyazi Berkes, *The Development of Secularism in Turkey* (Montreal 1964), 105.

16. Turkish text in A. Şerif Gözübüyük and Suna Kili (eds), *Türk Anayasa Metinleri* (Ankara 1957), 3–5; English translation by Halil Inalcik in J.C. Hurewitz (ed.), *The Middle East and North Africa in World Politics: A Documentary Record*, i (New Haven and London 1975), 270.

17. Mustafa Sami, cited in *Aylik Ansiklopedisi*, no. 5 (September 1944), 152–3.

18. In Ebüzziya Tevfik (ed.), *Nümûne-i Edebiyat-i Osmani* (Istanbul 1296–1878?), 239.

19. Şerif Mardin, *The Genesis of Young Ottoman Thought: A Study in the Modernization of Turkish Political Ideas* (Princeton 1962), 210.

20. Cevdet Paşa, *Maruzat*, ed. Yusuf Halaçoğlu (Istanbul 1980), 114–15; also, in Arabic characters, in *Tarih-i Osmani Encümeni Mecmuasi* (1341), 273. Partial English translation in Bernard Lewis, *The Emergence of Modern Turkey*, 2nd edn. (London 1968), 338.

21. On Sheikh Rifā'a's patriotic poetry, see James Heyworth Dunne, 'Rifā'a Badawī Rāfi' al-Tahtāwī: The Egyptian Revivalist' in *BSOAS*, ix (1937–9) 961–7; x (1940–2), 399–415.

22. *Nafīr Sūriya*, 25 October 1860, cited by Ami Ayalon in *Language and Change in the Arab Middle East: The Evolution of Modern Political Discourse* (New York 1987), 52–3.

23. *Ibret*, 22 March 1873. Reprinted in Mustafa N. Özön, *Namik Kemal ve Ibret Gazetesi* (Istanbul 1938), 265. English translation in Bernard Lewis, *Emergence*, 337.

Bernard Lewis

is Cleveland E. Dodge Professor of Near Eastern Studies Emeritus at Princeton University. His most recent publications include *The Political Language of Islam* (Chicago 1988) and *Race and Slavery in the Middle East: An Historical Enquiry* (Oxford 1990).

Barry Rubin

Pan-Arab Nationalism: The Ideological Dream as Compelling Force

The dream of pan-Arab nationalism — the idea that all Arabs could and must be united in a single state — has had an effect on Middle East history as compelling as that of Marxism on modern Europe. While both ideologies had lost appeal by the 1990s, that of pan-Arab nationalism continued to exercise an intellectual hegemony far in excess of that parallel utopian philosophy in Europe.

Whereas in Europe, nationalism focused predominantly on the individual nation-state, the nation in the Middle East was supposed to incorporate all Arabs; existing states were merely shards of the whole. Inasmuch as the Arabs chose a European model, it was the unifications of Italy and Germany. Identity was believed destined to create a state rather than the state consolidating a new identity.

This gap between reality and ideology was a major factor shaping the turmoil and seeming political perversity of the modern Middle East. Arab politicians and states engaged in constant battle; relations with the West were largely conditioned on the regional competition. Some leaders were reluctant participants in this game, pressured by foreign Arab rivals, domestic enemies, or fear of their own people's passions; others chased Arab leadership out of conviction or ambition.

The root motive of this restlessness was the perception that something was unacceptably wrong with the world. Arab and Islamic societies were weaker and poorer than those in the West, though they considered themselves superior. Their centuries-long decline left them asking, as in the title of a 1930s article by Shakib Arslan, 'Why are Moslems Lagging Behind the Christians?' Arslan believed in pan-Islam, seeing Moslem unity as the answer to Western predominance. His brother, Adil, became a pan-Arab activist, believing that all Arabs must unite under a single government. Both men were struggling with the same paradox.

Arabs and Moslems consider their societies and religion better than those of the West on theological and historical grounds. The early Arab nationalist Abdul Rahman al-Kawakabi wrote: 'Western man is a hard-headed materialist. He is fierce to deal with, he is by nature inclined to exploit others, and is ever ready to revenge himself on his enemies.' In contrast, Arabs and Moslems 'are morally motivated and are governed by kindness of heart, compassion and mercy, which they often misplace. They are gentle and kind even to their enemies.' The West, al-Kawakabi's compatriots wrote a century ago, as Islamic fundamentalists do today, was sick and barely civilized, a land of hunger, despair and death.[1]

It is usual to appreciate and exaggerate the virtues of one's own land and people. But the burning, agonizing problem for Arabs and Moslems was how to explain and eliminate the gap between what 'is' and what 'ought to be'. Modern history has been a humiliation for them. If Western exploitation has been at fault and some regimes are perfidious accomplices, the answer is a revolution to throw out the traitors and solidarity in confronting the powerful foreigners and their remaining lackeys.

These views partly reflect, though also exaggerate, the real history of Western intervention. Yet equally important are taboos blocking an unflinching self-examination of weaknesses at home. A direct critique of Islam's thought and culture is politically unacceptable in Moslem lands. Arab nationalism and radicalism are equally insistent on their absolute rightness. 'The most important goal . . . is opening our eyes to the mistakes and disasters of the past so that we can avoid them and prevent anyone else from repeating them while we build Egypt anew,' the great Egyptian writer Tawfiq al-Hakim wrote. 'The major task for the person who wields his pen and thinks is to expose the face of the truth.' But in the Arab-Islamic world the pen was most often employed at the service of ideology or the state. Even al-Hakim's book was able to be published only because the current government favoured a critique of its predecessor, and he was still fiercely attacked by many quarters.[2]

After all, Gamal Abdul Nasser, the object of al-Hakim's criticism, was hero of the Arab world despite his economic mismanagement and disastrous military defeats in the Yemen civil war and 1967 Arab–Israeli war, because he made Egyptians feel proud and strong. Nasser remained popular decades after his death, while his successor Anwar al-Sadat, who broke the rules by allying with the United States and making peace with Israel, was little mourned, though he gave Egypt peace and some prosperity.

It is difficult to challenge ideas that are simultaneously so popular and blessed with legitimacy. Many Arab and Iranian intellectuals understand that the slow pace of development, military defeats and cruel rulers are results of their own societies' structural shortcomings and political culture rather than foreigners' conspiracies. This knowledge may torture their consciousness and consciences, yet less commonly prods them to speak out. Instead, the contradiction between the existing and the proper order creates insatiable resentment and a basis for political instability. If a regime cannot meet impossible expectations — catch up on the West, develop prosperous societies, destroy Israel, expel foreign influence, unite the Arabs and Moslems — then it is not entirely legitimate.

But precisely because it is impossible to fulfil the commandments of theology or ideology, those who rule must compromise with reality. On the one hand, they have to speak and act in a manner consistent with pan-Arabism, Islamic unity and radicalism in order to survive; on the other hand, survival also requires taking into account the regime's interests and limited resources. The ideas become real forces because the ruler's subjects believe them and his enemies exploit them. But leaders who become fixated on the local rules may be destroyed by the universal rules of political power.

Arab disunity, then, was not the result of treason but of geopolitical realities, the inevitable fears or ambitions of regimes and individuals. Pan-Arabism furnished an arena for these conflicts. By providing a rationale for each state to interfere in others' affairs, it actually strengthened the individual regimes and weakened unity. Thus, after forty years of effort, the Arabs were more divided than ever before. Not a single leader could inspire a significant following outside his own country; rulers engaged in conflicts that wasted resources and sometimes caused bloodshed. The very effort to win pre-eminence, noted al-Hakim, 'has ruined us all'.

It is remarkable how the expenditure of so much Arab ink and blood made them less successful than other regions in productive cooperation. West Europe had NATO and the Common Market alliances, moving toward more co-ordination than the Arab world achieved. The Organization of African Unity, the Association of Southeast Asian Nations, and the Organization of American States all function more effectively — and with fewer disputes among members — than the Arab League.

Arab and Islamic politics operated in a pressure-cooker environment combining ideological rigidity — Islam and Arab nationalism
as absolute truths from which deviation is treason — with a ferocious
intra-state competition in which contenders made hypocritical use of
foreign support. The result often seemed a paranoid, intolerant style.
In American politics, moderation and centrism were a political
necessity since to be extremist is to be marginal. Ronald Reagan had
to show himself safely unradical to be elected and re-elected as
president; Barry Goldwater and George McGovern could not do so
and were defeated by landslides. But in the Arab-Islamic world, the
means of seizing or losing power are radical in themselves and, as
Goldwater noted, moderation rather than zealousness is sinful when
in pursuit of absolute righteousness. Instead, pluralism seemed to
endanger national survival. An Egyptian intellectual explained:
'Dialogue is the beginning of altercation. Altercation is the beginning
of internal war and disunity.'[3]

Lurking forces outside the Arab or Islamic communities,
Khomeini called them greater and smaller satans, await a chance to
sow their divisive doctrines. The organ of Egypt's Moslem Brotherhood thundered: 'The alliance of united enemies (Zionism,
Christianity, Marxism, Buddhism and cow-worshippers [Hindus]) is
working rapidly to gain new positions within the Islamic existence by
breaking, subjugating and smashing it under a barrage of both open
and malicious propaganda.'[4]

Since achieving an Islamic society or Arab unity is the highest
priority, individual rights or democracy must take a back seat.
Islamic fundamentalists cannot accept the Western revolutionary
notion that the voice of the people is the voice of God. The idea of
popular sovereignty is the very foundation of liberal-democratic
society. As an Islamic philosopher wrote:

> In Islam, the people do not govern themselves by laws they make on their own, as in
> a democracy; rather the people are governed by a regime and a set of laws imposed
> by God, which they cannot change or modify in any case. . . .Islam would not
> concur that the majority is sovereign, whatever its mistakes and errors.

Only the voice of God, as presented in the Koran and Islamic law, is
the voice of God. Dictatorship, then, is superior to democracy as long
as it is led by right-thinking leaders. As a Lebanese Sunni fundamentalist put it, 'The state in Islam obeys Divine Law, not the
people'.[5]

This view was held by traditionalists and revolutionaries, by those seeking a return to Islam and by those advocating radical nationalism. The Islamic reformer Mohammad Abdu claimed at the turn of this century,

> The Orient needs a despot who would force those who criticize each other to recognize their mutual worth, parents to be charitable, neighbours to be fairminded, and people generally to adopt his view of their interests, be it by intimidation or by joyful consent.

The argument, not unknown in Europe, is that the need for change is so profound and urgent that it can only be imposed from above.[6]

'Reactionary anthropologists,' wrote the iconoclastic Syrian sociologist Sadeq al-Azm, 'have declared showmanship and emotionality as constant traits of the Arab. These are in reality ill symptoms of a backward society and can be overcome as historic phenomenon.'[7] These characteristics are not innate but are historically rooted by principles shaping society which are simultaneously rigid and almost universally accepted. The mass audience is thus responsive to demagogic appeals demanding their fulfilment and to paranoid conspiracy theories demonizing the forces that allegedly threaten them.

If enough people believe that the revolution is necessary to fulfil their cherished values and destroy traitors and heretics, then the dictatorship is a representative government. This is what Khomeini achieved in Iran and the same pattern applies to Arab nationalist thought. What better fits Abdu's prophecy than Nasser's reign in Egypt? The result was a populist dictatorship where conformity is accepted voluntarily and dissent is literally unimaginable. Such arguments and beliefs justify the most extreme propaganda, violence or terrorism by both government and opposition.

Given the fact that the escalation of violent rhetoric often leads to violent events and each side's conviction of its absolute rightness, a freer atmosphere might give rise to more extreme demands as government and opposition seek to outbid each other. The American view is that free speech eases tensions and that repression only breeds more resentment, producing inevitable revolt. Concessions bring peace. But the prevailing pattern of Middle East politics is that leaders who cracked down with violence and sanctions were acting on their long experience and thorough knowledge of their own societies. For if a government permits criticism and demonstrations, the populace assumes it either secretly approves them or is too weak to

resist. The opposition's intimidation overcomes fear of the government and people hurry to be on the right side. This avalanche effect
was most clearly seen in Iran's revolution and Lebanon's disintegration. Westerners expect those battling repression or dictatorship
to be innately heroic and inevitably moderate but, as events in Tehran
and Beirut showed, they may be more ruthless and extremist than the
incumbents.

Thus, the Arab leader has a difficult task. He must cope with an
unfulfilled Arab nationalist and Islamic agenda, rivals at home and
abroad, a largely uneducated people whose political culture has made
them prone to demagoguery, and an army better versed in coup-
making than in fighting wars. Even the radical Syrians — who argued
that the PLO was too soft, refused any negotiation with Israel and
organized terrorist attacks on Americans — are attacked by their
own Islamic fundamentalists in a cartoon showing President Hafez
al-Assad as a dog led on a leash by the United States and Israel.

As Professor Adeed Dawisha puts it, 'The first major characteristic
of politics in the Arab world is the absence of enduring domestic
stability.' The ruler must show his willingness to repress opposition
while, at the same time, conforming to the proper slogans. 'He must
work, or rather appear to the populace to be working, to achieve the
goals of that value-system; and he needs to be seen as being successful
in achieving these goals,' Dawisha continues. 'If he is not, then his
survival in power cannot be guaranteed.' The 'goods' in this case
meant not only material benefits but also proper observance of Islam,
the pursuit of Arab unity, expulsion of foreign influence, the
destruction of Israel, strength, progress and social justice. When the
ruler cannot deliver, he must explain why things are not working out
and find someone to blame. Among his tools for doing so are
mobilizing the people against foreigners and launching intrigues
against neighbouring states.[8]

The Arab world has gone through different periods when alternative answers to shortcomings were in fashion. The thinkers of the
late nineteenth and early twentieth centuries argued that the Arabs
needed to imitate the West by adopting science and constitutionalism
while reforming Islam. The newly emerging states' political leaders,
beginning in the 1920s, claimed that independence would solve
everything. The next, radical generation came to power through
military coups beginning in the 1950s. It argued that the Arabs had to
fight the West and made big promises for the efficacy of anti-
imperialism, revolution, Arab socialism and activist pan-Arabism.

The neo-Marxists of the 1960s accused these new rulers of only paying lip service to revolution and socialism. They won little following, however, and their call for people's war soon turned out to be a euphemism for terrorism. Most recently, a wave of dissent in the 1980s insisted on Islam as the answer.

Consequently, modern Arab history has largely been the story of this succession of unsatisfactory solutions and destabilizing responses. The original effort to unravel the mystery of Western success in order to imitate it did not succeed. Writes Professor Hisham Sharabi: 'As long as intellectual activity remained bound to political, religious, and practical considerations — the scientific mentality could not be genuinely acquired nor attain autonomous existence [and] become self-generating.' Instead, 'haunted by a sense of impotence and fear, its leaders took to scapegoating [the West]'.[9]

The Arabs were not responsible for their own difficulties, ran the argument. Europe was to blame for

> social repression and economic manipulation . . . for the political fragmentation of the Arab world[,] the . . . polarization of power [, and the] . . . continued monopoly of oil . . . by patriarchal rulers and Western oil cartels. . . .Fragmentation of the national movement into separate independent movements . . . inimical to certain forms of social change.

It was the West that retarded modernization, actively encouraged ethnic and religious differences, 'backed the conservative and reactionary social groups and cemented class and economic distinctions'. The power of landlords, sheikhs, conservative clergy and a business class was its doing, arresting 'the growth of indigenous capitalistic formations'. Psychologically, this domination 'gave rise to a feeling of inferiority and frustration which often expressed itself in nihilism and despair'.[10]

This is the Arab case against the West. There is some merit and much exaggeration in it. Yet the underlying premise is deeply flawed, implying that only Western intervention prevented radical revolution, thoroughgoing social justice and the creation of a single pan-Arab state. After all, Arab political society did not spring fully-grown from the brow of Britain or France, it was largely a continuation of what had gone before. Fundamentalists criticize Europe for undermining traditional society; radicals complain they preserved it. Perhaps the worst 'inferiority and frustration . . . nihilism and despair' sprang not from the West's behaviour but from the radical interpretation's fatalism.

Still, if Arab nationalism was such an innately powerful force, why could it not overcome the existence of separate nation-states, even after the wave of radical nationalist coups that proclaimed this as their main goal? This concept of history was deeply destructive since it hinted at Western omnipotence and Arab helplessness.

The conflict with Israel was the latest, not the first, of these grievances. Again, Arab tactics rather than British perfidy was at the root of an Arab disaster. The Palestinian Arab leadership refused to compromise even with British efforts to hand the country over to them, eventually allying themselves with Hitler. With Arab regimes badly divided, internally corrupt and with each seeking Palestine for itself, the Arabs suffered a humiliating defeat in 1948. The well-known assessment of Constantine Zurayk contrasts the confident expectations with the dismal truth.

> Seven Arab states declare war on Zionism in Palestine, stop impotent before it and turn on their heels. The representatives of the Arabs deliver fiery speeches in the highest international forums, warning what the Arab states and peoples will do if this or that decision be enacted. Declarations fall like bombs from the mouths of officials at the meetings of the Arab League, but when action becomes necessary, the fire is still and quiet, and steel and iron are rusted and twisted, quick to bend and disintegrate.[11]

Israel's existence and survival symbolized for them the painful hollowness of Arab and Islamic ideology. It could neither be wished away with words nor crushed by force of arms. Yet only a portion of Arab or Moslem anti-Americanism was due to US support for Israel. Equally or more important, was US support for Arab states — Jordan, Morocco, Tunisia, Sudan, Saudi Arabia, pre-revolutionary Iraq (before 1958) and Libya (before 1969), or Egypt since the mid-1970s. Rival states and movements blamed Washington for blocking their ambitions. Those advocating an Islamic society or united Arab state would not attribute failure to the impossibility of these goals or their own people's refusal to rise up in support of them. Instead, the fault must lie with US interference. If only this could be banished, success would surely follow. The result was the wild anti-Americanism of Qadhafi, Khomeini, Arafat, Lebanese terrorists and others. But while one side demands that the Americans be kept out, an opposing faction or regime woos them.

The Arab military officers who seized power in the name of the people promised to solve everything. The new regimes intoxicated people with visions of victory, renaissance and revenge. The greatest of them, Egypt's Nasser, stepped forward as the hero able to unite all the Arabs and soon had followers in every country. Nasser asserted Egypt's pride and strength, ridiculed Western powers, smashed Islamic fundamentalist rivals and the Marxist left at home, intrigued the intellectuals and intimidated the foreign Arab regimes that opposed him. 'We would clap in proud surprise,' recalled al-Hakim, 'when he delivered a powerful speech and said about [the United States] which had the atomic bomb that "if they don't like our conduct, let them drink from the sea," he filled us with pride.' He continued:

> Whatever the fact, those glowing images of the accomplishments of the revolution made out of us instruments of the broad propaganda apparatus with its drums, its horns, its odes, its songs and its films. We saw ourselves as a major industrial state, a leader of the developing world in agricultural reform, and the strongest striking force in the Middle East . . . .No one argued, checked, verified or commented. We could not help but believe, and burn our hands with applause.

The regime's style was best symbolized by the massive Cairo rallies whose participants were transported, fed and housed at state expense. Each section leader carried instructions for the spontaneous celebration: 'Cheer in unison: "Nasser, Nasser, Nasser!" Cheer by section, "Long live the victor of Arabism!" Unison: "Long live the hero of the revolution . . . the leader of the Arab nation . . . !" '[12]

No one ever courted the masses so successfully. For the first time, the common people were mobilized, albeit as an ever-applauding audience. Since Nasser embodied right-thinking nationalism and militancy, only traitors could oppose him. The people cheered when he nationalized the Suez Canal Company, survived the 1956 Anglo–French–Israeli invasion (forgetting that US diplomatic intervention saved him), and built the Aswan Dam (mortgaging Egypt to the USSR). Egyptians felt themselves privileged to follow Nasser in advancing toward freedom, economic development and regional leadership.

But who would rule the new pan-Arab brotherhood? Each country saw itself as a candidate and the contenders divided into two quarrelling blocs. On one side, the new military regimes — Egypt, Iraq and Syria — wielded the sword of radical nationalism. On the other, Saudi Arabia and Jordan defended traditional society using the shield of Islam. Among ideologies, there was a battle for pre-eminence among Nasserism, Ba'athism, communism and monarchy. Within states, communal groups struggled for pre-eminence:

Alawites, Druse and Sunni Moslems in Syria; Christians and
Moslems in Lebanon; Sunni and Shiite Moslems and non-Arab
Kurds in Iraq. Country after country became a battlefield leaving a
toll of lost lives and wasted resources.

The pressures of the inter-Arab battle led Nasser and the radical
Syrian regime to blunder into the 1967 war. If the 1948 defeat
demonstrated the old governments' incompetence, corruption and
cravenness, the disaster two decades later seemed to do the same to
the revolutionary generation. One Arab scholar later called the war
'the Waterloo of Pan-Arabism'.[13]

In his post-mortem on Nasser's regime, al-Hakim voiced relevant
questions.

> Are the people made happy because they hear socialist songs although they are
> submerged in misery which everyone sees? The misery is seen not just inside their
> homes and their huts but also all over the streets where pressed masses of people
> wait for long hours in front of consumer co-operatives for a piece of meat to be
> thrown to them . . . .Or take Arab unity . . . . Did the revolution succeed in
> bringing it about by political means? Did it bring it closer and strengthen it, or
> rather did it scatter and weaken it by policies which included intervention,
> pretension to leadership, domination, influence-spreading, showering money in the
> planning of plots, fomenting coups d'état, and in the Yemen war inducing Arab to
> kill Arab, and Arab to use burning napalm and poison gas against Arab?![14]

The left would say that the solution was to go even further, toward
'real' socialism; the Islamic fundamentalist posed his system as an
answer. Yet neither of them, if actually tried, would fulfil these
expectations.

Similar recriminations followed the 1982 Israeli invasion of
Lebanon and everyone blamed others for their own failures. The PLO
leader Abu Iyad accused conservative Arabs of being accomplices to
the attack; Jordan's Prime Minister Mudar Badran said Syrian
sabotage of Arab solidarity caused the disaster. The Arab states did
nothing, commented a Palestinian writer, because they feared the
PLO's destabilizing effect on the region and were pre-occupied by
their own problems. PLO leader Khalid al-Hassan condemned Syria
at a mass meeting for not fighting hard or opening another front by
attacking Israel through the Golan Heights. Inter-Arab conflicts,
commented others, caused more damage to the Arab cause than all
external enemies. No one had any idea about how to resolve these
problems. Despite the fact that the United States generally supported
Israel, the Arabs' divisions made them more dependent on the United

States, while Washington's connection with Israel helped it continue to be the conflict's sole conceivable mediator.[15]

For the Arabs, the scene could hardly have been more gloomy. Egypt had made peace with Israel and was now a pariah; Lebanese Christians aligned themselves with Israel. Libya and Syria supported Iran against Iraq, a fellow Arab state. Morocco battled Algerian-backed guerrillas in the Sahara; Libya subverted Sudan. It seemed to be a war of all against all. And riches that once appeared so mountainous shrank as oil prices fell, surpluses were spent and the dollar's value declined. A typical analysis at the oil boom's onset claimed that Saudi Arabia 'has an economic power base unique in world history . . . .[It] can literally buy any future that is commercially "buyable".' But higher prices forced Western nations to conserve oil, switch to alternative fuels and find new sources. More impecunious oil-producers pushed production upward to make money.

The very differentiation among Arab states also signalled each one's growing objective and subjective identity. A study of textbooks in Egypt, Jordan, Syria and Lebanon found that they downplayed 'Arab unity' and the idea of a single 'Arab nation' in favour of local history.[16] Equally, high-flown language often merely dressed up a version of old loyalties. Behind talk of progressive and imperialist or leftist and rightist lurked real conflicts among communities and ruling groups for pre-eminence. The Ba'ath Party, representing pan-Arabism and socialism in theory, was a vehicle for the domination of Alawi and Sunni minorities in Syria and Iraq. The Progressive Socialist Party in Lebanon, with its universalist, leftist platform, was led by a hereditary clan chief and consisted almost exclusively of his Druze followers. Lebanese Hezbollah recruited along family lines. Of course, when a group joins one side, its traditional rivals choose the other one.

To hold together this explosive mixture, Arab rulers developed a sophisticated pattern of dictatorship to which their subjects evince submission as long as the government can force them to do so. 'For centuries,' explains Professor Adeed Dawisha, 'the pattern of political loyalty in the tribal and village communities was hierarchical,' reinforced by Islam whose 'normative imperatives . . . tend to bestow legitimacy on the centralized structure of political authority.'[17] The resulting system was 'absolute rule by the will of an individual', in al-Hakim's words. 'It has among its advantages rapid execution of what he sees as beneficial projects and among its faults precipitate decisions or . . . foolhardy gambles which may embroil the nation in a single hour and introduce the source of its destruction.'[18] Such devastating mistakes were made by Nasser in 1967, by provoking Israel to war, and by Iraqi President Saddam Hussein in 1980 by attacking Iran.

Neither Nasser nor Hussein fell from power, showing the system's strength and flexibility. Their type of government, the 'modern dictatorship', was designed to maintain simultaneously an organized hardcore base, through communal loyalties, privileges and institutions, and mass support through charismatic leadership, ideological demagoguery and populist reforms. This system rests as much on modern technology and ideas as on traditional ones. The former, Dawisha explains,

> placed in the hands of the rulers methods of social and coercive suppression that made earlier means of . . . control pale into insignificance . . . . A two-pronged maxim was followed: put fear in people's hearts, but also try to win their support, no matter how grudgingly given.[19]

This formula was practised even by the most seemingly traditional monarchs, who based themselves on tribal, religious and communal identity. They observed Arab nationalist and Islamic taboos as much as possible and deemed it safer to do nothing rather than to violate them.

Did the undoubted dissatisfaction with the nationalist dictatorships imply Islamic fundamentalism's triumph? Fundamentalists largely replaced neo-Marxist nationalists as the main opposition groups. 'Islam talked about labour relations and justice long before Marx, Lenin, Mao or Castro or any of those who speak of progressive ideology,' claimed Libyan leader Muammar Qadhafi. More important, Islam's appeal had far greater resonance among the masses than such complex, imported and atheistic ideologies.[20]

Further, the growth of an outward Westernization should not be confused with a concomitant acceptance of its philosophy or code of behaviour. Bahrain's Minister of Development, Yussef Shirawi, comments:

> Nobody was ready for all the money that descended on us, and right now the Muslim world is a mess. We accepted the manifestations of a modern civilization but refused its rulings. We accepted technology, for instance, but not science. People became confused, and they ran away to find comfort in Islam.[21]

Still, there is an important distinction between a stronger Islamic factor and a triumph for radical fundamentalism. Groups advocating revolution remained quite small. Khomeini's appeal did not extend far among Arabs. Governments used ferocious repression when necessary but most Moslems were satisfied with reforms bringing national laws more into alignment with the Islamic code.

In theory, all Moslems agree on their religion's primacy and basic principles. But practice is a different thing altogether. 'Certain poison pens in the service of imperialism have for several years been seeking to sow dissension in the ranks of the Moslems,' wrote Khomeini in 1971. Ali Shariati, a left-oriented Iranian fundamentalist who posthumously became a patron philosopher of the revolution, spoke of 'the dangers of the superpowers and their agents who have infiltrated Muslim nations' and the need 'to fight against brain-washing, propaganda, disunity, heresy and false religions'. But whose religion is false? Who is provoking disunity? Around whom should everyone unite? What is heresy? Who is the true Moslem and who the victim — or purveyor — of brainwashing and propaganda? The inability to agree crippled fundamentalism's appeal. It became simply another cause of division in the Arab world.

The Islamic movement's strength lies in the very fact that it is the product of very modern forces and ambitions, rather than being a throwback to the Middle Ages. Fundamentalists became more active in direct proportion to modernization's impact on their society. If Arab nationalism was the response to Western political power in earlier decades, the Islamic resurgence takes its cue from Western cultural penetration. The fundamentalist claim, virtually undeniable by Moslems on theological and historical grounds, is that Islam must necessarily define politics and society. According to Ayatollah Khomeini, Islamic law

> has answers for the needs of men from the beginning to the end . . . for daily [life], and for issues that might arise in the future and about which we know nothing now. There is no need for anyone to engage in false interpretations.

Islamic law, the Koran, 'and the traditions of [Mohammad] . . . satisfies all the material, spiritual, philosophical, and mystical needs of all humanity at all times until Judgement Day'.[22]

It is equally imperative that Moslems work and fight to put these teachings into authority over all Moslems.

> Had the prophet remained in the Medina mosque all his life just to preach the Koran, we would have followed his example. Instead he began his mission in Mecca with . . . an armed struggle and established a government. He then sent

missionaries and representatives everywhere, as far as he could. He brought the glad tidings that we are going to conquer the entire world and destroy everybody. He said: We are going to destroy the Roman Empire, Persia and others. By destroying them, he meant eliminating their religious rituals . . . .They should say: We should do what our Prophet did. He set up a government, we should do the same. He participated in various wars, we should do the same. He defended Islam, we should also defend it. Therefore, if we are the followers of this noble Prophet, if we are the followers of the holy imams, we should follow their example. What did they do during their lives? Did they just sit and issue religious instructions? If they had limited their achievements to preaching alone, why were they persecuted, imprisoned, expelled, isolated and killed by the arrogant? Despite all these restrictions, you see the extent of the popularity of [Islamic law], and you have not seen its full extent yet.[23]

The huge crowd shouted its approval.

Yet there are many flaws in Khomeini's arguments from an Islamic standpoint. After all, Moslems purported to believe many of his ideas for centuries without ever acting as he insists. They gave allegiance to rulers, in accord with long-standing Islamic teachings, even when their behaviour contradicted these interpretations. It is easy to find many statements by respected clerics preaching passivity and obedience. Fundamentalists were also hard put to deal with the cultural onslaught of modernization and Westernization.

Nor did they easily win the ideological battle against Arabism. The influential Egyptian preacher, Sayyid Qutb, said pan-Arabism 'had exhausted its role in universal history'. Still, nationalists, not fundamentalists, continued to rule the Arab lands. Similarly, the individual state remains the power centre; Arab nationalism can retain power but cannot accomplish a pan-Arab mission. Ajami says it best: 'Pan-Arabism had dominated Arab political life for nearly half a century. It had gripped the young and made life difficult for many rulers. But it was never able to transform the Middle East.'[24]

Impotent yet unchallengeable, extremist nationalism and Islamic politics become roadblocks to development and induce disunity and violence. Blaming foreigners engenders fatalism and inhibits a desperately needed rethinking of the issues. 'I sometimes ask,' writes the great Egyptian novelist Najib Mahfuz,

what is happening in the region, and they tell me that it is all a game being played by the Great Powers. I then ask myself: Are we rubbish? Have we no minds? Is it the Great Powers who are treating us like playthings? Have we Arabs become a kind of toy or plaything? Is there humiliation greater than this?[25]

These deadlocks drive even Arab leaders to despair. Egypt's President Husni Mubarak said, 'The general Arab situation has, with this dismemberment, estrangement, and infighting, deteriorated.' Even Arab League Secretary-General Chadli Klibi admitted that the Iran–Iraq war, not the Arab–Israeli conflict, became the top Arab concern. And even the militant journalist (and Nasser's ex-ghost-writer) Mohammad Heikal mourned, 'All dreams are gone and no dreams are replacing them.'[26]

The adjustment to experience, though, is imperfect. The official line is still that pan-Arab nationalism is pre-eminent. Heikal considers the crisis to be only temporary; Palestinian intellectual Walid Khalidi sees Arab nationalism as a 'super-legitimacy' next to which each individual state 'shrinks into irrelevance'. Just because 'the idea of "one Arab nation with an immortal mission" has never been translated into a viable political project', means nothing for the future, argues an Arab writer. Does Marxism not exist because 'it failed to unify the workers of the world!'[27] But Marxism, originally billed as a movement of liberation and progress, came to rule the most oppressive societies and then largely collapsed. Similarly, pan-Arabism came to justify each state's dictator and inhibit economic progress, political moderation, and even inter-Arab co-operation. 'Today the Arab reality and the Arab dream,' writes Hisham Sharabi,

> appear separated by an unbridgeable gap. The hope that has animated the past generation's struggle . . . turned into cynicism and despair . . . .Power-holders throughout the Arab world seem to have found it fairly easy to get away with the contradiction between their verbal and actual behaviour.

Even Edward Said notes that the struggle to obtain the unattainable leaves the Arab 'embittered or apathetic'.[28]

Many dream of new revolutions to smash the status quo, activate the masses, and create a new society. The last generation's dream had produced Nasser, the Ba'ath and Qadhafi. When the perverse genie of history again granted a wish it was in the form of Iran's revolution. Yet if what actually exists is so disappointing, potential victories and ongoing struggles still have the power to excite passions and political activity.

Notes

1. Hisham Sharabi, *Arab Intellectuals and the West* (Baltimore 1970), 98–101.

2. Tawfiq al-Hakim, *The Return of Consciousness* (New York 1985), xv, xiii.

3. Lewis Awad, 'The Arab Society: Possibility of Dialogue, The Egyptian Experience', in Edward Said, *The Arabs Today: Alternatives for Tomorrow* (Colombus, OH 1973), 62ff.

4. Hilmi al-Qa'ud, 'Relaxation . . . Then What?', *Al-Da'wah* (July 1979). Translated in Joint Publications Research Service (JPRS), 29 August 1979, no. 201, 28–30.

5. Quoted in Emanuel Sivan, *Radical Islam*, 74. See also Barry Rubin, *Islamic Fundamentalists in Egyptian Politics* (New York 1990).

6. Anouar Abdelmalek, *Contemporary Arab Political Thought* (London 1983), 40.

7. al-Azm in Said, op. cit., 42.

8. Adeed Dawisha, 'Comprehensive Peace in the Middle East and the Comprehension of Arab Politics', *Middle East Journal* (Winter 1983), 44–5. See, for example, Awni Farsakh, 'History and Identity in the Arab Homeland', *Al-Mustaqbal al-Arabi*, vol. 6, no. 51 (May 1983), 24–53, and the aptly titled article by Sabri Ismail Abdallah, 'The Arab Nation: The Scientific Truth Versus Error and Confusion', *Al-Mustaqbal al-Arabi*, vol. 8, no. 82 (December 1985), 4–19.

9. Sharabi, op. cit., 130–1.

10. Ibid., 133–6.

11. Constantine Zurayk, *The Meaning of the Disaster* (Beirut 1956), 2.

12. al-Hakim, op. cit., 20–1, 28.

13. Fuad Ajami, 'The End of Pan Arabism', *Foreign Affairs* (Winter 1978–9), 357.

14. al-Hakim, op. cit., 50.

15. Radio Amman, 14 June 1982; British Broadcasting Company, *Survey of World Broadcasts*, 16 June 1982; Yasser Arafat on Voice of Palestine, 17 June 1982; Ali Hashim, Ali, 'The Media Repeats its 1967 Performance and the Lebanese are Strangled', *Al-Nahar al-'Arabi w-al Duwali*, 23 August 1982, vol. 6, no. 277 (23August 1982), 24–5; Ahmad Shanin, 'The Extent of Arab Participation in the War and Factors Behind It', *Shu'un Filastiniyyah*, no. 129 (August 1982), 33–7; *Al-Dustur*, 'Khalid al-Hasan: Why Did Syria Not Take Advantage of the Opportunity to Liberate the Golan?' vol.12, no. 264 (13 December 1982), 20–1; Tamam al-Barazi, 'Hisham Sharabi: "These are Arafat's Mistakes" ' , *Al-Watan al-'Arabi*, vol. 7, no. 339 (12 August 1983), 24–6; Isam Ni'man, 'Peace Between the Arabs', *Al-Watan al-Arabi*, vol. 7, no. 333 (1 July 1983), 36–7.

16. Hasan Madiyah Salim, 'The Fostering of the Arab Child's Political Consciousness', *Al-Mustaqbal al-'Arabi*, vol. 6, no. 51 (May 1983), 54–68. See also Tawfiq Abu Bakr, 'The Flourishing of Arab Regionalism: Between Truth and Exaggeration', *Al-'Arabi*, no. 310 (September 1984), 61–3, and Stewart Reiser, 'Pan-Arabism Revisited', *Middle East Journal*, vol. 37, no. 2 (Spring 1983), 218–33.

17. Adeed Dawisha, 'Arab Regimes, Legitimacy and Foreign Policy'. Paper presented at the American Political Science Association meeting, November 1984.

18. al-Hakim, op. cit., 49–50.

19. Dawisha, 'Arab Regimes . . . ', op. cit. See also Hasan Hanafi, 'Arab National Thought in the Balance', *Jerusalem Quarterly*, no. 25 (Autumn 1982), 54–67.

20. Nabeel A. Khoury, 'The Pragmatic Trend in Inter-Arab Politics', *Middle East Journal*, vol. 36, no. 3 (summer 1982), 384.

21. David Lamb, 'Arab Power on the Wane Despite Oil', *Los Angeles Times*, 14 July 1985.

22. Speech broadcast on Tehran radio, 10 November 1987, in *FBIS-South Asia*, 12 November 1987.

23. Ibid.

24. Ajami, 'Stress in the Arab Triangle', *Foreign Policy*, no. 29 (Winter 1977-8), 100–1.

25. *Al-Mustaqbal*, July 1984, cited in Elie Kedourie, 'Critics in Despair', *New Republic*, 24 March 1986, 33.

26. Speech of 15 November 1985, in *FBIS*, 15 November 1985, D-11; Interview with Qatar News Agency, 6 March 1986, in *FBIS*, 7 March 1986, A-1; Christopher Dickey, 'Egypt Has an Air of Calm But . . . ', *Guardian Weekly*, 21 July 1985.

27. Hassan Nafan, Hassan, 'Arab Nationalism: A Response to Ajami's Thesis on the "End of Pan-Arabism" ', *Journal of Arab Affairs*, vol. 2, no. 2 (Spring 1983), 173–4, 182.

28. Hisham Sharabi, 'Unity, Disunity and Fragmentation in the Arab World', in Said, op. cit., 137–8; Said, 5–6.

Barry Rubin
is a Fulbright Fellow (1990–1), teaching at
Haifa and Tel Aviv Universities. He is the
author of several books, including *Modern
Dictators: Third World Coupmakers,
Strongmen and Populist Tyrants*; *Paved with
Good Intentions: The American Experience
and Iran*; and *Islamic Fundamentalists in
Egyptian Politics*.

Yaacov Shavit

The 'Glorious Century' or the 'Cursed Century': *Fin-de-Siècle* Europe and the Emergence of Modern Jewish Nationalism

I longed to dwell in Europe, where I was born — but in vain. (Uri Zvi Greenberg, *In the Land of the Slaves* [Berlin 1923])

We — the youngsters of Israel — have experienced with all the warmth of our youth the life of Europe, its shakings, its anxieties. We were like a seismograph which records every slight tremor. ('Our Position in the Labour Movement', *Kehilatenu* [Our Community] 1922: 149)

'For a continent that has been declared dead many times during the last thousand years, Europe has shown a surprising capacity for survival. Prophets of doom have appeared and found a public eager to listen to their message, not just during the last generation or two, but throughout the history of European civilization . . . .The age of European political predominance has ended, but no other centre has so far wrenched from Europe the torch of civilization. In a wider sense, the European age has only begun.'

This statement was written by Walter Laqueur in 1969, in the conclusion to his book *Europe since Hitler*, published in 1970. Three years after it was written, the oil crisis occurred as a result of the Yom Kippur War, and articles prophesying the decline of Europe and its political and moral surrender to the Third World and its oil and petro-dollars again became an almost dominant intellectual fashion. The oil embargo and the huge financial reservoir which backed it up were seen as the revenge of the Third World against European colonialism and imperialism. What the Muslim army failed to achieve before Poitiers and where the Ottomans failed before the walls of Vienna, petro-dollars succeeded. The decadent West, hedonistic and materialistic, now lost all its vitality and had no choice but to crawl on its knees. The pessimistic consciousness of the *fin-de-siècle*, the Cassandra-like prophesies of the previous century and the metaphor of the 'decline of the West' expressed the mood of the mid-1970s.

Professor Laqueur always stood outside this fashionable mood and the oil crisis did not change his views, which he expressed so concisely in the concluding paragraphs of his book. The 1980s confirmed his outlook; not only was Europe not in decline, she was reborn. In a historic upheaval which has an almost eschatological colouring — albeit without the violence usually attendant upon such a major transformation — Europe underwent deep structural and ideological changes. Europe at the twilight of the twentieth century seems nearer than at any time before to the 'European utopia'. At any rate, we can no longer speak in terms of the decline of 'European' status or hegemony in world politics or within the scope of universal history. Neither can we speak about a cultural decline or the loss of European vitality.

This recreation of Europe, with the shattered Russian Empire in East and Central Europe on the one hand, and the reunification of Germany as a first-rate European power on the other, raised mixed opinions and ambivalent reactions in the Israeli and Jewish public. These reactions are in a certain sense a continuation and meta-morphosis of the ambivalent reactions of the Jews to the French Revolution at the end of the eighteenth century,[1] and to the general history of the nineteenth century (i.e. European history). These popular reactions indeed created, at the beginning of the nineteenth century, the typical patterns of response, inherent since then in the Jewish historical consciousness, formulating its attitude towards 'Europe' and the 'West' from the outset of the nineteenth century to the present. There are several reasons for the current ambivalent response. First and foremost, there are the contradictory attitudes towards the reunification of Germany and the awakening of nationalism and particularism in East and Central Europe on the one hand, and the collapse of communism on the other. But there is also another reason: the attitude towards 'Europe' very often plays a major role in debates concerning the future cultural orientation of Jewish-Israeli society and the nature, essence and content of modern Jewish culture. The prophesy and metaphor of 'the decline of Europe', and the negative image which derives from it, seem to strengthen those trends which argue in favour of cutting off cultural links with Europe, not only because of its recent diabolic history, but also as a result of its decadent nature, its rotten and degenerate values, and because its future is inevitably doomed. The 'West' is considered to be a sinking ship, while the 'East', this abstract, metaphorical construct, is considered by many as a real political and cultural entity, fated to be victorious in the long run. No wonder, therefore, that the 'revival of Europe' began, even in a small measure, to occupy part of Israeli public opinion with regard to Israel's future cultural orientation and essence.

It seems right to speak of the fifth historical chapter of the Jewish web of interpretation and response to the European essence, characteristics and changes during the last 200 years. Almost a hundred years after the pessimism of the *fin de siècle* dictated part of the Jewish general mood, a new response is needed. Should the Jews welcome the revival of Europe with new expectations, or should they remember what it did not long ago and not let themselves be deceived once again?

The first historical chapter began during the years of the French Revolution and the Napoleonic Wars, which created the cornerstones of nineteenth-century Europe. Only in the eighteenth century, we must recall, did the idea of 'Europe' reach its peak and become a widespread *topos*. The Jewish response was mainly one of heightened expectations; high hopes from the 'new Europe' of the inevitable progress which, in due course, would open the gates to a new and better world for the Jews. The French Revolution was not the main cause of this optimism, but rather the reformist trends in the 'Enlightenment monarchies' in Europe. The 'Tolerance Edict' of Josef II (1782) rather than the Declaration of the Rights of Man and Citizen was regarded as a sign of the new horizons. The first signs of pessimism both in the 'East' and 'West', as a result of and in response to different events, were already discernible in the 1870s.[2] The optimistic utopia of the Jewish Haskala had changed, within certain circles, into deep disappointment, which grew faster in the 1880s and thereafter. The response of the Jewish intelligentsia to the rise of modern anti-semitism thus became intertwined with the general mood of pessimism and was fed by it. They saw anti-semitism both as a major pathological symptom of the European essence and as a result of *fin-de-siècle* decadence. The different varieties of Jewish radicalism, including radical nationalism, were one of the sharp responses to this general *Kulturpessimismus*, and a manifestation of the conclusion which the Jewish intelligentsia drew from it. Eschatology of many types — revolutionary and national — was the reaction to the deep pessimism. It was an inevitable result of the eagerness to find redemption in the midst of a crisis. Therefore, it would be right to claim that the nationalism of the Jewish intelligentsia and semi-intelligentsia was not a product of great optimism, but a result of deep disappointment and frustration, which sought compensation and new horizons. So high was the expectation, and so deep were the disappointments, that an alternate utopic-eschatological world-view was needed in order to replace the decaying ones and to provide adequate answers to the crisis. The disappointment with emancipation blended with the new negative attitude towards 'Europe', in which Jewish intellectuals longed to be rooted.

The third historical chapter opened after the first world war. It was manifested by a combination of the general reaction to the great war and its upheavals, and the mood of the 'decline of the West', which was strengthened after the war, and was accompanied by the belief that new vital civilizations were going to take the place of Europe. The deep influences of this intellectual mood on European politics and culture are well known. To this general background one should add the Jewish reaction to the great and bloody pogroms against the Jews in the East during the war and after.[3]

The fourth historical chapter began with the rise of nazism and needless to say, became a main issue on the Jewish agenda and in the Jewish world-view after the Holocaust. The question which engaged Jewish understanding of history in general and Western history in particular was: had Europe exposed its real face, its real nature, or was it only a part of it, only one layer of its entire entity? Was nazism an inherent feature of the 'European essence' or was it a diverted characteristic, an 'historical accident'? Since the late 1940s, this crucial question has occupied Jewish philosophy and polemics and has become a central topic within the Jewish *Zeitgeist*. The question, and the different answers given to it, shaped the world-view of the Jews and their attitudes towards the past, present and future history of the Jewish people (and its active behaviour in history).

The fifth historical chapter began in the late 1980s.

This article focuses on several manifestations from the second and third historical chapters — in other words, on the ambivalent reaction of modern Jewish nationalism to the pessimistic mood and formulations of the *fin de siècle* in Europe, and the conclusions it drew from this reaction. It is not the intention of this article to present the vast scope of these expressions and reactions. The main aim here is to present several characteristic responses, which serve as an illustration to the main argument.

The main argument is that while quite a large number of Jewish intellectuals and men of letters became nationalists in response to the pessimism of the *fin de siècle* and, by adapting its world-view, derived radical national and cultural conclusions from it, Zionism as an organized, active, historical phenomenon, acting on the stage of modern history, was able to gain power and strength, and to achieve international status and momentum, mainly due to the fact that the Europe of the late nineteenth century was not a declining continent, but rather a world at its apogee — a Europe which shaped the world outside itself in almost every sphere of human life. Those who expressed a negative attitude to Europe in general were far from rejecting the basic components of European civilization (or 'modernism').

Hence, we are faced with a sharp contradiction, even a deep gap, between historical consciousness and moods of reaction and expression, feelings and attitudes, as were formulated and internalized in the self-awareness of the Jewish intelligentsia, in its 'historical reality' as 'it really was' and its cultural behaviour. It was Max Nordau who, perhaps more than any other Jewish intellectual of that period, profiled and canalized the nature of the prevailing *Kulturpessimismus* that emphasized the existence of a gap between a world-view and objective reality. Nordau claimed that the 'mania of sadness', in his own terms, of the fashionable pessimism, represented the victory of the imaginative forces over reality.[4] Such was also Auerbach's criticism of Hess, when he wrote that Jewish intelligentsia tends to interpret the world in accordance with its own personal biography. In fact, what he had meant to say was that the sensitive threshold of the intellectual drives him to enforce his own biography on 'history' at large and to interpret it according to his own despair and expectations.[5] From the view-point of a provincial town (Tomashpol), Yehuda Leib Levin (Jepalel) found that the consciousness of decadence was a mere fashionable sickness, by which the Jewish intelligentsia had been afflicted, under the influence of the Russian (and German) intelligentsia. In his view, it was an expression of a confusion of concepts and romantic daydreams, and the ardour with which Jews grab fashionable intellectual and literary ideas. It was a result of 'a panic which had been transferred into boredom'.[6] He himself rejected the notion that Jews must sever their cultural links with Europe.

We should remember that a distinction must be made between the awareness of change and the more concrete descriptions of the society and culture in Europe at the crossroads of the nineteenth century. We must also be aware of the fact, already mentioned, that only during the eighteenth century did the concept of 'Europe' as a geographically and culturally united entity take its place as a superstructure under which its divisions, differences and national diversity could exist.[7] The topic here is 'Europe' as a unity and uniformity, but Jews were, of course, well aware of the fact that every European culture had its own nature, and therefore approached each of them separately. The variety which is Europe, wrote Ber Borochov before the first world war, is under the threat of the German spirit.[8] The statement that 'Europe inevitably meant Germanness'[9] is not far from the historical truth, but fails to distinguish between different and contradicting images of 'German culture', and, of course, the influences of other European cultures. More than that, Jewish intellectuals were well aware of the existence of different layers of 'European culture'. The images of the different European cultures and the different attitudes towards them is a separate subject. Dealing with it, we should distinguish between the Jewish images of each and every culture, on the one hand, and the real contacts between Jewish culture and every European national culture on the other. However, it is not in any way astonishing to find Jewish intellectuals and writers in the front line of those who revere the 'general European culture'.

When the great Jewish historian, Simon Dubnow, a great believer in the prospect of recreating a new Jewish national life (a *Kulturnation*) within the framework of Eastern Europe before the second world war, portrayed the closing of the nineteenth century from the perspective of the watershed year of 1900, he wrote:

> The nineteenth century, which began with a wave of glowing youthful hopes, came to a close worn out and enfeebled and in an esthetic and ethical condition described by the term *fin de siècle*. One of the powerful antitheses of Jewish history created by this turbulent century is now gradually drawing to its close.[10]

The radical shift from high optimism to the depths of pessimism signals the change from the optimism of the Haskala and radicalism, each of which in their turn believed in the integration of the Jews into the surrounding societies, either in a revolutionary mood, aspiring to be involved in the struggle to change those societies, or in a national mood, desperate for any future possibility of such integration. The shifts in attitude were indeed very sharp. For example, in 1863, one of the leading figures in the Haskala movement in Russia, Y.L. Gordon, who preached in favour of Jewish acculturation and integration in the tsarist empire, expressed his hopes in a famous poem. The land in which we are born and dwell, he wrote, is now becoming part of Europe; this Europe is the smallest of all continents, but her wisdom is the most abundant. This elaborate paradise is opening its gates to the Jewish people, calling the Jews 'our brothers'. Jews must, therefore, accept this warm invitation and stop feeling like foreigners.[11] These longings for Jewish redemption, during the period which Leopold Zunz referred to as the *Erlösungsjahre*, were grounded in a belief in reform, not revolution. The hope for Jewish redemption in Russia was strongly connected to the belief that Russia had undergone a deep 'Europeanization' process and would very soon become an integral part of Europe. Europe, which symbolized (to use Kalman Shulman's description) the evil of all evils, the most brutal and murderous instincts of humanity, was now changing its nature, and new horizons had begun to open up wide and clear.[12] From this assumption rose the belief that under the enlightened rulers Jews would be safe and sound, since these rulers did not expect in return full-scale integration and the renunciation of their Jewish identity. For this reason, Jews must respond to this kindly gesture by behaving like trusting, obedient and good citizens. In the world-view of the *maskilim*, Europe was indeed the heart and centre of humanity. They adopted with excitement and expectation the idea of the 'white man's burden', and its Eurocentric outlook. Europe, wrote one Jewish newspaper in the middle of the century, willingly opens its heart and treasures for all humankind. It is ready to spread its wisdom and its many achievements in the far-off lands of India, China and Japan, being like dew to these far-away dry fields.[13] This was how a newspaper (which was published in the provincial town of Lück, on the border of Prussia and Russia) saw the 'new imperialism'.

Less than thirty years later, another Hebrew newspaper bitterly expressed its conclusion with regard to the deep crisis of Jewish optimism. Europe, the fortress of progress, had revealed itself as the bosom of the anti-semitic monster. This was the 'real' new Europe, the Europe that Jews worshipped, whose wisdom and education they praised, and in order to be accepted by whom they were ready to betray their most treasured national possessions.[14] Some of them found compensation in the theories which distinguished between the progress of civilization and the state of morality. There was no link, they claimed, between progress in the material sphere and the degenerate state of morality.

Our present, enlightened, educated age,
The glorious nineteenth century,
Is now the scene of every crime.[15]

Thus, in this painful, sarcastic verse, Y.L. Levin summarized the nineteenth century in his poem *Our Time Questions*. For him, it was a painful emotional departure from 'Europe', since as a 'westernized' Jew he did not find it easy to say farewell to 'Europe' and everything it represented. To depart from Europe was not a happy journey, he admitted. It was the abandonment of a place which was, from the Jewish side at least, 'a homeland'. The distinction he made between the progress of civilization and the degeneration of morality gave him a useful solution: it was possible to separate European progress and ethics. It was possible to stress the superiority of Jewish ethics, while adopting Europe's material achievements. This distinction was made by many non-western intellectuals and became a fundamental cornerstone in their response to the 'Western challenge'.[16] From this point of view, the grave and plain mistake of the *maskilim* of the first half of the nineteenth century was that they failed to understand that very often 'material civilization' is only a tool, and ethics are the driving force which determine the uses and aims of these tools. The negative aspect of European culture was encouraged by scientific and technological inventions and innovations, since instead of serving the cause of morality, they served as new and powerful tools for injustice, oppression and brutality. It was not 'European imperialism' in Asia or Africa which reflected this ugly face. From the viewpoint of the Jews in the provinces of tsarist Russia, the ugly face of Europe was reflected in its new anti-semitism. The 'wisdom of Europe' thus turned out to be a poison. Material inventions do not serve the salvation of mankind, but instead become means of oppression.

Another radical intellectual, M.Y. Berdichevski, from his Berlin vantage-point, expressed a similar, but far more pessimistic vision. It would take Palestine, he wrote in 1891, 500 years to reach the same level of culture that Russia presently enjoyed! Turkey was the cradle of savagery — and of witlessness. He also claimed that Russian Jews were merely building castles in Spain, dreaming that Western Europe was a paradise. The hard truth was that Western Europe, contrary to dreams and wishful thinking, was in reality a hard place to live; hard and depressed conditions of life prevailed: radical individualism, internal class struggle, national and political division and spiritual decadence. 'Those who say that in the West the sun is shining, are terribly mistaken.'[17] These are depressing words indeed, coming from the pen of one whose point-of-departure was that the revival of Hebrew national culture was possible only in Palestine; from one who firmly believed that even national-cultural autonomy in Russia could not provide the Jews with the necessary framework for a real and deep cultural revival. If 'Europe' was far from being the ideal model, and Palestine under the Ottoman lay in the shadow of the deep and heavy darkness of the Middle Ages, what could a Russian Jew expect from the future?

It is clear that Jewish intelligentsia, both in the 'West' and in the 'East', saw in the nineteenth century a mirror of the nature and soul of the 'West' in general. Their verdict on the prospect of Jewish integration in this kind of Europe was negative. Since this Europe was a whole and total cosmos, they were forced to formulate a vision of a whole and total cultural alternative: the alternative of a Hebrew national culture as a new Jewish-Hebrew cosmos. Here lay their eagerness, desire and need to formulate the utopia of the Hebrew culture as a new Jewish mode of existence — a utopia which was too heavy a burden to carry.

We now briefly consider three responses by Jewish intellectuals. Although they came from different backgrounds, they each reached similar conclusions.

'Pouvez-vous nous déseuropéaniser?' — will we be able to discard our Europeanness? — so wondered the 'English lady', Heinrich Graetz's 'second voice'. 'Europeanism,' she mused, 'covers the whole Jewish field of vision.' It is an integral part of their essence. But what is the real nature of this Europe, she wondered rhetorically. Heinrich Graetz, in his response, did not hesitate to use the data of the new science of social statistics to portray European society as a sick society, a reflection and continuation of the ancient pagan cultures; corrupted and divergent from top to bottom. He sought to prove, utilizing the statistics of the spread of syphilis in Germany and the incidence of illegitimate births in Europe (in the same way, one may add, that Jewish writers today use the data on AIDS) to prove the utter immorality of contemporary 'Western culture'. Europe, Graetz wrote, was a hospital for the incurable, a terrible monster, a moribund culture, which would pass away very soon. There was no future for Europe, and only those who believed that salvation would rise from decay could really believe in its prospects. Beyond the magnificent façade of its artistic creations, behind the many shrines of art and the palaces of science, the 'English lady' fully agreed with him, a great sickness was hidden: Europe was rife with many unknown sicknesses which corroded its soul. Was it not a depressing thought, she queried, that there could not be any compromise between the spirit of the Jew and the spirit of Europe? The inevitable conclusion must be, therefore, that in order to free themselves from this evil spirit, Jews must depart from Europe and sever all their links with it. Hence the drive to call for the 'revival of the Jewish race'.[18]

How remote is the spirit of these words from what Zunz wrote in the last chapter of his monumental study, *Die Gottesdienstlichen Vorträge der Juden: Historisch Entwickelt* (1892, second edition). Here Zunz identified the 'European spirit' and 'culture' with the 'German spirit' and German *Kultur*, and expressed his belief that *ex Germania lux*: the light should flow from now on, not from Babylon, but from Germany — the *Vaterland*, where her citizens would combine wisdom, patience, industriousness and honesty in a fine mixture, where side by side with legal equality and the indulgence of culture, the emancipation of the Jews, both civil and spiritual, would progress unimpeded.[19] This utopia, as is well known, shaped the world-view of German Jews during the nineteenth century and into the twentieth. They urged their fellow Jews to shed their 'Asiatic' characteristics and to become 'true and full Europeans'. Indeed, it is hard to find more illuminating illustrations of a simultaneously pessimistic and optimistic response to the *fin-de-siècle* mood. However, we must not forget that Graetz's conclusions were far from radical. In spite of his intellectual and aesthetic dislike of and recoiling from 'Europe', he was very far from any readiness to 'divorce Europe'. The question posed by the 'English lady' — can the Jews sever their European roots? — was answered with a negative. Graetz and the Jewish world he represented could not really give a convincing positive answer.

Lilienblum is a different case. He was by no means a 'westernized' Jew in his convictions and beliefs, far from the mystic-exotic nuances of some of his Jewish contemporaries. He was never taken with the idea that 'the East' could be a substitute for 'Europe' as a cultural environment. Indeed, he drew a sharply negative portrait of Europe, comparing it to decadent Rome, replete with blood and fiery beastly passions. Europe of the Middle Ages and of our times is a licentious culture, he wrote time and again. Turning Zunz's optimism into a pessimistic vision, and Graetz's pessimistic outlook into ideology, Lilienblum's radical conclusion was that there was a crucial need for a real national and cultural revival of the Jewish people in Palestine. But in contrast to the admirers of the 'East', who were inspired by some of the Slavophiles of their time,[20] and despite what he himself wrote against Europe, Lilienblum never saw in the 'East' a desirable alternative. He claimed that Judaism had to demolish its windows to the 'West' to let the cobwebs blow away for ever. But these windows he wished to open wide in Palestine. Only there could 'open windows' not turn out to be open gates to assimilation. No wonder he found himself struggling on three fronts: with those who believed that the modernization of the Jews was possible only in Europe; with those who believed that America offered the only escape from both Russia and the 'East',[21] and with the Orthodox Jews who hoped for an Orthodox conservative Jewish society in Eretz Israel.

Y.L. Levin reached the same conclusion. In a series of articles he published in *Ha-Meliz* during April–May 1899, entitled 'The End of the Century', he discussed Simon Bernfeld's article, which was published in *Lu-ach Ahiasaf* the same year.[22] Bernfeld, according to the 'Nietzschean fashion' of the time, claimed that the origins of the nineteenth century's sickness lay in the victory of democracy all over Europe. The new political culture had given birth to a mass culture which lacked real education (i.e. real *Bildung*). Bernfeld thus only repeated the fear and even horror with which many European intellectuals and literati greeted the emergence of 'mass culture' and of the 'masses' on the stage of history. As a radical *maskil* and even a populist, Levin firmly rejected the characterization of democracy as the realm of degenerate culture and the source of evil and sin. He truly believed that the real cause of the nineteenth century's sickness was the deep gap created between mind and soul, that is, between the rational and the irrational. The deterioration of the century, he went on to argue, was a result of the 'assault of passion and the petrification of the mind'. This gap was increased by the effect of the many innovations and achievements of this century in every sphere of life. It was not the 'rule of the mob' which was the cause of all troubles, rather the fact that the vast majority of the population, who, until recently, were guided by morality (i.e. religion), had been corrupted by modern 'materialistic secularism'. He rejected the slogan of the 'danger of the masses' and the description of its effects on 'culture', since Jewish history proved that the 'masses' could be dominated by morality and knowledge of the *Torah* (the Laws of Moses, i.e. its moralistic values). At any rate, he totally accepted the description of contemporary Western culture as degenerate, full of despair and emptiness. The salvation of the Jews, therefore, would only be achieved by 'national romanticism', by the so-called 'volkish revival' of the 'national soul' in its 'motherland' — the resurrection of the 'Hebrew soul'.

Jewish literature of the late nineteenth century is full of this kind of bitterly negative criticism of Europe. It blended the pessimism of the *fin de siècle* and the horror of the cold, threatening emptiness of existence as expressed by different trends in the European world-view, with Jewish reaction to the new European anti-semitism which appeared in the 1880s. Paradoxically, but logically, it was the Jewish intelligentsia and semi-intelligentsia, the most 'westernized' group within Jewish society, that created the most demonic image of Europe. However, this demonic image did not cause them to turn away from Europe. On the contrary, their first encounter with the realities of Palestine of the late nineteenth century only sharpened and strengthened their European outlook. Europe became a 'lost cultural paradise'.

On 21 September 1882, Vladimir Dubnow, a young member of BILU (one of the first modern Zionist movements), wrote from Jafa to his elder brother, the historian Simon Dubnow, in Petersburg:

> Newspapers are so rare here that it is even impossible to know what is going on in Turkey itself. We are all walking in the dark. To sum up, here is wild Asia and not cultured Europe, which every day becomes more and more precious to me.[23]

A brief impression of the Palestinian scene was sufficient to impress him, and what he saw was automatically translated in terms of the common topos of the 'wilderness of Asia'. These longings for 'Europe' were expressed, we must recall, not by immigrants who had left behind the centres of Western European culture, but very often by those who came from small towns in Eastern Europe. However, from their point of view they were Europeans in every sense. These expressions are to be found in the literature of the First *Aliya*, the second *Aliya* and thereafter. From its outset, the new Jewish society was urged to model itself on 'European standards'.[24] Thus, even a radical nationalist was unable to divest himself of all that 'European culture' presented and meant to him. The geographic remoteness of Europe transformed its many flavours into treasured memories, since the common, ordinary and daily became rare and precious.

One of the major challenges a radical nationalist had to face was the need first to refute and then to convince his anti-national and anti-Zionist opponents, who promoted acculturation and integration in Europe, that departure from 'Europe' was by no means exile to a 'cultural wilderness'. Time and again he argued that 'Europe' was a 'portable culture' and could be carried away to Asia and planted there: a Jewish-European island in the midst of the 'East'.

For the modern, westernized Jew, Europe was not only the Europe of the 'big ideas', of humanism, liberalism, etc., but the Europe of everything that meant culture: libraries and art galleries, modern schools and houses, medicine and electricity, and so forth. In other words, the 'westernized' Jew held the opposite view to that which claimed that 'a civilization cannot simply transplant itself, bag and baggage' outside its 'natural space', and believed that such a 'transplantation' was possible.[25]

> I'm convinced that you too will share my view that the genuine works such as those of Heine, Schiller, Börne, Goethe, Lessing and others will still be of world interest hundreds of years from now, and that we, who are cut off from European civilization, need them in order to rest while reading them and to meditate after our hard day's work — they, the great and sincere friends of humanity.[26]

The missing books (this letter was written in 1887) were of course only one aspect of Europe, a central aspect indeed, but not the only one. The departure from Europe and the settling in the 'desert of the East' was considered an existential necessity, and not always an act of free will and free choice, a fact that was a driving force behind the visions of a total renaissance of the Jewish existence in Palestine.

Uri Zvi Greenberg, the poet who was imbued with an apocalyptic, pessimistic outlook and who declared his hatred towards 'Europe', gave an illuminating example of this ambivalent attitude:

> We ought to go
> The lands cried out under our feet . . .
> We ought to hate what we loved so dearly
> We have loved the wood, the stream, the well, the mill
> We have loved the falling leaves, the fishes, the bucket and the
> *halla*, and in deep secrecy we have loved their bell-ringing
> We have loved the harmonica, flute and Ukrainian folk-songs, the
> village girls in their dancing with their coloured ribbons
> We have loved the white shed with the straw gardens and the red roofs,
> We have loved deeply the smokey hours in the coffee shops,
> And operas, parks, a perfumed head and dancing places. Opium.

Ballet. Boulevards and brothels
And electricity, museums of antiquities and city libraries . . . [27]

It is indeed a desperate and painful love-cry. This longing for
Europe is transfigured into a vision of a Hebrew revival and a whole
Hebrew universe. This universe or cosmos included all the features
and characteristics of Europe: of rural Europe with its village and
country 'organic life', of urban, bohemian, educated, licentious
Europe — nothing was missing! This cultural eschatology was
needed, since the culture of the 'westernized Jews', and mainly the
Jewish intelligentsia left behind, was indeed a 'whole world', toward
which they felt deep historical and cultural linkage, and since the
alternative culture they intended to create was as yet only an
imaginary one.

However, despite his Europhobia, Greenberg often proclaimed
that his model of organic-national culture was a European model,
mainly Slavic (and communist). When he referred to the cultures of
East European nations, he stressed the fact that all of them were
'natural cultural entities'. And how he envied them this! They had the
'natural roots' that Jews now had to grow in a hurry. When he
referred to the 'East', and the 'Hebrews' returning to their 'Eastern
natural birth-place and natural historical environment', he used
'Western images' of the 'East', created and formulated by European
conservative romantics and mystics in the 'West' as well as in the
Russian literature of the late nineteenth century.

It must be stressed at this point that this mystical longing for the
'magic East', which possessed the secret cure to all the sickness of the
soul of the 'West' and of Judaism, was a reaction and perception of
the few, and had only a marginal influence on cultural behaviour. The
'East' they raised in necromancy was an imaginary entity, and not a
'real' and concrete one. Very often its Islamic nature was not
mentioned, as if it did not exist. Yaacov Rabinovitz, in a very
sarcastic and sharp article, pointed to the fact that the Jewish
intelligentsia who expressed 'reactionary-European' notions about
'the return to the East', did not take their own phrases and slogans
seriously, and had no intention of 'living in the East', that is to say, of
adopting 'the Eastern ways of life'. They would always prefer to live
in the 'East' as Europeans.[28] Those who sought 'spiritual salvation' in
the 'East' of their pure imagination were ignoring the real character of
'Eastern society' and 'Eastern culture'. They were idealistic and
reactionary. The paradox lay, therefore, in the fact that 'escape' from

Europe to the 'Eden of the East' represented one of the many 'European components' of the Jews as 'Western Jews' (the usage of the term 'East' by itself is evidence of this).

Herzl, one of the outstanding 'westernized' Jewish intellectuals and leaders of the national movement, pointed very clearly to the central role of daily life as an integral part of 'culture'. 'East' and 'West' were not only two different metaphors or two contradicting topoi, but were real and dynamic differing complexes of everyday life, of 'culture' as human environment. In a paragraph which, from a historical perspective may be regarded as naive and even pathetic, Herzl wrote that daily habits were portable and could be transplanted from one place to another. Not only ideas, laws and beliefs could be taken in one's travelling-bag, but also one's 'small habits'. The history of colonization movements, certainly in the modern age, provided solid and indisputable evidence of this, and explained why Herzl had no difficulty in portraying the establishment of a modern European Jewish society in Palestine. His Europe was not only the Europe of trains, theatres, parliaments, art galleries, electricity, etc., nor was it an 'organic Europe'. It was a Europe of daily life, containing the many things people were used to, all of which were included in the 'fleshpots' that Jews would not leave behind in Europe. In the *Judenstaat*, Herzl therefore stressed the fact that modern technology was used everywhere mainly in order to transplant these 'small habits' to the new homelands: there were English hotels in Egypt and on the top of the mountains in Switzerland, Viennese-style coffee-shops in Latin America, French theatre in Russia, German operas were performed in North America, and the best Bavarian beer was to be found in Paris! In leaving Egypt behind, he declared, we would not forget the 'fleshpots of Europe'. We would take them with us.[29]

By this Herzl intended not only to calm those who feared that leaving Europe would mean leaving behind for ever all that was so dear to the bourgeois Jew, whose main concerns were his daily comforts and conveniences. Certainly, he never saw himself as advocating 'cultural colonization', i.e. transplanting a certain 'culture' from its 'natural place' to a strange, alien environment and imposing it on a place (and its people) where it did not belong. His main aim was not only to gain the support of middle-class Jews, but to reject the common and widespread theory that there existed a deterministic linkage between a place and a culture, and that as a result of this linkage, the creation of a Jewish culture in Asia would not mean the creation of an 'Asiatic Jewish culture'. Cultures, Herzl voiced very clearly, were man's creations, and it was the human spirit and human initiative which gave a place its identity and character. It was culture that endowed a place with its uniqueness and not the other way round. Therefore, for the 'West', the 'East' was not a geographic border.

As is well known, Herzl was branded 'messianic' or 'utopian' and certainly as one who held 'European prejudices'. Eurocentric he was indeed, but at the same time he was far more realistic than many of his contemporary critics, for whom the question of modern Jewish *Kultura* was the main concern. For them, culture meant mainly ideas, values, an organic whole, spirit, etc., while for Herzl it was a dynamic complex of human existence and environment in its total scope and its many aspects. His concept of culture was not an idealistic and abstract one, like that of most of his critics. At the same time, his notion of modernity was also not of a poetic nature. He was very well acquainted with the nature of modern, urban-industrial society.

Herzl did indeed draw a very clear picture of the political, economic and social structure of Western civilization at the *fin de siècle*. He emphasized the influence of 'mass politics' on political culture, the conflict between capital and work, the hard conditions of the working class, etc. He even drew a parallel between the European proletariat and the Jews. Both were longing for salvation and were thus prone to utopias or visions which promised them redemption in the near future. He even went as far as to argue that it was impossible to predict what kind of misery would emerge from these future remedies, and had some doubts concerning the influence of advanced technology on modern society. He was not a simple-minded utopian who believed in modern progress. But while he was very cautious about the prospects for socialism and the chances of success in constructing a 'new world', he was very strong in his conviction that the prospects for Zionism were bright. It is correct to describe his Zionism as 'scientific Zionism' (on the model of 'scientific socialism').[30] He firmly believed that the new forces created by man during the nineteenth century could be used in the service of progress and humanity. Zionism, in his view, was composed of national aspirations and social longings made possible by the power of science and technology. In other words, while he was very pessimistic about the prospect of a 'European utopia', he believed in the reality of the 'Zionist utopia'. Without trains, steam-power, electricity, etc., the mass migration of the Jews would remain a day-dream, and the creation of modern Jewish society only a vision. Zionism was the offspring of modern Europe, and was an active national — and social — force because it acted within the modern world, adopting and using its skills and inventions. If Herzl was messianic, his was a scientific messianism. His utopia could become a reality only through scientific messianism. *Fin-de-siècle* Europe was a creative force which changed the world around it, and the Zionist revolution was part of this revolutionary change. His optimism, therefore, originated in a deep belief in modernity and in the new human horizons it opened up. Only against this background would the Jews be able to forge through to new horizons.

In the limited space available, it is impossible to give even a brief survey of the romantic longings and their expression in the Hebrew literature of that period. There were two types of romanticism. One embodied a longing for the landscape of Europe. 'My dreams ripened among pines, not among palms,' wrote a Jewish German intellectual. 'When we worked in the fields, some of us felt deep longings for the misty woods of Europe and their bubbling damps,' wrote a young pioneer in 1922.[31] The second was a new Eretz-Israeli romanticism, trying to create deep intimate linkage with the new landscape and its nature. In both types we can easily recognize the longing for an 'organic whole', and the eagerness to create an intrinsic, atavistic affinity to the land.[32] However, all these expressions were a mirror, and a manifestation, of only one dimension of their world-view. No less powerful were their strivings for modernity — modernity as a superstructure on the basis of this new-born atavism and organic *Weltanschauung*. The socialist and liberal visions of modern society were no less influential than the romantic mood. Industrialization was just as important and decisive a factor as were the new feelings towards landscape and nature. Zionist romanticism did not turn out to be Zionist primitivism. What Frankel defines as the 'advantages of backwardness'[33] must be understood as the advantages of building, without any 'outside' interference, a new and modern society — and not a primitivist one, rejecting modernity. One of the fundamental myths of the modern Jewish *Weltanschauung* was the Promethean myth: the myth of a collective effort to change nature and to 'conquer' it in order to build in this backward province the most advanced society.

We must remember that literature and literary works, with their romantic mood of expression, are often misleading in this connection. Our historical reading must carefully distinguish between mood, images and modification of reality, and the real cultural process and development. Many contemporary plans reflect very clearly the wide vision of progress and modernity of that period. The real *Weltanschauung* of Jewish society in Palestine was a complex combination of romanticism and modernity, and the foundations and the structure of its culture were modern indeed. The anti-European motifs were marginal and had no influence. Y.H. Brenner clearly understood this when he wrote that 'we want the culture of the Gentiles in our streets, on our land, within our people, and what we were intended to do if we were to mix among them, we are ready to do by ourselves, according to our own ways'.[34]

For the major part of the Jewish intelligentsia, the West of *fin-de-siècle* Europe was the model for a modern Jewish society. They rejected romanticism and anti-Westernism and cleaved to the idea that Zionism was the only way to achieve 'acculturation without assimilation'. The great historical advantage of Palestine lay in the unique opportunity it gave to transfer and transplant 'Europe' to the 'East', while selecting its positive components and rejecting the negative ones. Zionists were the pioneers of Western civilization in the East. In other words, only in Palestine would the national Jews become 'real Europeans'.

These notions and concepts underwent several changes between the two world wars, not to say after the Holocaust. However, beyond the mood and the formulation of expressions and ideas exists the 'cultural reality'. Jewish society was created and institutionalized during the period of *fin-de-siècle* Europe as a modern European society. Most of its institutions, norms and values were based on European models.

Here indeed we face a paradox: a society which was created by, among other forces, the pessimistic response to *fin-de-siècle* Europe, and by a sharp critique of the values Europe represented, was, from the outset, a European society in essence and in framework. So strong was the Jewish bond with Europe that even the Holocaust was unable to sever it. There was no fleeing from Europe, and the different efforts to escape from it merely emphasize this deep link, and the impossibility of cutting off its roots and its heritage.[35]

Notes

This article is part of a study in the history of 'cultural models' in modern Jewish perception. It was written when relations between the 'Jews' and 'Europe' were taking a new step: the 'shadow of the Holocaust' was fading in European public opinion, the mass immigration of Jews from Russia to Israel might bring down the curtain on the presence of Jews in Russia, and would thus accomplish the mass Jewish emigration from Russia which began in the 1880s, and many Jews felt a deep new affinity toward 'the world of their forefathers' in Eastern Europe.

I should like to thank Jeffery Kaplan of the University of Chicago Committee on the History of Culture for his editorial assistance in the preparation of this article.

1. Samuel Verses, 'Hamaapechah Hazarfatit baaspaklaryah shel hasifruth aivrit' (The French Revolution in the Mirror of the Hebrew Literature), *Tarbiz, Quarterly for Jewish Studies*, 54, April–September 1989, 483–521. I am indebted to Samuel Feiner for his yet unpublished studies on the attitude of modern Jewish historiography toward the French Revolution.

2. The pessimistic mood of the Jewish radical intelligentsia in Russia was the result of 'minor' events, such as the pogroms in Odessa in 1871, the expulsion of the Jews from Kiev in 1872, etc.

3. It is worth mentioning here that Jewish literati in the second historical chapter did not write under the influence of Spengler's *Der Untergang des Abendlandes: Umrisse einer Morphologie der Weltgeschichte* (*The Decline of the West*), which appeared between 1917 and 1922 (the English translation appeared between 1926 and 1928), but they were surely impressed by other literary echoes of this pessimistic mood and mainly by D.S. Merezhkovsky's *On the Causes of the Decline of Russian Literature and its New Trends* (1893). This essay had a great influence on modern Hebrew literature of that period. See Bar-Yosef, Bialik and Russian Literature, *Moznayim*, 62, nos 9–10 (May–June 1990). See B. Glatzer Rosenthal, 'Stages of Nietzscheanism: Merezhkovsky's Intellectual Evolution' in Glatzer Rosenthal (ed.), *Nietzsche in Russia* (Princeton 1986), 69–93. See also Andrzje Walicki's studies on the Slavophiles and the westernizer in the second half of the nineteenth century in Russia and the anti-Enlightenment trends there, *A History of Russian Thought from the Enlightenment to Marxism* (Oxford 1980), esp. chaps 4, 6: and his *The Slavophile Controversy* (Oxford 1975). However, the Jewish intelligentsia could not accept the anti-Western ideas which gained some credibility in Germany. See Fritz Stern, *The Politics of Cultural Despair: A Study in the Rise of Germanic Ideology* (Berkeley, CA 1962). See also K.W. Swart, *The Sense of Decadence in Nineteenth-Century France* (The Hague 1964); Saul Friedlander, 'The Nineteenth Century and the End of Mankind', *Smanim — A Historical Quarterly*, vol. 1, no. 2 (January 1980), 16–25; P. Mendes-Flohr, 'Fin de Siècle Orientalism and the Aesthetics of Jewish Self-Affirmation' in *Mehkarei Yerushalayim bemahshevet Israel* (*Jerusalem Studies in Jewish Thought*), vol. 3, no. 4 (1983–4), 623–82. Carl G. Schorske, *Fin De Siècle Vienna: Politics and Culture* (New York 1981); Peter J. Bowler, *The Invention of Progress: The Victorians and the Past* (Oxford 1989), 192–201 ('Progress and Degeneration').

4. Max Nordau, *Paradoksim* (the Hebrew translation of *Paradoxes* [1885] by Dov Stock, Tel Aviv 1930), 5–25. See also Nordau's *Hasekarim hamuskamim shel haenoshut atarbutit* (the Hebrew translation by H. Goldenberg of *Die conventionellen Lungen der*

Kulturmenschheit [1883], Tel Aviv 1930), 182–3. Nordau portrays Western decadence, but at the same time believes in the possibility of change and progress.

5. Quoted in Jonathan Frankel, *Prophesy and Politics: Socialism, Nationalism and the Russian Jews, 1862–1917* (Cambridge 1981), 48. He wrote: ' . . . You take the stages of the development of your personalities and your momentary thought processes very easily for the development of the actual period and real world.'

6. Yehuda Leib Levin, 'Pirkei zikhronot' (Memories) in Yehuda Slutsky (ed.), *Zikhronot vehegyonot* (*Memories and Reflections*) (Tel Aviv 1968), 81–2.

7. Denys Hay, *Europe: The Emergence of an Idea* (Edinburgh 1968); Jurgen Fischer, *Oriens, Occidens, Europa: Begriff und Gedanke 'Europa' in der späteren Antike und im frühen Mittelalter* (Wiesbaden 1957).

8. Quoted in Matityahu Mintz (ed.), *Mikhtavei B. Borochov* (B. Borochov's Letters 1897–1917) (Tel Aviv 1990), 615.

9. Quoted from an article by Robert Weltsch in George L. Mosse, 'Influence of the Völkish Idea on German Jewry' in *Germans and Jews* (Detroit 1987), 78. See also Mosse's remarks on the influence of the atmosphere of the *fin de siècle* on the acceptance of the völkish ideas all over Europe. These ideas were also adopted by the new Jewish national *Weltanschauung*.

10. Simon Dubnow, 'Autonomism, the Basis of the National Program' in S. Dubnow, *Nationalism and History, Essays on Old and New Judaism*, edited with an introductory essay by Koppel S. Pinson (Philadelphia 1959), 131. See Dubnow note on the 'law of the evolution of *Weltanschauungen*, the law of spiritual progress', ibid., 131–2.

11. *Kol shirei Judah Leib Gordon* (Tel Aviv 1956, 3rd edn), 17.

12. Kalman Shulman, *Sefer divrei yemei olam* (Vilna 1875, 2nd edn), part 4, 19–20.

13. See Yaacov Shavit, 'Halonot laolam' (Windows on the World), *Qesher*, no. 4 (1988), 3–10. (These quotes are from the newspaper *Hamagid* of 1858.)

14. See Jehuda Leib Winz's article 'The Enlightenment of the 19th Century and the Hope of Israel in Germany', *Hameliz* (7 March 1896). He stressed the fact that anti-semitism became popular in Germany, 'the country which stood in the front line of our age of Enlightenment'.

15. The poem *Sheeloth azman* was reprinted in Levin's *Zikhronot ve hegyonot*, ibid., 140–3.

16. See his articles on H.T. Buckle's concepts of morality and progress which are summarized in my article 'Hashimush shel maskilim yehudiim bemisrach Eropah bemishnato shel H.T. Buckle' (The Works of Henry Thomas Buckle and their Application by the Maskilim of Eastern Europe), *Zion*, 49, no. 4 (Jerusalem 1984), 401–12. On the same attitude of Muslim thinkers see, for example, Fazlu Rahman, *Islam and Modernity: Transformation of an Intellectual Tradition* (Chicago 1982), 43–83. These Arab thinkers wished also to distinguish knowledge (philosophy) from the practical technological spheres.

17. This letter was recently published in Avner Holzman (ed.), *Ginzei Mikhah Yosef Berdichevski* (Holon 1990), 16–19.

18. I used Yeruham Tolqus's Hebrew translation of the 'Correspondence of an English Lady on Judaism and Semitism' (Stuttgart 1883) in Shmuel Ettinger (ed.), H. Graetz, *Darkei hahistoryia hayehudit* (Jerusalem 1969), 126–76. And see also Graetz's article 'The Rejuvenation of the Jewish Race', ibid., 103–9. See the English translations in Ismar Schorsch's collection of Graetz (The Jewish Theological Seminary of America, New York 1975), 141–50, 191–258. Graetz thought that Europe

must be considered as the main seat of Judaism (and not Russia). On the background of the 'Briefwechsel' see Schorsch, 59–60, note 152, and on Graetz's use of 'Moralstatistik' see ibid., 311, note 6.

19. There is a vast literature on the German–Jewish optimistic outlook and attitude during the last half of the nineteenth century and therefore I feel no need to suggest references to the literature on this subject.

20. See also Shlomo Breiman (ed.), *Mikhtavei Moshe Leib Lilienblum le Yehuda Leib Gordon* (Lilienblum's Letters to Gordon) (Jerusalem 1968), 198–203. See also Lilienblum's autobiography, *Kitvei M.L. Lilienblum*, vol.2, 1874 (Jerusalem 1970), 148. There he writes about the 'loathsomeness of Europe'.

21. On Lilienblum's debate with David Frishman (who argued that Jews should emigrate to America and not to Asia, the symbol of enlightenment, freedom, good, etc., 'since the spirit of haskala moves from East to West and will cross now the ocean to reach the "West" '), see Yosef Klausner, *Historia shel Ha-Sifrut Ha-Evrit Ha-Hadasha* (*History of Modern Hebrew Literature*), vol. 4 (Jerusalem 1953), 280–1.

22. S. Bernfeld's article was published in *Luah Ahiasaf*, 3–42.

23. Quoted in Shulamit Laskov (ed.), *Ketavim letoldot Hibat Zion veyishuv Eretz Israel* (*Documents on the History of Hibbat Zion and the Settlement of Eretz Israel*), vol. 1, 1870–1882 (Tel Aviv 1982), 504.

24. In the 'Documents', and other contemporary literature, there are many references to the need for 'European standards'. See, for example, the memorandum of BILU headquarters in Istanbul from June 1882, ibid., 367. The memorandum speaks about the 'updated results' of European science and culture. The German colonies in Palestine were models of 'European villages'.

25. Fernand Braudel, *The Mediterranean and the Mediterranean World in the Age of Philip II*, vol. 2, translated by Sian Reynolds (New York 1966), 770. Here Braudel expresses his 'organic concepts', but he also believes that culture can be transferred, not by anonymous carriers, but by organized conscious enterprise.

26. Quoted in Dov Schidorsky, *Sifria vesefer beEretz Israel Be shalhe tekufah haosmanit* (*Libraries and Books in the late Ottoman Palestine*) (Jerusalem 1990), 103.

27. Uri Zvi Greenberg, 'Yerushalayim shel matah', *Eimah gedolah veyareah/Poems* ('The Earthy Jerusalem', *Grey Fear and the Moon*) (Tel Aviv 1925), 55. Europe, he wrote, cannot bear Jews anymore, 'Therefore I give her back my Frack [evening dress], my tie, my lack shoes [patent leather shoes], and also my graveyards . . . '

28. Yaacov Rabinovitz, 'Al mizrah vemaarav' (On East and West), *Hatekufah*, no. 17 (Elol/September–October 1921), 443–54. See also Zeev Jabotinsky's articles 'Hamizrah' and 'Hamizrah Haziuri' (The East and The Pictorial East) from 1926 and 1932, re-printed in Yosef Nedava (ed.), *Principal Foundations for Current Problems* (Tel Aviv 1981), 90–6, 97–100. Jabotinsky not only emphasised the 'European nature' of Jewish civilization, but, like many others, stressed the fact that 'European civilization' itself has fundamental 'Jewish' components.

29. I used M. Yoeli's Hebrew translation of Herzl's *Medinath ayehudim* (Tel Aviv 1978), 55 ('Hergelim ketanim' — 'small habits').

30. See Herzl's articles from his 'Parisian Period' in *Heikhal Bourbon-miBoulanger ad Dreyfus 1891–1895* (*From Boulanger to Dreyfus*), vols 1–3 (Jerusalem 1974), mainly the articles from August 1893 (vol. 2, 522), and December 1891 (vol. 1, 48). See also Daniel R. Headrick, *The Tools of Empire; Technology and European Imperialism in the Nineteenth Century* (Oxford 1981).

31. Moses Calvary (in 1912–13), quoted in Mosse, ibid., 94.

32. *Kehilatenu* (*Our Community: Collection of Reflections, Exertions and Longings of Pioneers*), 1922, introduction and annotations by Moki Zur (Jerusalem 1988), 277. This collection of testimonies is saturated with reflections about the nature and the destiny of Europe and the linkage between the Jews and Europe. At the same time the writers express their hopeless desire to reach in Palestine the 'cultural stage' of Europe, and portray 'Europe' as an 'old', 'cursed' continent; they long for European landscape (regard the 'East' as a region somewhere behind the Sambation River), and try to create a 'natural' linkage to the new unknown and different landscape of Palestine. Ibid., 136–7, 181, etc. Another type of rural romanticism (based on Eastern European model); see, for example, David Ben-Gurion's memories from his life in Galilee, 'Bi yehudah uvaGalil: Kitvei zkhronot' (In Judea and Galilee: Fragments of Memories) in *Anahnu vekchinenu* (We and our Neighbours) (Tel Aviv 1931). See Motolensky's criticism of this 'reactionary romanticism' in *Haahdut* (*The Unity*), no. 35 (June 1911). If romanticism moves from the sphere of poetry to the 'real world', it can endanger the ideal of progress, this critic wrote.

33. Frankel, *Prophecy and Politics*, chap. 8, 366–452. In this backwardness he sees an 'advantage', since the pioneer socialists in the USA comprise only a national and class minority within American society. However, since most of them envisioned a modern Jewish society and not a rural-agricultural one, this backwardness was also a hard and insurmountable obstacle.

34. Y.H. Brenner, 'Bahayim u basifrut' (I in Real life and in Literature) in *Kol kitvei Y.H. Brenner* (*Y.H. Brenner's Writings*), vol. 2 (Tel Aviv 1960), 61. See also Frankel, 89. Zalman Epstein wrote: 'We have lived to hear . . . words worthy of Aksakov and his school which pours out abuse against the west and all its Enlightenment'. Lilienblum expressed this common view by writing that only in Palestine would Jews be able to adapt 'European civilization' without being forced to become only 'Benei Dat Moshe' — that is, Jews by religion only. In Palestine they would be able to graft the twig of Yapeth onto the genus of Israel.

35. On this chapter, and the more recent one, I intend to write separately in a forthcoming article, 'The "New Germany" and the "New Europe" as an Old–New "Jewish Problem" '.

Yaacov Shavit

is a Professor at Tel Aviv University where
he teaches the history of Zionism and Jewish
intellectual history. He is the author of
numerous articles and books, including *The
New Hebrew Nation: A Study in Israeli
Heresy and Fantasy* (London 1987),
Jabotinsky and the Revisionist Movement
(London 1988), *History in Black: Race,
History and Culture in African–American
Writings* (forthcoming) and *Judaism in the
Greek Mirror* (forthcoming).

Billie Melman

Claiming the Nation's Past:
The Invention of an Anglo-Saxon Tradition

The reconstitution of continuities, of a suitable history which links present to past, characterizes most societies in moments of transition. The past alone, observed Disraeli, energizes an atrophied race when all else fails. An invented past, wisely manipulated, not only 'explains the present', but 'moulds the future'.[1] Invented continuities, to paraphrase Hobsbawm's over-used expression, are most likely to develop in modern communities.[2] Indeed, the quest for historic continuities is to be looked for especially in those places and at those times in which a national identity emerges and crystallizes.[3]

But not only new or immature nations, or groups seeking to attach themselves to a real or an imagined 'nation', legitimize innovation by inventing a tradition. In some of the oldest national communities, exemplified in the 'mature' nation-states, identities have been challenged, defined and re-defined in diverse processes of inclusion (in the nation), exclusion (from it) and transformation.[4] The case of the construction of an integrative English identity, through the possession and reinvention of an Anglo-Saxon inheritance, may illustrate the usages of the remote past in a society which was the first to be exposed to the related effects of industrialization and modernization.

Although a great deal has been written on the meaning of medievalism in the 'age of industry', most studies of the Victorian usages of the Middle Ages focus on neo-feudalism and the cult of chivalry related to it.[5] Little attention has been paid to the development of Saxonism, or English Teutonism and the cultural significance of the veneration of pre-Norman England. The few studies we do have fix on the period after 1870, thus conveniently relating the preoccupation with ethnicity to modern imperialism and the ascendant, new 'democratic' Toryism.[6] Earlier and formative phases in the evolution of a racial notion of Englishness are quite neglected.

This gap is attributable to the state of the study of nationalism. In a pun on Hobsbawm, the history of nationalism in Britain is, itself, 'an invented tradition', claimed and taken possession of by impassioned scholars of both left and right. Nationalism, or, as it is more comfortably designated, 'patriotism', had been, until about 1982, quite an embarrassing topic, especially to socialist historians. The Falklands War gave issues like national identity and historical continuity political relevance and urgency.[7] The history of nationalism is hence constructed by historians identified with the left and with considerably less persistence and vigour by neo-conservatives. Furthermore, historians fully realize the usefulness of 'nation' and 'nationalism' as analytical categories which may supplement the category of class in the study of modern political culture.

Naturally enough, ideological sympathies and antipathies shape the approach to the topic; the selection of *kinds* of source materials; the strategies of narrative, and, most relevant here, the employment of the nineteenth century as a nationalist era. Thus, where 'radical' historians concentrate on diversity and discontinuity in national traditions, on the potential oppositional character of patriotism, or, conversely, on the usages of patriotism by ruling élites, conservatives are obsessed with unities and with the 'great lines' in British history.[8] Symptomatically, research focuses on the period before the Great Reform Bill and the demise of Chartism, and on that after 1870. The interim between oppositional nationalism and the consensus patriotism of the late nineteenth century is still considered either as an epilogue to the 'age of reform', or as a prelude to the conservative 'age of empire'.[9]

It is precisely on the interim period and on the conservative discourse *before* the new Toryism came into power that this essay concentrates. The patriotic language and images it examines are not directly political or partisan. The source material comprises historical fiction and conventional histories, literary forms which evolved together and cross-fertilized. The historical novel, which even before Lukács had been regarded as a patriotic genre (indeed, as a generically 'nationalist' artefact), is regrettably neglected by students of British nationalism. In fact, national identities developed in historical fiction from the late 1840s, a period which Lukács, in his famous tripartite division of the history of the genre, regards as socially rather than nationally oriented.[10] The middle decades of the nineteenth century saw the rise of the post-Scott 'serious' novel, in which new standards of scholarship and accuracy were sought. And it was precisely during that period that history was gradually transformed from an amateur occupation to an academic, specialized 'profession'. The achievement of British history of the mid-nineteenth century is the historiography of the early Middle Ages. Thus, the first — and by far the longest — section in this essay examines the relationship between the novel on pre-Norman England and 'conventional' history of the Anglo-Saxon period. No attempt is made to provide a genealogy of the two genres. Instead, a few texts which best represent the conservative discourse were selected. They include the works of Edward Bulwer Lytton, Charles Kingsley, Benjamin Disraeli, Carlyle, and, among the historians, Stubbs and Edward Freeman. The selection of the material and use of the term 'conservative' may seem rather arbitrary and even eccentric. For at least two of these writers would qualify as 'Whigs' or even Liberals. Freeman was a Gladstonian Liberal, and Bulwer, at the time he wrote the prototype to all the 'Saxon' novels, *Harold*, had not yet become a Tory, but was still attached to radical politics. The term 'conservative' is used in a rather broad and inclusive manner, and denotes an attitude or a temper rather than a political creed or filiation. It is anti-modernist, paternalist, ruralist and nationalist. In its radical form, which is examined here, it opposes Peelite reformism (based on an alliance between the landed class and the middle classes) and adopts a popular and even 'folkish' rhetoric. Notwithstanding an acceptance of the Whig doctrines of continuity and improvement, the conservative writers cultivate a sense of the irrevocability of the past that underpins their version of continuity. Most significant, the tradition they invent is potentially integrative and seeks to include in the nation groups hitherto excluded from it. This is done by means of the construction of inclusive histories. Events in the past are rearranged, dates are canonized and inscribed in the national memory. The first section focuses on the canonization of 1066 and its relocation in history. The second section moves from the sense of time to that of places, those loci identified with Anglo-Saxon England. As most students of nationalism agree, it grew from 'territoriality', a loyalty to, and veneration of, territories or places — real or imagined. The national geography defining England is central to the development of national identity. The third section is about the construction of identity through national Saxon heroes and heroines. It particularly looks at the relationship between the construction of the nation and that of gender. The historiography of nationalism writes out women, perhaps because nationalism is perceived as political and public, while women's history is still seen as 'private' and 'domestic'. But as Joan Scott points out, by introducing gender to the study of nationalism, we may enrich our understanding of its language and symbols.[11] The integrative character of the conservative notion of Saxonism and Englishness is manifest in the construction of images of masculinity and femininity, the public and the private.

The historical imagination took possession of the Anglo-Saxon past relatively late. *Political* fiction about Gothic, Teuton freedoms preceding the 'Norman yoke', is, of course, quite old. The notion of an 'ancient' national 'constitution' loomed large in discussions on the modern one even before the seventeenth century. The Saxon character of representative government, of English freedoms and of the limited monarchy, are motifs which recur in the writings of constitutionalists — Whig and radical alike. Yet, towards the end of the eighteenth century, the Saxon past no longer had a political meaning. As Christopher Hill argues, the 'ancient constitution' and the 'Norman yoke' survived as rhetoric, not as mobilizing political slogans. The argument for change drew increasingly on universal rights — sought *de novo* by each generation — and less and less on what Burke had called 'descent'.[12] As a result, the issue of continuity, or the lack of it, between what *had been* before the Norman Conquest and what *was* after it, lost its urgency. As Stubbs stated in his inaugural lecture as Regius Professor of History at Oxford in 1866, early medieval England was remote enough to be politically un-controversial, and close enough to modern times to teach students of modernity instructive lessons.[13] What makes this statement so meaningful is that Stubbs, the first professional medievalist, was also the first historian to be appointed Regius Professor. The Professor of Modern History at Cambridge at that time was the novelist Charles Kingsley, an enthusiastic Germanist and the author of best-selling patriotic fiction in which the early Middle Ages figured prominently.

Because of its remoteness, the pre-Norman era could be recon-structed as an inclusive fiction. Unlike the myths of the Great and Glorious Revolutions, that of 1066 could cut across political loyalties and appeal to a wide national sentiment. As J.W. Burrow wryly puts it: 'No defiant supporters to the prerogative toasted the memory of King John',[14] let alone that of the unfortunate Edward or Ethelred. Thus, when Saxon England fades away from the political discourse, the Anglo-Saxons as a nation and race are discovered by novelists *and* Germanist historians.

Of course, Scott himself was interested in the tension between the Latin-Norman and Teuton-Saxon elements in the English language and culture. This was pretty obvious to nineteenth-century readers of *Ivanhoe*. The opening chapter of the novel, with the dialogue between the Saxon Gurth and Wamba on the Normanization of English-Saxon, was regarded by historians as different as Carlyle and Thierry as a human and historical document on the national past. However, the Conquest functions as a point of reference rather than being an integral part of Scott's emplotment of the Middle Ages. The eleventh century was considered by most writers as a dark and unknown period. 'The period *ante Agamemnone*, before the brilliant age of mature chivalry.' 'The Norman Conquest', writes Bulwer in the Dedicatory Epistle to Tennyson D'Eyncourt, prefacing the first edition of *Harold*, 'was our Trojan War; an epoch beyond which our learning seldom induces our imagination to ascend.'[15] Both the Epistle and the Preface to the third edition consider the novel an experimental historical genre, planted 'on a ground so new to fiction'.[16] This new kind of scholarly literature substitutes rigorous standards of scholarship for Scott's slapdash romantic notions of the pre-Norman era.

Bulwer was not the first to capitalize on the new appeal of the eleventh century. Charles Macfarlane's *Camp of Refuge*, covering the reign of Edward the Confessor, appeared in 1844. More significant, Disraeli's *Sybil, or the Two Nations*, which appropriates the radical rhetoric of the 'Norman yoke' for Tory propaganda, was published in 1846. The novel is conventionally read as 'social' or 'industrial' fiction. But it is also an attempt to lay claim to the national past and 'wrench' the Middle Ages from Whig historians. Specially relevant here is Disraeli's exploitation of the myth of the Conquest. 'Saxons' and 'Normans', or 'conquered' and 'conquerors', are metaphors for 'the poor' and 'the rich'. This was conventional enough. Disraeli probably borrowed the terms from Chartist rhetoric. And his identification of 'Saxons' and 'Chartists' is an interesting reversal of Carlyle's analogy in *Past and Present* between the popular movement and the Norman invasion. But the novelist goes further. In a scene which is ignored by the critics, the heroine, the Saxon 'daughter of the people', reads to her father, the Chartist leader Walter Garard from 'A History of England in the Norman Occupation'. The domestic scene is witnessed by Harold, Sybil's bloodhound, who immediately responds to the mention of his illustrious namesake, Harold II, the last Saxon King. Garard warms to this canine exhibition of patriotic feelings, remarking that 'a live dog they say is worth a dead King'. To which Sybil retorts, 'Why have we not such a man now.'[17] Disraeli is referring to Augustine Thierry's *Conquête de l'Angleterre par les Normands* (1825), an examplar of romantic historiography which, despite its lack of scholarly standards, influenced a number of the later Teutonists. The study of Anglo-Saxon history is identified as a working-class tradition. Disraeli shrewdly juxtaposes the popular history with the cult of chivalry of aristocrats like the young Lord Valentine. What the writer quite openly preaches is a transformation of the myth of a class to a national myth.

It was, however, Bulwer's less directly political fiction and rhetoric which found numerous imitators. *Harold, Last of the Saxon Kings* inspired novelists, conventional historians and artists. The novel, written in the form of an epic, became the model for romances set at the time of the occupation. Charles Napier's well-documented novel, bearing the same title as Bulwer's, appeared posthumously, in 1858. Charles Kingsley's *Hereward the Wake, Last of the English*, came out in 1866, on the 800th anniversary of the Battle of Hastings. In the 1870s, both Edward Freeman and Alfred Tennyson paid tribute to Bulwer in the *History of the Norman Conquest* and the verse epic *Harold*, respectively. During the 1880s there appeared A.D. Crake's series of juvenile novels, *Chronicle of Aescendune* and Emma Leslie's *Gytha's Message* (Gytha was Harold Godwinsson's mother, and wife of the king-making Saxon Earl Godwin). Later Teutonists, including Henty, Buchan and Kipling, capitalized on the success of the novel on the eleventh century.[18]

The flourishing of fiction on the Conquest roughly coincided with the revival of antiquarian and historical interest in Saxon England. Novelists could make use of translated chronicles and poetry (both Anglo-Saxon and Nordic), and legal documents, which poured from the presses of the antiquarian and ecclesiological societies, and later, the Rolls Series. A number of histories of the pre-Norman era appeared. Sir Francis Palgrave's *History of Saxon England* (1832), which Bulwer used as a textbook, succeeded Sharon Turner's *History* (1799–1818) as the authoritative work on Anglo-Saxon history. J. Mitchell Kemble's *Anglo Saxon England* appeared a year after *Harold*. Freeman's monumental *History* was completed in 1877 and Stubb's *Constitutional History* in 1878. To these may be added the works of antiquarians like Thomas Wright (1810–77) and the earlier effort of Henry Hallam (1777–1859).

It is difficult to decide which of the two confluent forms of historical narrative, the novel or 'straightforward' history, contributes more to the shaping of the other. But as critics like Fleishman, Chandler and Sanders convincingly demonstrate, the Victorians saw the historical novel as a form of history. Indeed, readers of historical fiction (especially fiction on the remote past) looked for what we now seek in social history. The 'medieval' novel, it was argued, reconstructed the lives of ordinary English men and women, their moods and feelings. Conventional histories failed to do this.[19] 'Monuments of dead ashes,' writes Carlyle in 1842, 'does assiduous pedantry dig up' from the ruins of the Middle Ages. 'Over our Historical Library it is as if all the Titans had written for themselves: Dry Rubbish shot here!'[20] To penetrate beyond the great political events, or the structures of the constitution, to the spirit of a people, a literary-historical mind was needed. Carlyle's words are echoed by historians like Thierry, Palgrave, Michelet and Freeman.

The contiguity of the two genres is not merely one of time. Common to both novelists and historians is an emphasis on the irrevocably past, on a lost heritage. There is also a growing attraction in viewing national character and race as unifying elements in history. Both these features manifest themselves in the fascination with the Norman Conquest: 1066 is elevated to an iconic year, more important than either 1642 or 1688. The war in 1066 is reinterpreted as a national struggle; it becomes the key to an understanding of modern English history. This naturally is a challenge to the hegemonic Whig version of the past. Whigs, as Burrow points out, came to be embarrassed by the myth of the 'ancient constitution'.[21] They tried to gloss over the Conquest. Macaulay devotes to the eleventh century less than a page in his *History of England*, and the period 1066–1200 is summarily treated by him as 'not English': 'During the century and a half which followed the Conquest, there is, to speak strictly, no English history.'[22]

Between 1830 and 1880 the dark period in the national history is gradually transformed into one of apotheosis. Freeman sees 1066 as the beginning of *English* history, 'a great year whose effects on all later English, on all later European history can for a moment compare, in lasting importance to the year which with some exaggeration we may call the year of the Norman Conquest'. Not one day in the history of England can compare to the day of St Calixtus, on which the Battle of Hastings (pedantically and mistakenly called by Freeman Senlac) took place.

There is no one day in later times to compare [to] the memorable morning when Northern and Southern Europe, when England and Normandy, when Harold and William met face to face in the great wager of battle on the eve of Saint Calixtus.[23]

Bulwer's *Harold*, like Freeman's *History*, was designed as an *epos*. The earlier work had been inspired by the *Iliad*. Recall Bulwer's analogy between the Conquest and the Trojan War. The events at Hastings are represented as heroic encounters between Homeric figures. Yet the defeat of the Saxons is inverted in the *dénouement* to a victory. Far from destroying England — Troy — the Normans are overcome by her. English freedoms are not extinguished. English religion, commonsensical and humane, wins over Norman religious excesses. The land itself remains English:

In many a noiseless field with thoughts of Armies, your relics, O Saxon Heroes, have won back the victory from the bones of the Norman Saints; and whenever with fairer fates, Freedom opposes Force, and Justice, redeeming the old defeat, smites down the armed Frauds that would consecrate the wrong, — smile, o sons of our Saxon Harold, smile appeased, on the Saxon land![24]

Kingsley's claim to originality lies in his arrangement of the events of 1066 and their aftermath. Hastings is allocated a secondary place in the plot. Instead, the local rebellion under Hereward, erroneously styled the 'Wake', which took place in the Fens in 1069–70, is elevated to a war of national liberation: 'It was the year of 1069, a more evil year for England than the year of Hastings.'[25] Accordingly, in *Hereward the Wake*, the story of the defeat is reconstructed piecemeal from contradictory sources. No version of the Battle of Hastings is regarded as definite: each is reported rather than directly narrated. Such an employment of historic events suggests the probability of more than one history. This is the very opposite of the Whig linear story of progress. That is not to say that the conservative authors reject the notion of continuity, or the idea that English history was an ameliorative process, for they do not. However, the continuity was perceived not in the constitution or in structures, but in the people, a national English character, in landscapes (see pp. 584–7). Moreover, the narrated part of the national past is one of *losses*, not gains. And it is told from the point of view of the losers — 'the last of the Saxon Kings', 'the last Englishman'. Whig fictions are success stories. Kingsley and Bulwer, like Carlyle and Disraeli before and Freeman after them, react to the ethos of success, which all of these writers identify with utilitarianism and mammonism. Disraeli's rewriting of national history in the *Vindication of the English Constitution* and *Coningsby* is comparable to the medievalist writers' restructuring of the defeat of Harold at Hastings as a victory. 'Losers', neglected by chroniclers and modern historians alike, are rehabilitated and replace the Whig heroes (Charles II replaces William II; Bolingbroke, author of *The Idea of a Patriot King* takes the place of Walpole and, in the novel of the eleventh century, Harold replaces Edward the Confessor, the latter being cast as a 'foreign', Normanized king, detached from the national spirit).

The invasion carries another cultural meaning, reflecting collective anxiety in the face of the revolutionary wars on the continent. British patriotism, regardless of political affiliation, had been notoriously Francophobe. The French, the historic enemy, and well into the nineteenth century Britain's chief rival on the continent, had traditionally featured as that nation's 'other'. Proximity and France's cultural predominance rather complicated this notion of the alien, threatening England's integrity, yet at the same time, appealing. While there was no danger of a physical invasion — at least not since 1803 — the threat of a cultural or 'moral' one seemed real enough, particularly during the revolutionary upheavals between 1815 and 1848. The Norman invasion and its subsequent impact on the language, manners and morals, all these are represented as prototypical.[26] The first Conquest prefigures future corrupting 'foreign' influences, as well as the fortitude of the invaded people. The analogy between the Conquest and the feared invasion from republican France is quite common and explicitly drawn in patriotic propaganda. Napoleon I and Napoleon III are likened to 'the bastard', the revolutionary armies to the Normans, and working Englishmen to Saxons. Thackeray lampoons the popular analogies in a series of burlesques on modern historiography, entitled 'Miss Tickletoby's Lectures on English History', probably written in 1841 for *Punch* and published in 1847 in the *Book of Snobs*. Half the lectures are spoofs on the popular 'histories of Anglo-Saxons', and one is a knockabout pastiche on the treatment of the Norman Conquest by patriotic historians. The lecturer — predictably 'a delicate and sensitive female' — gets mixed up with basic chronological details: 'The Battle of Hastings occurred — let me see, take 1066 from 1842 — exactly seven hundred and seventy years ago; yet I can't help feeling angry to think that these beggarly, murderous Frenchmen should have beaten our honest English as they did (cries of "Never mind we've given it'em since").'[27]

The local, regional character of British patriotism has often been noted. Limited loyalties, what Burke designated 'the little platoons', existed alongside allegiances to centres: the Crown, the State and the Empire. National literature, but particularly historical fiction, was instrumental in the propagation of a geographical tradition of England, the notion of specific English places as historical *loci*. As Herbert Butterfield notes in the first critical monograph on the historical novel (anteceding Lukács' work by almost a decade): 'In the historical novel there is a devotion to locality and a feeling for history that breathes through the soil, all this comes large and most complete where geography and tradition, love of place and pride in its heritage of history combine in patriotism.'[28] Note the characteristic approval of local chauvinism as a refined form of the national consciousness, an approval which a number of radical historians of nationalism seem to share.

What is England in the 'Saxon' tradition? What are its geographical boundaries? How did historical geography relate to contemporary changes in the landscape, particularly to urbanization? England is a literal and geographical term, covering those parts of the country which, until the Conquest, had been populated by Saxons and Danes. 'English' territory comprises East Anglia (notably Norfolk, Suffolk and the Isle of Ely), the central Kingdom of Mercia, and Northumbria extending north of the Humber into all the parts of Scotland south of the Firth of Forth. These regions receive special attention because they present a successful mixture of Germanic people, notably the Saxons and Danes. 'The war sons of the old North,' notes Bulwer with obvious satisfaction, 'as a main cause of civilization [they] were wonderfully pliant and malleable in their admixture with the peoples they overran.' This 'malleability' distinguished the Anglo-Saxon (the term includes the Danes) from the barbaric Celt, 'who refuses to mingle, and disdains to improve'.[29] Celtic Britain and the Gaelic North and West (Scotland and Ireland) are excluded from the new notion of England and reduced to the uncivilized periphery. The Welsh and Cornish are reduced to ethnic antitypes. Enough to cite here Bulwer's representation of Gryffyth, the rebel Welsh King, in the chapters on Harold's Welsh campaign and Kingsley's treatment of the barbaric Cornish and Scottish aristocracies.

However, anti-Celtic biases *should not* be read as simple-minded racism. The emerging national geography is an interesting reaction to Whig and romantic notions of centre and margins in British history. The geographical 'margins' of the island, notably Scotland and

Ireland, played an important role in the story of the Whig revolution and the subsequent conflict between Jacobites and Hanoverians. Indeed, as Burrow notes, readers of Macaulay knew more about Scotland than about the Shires. Apart from Whig historiography, there had been an idealization of the Celtic heritage which particularly characterized the nationalist romanticism of the eighteenth century. Most important, the geographical periphery was familiarized in the novels of Scott. The Highlands and Scottish Borders became nationally admired places, the objects of veneration and identification.[30]

The Germanist writers' geography should be regarded as a reaction against the three influences mentioned above. Kingsley is quite outspoken on the matter. *Hereward* opens with a challenge to the Tory novel, to romantic sympathies and Whig history:

> The heroic deeds of highlanders, both in these lands and elsewhere, have been told in verse and prose. . . . But we must remember, now and then, that there have been heroes likewise in the lowlands and the fen.

Hence Kingsley's own admiration of the Fens, which he chose as the *locus* of the saga of national resistance. What he emphasizes is the lack of Romantic qualities in the English landscape when compared with Scotland and Wales:

> The lowlands and those who live in them are wanting in the poetic and romantic elements. There is in the lowlands none of that background of the unknown, fantastic, magical, terrible, perpetually feeding curiosity and wonder, which still remains in the Scottish highlands.[31]

The achievement of the lowlander is the taming of nature, particularly the clearing and dyking of the Fens. It is no wonder that the writer finds an analogy between the patriotic English and the Dutch, tamers of the sea and freedom fighters. Kingsley's unromantic ruralism is comparable to the reconstruction of the Saxon village community in the structural histories of Palgrave (notably his *History of the Commonwealth* [1831]), Kemble and, most notably, Stubbs.[32]

The break away from the older notions of centre and geographic periphery is completed in representations of London as the national capital. British patriotism, in contradistinction to eighteenth- and early nineteenth-century French nationalism, had not only been non-centralist but hostile to the metropolitan city. Indeed, hostility to London cut across political allegiances. Radicals as well as Tories juxtaposed the corrupt, parasitical city, embodied in the court, the centre of foreign intrigue, to the country. In Whig–Liberal discourse, too, London features as an anomalous growth which thrives on the profits of the Industrial Revolution (identified with the northern towns), without contributing to *national* prosperity. In the new geographical tradition, the capital is dissociated from the processes of urbanization and modernity and represented as a symbol of unity. Like East Anglia, eleventh-century London was perceived as representing the desirable Germanic racial mixture mentioned before (and very unlike, of course, the ethnic pluralism of the modern capital). The architecture of the pre-Norman city still displayed Roman and Briton influences, both distinctly pagan. May Day and popular festivals were celebrated together with the Christian holidays. Unities, however, are particularly associated with monuments which present historical continuities. Interest in the national architecture gained enormous popularity thanks to a sub-genre of historical romance which may be identified with a single writer, John Harrison Ainsworth. Ainsworth probably had the longest novel-writing career in the nineteenth century, made up entirely of historical romance. His speciality was late medieval and Tudor melodrama. But his fame came from the series of novels on national monuments which he published in the 1840s and which combined romance with topographic detail and guide-book techniques. The novels on the monuments of London, illustrated by Cruikshank, were smash hits in multi-volume, volume and serial form. Most celebrated were the *Tower of London* (1840) and *Old St Paul* (1844).[33] In 1846, Disraeli could safely include descriptions of Westminster Abbey in *Sybil*, together with more conventional representations of fashionable private houses and clubs. *Harold* includes an abundance of references to public, national buildings, most notably the Abbey, the place of coronation of the last Saxon king. But it is neither the Tory Disraeli nor Bulwer who provide us with the most patriotic, most deliberately traditional discussion of nationalism and architecture, but the democratic-liberal Freeman (whose inclusion in the category 'conservative' was explained earlier). Freeman devotes a chapter to the Abbey, on 5 January 1066, the day of Edward's death and Harold's coronation, coinciding with the Feast of the Epiphany.

On that day began the long series of national ceremonies which has gone on unbroken to our own time, and which has made the Abbey of Saint Peter the hearth and *pny taneion* of the English nation . . . of all the gorgeous sites celebrated by Kings and Prelates beneath the vaults of the West Minster, the twofold site of the great Epiphany, which haste and urgency may well have made the least gorgeous of them all, is that around which the national ceremony of Englishmen may well centre most fondly. The first royal burial, the first royal consecration, within the newly-hallowed temple, have an historic interest and an historic import beyond all those which have followed them.[34]

Freeman's handling of the coronation could hardly be more royalist and patriotic. To the populist liberal, 'continuity' is not the principle of descent as embodied in the constitution, but the unity of monarch and people as apotheosized in the succession of kings.

The national capital and rural England are mirror images of city and country in the nineteenth century. After 1851, the physical world of the majority of the British people was urban. The landscape manifested changes brought about by the industrial and urban revolutions and the subsequent revolution in transport. Most significant, the cradle of the Saxon-Danish nation, East Anglia, was now a declining area, demographically, politically and economically. And London had not yet become the capital of an Empire. The fiction of Great Britain as 'Little England', a rural, racially 'pure' community, undoubtedly helped people come to terms with the processes related to industrialization. Furthermore, the new 'national geography', with race for its basis, made it possible to exclude and marginalize sections and groups which both literature and historiography had treated as 'central' (the Scots and Celts in general). However, as the third section demonstrates, race was so attractive to the Germanist writers *because* it could be used both ways: to exclude the non-Saxon ('non-English') from the notion of 'nation' *and* to extend it to groups and spheres hitherto perceived as apolitical: women and the domestic sphere.

Characterization and, more broadly, the interpretation of the relationship between character and history, present the most significant challenges to the older historical fictions. Scott focused on minor historic figures, or on altogether imaginary ones. Most critics would agree with Lukács that the bane of the historical hero is his neutrality. This protagonist stands for sanity and moderation, epitomizing the 'golden mean' between extremes. He is capable of comprehending and sympathizing with opposing political and economic forces: Jacobites and Hanoverians; Saxons and Normans;

the emerging bourgeoisie and the feudal land-owners.[35]

It is here, in the view of the juncture between the historical man and a historic situation — characteristically a crisis — that the new patriotic fiction departs from familiar Tory formulae. The new model eludes Lukács' dialectical paradigm. This hero is certainly not neutral. He sides with lost causes. He is a familiar historic figure, characteristically a statesman. In overall literary terms he may be described as a Carlylean hero, an individual destined to grasp the 'spirit of the time' and, during moments of crisis, translate it to actions whose course has already been determined.

Heroes' biographies could be used as a weapon both against the Whig version of the early Middle Ages and the 'new' scientific history, identified with political economy and, from the 1860s, with Comtean positivism, or alternatively with professional 'structural' history. To conservatives, both kinds of history were dangerously inhuman. To be sure, the Whigs had their fair share of hero-worship. But neo-feudalists like Cobbett, Carlyle and Disraeli, and, following them, Germanists like Kingsley and Freeman, vehemently criticized the influences of Mancunian *laissez-faire* and of utilitarian thought on the Whig historians. 'Laws' substituted for people and human relationships. The 'new' histories seemed even more offensive. They ignored biography, the heart of *all* history, and sought to write people out of the narratives of the past. The secularization of historical plots which replaced providence with natural rules or laws, was equally threatening. Kingsley devoted his inaugural lecture as Regius Professor of History to the refutation of 'scientific history', a term which he uses quite liberally. His words tally with Carlylean rhetoric. Students

> should try to understand men and women. For History is the History of men and women and of nothing else: and he who knows men and women thoroughly, will best understand the past work of the world. . . . The men who governed the world have been those who understood the human heart.[36]

The lecture, appropriately entitled 'The Limit of Exact Science as Applied to History' was printed in a collection of Kingsley's greatly influential talks to undergraduates on *The Roman and Teuton*.

The narrative best suited to such an approach was that of the biographical novel. As Bulwer argues, in order to read the past we need to know the lives of world-historic figures, and their relations to politics and 'morals'. 'Manners' are of minor importance. The great moments — characteristically battles — in the national history are shaped by great men. So in *Harold* (and its many imitations) the bloody events at Hastings are emplotted as a series of encounters between individuals of Homeric stature, and modelled as an archetypal epic narrative (to use Hayden White's terms). At intervals the story is interrupted with exhortations like: 'Live Harold; live yet, and Saxon England shall not die.'[37] And Bulwer is quite restrained in comparison to Freeman who includes many addresses to the putative reader on the role of heroes in history.

> On its historic importance [that of the Battle of Hastings] I need not dwell; it is the very subject of my history. . . . Had Harold lived, had another like Harold been ready to take his place, we may well doubt whether, even after the overthrow of Senlac, England would have been conquered at last.[38]

In contradistinction to the Carlylean statesman, the Saxon hero is a private as well as a public person. Indeed, the construction of the new tradition is hardly separable from the development of notions of the public and private, masculinity and femininity. The enormous literature on the Middle Ages, especially on chivalry, set models for masculine conduct which were internalized by the Victorian élites and propagated by the public school system. Enough to mention here that Kingsley, 'inventor', with Thomas Hughes, of the ideal 'muscular' Christianity, locates his protagonist in a tradition of folk heroes which includes Robin Hood, the eighteenth-century bandit Dick Turpin and the product of the public school system. Indeed, *Hereward* may also be read as a *Bildungsroman* describing, as it does, the development of the hero from savage 'berserker' to a Christian knight.[39]

Yet this novel, indeed the Anglo-Saxon novel in general, may not be regarded as a masculine genre. It offers feminine models of heroism which are projections of Victorian gender ideology. At the same time, the roles offered are active and suggest degrees of freedom denied to contemporary women. It is necessary to stress this point because in recent studies on nationalism and sexuality the passive role of women is emphasized.

The identity of the heroine is Germanic (Saxon) and Christian. This particular combination is quite new. Before the middle of the century personifications of the nation are ethnically and culturally syncretic and predominantly Celtic, though in the figure of *Britannia* (the oldest and most enduring symbol of England) Roman and Christian motifs are soldered to the British/Celtic ones.[40] In the mid-century novel, heroines are purified of non-Germanic influences and

Germanic-Nordic representations of the nation as female replace the
Celtic ones. The Christian aspect is equally important. Female piety is
central to the positive model of the Englishwoman, though religious
excesses are condemned as 'Norman' or 'foreign'. Similarly, pagan-
ism is associated with witchcraft, as in Bulwer's Danish *vala*
(prophetess) Hilda, a figure which became the centre of a public
debate in the periodical press.[41]

Very little was known about the life of Anglo-Saxon women. The
novelists did not use court-rolls but relied almost exclusively on
chronicles — composed by misogynist churchmen — and on Anglo-
Saxon, Nordic and medieval German poetry. Both Bulwer and
Kingsley draw on the *Edda* and Snori Sturluson's *Heimskingla*, the
twelfth-century Norwegian epos, for characterization and detail. But
this was not enough and, as Bulwer frankly admits in a letter to the
Edinburgh Review, the female heroes were 'inventions'.[42] The figure of
Edith, the 'betrothed', probably draws on 'Edith of the Swan's Neck',
or Edva Fayva, Harold's mistress and the mother of his children
(there is mention of her in the *Doomsday Book*). In Bulwer's chaste
version, she is Harold's platonic love and a paragon of Saxon
femininity: 'Edith would not love thee as she doth, and will till the
grave clasp her, if thou didst not love England more than Edith.'[43]
The phrase captioned a drawing of the patriotic betrothed on the
frontispiece in successive editions of the novel. Edith's entrance to the
cloister, parallel to that of Torfrida in *Hereward*, is not merely a
sacrificial act. Neither heroine gives up sexuality unthinkingly and the
sacrifice has patriotic rather than religious grounds.

Heroines are represented not only in the cloister but on the
battlefield. The association between purity — in men and women —
and the integrity of the nation is conventional and, as Mosse has
argued, characterizes middle-class discourse on nationalism.[44]
Examples abound. Torfrida leads the rebels of Ely to battle guided by
the three sibling saints Etheldreda, Withburga and Sexburga, Saxon
warrior virgins and patronesses of East Anglia. Impurity destroys
domesticity and threatens the national integrity, and more specifically, impurity is a metaphor for Normanization — both political
and cultural. Characteristically, the values of home and country, and
the absence of these, are embodied in pairs of female figures, which
personify virtue and transgression. The binary model is developed by
Scott in *Ivanhoe*, in the juxtaposition of Rowena, the Saxon virgin,
and Ulrica, the Normanized prostitute and murderess. Edith and
Aldyth in *Harold*, and Torfrida and Alftruda in *Hereward*, are

elaborations on the earlier model.

Yet, the usage of conventional ideas about domesticity and patriotism does not preclude the development of new attitudes. Take, for example, representations of bereavement. The familiar figure of the Saxon mourner appears in most of the medieval chronicles of the Conquest. Most chroniclers mention the discovery of the body of Harold by Edith of the Swan's Neck. The body had been so mutilated by the Norman arrows that it could not be recognized, not by the loyal monks of Waltham, nor by Gytha, the hero's mother. Edith alone could identify the King's body, by marks known only to her. Freeman, merely by praising the loyalty of this unlawful love, breaks through Victorian conventions. The hero's wife and sister do not come to claim the body. Only Edith, 'a true daughter of the people', embodying the people's love for the country, comes to mourn for the dead King.[45] Bulwer, who wrote a novel for domestic consumption, is less outspoken. Nevertheless, in what appears to be a bowdlerized version of the 'real' story, he manages to be quite unconventional. Edith, the patriotic Englishwoman, claims Harold, and implicitly her sexuality, from England. In a rather morbid scene, Bulwer describes how

> Her hands bled as the mail gave way to her efforts; the tunic beneath was all dabbled with blood. She rent the folds, and on the breast, just above the silenced heart, were punctured in the old Saxon letters, the word 'Edith'; and just below, in characters more fresh, the word 'England.' 'See, see!' she cried in piercing accents; and, clasping the dead in her arms, she kissed the lips, and called aloud . . . .'Wed, wed . . . wed at last.'[46]

The last phrase captioned illustrations of the scene which were reproduced in most British and American editions of the novel. More significantly, Kingsley modelled his representation of female bereavement on Bulwer's. In one self-consciously unsavoury scene (bloody even by Kingsley's standards), Torfrida claims Hereward's mutilated body from his Norman murderers. In the penultimate chapter of the novel we see her carrying the hero's decapitated head, to anoint and decorate it,[47] this being, of course, a reversal of the theme of St John's decapitation by Salomé.

All these public and private freedoms derive not from an equality between the sexes, nor from 'rights', but from ethnicity. It is English identity, perceived as primarily racial, which entitles men *and* women to liberties. The freedoms deriving from descent and embodied in the representative institutions (such as the *Witenagemot*, or the Anglo-

Saxon council) or the elected monarchy, are also identified with ethnicity. Race cuts across the differences between class, or those deriving from gender. And this makes heroic biography a potentially inclusive tradition.

To conclude, the nationalism discussed in this essay is a literary phenomenon. Conservative and oppositional, it characterized the period before the rise of consensus patriotism, associated with the advent of modern party politics. I do not deny the political meaning of the invented Saxon tradition. The conservative attempt to hijack history from the Whigs and Radicals took place in a moment of transition in British politics. This transition may be conveniently characterized by the disintegration of Peelite conservatism and the related rise of what is known as conservative, non-reform liberalism. At the root of the worship of Saxon heroes is the disappointment with leadership and political reform. We should be wary of arguing for continuities within a 'conservative tradition', continuities which link radical Toryism in the 1840s to 'mature' conservatism in the 1870s. Attempts to prove such continuities 'from Peel to Thatcher' (I have in mind Robert Blake's work), are not very convincing. Instead, we should concentrate on those unities in the early example of Saxonism, which have a bearing on the history of national identity, on developments of symbolic representations of the nation, and on changes in constructs of 'England', 'Englishness' and race. First, the notion of the English people as a Germanic race antecedes modern imperialism and emerges *outside* imperialist discourse. Saxon England, as perceived by the mid-Victorians, has the attributes of 'Little England', not of a 'Greater Britain', let alone the Empire. More significant, the evolution of an English identity depends on that of the Celt as anti-type. Secondly, the fiction of race is not only exclusive, but may be used to broaden the perception of the nation. As the last section illustrates, notions like 'freedom' and patriotic virtues which build on ethnic identity may be extended to include in the nation marginal groups hitherto excluded from it. There was no place for women in the Whig definition of freedom which was legal and political. The 'Englishman's freedom' was not only generic, but also a literal term. In the new Tory rhetoric women are offered liberties. These, of course, are not political and bestowed upon them solely on the strength of their racial identity. Third, and parallel to the preceding two unities, is the extension of the 'nation' from the political to the private sphere, a development which manifests the interrelations in Victorian culture between the construction of nationality and that of femininity or masculinity.

It is the particular combination of these three notions that elevates the Saxon tradition from being merely an invention to a culturally significant myth.

Notes

1. Benjamin Disraeli, *Sybil or the Two Nations* (reprinted 1845) (Harmondsworth 1984), 496.

2. Eric Hobsbawm, 'Inventing Traditions', in Eric Hobsbawm and Terence Ranger (eds), *The Invention of Tradition* (Cambridge 1984), 1–15, especially 1–2.

3. Ibid., 13.

4. On processes of inclusion and exclusion, see Philip Dodd, 'Englishness and the National Character' in Robert Colls and Philip Dodd (eds), *Englishness, Politics and Culture 1880–1920* (London 1987).

5. See Alice Chandler, 'A Dream of Order', *The Medieval Idea in Nineteenth-Century English Literature* (Lincoln, NE 1970); Mark Girouard, *The Return of Camelot, Chivalry and the English Gentleman* (Yale, New Haven 1981); Charles Dellheim, *The Face of the Past, the Preservation of the Medieval Inheritance in Britain* (Cambridge 1982).

6. The meaning of Saxon England to Liberal historians is briefly discussed by J.W. Burrow in his brilliant monograph on *The Liberal Descent, Victorian Historians and the English Past* (Cambridge 1981). See particularly the section on Stubbs. Later scientific racism is discussed by Christine Bolt, *Victorian Attitudes to Race* (London 1971); Hugh MacDougall, *Racial Myth in English History, Troyans, Teutons and Anglo-Saxons* (London 1982). On the connections with jingoism and democratic Toryism, see Hugh Cunningham, 'The Conservative Party and Conservatism' in Colls and Dodd, 283–308; 'Jingoism in 1877–8', *Victorian Studies*, XIV (1971), 429–54, and 'The Language of Patriotism, 1750–1914', *History Workshop Journal*, 12 (Autumn 1981), 8–23.

7. On the embarrassment of historians, see Gerald Newman, *The Rise of English Nationalism, a Cultural History* (New York 1987); Eric Hobsbawm, *Nations and Nationalism since 1870: Programme, Myth, Reality* (Cambridge 1990). Among the very few early works is Hans Kohn, 'The Genesis and Character of English Nationalism', *Journal of the History of Ideas*, I (1940), 69–94. The diversity of work after the Falklands War is exemplified in Raphael Samuel (ed.), *The Making and Unmaking of British National Identity*, 3 vols (London 1989); see particularly Vol. I, *History and Politics*, and Vol. II, *National Fictions*. See also J.H. Grainger, *Patriotisms, Britain 1900–39* (London 1986).

8. Samuel, 'The Little Platoons', *Patriotism*, III, i–xxxv; Christopher Hill, 'History and Patriotism', *Patriotism*, I, 3–9, for the tradition of pluralist nationalism. For the conservative interest in 'unities', see Alun Hawkins, 'A Defence of National History', ibid., 18–26.

9. See notes 6 and 7 above. For the problematics of the distinction between opposition and consensus nationalism, see Linda Coley, 'Whose Nation? Class and

National Consciousness in Britain, 1750–1830', *Past and Present*, 113 (1986), 96–117.

10. Georg Lukács, *The Historical Novel* (transl. Hannah and Stanley Mitchell) (London 1962), and before him, Herbert Butterfield, *The Historical Novel* (Cambridge 1929). For criticism, see David Brown, *Walter Scott and the Historical Imagination* (London 1979), 4–5; Paul De Man, 'George Lukács's Theory of the Novel', *Modern Language Notes*, LXXXL (1966), 527–34.

11. Joan Scott, 'Gender: A Useful Category of Historical Analysis', *American Historical Review*, 91 (5) (1986), 1053–76.

12. Christopher Hill, 'The Norman Yoke' in *Puritanism and Revolution* (1958; repr.) (Manchester 1969), 58–126; Burrow, op. cit., 100–3; Gertrude Himmelfarb, 'Who Now Reads Macaulay?' in *Marriage and Morals among the Victorians* (London, reprinted 1986), 163–78.

13. Quoted in Burrow, op. cit., 99.

14. Burrow, op. cit., 100.

15. Dedicatory Epistle to the Right Honourable C.T. D'Eyncourt, MP, *Harold, Last of the Saxon Kings* (New York 1886).

16. Bulwer, Preface to the 3rd edn, ibid., xiii–xvi.

17. Disraeli, *Sybil*, 210.

18. For a check-list of historical novels on the eleventh century, see Jonathan Nield, *A Guide to the best Historical Novels and Tales* (New York 1902, reprinted 1929).

19. Chandler, *A Dream of Order*; Arron Fleishman, *The English Historical Novel, Walter Scott to Virginia Woolf* (Baltimore 1971), especially chap. 2, 'Origins: The Historical Novel in the Age of History'; Andrew Sanders, *The Victorian Historical Novel 1840–1880* (London 1978), especially the Introduction; J.C. Simmons, 'The Novelist as Historian: An Unexposed Tract of Victorian Historiography', *Victorian Studies*, XIV (March 1971), 293–305.

20. Thomas Carlyle, *Past and Present* (reprinted New York 1843), 7.

21. Burrow, op. cit., 101.

22. Lord Macaulay, *The History of England from the Accession of James the Second* (London 1895); 'Before the Restoration', 7.

23. Edward Augustus Freeman, *The History of the Norman Conquest of England*, T.W. Burrow (ed.) (reprinted Chicago 1971), 3–4.

24. Bulwer, *Harold*, vol. 2, 316.

25. Charles Kingsley, *Hereward the Wake, Last of the English* (London 1866, reprinted 1898), 161.

26. Gerald Newman, 'Anti-French Propaganda and British Liberal Nationalism in the Early Nineteenth Century: Suggestions Toward a General Interpretation', *Victorian Studies*, XVIII (1975), 385–418; *The Rise of English Nationalism*; Stella Cottrell, 'The Devil on Two Sticks: Franco-Fobia in 1803', *Patriotism*, I, 259–74.

27. William Makepeace Thackeray, 'Miss Tickletoby's Lectures on English Literature', 'Edward the Confessor — Harold — William the Conqueror', *Works*, XXIV (London 1886) 28.

28. Herbert Butterfield, op. cit., 42.

29. Bulwer, *Harold*, vol. I, 20–1.

30. Hugh Trevor-Roper, 'The Invention of Tradition: The Highland Tradition of Scotland', in Hobsbawm and Ranger, op. cit., 15–43.

31. Kingsley, *Hereward the Wake*, 'Prelude of the Fens', 1–3.

32. See Paul Vinogradoff, *Villainage in England* (London 1892), 12–20.

33. On literature on monuments, see J.A. Sutherland, *Victorian Novelists and*

Publishers (London 1976), 152–66; Sanders, op. cit., 32–47.

34. Freeman, op. cit., 19–20.

35. See for example Sanders and Fleishman, op. cit.

36. Kingsley, *The Roman and the Teuton* (London 1881), 309.

37. Bulwer, *Harold*, vol. 2, 302.

38. Freeman, op. cit., 211.

39. Kingsley, *Hereward*, 370.

40. On Britannia, see Marina Warner, *Monuments and Maidens, The Allegory of Female Form* (London 1987), 42–53; Madge Dreiser, 'Britannia' in Samuel, *Patriotism*, III, 26–42; George L. Mosse, *Nationalism and Sexuality* (New York 1985).

41. Bulwer, Preface to the 3rd edn.

42. Ibid.

43. Bulwer, *Harold*, vol. 1, 162.

44. Mosse, *Nationalism and Sexuality*.

45. Freeman, op. cit., 217–18.

46. Bulwer, *Harold*, vol. 2, 314.

47. Kingsley, *Hereward*, 367.

Billie Melman

is Senior Lecturer in Modern History at Tel
Aviv University. She is the author of *Women
and the Popular Imagination in the Twenties*
and *Women's Orients: Englishwomen and the
Middle East 1718–1918, Sexuality, Religion
and Work*. She has also written on terrorism
in literature, exoticism and orientalism.

Zvi Yavetz

An Eyewitness Note:
Reflections on the Rumanian Iron Guard

As an ancient historian, I became interested in anti-semitism in the Roman world. I am convinced that Mommsen's terms *Judenhass* and *Judenhetze* are more appropriate for the ancient world than 'anti-semitism' and, in an attempt to coin a better concept in English, I studied various forms of anti-Jewish propaganda through the ages. Having been born in Rumania, I had the feeling that the anti-semitism of Cuza, Goga and Codreanu was somewhat different from that of the Hungarians and Poles, but I knew very little about it. I thus read the writings of Eugen Weber, whose magisterial studies on the Iron Guard offer the definitive clue to this rather strange and unique 'variety of fascism'. A few years ago, Arnim Heinen published a new study on the Iron Guard, *Die Legion 'Erzengel Michael' in Rumanien* (Munich 1986), and on the basis of these works, I reflect here on some issues which intrigued me as an amateur and as an eyewitness.

The surprising results of the Rumanian general elections of 1937 are still vivid in my memory. I knew some leading Iron Guardists in Czernowitz (Bucovina) — two of whom were my teachers in high school — and in spite of the fact that I have never scrutinized archives nor studied electoral statistics, I am nevertheless able to attest that the prevailing atmosphere in those days is not always reflected in documents, newspaper editorials, and/or political writings of the protagonists. No ancient historian would disregard the memoirs of a private Roman soldier in the praetorian guard in the days of Tiberius, little as he may have understood the situation on the eve of Sejanus's downfall. It is clear that, eventually, the information coming from the *Acta Senatus* would prevail in history books, but the memoirs of a private soldier (if indeed recovered) would certainly merit a footnote, and it is precisely a footnote of this kind that will be provided here.

Heinen mastered practically everything available on the Iron

Guard. He knows the Bundesarchiv in Koblenz, the collection of Schuhmacher, and the testimony of General Erich Hansen, who played a major role in the annihilation of the remnants of the Iron Guard in 1941 in Bucharest under the leadership of Horia Sima. He is familiar with the memoirs of non-Iron Guardists like Argetoianu, Jorga, Duca (for some reason Gafencu is missing from his bibliography), as well as those of Iron Guardists like Papanace and Palaghita, who survived the second world war and still live in exile, and of sympathizers of various degrees like Pamphil Seicaru and Mircea Eliade. Needless to say, he read all the secondary literature published in the West, especially Eugen Weber, Martin Broszat, Bela Vago, and Nagy Talavera, and the recent Rumanian studies by Gh. Matei, P. Ilie, A. Savu, M. Fatu, I. Spalatelu, F. Nedelcu, S. Neagoie, and C. Neagu. Rumanian archives in the days of Ceaucescu, however, were inaccessible to Heinen and one wonders whether Rumania under Iliescu will at last put all the documents at the disposal of the international community of scholars. It is possible that Rumanian glasnost will offer some answers to many queries, but even if the new material might make Heinen change his mind on some major issues, nothing should minimize the value of his scholarly achievement.

I am in no disagreement with Heinen concerning his chapters dealing with the emergence and growth of the Iron Guard from the year 1919 until 1933. He is right in taking us back to the small group of twenty people led by the plumber Constantin Pancu in 1919, which consisted of a printer, a student, a lawyer, an orthodox priest, four mechanics, and some twelve free artisans, such as a carpenter, a locksmith, and so on. It was precisely this heterogeneous composition that characterized the Iron Guard in its heyday. Pancu was the founder of the Guard of National Conscience, and dreamt of a national Christian socialism (*Socialismul National Crestin*). His influence on Corneliu Zelea Codreanu was enormous. However, were it not for the terrorist group *Frati de cruce* (Brothers of the Cross), led by the Transylvanian Amos Francu (*Regele Motilor*), the violent character of the future Iron Guard could never be understood. Heinen has analysed correctly the impact of the annexation of Transylvania, Bucovina, and Bessarabia to pre-first world war Rumania, which in 1914 consisted only of the Danubian principalities, Wallachia (which comprised Muntenia and Oltenia) and Moldavia, from the Carpathian Mountains to the River Pruth, not to be confused with the present Moldavian Republic, which consists of

Bessarabia and the plain beyond the River Dniester to the east. The high standard of living of the ethnic minorities (Hungarians, Germans and Jews) who lived in the newly annexed territories, gave the autochthonous Rumanian population a feeling of deprivation and discrimination, and turned Greater Rumania (*Romania Mare*) into a breeding ground for extreme nationalism and xenophobia. In 1918, Rumania was a primitive country, where between 43 and 60 per cent of the population were illiterate, infant mortality ran at 17.4 per cent, and the annual per capita income was sixty dollars. Productivity was extremely low, industry at an embryonic stage, protective tariffs were very high, and most experts agree that 80 per cent of the population lived below the poverty line.

At the end of the first world war, Rumanian youth was full of hope. Rumania had doubled its area and population. There were plenty of openings in government bureaucracy and an academic degree could easily open doors. This is how the university turned into the main agency of social mobility, and Rumanian students practically stormed the doors of nearly all faculties, not just the schools of law and medicine where academic requirements were high and minority students formed the majority. Any academic degree could guarantee some government job and would satisfy most Rumanian students, who came from primitive villages, were poor, and hoped to be absorbed into the growing cities. However, the number of places in the student dormitories was limited, rents were high, and government scholarships few. Jewish students, however, came from urban areas, lived at home with their parents, and even if they were not rich, appeared as such in comparison to Rumanian students. Any anti-semitic propaganda thus fell on fertile ground.

Anti-semitic ideas, which can be found in abundance in the Rumanian literature of those days, have been impressively analysed in Heinen's book, and rightly so, because literature and politics were closely knit together, and because university students were those who not only read works like that of Hasdeu on the Talmud, but could also recite by heart poems of Alecsandri, Eminescu and Coshbuc, which were saturated with anti-semitic insinuations. Having said all that, and assuming that Heinen's book will be regarded as the standard work on the Iron Guard by younger scholars, I would like to make three observations, which should be taken as critical reflections rather than as dissenting remarks.

My first observation concerns the problem of the true character of people versus their public image. In spite of Heinen's criticism of

Nicolae Iorga, historian, journalist, politician and educator, whose
list of publications extends to over 1,100 entries, Heinen is at pains to
make clear that there was serious disagreement between him and A.C.
Cuza on anti-semitism, and that there was certainly no direct link
between Iorga's and Codreanu's political thought. This is nowadays
commonplace and is also shared by communist Rumanian historians.
I dare to challenge it.

   Iorga, who in 1940 was brutally murdered by the Iron Guard gangs
led by Horia Sima (Codreanu had been shot earlier, on 30 November
1938), was completely rehabilitated under the communist regime. In
the days of Ceaucescu, his enormous library became an important
centre for historical studies, a place of pilgrimage for young scholars,
and Iorga's contributions to the understanding of Rumanian history,
and especially his views on the continuity of the Rumanian people
from the days of the Dacians and Romans to our own period were
continuously hailed and stressed. It is of course true that Iorga's anti-
semitism was far more sophisticated than that of A.C. Cuza, a
Professor of Economics at the University of Jasy, who propagated
almost blindly Malthus's theories in Rumania, arguing that Rumanian natural resources were limited, and that the Jews were plundering
them relentlessly. Jews should therefore be blamed for all the
miseries, misfortunes, and afflictions that befell the Rumanian people
and should be expelled from the country. Cuza also took pride in
having introduced the swastika to Rumania as early as 1907. Almost
every Rumanian student could quote the Rumanian saying:

> Muntii nostri aur poarta
> Noi cersim din poarta in poarta
>
> (There is plenty of gold in our mountains,
> But we beg from door to door)

Iorga, of course, knew better, but nevertheless joined Cuza in 1910 in
establishing a National Democratic Party (Partidul Nationalist
Democrat). Many students and schoolteachers joined them, attracted
by the authority and prestige enjoyed by these two distinguished
professors. Among their followers was Ion Zelea Codreanu, the
father of Corneliu Codreanu, the future leader of the Iron Guard.
After the first world war, the alliance between Iorga and Cuza fell
apart. Heinen thinks that Iorga could not go along with Cuza's
uncompromising anti-semitism, but I have no doubt that had anti-
semitism been the main cause of friction, they could have found a

comfortable compromise (just as Juliu Maniu made a compromise with the Iron Guard in 1937, as I show later in this paper). Nor was the split an ideological one, and in the 1930s *vox populi* interpreted the split between them as a personality clash, since there could not be two 'number ones' in a single party. As a matter of fact, Iorga and Cuza founded two new parties, the identical names of which are instructive. One party was called the Nationalist Democratic Party Under the Leadership of A.C. Cuza, and the other was called the Nationalist Democratic Party Under the Leadership of N. Iorga. That anti-semitism was no vice in Iorga's opinion can easily be established by looking through the journal founded by him, *Neamul Romanesc*, which started to appear before 1910. In those days, Iorga enthusiastically supported the notorious Karl Lueger from Vienna, mainly because of his 'courageous fight against Judeo-Magyars'. Had Heinen written a simple history of ideas using a pedantic method of *Quellenkritik* as practised in German classical philology, he could have easily been proven right. There is indeed a great difference between Iorga's writings, Cuza's primitive pamphlets, and Cod-reanu's terrorist acts.

But Heinen has written an exhaustive study on the Iron Guard, and not a plain history of ideas. For all practical purposes, it hardly matters that Nietzsche was not a racist and that the nazis misrepre-sented and abused his theories. What matters is that a third-rate Gauleiter made fifth-rate henchmen believe that the nazi superman was theoretically based on the great thinker Friedrich Nietzsche. All those who lived in Rumania in the 1930s can remember that Codreanu made everyone believe that he adored Cuza and Iorga alike, that he deeply deplored the rift between these two great intellectuals, and that only dirty Jewish intrigues had made the two great men quarrel. University students in Czernowitz, especially from the School of Theology, many of whom I knew personally, spread precisely this view. Today we know better, and understand why Codreanu broke with Cuza in the 1920s, but very few in the Rumania of those days knew about the affair between Cuza's son and Codreanu's sister, and Cuza Jr's refusal to marry her when she became pregnant. In Czernowitz, Codreanu's supporters made us believe that in the depths of his heart, Iorga supported the brilliant, dedicated, and idealistic young intellectuals of the Iron Guard. The three sons of a school headmaster by the name of Scarlat (Mircea, Caesar, and Doro), who led the cell (*cuib*) of the Iron Guard in my neighbourhood, constantly claimed that Iorga was the intellectual and spiritual father of the Iron Guard, and that his occasional disagreements with Codreanu were only matters of temporary tactics. Public images play a tremendous role in history, and they do not always coincide with people's true character. In Iorga's case, the image can easily be substantiated. Two examples will suffice.

On 29 December 1933, Prime Minister Duca was shot by three members of the Iron Guard at the railway station in Sinaia. At the trial, which took place the following year, respectable gentlemen like Vaida Voievod, Argetoianu, Maniu, Mihalache, and Gheorghe Bratianu, testified in favour of Codreanu's legion. True, Iorga did not speak in favour of Codreanu, but he did not criticize him either, and in the summer of 1936, he agreed to address, together with Constantin Giurescu, a congress organized by Christian national students in Tg. Mures. Everybody knew that the congress was dominated by Iron Guardists, but many respectable people were still hoping to win their benevolence by appeasing and flattering them. From this point of view, Iorga's image was no different from theirs, at least not before 1937, and it is therefore essential that Iorga's impact on anti-semitism and the Iron Guard be reconsidered, taking into account his articles in daily papers, like *Curentul*, and not merely his more strictly political writings.

My second observation recommends a switch of emphasis in the surprising results of the elections that took place in 1937. Here I juxtapose history and memory.

The elections held on 20 December 1937 were unique for three main reasons. Firstly, not since 1918 had the ruling party lost an election. As a matter of fact, no one in the West respected the Rumanian parliamentary democracy that was established in 1918. It was an open secret that governments rigged elections, that voters were easily corrupted, and the entire issue of electoral ethics produced more questions than answers. In 1937, the ruling Liberal Party (Partidul National Liberal), headed by Tatarescu, was expected to win at least 40 per cent of the votes, and thus easily form a majority government. According to the Rumanian constitution of 1923, the winning party automatically received 50 per cent of the seats in the Lower House and, in addition, *further* seats in proportion to their electoral showing. Thus, a party which won 40 per cent of the vote might receive 90 per cent of the seats in the Lower House. But the Liberals lost. However, there is another reason why the elections of 1937 should be considered unique. For the first time in Rumanian history, the government completed its legal term of four years. This in itself was considered a miracle in Rumania, which had twenty-eight governments between 1918 and 1938, some of which lasted for only a few weeks. Thirdly, it was in 1937 that the electoral success of the Iron Guard surprised everyone. The ruling Liberal Party received 1,103,353 votes (35.92 per cent), which gave them 152 seats. The National Party of the Peasants (Partidul National Taranesc), headed by Maniu and Mihalache, received 626,612 (20.4 per cent) and thereby 86 seats. The Iron Guard, which ran under the name Total Pentru Tara won 478,368 votes (15.58 per cent), which gave them 66 seats. The National Christian Party, led by Cuza and Goga, won 281,167 (9.15 per cent), 39 seats. This came as a complete surprise. Between 1933 and 1937, King Carol II seemed to succeed in stabilizing the Rumanian government. This stability had been shaken neither by Italy's invasion of Ethiopia, nor by the outbreak of the Spanish Civil War. It appeared that King Carol played his delicate game very skilfully, and did the right thing at the right moment, whenever the neutrality of Rumania was at stake. At a certain moment he fired the only real democrat in the Liberal government, Titulescu, who recognized early on the danger presented by fascist governments and pressed for a rapprochement with the Soviet Union. In 1937 the Rumanian economy started to grow; the government promoted foreign investment, and foreign capital began to flow into Rumania. The balance of payments improved, and the wounds caused by the crisis of 1929 began to heal. Everyone in Rumania expected the ruling party to win easily and very few doubted that Tatarescu would become the new Prime Minister. Since democracy is a form of government in which surprises are possible, it should be pointed out that the elections of 1937 were the first and last democratic elections in Rumania. The big surprise was not only the failure of the Liberal Party to achieve the necessary 40 per cent to form a stable government, nor the poor showing of the Peasant Party and the party of Cuza and Goga, but the surprising success of the Iron Guard.

Heinen was aware that this was a major issue, and tried to interpret it. He gave two main reasons for the unexpected success of the Iron Guard. Firstly, as a result of Codreanu's primitive ideology, Rumanian voters directed their anger against corrupt politicians, cynical party politics, Jewish parasitism, and especially against the camarilla of King Carol II, headed by his Jewish mistress, Helena Lupescu. Secondly, Heinen believed that the despair felt by the people in the face of crooked politicians prompted them to turn to a less corrupt form of government. Heinen's view is beautifully documented, but by juxtaposing history and memory, I may add that according to the Jewish circles of Czernowitz in the 1930s, two other major factors enhanced the reputation of the Iron Guard and helped it win such an impressive electoral victory. Jews believed that it was the mild and appeasing attitude of the Rumanian establishment towards the Iron Guard that enhanced its attractiveness. Until 1935 or 1936 it was not considered respectable to admit that one was a member of the Iron Guard, and many staunch supporters of Codreanu hesitated to appear in public in their green shirts. Many of them were of German and Ukrainian extraction and had Rumanian names. They were in good company. Between the years 1935 and 1937, more and more respectable gentlemen praised the idealism of the youngsters who joined the Iron Guard, and praise came not only from the likes of Vaida Voievod and Gheorghe Bratianu, but also from court circles (including the King himself), and especially from the Patriarch and his Orthodox Church. Heinen knew all that, but underestimated its importance.

Jews were shocked when news spread in the synagogues that even the decent, non-anti-semitic leader of the National Peasant Party, I. Maniu, had signed an agreement with Codreanu. Maniu was a Transylvanian intellectual, a devoted Christian, and a supporter of Western parliamentary democracy. The National Peasant Party led by him came to power in 1927, but under economic and social pressures in 1930, Maniu decided to bring back Carol II, then living in exile because of his eccentric love affairs which embarrassed the Rumanian court. Maniu, a bachelor and a Puritan, was hoping to convince King Carol to abandon his Jewish mistress, and establish a constitutional monarchy in Rumania. He was also hoping to be offered the same authority in government as the Liberal Ionel Bratianu enjoyed in the days of King Ferdinand. But Maniu was very quickly disappointed. Carol came back, followed by Mrs Lupescu, and declared openly that he intended to rule, and that constitutional monarchy was an idea which suited Western countries, but that Rumania was neither Sweden nor Belgium. He once said to an English journalist that in England the King says what his ministers tell him to say, but that in Rumania the ministers should do what the King tells them to do. Carol did not hide his intention of ruling as an absolute monarch. Maniu resigned in despair in 1930, and opened the way for a Liberal come-back in Rumania, but instead of fighting openly for a constitutional monarchy and for parliamentary supremacy, he preferred an easy way out. He put the blame on the Jewish mistress, and on the corrupted court camarilla. Before the elections in 1937, he signed an electoral non-aggression pact with Codreanu, which was published in the Bucharest *Tageblatt* of 17 November 1937. In May 1938, when Codreanu had to stand up in court, Maniu testified to this non-aggression pact. He said explicitly that he did not agree with Codreanu on anti-semitism, but that in all other respects their views were identical, because both were convinced Rumanian nationalists, and both believed in decency, honesty and Christian ethics, which were part and parcel of Rumanian Christianity.

Once Maniu gave the Iron Guard his moral legitimation, thousands of people decided to vote directly for Codreanu. They no longer needed Maniu as a mediator, and Codreanu was young, charismatic and much more attractive to the Rumanian voter. As I point out later, the Iron Guard indeed won many seats in rural areas, which previously had been dominated by the National Peasant Party. When the results of the December 1937 election became known, it was clear that no party could form a majority government, since no party had reached the necessary 40 per cent, but had Maniu been less dogmatic and more devoted to a pro-Western democratic government, he could have easily supported a coalition with the Liberals. But Maniu hated Tatarescu and the King more than the Iron Guard, and it was his obstinacy that forced the King to ask Goga to form a minority government, because he was less afraid of the National Christian Party than of Codreanu. After the Soviet occupation of Rumania in 1944, Maniu was arrested, condemned and later died in captivity. It was only after the second world war that Maniu became a martyr and was completely exonerated. But many in 1938 believed that his non-aggression pact with Codreanu gave the Iron Guard more respectability than the trust of some Rumanian aristocrats like Cantacuzino, Flondor and Sturdza.

Another factor that consolidated Codreanu's position was the rise of Hitler in Germany on 31 January 1933. It is on this issue that my memory totally contradicts Heinen's views. Having scrutinized all the documents, Heinen reached the conclusion, which I do not challenge, that the sympathy of the Iron Guard towards Hitler was far from mutual. The Iron Guard admired Hitler, but Hitler did not admire the Iron Guard. Once the nazis came to power in Germany, they treated Rumania with great caution. They intended to establish links with various opposition groups, but preferred not to shake the monarchy and refused to hurt the King. Believing that the national poet Octavian Goga, who allied himself with Cuza, had a better chance of toppling the pro-Western government of the Liberals, the nazis preferred Goga and Cuza to Codreanu. In the spring of 1933, a Cuzist delegation was received by Hitler, Goering and Goebbels, and in September 1933 Goga was personally invited to Berlin. In those days, Hitler believed that Goga would one day become Prime Minister, and preferred him to Codreanu, who was known for his hatred towards all ethnic minorities. Hitler was not troubled by Codreanu's anti-semitism, but he could not neglect the future of the large German minority in Rumania. Heinen, as Hillgruber and many other historians before him, could easily prove that a good deal of money was sent from Germany to the National Christian Party of Goga, and not to Codreanu. This is what the documents show, but not everything that is in the documents actually occurred in real life. Documents can never reproduce an atmosphere, and it is precisely this atmosphere which I would like to record here. I can testify that my Rumanian, Polish and Ukrainian neighbours, whose names and addresses I can still remember, joined the Iron Guard with great fervour, and started to appear proudly in their green shirts, especially after the funeral of Mota and Marin, who were killed in Spain fighting for Franco. They never read the documents and reports of the German ambassador in Bucharest to the German Ministry of Foreign Affairs. Nor did they know about the serious differences between the office of the National Socialist Party which was in charge of foreign affairs (it was headed by Rosenberg and called A.P. Amt), and the Ministry of Foreign Affairs (Auswärtiges Amt), headed by the Minister of Foreign Affairs.

The Rumanian man in the street was convinced, erroneously, as historians can now show, that the Iron Guard, more than any other group in Rumania, was fully supported by the Third Reich. This belief not only gave it enormous self-confidence, which it had lacked before Hitler's accession to power, but also gave it great hopes of recruiting more people into its ranks. Indeed, after 1933, the Iron Guard was transformed from an élitist group into a mass movement. In the late 1920s, individuals who joined the Iron Guard were sworn in singly in a special ceremony. After 1933, this was impossible, because in one ceremony alone, some 1,500 people were sworn in. It hardly matters that leading SS members viewed Codreanu's movement with contempt. It is more important to remember that Codreanu organized his movement on the German model. He established a 'Death Team' (*Echipa mortii*) in imitation of the notorious *Todesmannschaft*. The general public believed that Codreanu enjoyed full German support, and looked upon this imitation with respect. Nazi songs praising death (e.g. *The Legionary Death is the Most Beautiful of Weddings*[1]) were imitated in many Rumanian versions, and this can easily be shown by comparing the song-book of the Iron Guard (the *Carticica de cantece*) with the German originals. In Rumania, as in Germany, the dead marched with the legions of the Iron Guard: 'Marschieren im Geist in unseren Reihen mit'. Codreanu's statement that forty-eight hours after his electoral victory he would establish a firm axis between Bucharest and Berlin made a tremendous impression in the Rumanian streets.

This is the place to stress that I do not believe that emphasizing the uniqueness of the Iron Guard as a special variety of fascism (i.e. based more on romantic and religious fanaticism than on racism) is fully justified. This argument is more applicable to Italian fascism. Indeed, Italian anti-semitism was based more on spiritual and cultural ideas rather than on biological concepts, and as such was consistent with Italian traditions and teachings of the Italian Church. Italy was extremely popular in Rumania because Latinity was one of the major slogans in Rumania which tried to show the difference between Rumanians and their Slavonic and Mongolian neighbours. Italian and French were much more popular in Rumania than German, since German reminded Rumanians primarily of Austria, which together with Hungary had ruled for many years in Transylvania and Bucovina. In the first world war, Rumania did not join Germany in spite of the fact that its ruling monarch was of German extraction. In 1916 it joined forces with England and France, and had to fight German troops in some ferocious battles. At Versailles, Rumania came out as a victorious country and annexed huge territories, only to discover to its distress that the Italians sympathized first and foremost with the Hungarians because both opposed the Versailles Treaty which Rumania supported wholeheartedly. On 1 November 1936, Mussolini openly declared his support for Hungary's territorial demands, i.e. the restoration of Transylvania and the Banat to Hungary, and the Rumanians understood the implication.

However, as early as 26 October 1930, an article was printed in the journal of the Iron Guard, *The Land of Our Forefathers*, in which the nazis were praised and the Weimar democracy depicted as rotten and corrupt. Among other things, it explicitly stated that Hitler's victory would be a victory of the Aryan race and symbolize an awakening of our entire race. I can therefore not agree with Heinen, and many other scholars who try to clear the Iron Guard of racism. If necessary, the Legionaries could easily have turned into racists because they were basically just as pragmatic as the partisans of Goga. True, some Rumanian intellectuals who joined the Iron Guard, like Nichifor Crainic, opposed racism because they saw in it a secular religion which might undermine Rumanian Orthodoxy. But the thousands of people who joined the Iron Guard and voted for it in 1937 hardly needed a theoretical foundation for racism. They hated Jews, demanded their expulsion, and even their annihilation, even on the sole basis of the perceived fact that they had been responsible for the death of Christ. Codreanu, who was a devout Christian and 'spoke' with the Archangel Michael, was once asked how he, as a religious man, could reconcile his faith with terror, murder, and wild hatred for the Jews. He answered that although one must strive for a purely Christian government, in an imperfect world we are sometimes called upon to perform acts which will not be required after the Redemption.

My third observation concerns sociological generalizations based on statistics. The palm should go to Eugen Weber for being the first to analyse seriously the results of the 1937 elections. He was aware, of course, that the figures known to him were not always reliable, but his attempt is still praiseworthy. In his paper, 'The Men of the Archangel', published in the *Journal of Contemporary History* in 1966, he compared the number of votes given to the Iron Guard with those received by Goga's party (PNC — Partidul National Crestin). One of his stimulating conclusions was that the Jewish problem was less acute in Legionary counties than in those dominated by Goga's party. Between 1932 and 1937, the legion grew six-fold, but Goga's party hardly grew at all. This indicated, according to Weber, not only the superior dynamism of the Legion, but also the limits of the anti-semitic appeal. Codreanu won in remote, isolated, and extremely poor areas, untouched by modern life, like Vlasca and Teleorman, where an old tradition of peasant socialism prevailed, and where Jews were conspicuous by their absence. He was also victorious in malady-stricken areas where malaria and syphilis were an ever-present problem, such as Teleorman and Dolj. In those places, the Jewish problem was hardly an issue, but Codreanu's party inspired the peasants in these backward areas, who were attracted more by his youth and enthusiasm than by his theories. He gave these people new hope and Weber rightly concludes that the major factors in a radical or revolutionary orientation are less strictly sociological than psychological. Weber is certainly convincing when he analyses the various age-groups and shows that the majority of voters for the Iron Guard were young people.

In an important chapter, Heinen challenges Weber's conclusions, based on figures issued by the Rumanian Ministry of the Interior rather than Enescu's more trustworthy report of the elections of 1937. This is why Weber's list of the Legionary strongholds seems incomplete: he missed out Campolung, Radauti, Tecuci, Ramnicul Sarat, Putna and Suceava. On the other hand, he wrongly included Prahova, Ialomita, Gorj, Vlasca and Timis Torontal. According to Heinen's analysis, the Iron Guard was successful precisely in those areas where modern influences started to be felt, and had a disintegrating effect on the local peasantry. Thus, the victory of the Legion in southern Rumania can be explained, and this is why Goga's party won in the north-east.

At first, Heinen's emphasis on 'die auflösenden Erscheinungen der Moderne' appears as an important corrective to Weber's analysis. Heinen's method is more sophisticated, and he takes into account ethnic composition and the religious beliefs of the population. Yet some loose ends still remain. The term 'north-east' is too general, because of the significant differences which existed between Bucovina and Bessarabia.

When I was a boy, popular wisdom had it that in the more primitive areas of Bessarabia, peasants voted for Cuza and Goga. Most of them were illiterate, and behaved like hooligans when they came into the towns. In more advanced areas, where German influence was greater and university students from the cities agitated among the peasants, the Iron Guard was stronger. Table 1 shows clearly the difference between the election results in Bucovina and Bessarabia.[2] But it is hardly possible to interpret these results on the basis of the model which fits Vlasca and Teleorman. Nor can it explain why three other districts of Bessarabia, Cahul, Cetatea Alba and Ismail, show a decisive victory for the Iron Guard over the PNC. It is, of course, correct to assume that popular wisdom can never replace proper scholarly criteria. But we should still ask, how can one explain that in Sadagura, the seat of one of the most famous rabbis, the Iron Guard won 203 votes, and the party of Goga only 43? It appears to me that because of the tremendous regional differences between Moldavia and Dobrogea, Bessarabia and Transylvania, a general model for the whole of Rumania would be very nearly impossible to devise and to implement.

TABLE 1

	Iron Guard	PNC
Bucovina		
Campulung	6,623	1,132
Cernauti	10,998	2,173
Radauti	10,165	3,627
Storijinet	4,652	3,412
Suceava	6,124	5,413
Bessarabia		
Balti	1,469	15,996
Hotin	2,581	17,393
Orhei	1,399	6,713
Soroca	4,170	11,064
Tighina	2,121	6,983

Notes

1. 'Moartea numai moartea legionara, este cea mai frumoasa numta dintre nunti.' (Liviv Russu, who wrote the book, *What is the Legionary Song*? was my music teacher in high school between 1937 and 1940.)
2. These figures are taken from the marvellous article by Paul H. Shapiro, 'Prelude to Dictatorship in Rumania', *Canadian-American Slavic Studies*, viii (1974), 45–88.

Zvi Yavetz
is Fred Lessing Professor of Ancient History
at Tel Aviv University and Distinguished
Professor of History at the City University
of New York (Queens). He is the author of
Plebs and Princeps (Oxford 1969), *Caesar's
Public Image* (London 1979) and *Slaves and
Slavery* (New Brunswick 1987; Augustus, Tel
Aviv 1988). He is currently working on a
book on Czernowitz between the world wars.

Michael Confino

Solzhenitsyn, the West, and the New Russian Nationalism

Present events in the Soviet Union have brought about changes which not long ago would have been thought of as pure fantasy or extravagant futurology. Well-entrenched institutions have been shattered or abolished; new forces have appeared in the social and political arena; currents of ideas considered yesterday as marginal have moved to centre stage. Aleksandr Solzhenitsyn's views belong to this category. Their examination has now acquired a particular interest as a result of two main developments. First, because various right-wing groups in Russia, including Pamiat and other anti-semitic nationalists, repeatedly use Solzhenitsyn's name and moral authority to boost their political propaganda. Second, because some of Solzhenitsyn's works, fictional as well as non-fictional, are now published in the USSR.[1] The ensuing debate in the Soviet public has focused not only on the literary merits and aesthetics of these works, but also on the political, social and ethical ideas of their author. Of course, some Western intellectuals feel differently; not long ago John Bayley observed in the *New York Review of Books*:

> It has become the fashion to write off Solzhenitsyn as a has-been, an old fuddy-duddy, still lamenting in voluminous pages at longer and longer intervals the disappearance of Holy Russia, and castigating now not so much the Soviet regime as the new-style Russian intelligentsia, both those in exile and those still in their own homeland.[2]

But this intellectual fashion is specious, and Solzhenitsyn's views should be taken seriously — for what they are and for their actual and potential influence. In today's dynamic developments in the USSR, when the present is exhilarating and the future uncertain, it is appropriate to take a closer look at the perceptions of a thinker who has become a *maître à penser* of a diffuse, but non-negligible, segment of the nationalist political forces that are shaping Russia's present and future.[3]

The purpose of this essay is to examine some major ideas in Solzhenitsyn's political thought, which appear to have influenced the orientation of Russian nationalist groups. Its major themes will focus on the image of the West in Solzhenitsyn's representations and on their role in the formation of nationalist attitudes. These themes include his views on the course of Russian and Western history; his perception of the roots of 'the present crisis of the West'; the guilt of the West toward Russia; and the place of these ideas in contemporary Russian nationalism.

The main documentary basis of the essay are Solzhenitsyn's non-fictional writings and pronouncements, his speeches and *publitsistika*, about which he recently reiterated that he stands by all the views he has expressed in them.[4]

In Solzhenitsyn's world-view, the West is at present in a state of deep crisis which may lead to its imminent collapse. How did this come to be?

The fatal mistake, he says, lies at the very foundation of Western thought in modern times, and stems from 'the prevailing Western view of the world which was born in the Renaissance and has found political expression since the Age of Enlightenment'.[5] It became the basis for political and social doctrine and could be called, in his words, 'rationalistic humanism' or 'humanistic autonomy', that is the proclaimed and practised autonomy of man from any higher force above him: an 'anthropocentric' view, according to which man, and not God, is the centre of everything. To the extent that the teaching of the *philosophes* of the eighteenth-century Enlightenment was crucial in this shift of focus from God to man, Solzhenitsyn seems to repeat in different words the well-known persiflage, '*C'est la faute à Voltaire, c'est la faute à Rousseau*', a proposition forcefully defended in the recent past by the late Jacob L. Talmon.

Historically, the turn introduced by the Renaissance was probably inevitable: the Middle Ages, he says, had come to a natural end by exhaustion, having become 'an intolerable despotic repression of man's physical nature in favour of the spiritual one'.[6] From the Renaissance onward, the West recoiled from the spirit and embraced all that was material. The humanistic way of thinking did not admit the existence of intrinsic *evil* in man, nor did it see any task higher than the attainment of *happiness* on earth. These two notions are central to Solzhenitsyn's world-view, and they command his attitude toward both Russia and the West: first, man is evil; second, the pursuit of happiness is an unworthy goal.

The humanistic way of thinking led modern Western civilization on the dangerous downward path of worshipping man and his material needs. Thus,

> everything beyond physical well-being and the accumulation of material goods, all other human requirements and characteristics of a subtler and higher nature, were left outside the area of attention of state and social systems, as if human life did not have any higher meaning.[7]

Human rights and freedom, which were given to the individual conditionally, on the assumption of his constant religious responsibility, became unlimited, as if they were granted for no purpose and simply for the satisfaction of man's whims. Thus, all limitations were eroded in the West, and a total emancipation occurred from the moral heritage of Christian centuries with their great reserves of mercy and sacrifices. The West has finally achieved the rights of man, and even to excess, but man's sense of responsibility to God and society has grown dimmer and dimmer. In the past decades, the legalistic selfishness of the West has reached its peak and the world has found itself in a deep spiritual crisis and a political impasse.

As a result of this evolution, materialism and atheism have now reached their logical conclusion in *both East and West*, thus creating between them 'an unexpected kinship'.[8] Surely, there are differences between capitalism and communism, but what has been overlooked are the similarities, and 'both systems are defeated by a common defect'.[9] This defect is the materialistic world-outlook and its corollaries: the elevation of man above all else, the sacrifice of moral principles to the pursuit of present interests in a selfish and wasteful way, and the stress on an ecologically harmful economic growth. However, this 'kinship' exists not between the West and *Russia*, but between the West and the Soviet communist system, and the values which it symbolizes are seen by Solzhenitsyn as deeply 'anti-Russian'. This is probably one of the reasons why this view has been adopted and repeatedly voiced by nationalist circles in Russia.

How did matters in the West reach this dismal situation? On the way from the Renaissance to the present (and in Russia, from Peter the Great's time on), man has lost the concept of a Supreme Entity which used to restrain his passions and irresponsibility. We have placed, he thinks, too much hope in politics and social reforms, only to find out that we are being deprived of our most precious possession: our spiritual life.

> This spiritual life is trampled by the party mob in the East, and by the commercial mob in the West. This is the essence of the crisis: the split in the world is less terrifying than the similarity of the disease afflicting its main sections.[10]

Thus, the key to understanding the present crisis, East and West, is in the course of events since the Middle Ages: 'Renaissance, Reformation, Enlightenment, physical bloody revolutions, democratic societies, socialist attempts',[11] and finally the 'Bolshevik coup d'état',[12] which was 'the logical result of doctrines that had been bandied about in Europe for ages and had enjoyed considerable success'.[13] (How the Bolsheviks fit into this sequence — another proposition that has also been argued by Jacob L. Talmon[14] — will be examined below.) All that cycle was wrong, concludes Solzhenitsyn, everything in it was wrong, and it is urgent to get out of it. But how? The key to salvation, the way out from the crisis (which, incidentally, is symmetric to what other authors call 'the crisis of bourgeois society') is in the hands of the West, which must undergo a major transformation, a political, economic, and spiritual upheaval, and 'a moral revolution'.[15]

Solzhenitsyn's understanding of the course of Western civilization appears to be based on a dogmatic (and at times utterly flawed) historiosophic vision which postulates that evil comes from humanism and anthropocentrism, born in the Renaissance and imported into Russia by Peter the Great's reforms. Moreover, his historical outlook is closely linked to an uncompromising conception of the role of *spirituality* in modern life, which commands entirely Solzhenitsyn's evaluation of social and political developments: a topic to which we now turn.

If this is 'the mistake at the root' of Western civilization, what are its expressions in the political sphere? And how do Solzhenitsyn's views in this respect relate to the nationalists' outlook?

The two main weaknesses of the West are the democratic regime and the party system; its two main illusions and deceptions — the so-called political and intellectual freedoms.

For Solzhenitsyn democracy is a 'sham' because it is based on the principle of voting and elections. But elections — the heart of the system's legitimacy — are a 'grotesque hypocrisy', and the rule of the majority over the minority is a false ideal. 'I do not think', he writes,

> that the will of the English people was implemented when England was for years sapped of its strength by a Labour government — elected by only 40 per cent of the voters. Nor was the will of the German people served when the left bloc had a majority of one seat in the Bundestag. Nor is any nation served when half the electorate is so disillusioned that it stays away from the polling booths [an allusion to the United States].[16]

To this unsatisfactory system Solzhenitsyn prefers the wisdom of an old traditional Russian concept which postulates that

> the truth cannot be determined by voting, since the majority does not necessarily have any deeper insight into the truth. (And what we know about mass psychology would suggest that the reverse is often true.)[17]

(But if this so, why is he so critical of a minority government, 'elected by only 40 per cent of the voters', ruling over England?) What Solzhenitsyn would like to see applied in politics is the old Russian concept of pre-Petrine times: no majority, no minority, no voting. How, then, will matters be decided in the polity? His answer is:

> When representatives of the entire country gathered [in the sixteenth and seventeenth centuries] for important decisions (the so-called Assemblies of the Land) there was no voting. Truth was sought by a lengthy process of mutual persuasion, and it was determined when final accord was reached.[18]

But this example of the old Russian Assemblies of the Land (*Zemskie Sobori*) requires some comment. The search of 'truth' was not the purpose and the agenda of their gatherings, always summoned by the tsar, but taxation, quite often because of impending or ongoing wars for which he needed monies. The participants at these Assemblies (whose Western counterparts were the French Etats Généraux, the Spanish Cortes and the Swedish Ricksdag) were representatives nominated or elected on the basis of locality, profession, status or membership in one of the Estates (*Sosloviia*; *Stände*), such as noblemen, state officials, clergy, merchants, Cossacks and free peasants. Transposed into twentieth-century societies, such assemblies, representing professional associations and suchlike corporations, would resemble much more those devised by Mussolini and Perón than their seventeenth-century Russian prototype. Further, Solzhenitsyn's idea about decisions arrived at by 'a lengthy process of mutual persuasion' and without votes, has been borrowed from the ethos of the peasant commune, indeed an authentic Russian institution in the past. But one wonders whether a collective device that worked in well-integrated small communities kept together by strong traditional ties during many generations, could be a workable procedure in complex, diversified and stratified societies, facing a multitude of problems and conflicting interests. Paradoxically, it is precisely the existence of these conflicting interests that Solzhenitsyn sees as basically harmful and which, for that reason, should be eliminated. For he proceeds to elaborate:

> While the decision of the Assembly was not legally binding on the tsar, it was morally incontestable. From this perspective the creation of *parties*, that is of segments or parts which fight for their *partial interests* at the expense of the other segments of the people, seems an absurdity. (Indeed, this is less than worthy of mankind, at least of mankind in its potential.)[19]

Thus, the parties appear as the epitome of the West's debased political system. Why is that so? Why does Solzhenitsyn consider them as an 'absurdity' unworthy of mankind? Basically because, in his view, the people, the *nation*, represent an *organic whole*, a unity, a marvellous and mysterious web of links, of traditions and of historic memory. Everything that breaks or weakens this organic unity is harmful to the nation's soul and body:

> Do we not discern in the multiparty parliamentary system yet another idol, but this time one to which the whole world bows down? 'Partia' means a *part*. Every party known to history has always defended the interest of this one *part* against — whom? Against the rest of the people.[20]

In a way Solzhenitsyn holds that parties do not exist *because* there are different views and interests in society, but that such views and interests emerge because of the existence of political parties. Although this may sound as logical as the belief that an increase in the production of caskets would produce higher mortality rates, this condemnation of the political parties is an important indication of how far Solzhenitsyn stands, not only from the West's political system and from the communists, but also from the trends in Soviet Russia oriented toward more liberty and democracy by means of diversification and greater activity of political movements. Indeed, this view too has been adopted by the nationalists who speak of 'the wholesomeness and unity of the Russian people', which are being shattered by 'harmful internal dissensions' and by 'other nations' hatred for Russians'.

But on a higher level of thought one may also ask, why is the party system 'unworthy of mankind and of man'? There are two answers. The first postulates that it is so because man is evil. As a result, democratic political regimes and their party system appeal to, and encourage, his deep-seated vices and human weaknesses. This leads to the emergence of

> old atavistic urges — greed, envy, unrestrained passion, and mutual hostility — readily picking up respectable pseudonyms like class, race, mass, or trade-union struggle, [which] claw and tear apart our world.[21]

In this kind of society and political regime, 'any professional group, at the first opportunity to *get their hand on something extra* — though unearned and even unneeded — grab it and the rest of society be damned'.[22] This is the cause, too, why Western society is approaching 'an amplitude of fluctuations beyond which a system becomes metastable and must disintegrate'.[23]

The second answer goes even deeper into the springs of human nature and social action, and is closely linked to Solzhenitsyn's *primat* of spirituality. It postulates that if the Western democracies are in a state of 'political crisis and confusion',[24] this is due to the fact that 'a society in which political parties are active does not rise in the moral scale'.[25] This explains why, in his view, such a kind of society is doomed and could be redeemed only through the elimination of the parties and a 'moral revolution'. Would Solzhenitsyn be surprised that it was Saint-Just who proclaimed that 'a country where there are parties [factions] is not a free country', and that it was Robespierre who advocated the 'revolution of virtue'?

We thus reach a point in Solzhenitsyn's thought where the *moral* and the *political* dimensions meet, and even merge. At bottom, Solzhenitsyn is interested in the form of political regimes only from the point of view of *moral values* (and for Russia, Christian Orthodox moral values). The basic question he keeps raising in different ways is, which is the political regime allowing the greatest moral and spiritual elevation? His answer is:'ethical authoritarianism'.[26] In such a regime (as distinct from democratic or totalitarian ones), *society* would be completely separated from *state* and *government*. This separation implies, first and foremost, the non-interference of one entity in the sphere of the other; the sphere of the state being the political one, and the sphere of society the moral and spiritual. It is in the light of this conception that a famous passage of Solzhenitsyn's *Letter to the Soviet Leaders* becomes clear, namely his proposal (whether naïve or shrewd does not concern us here) that the Soviet government continue to rule the country (i.e. manage all matters in the political sphere), on condition that it gives up *ideology* and stops interfering in the social and spiritual life of the people.[27] This conception has two interesting aspects.

The first represents a curious paradox, since Solzhenitsyn, an anti-liberal, adopts implicitly one of the basic assumptions of Western European liberal doctrine — the principle of the total separation of the political and social spheres. But at the same time he rejects both liberal constitutionalism and the very content of the liberal idea of freedom. Instead, the content of this ideal of freedom is replaced by his version of Russian Orthodox spirituality.

Second, this peculiar concept of separation of state and society has deep roots in an important current of Russian political thought. Here is an example that might have been written by Solzhenitsyn or one of his disciples a month or a year ago:

> The [Russian] people want these things only: freedom to lead their own life, spiritual freedom, freedom of speech. As they themselves do not meddle in matters of state, they do not want the state to interfere in their spiritual life and their ways, which the state has meddled with and has been repressing for 150 years — even to the point of telling them what to wear. The government must once again grasp the basic relationship between the state and the land — and restore it. Since it was the government itself that violated this relationship when it encroached upon the people's rights, it can eliminate the violation. This is not difficult and calls for no forcible action. As soon as the oppression of the land by the state is done away with, it will be simple for the government to establish the true Russian relationship between itself and the people.

This passage is taken neither from Solzhenitsyn's *Letter to the Soviet Leaders*, nor from some dissident publication in the recent past. It was written 135 years ago by the Slavophile thinker, Konstantin Aksakov, in a long memorandum submitted by him in 1855 to tsar Alexander II.[28] Solzhenitsyn's conception fits very well into the pattern of Russian conservative, nationalist and religious political thought. The special 'Russian' path of salvation for mankind,[29] which the conservative thinkers (like Dostoevsky, for instance) have constructed, has always consisted *not in the control of society over politics*, but in the *removal* of society *from* politics, which inevitably results in some form of authoritarianism. And for Solzhenitsyn, as mentioned above, authoritarianism is a desirable form of political regime.

Underlying this conception, which I would term 'non-politics as the Russian nationalists' way of politics', is also the belief that politics, in the everyday sense of the word, is not an important part of life, and is even, to a certain degree, an unworthy, if not immoral one. 'Life' is above all spiritual life, and it should stand above politics. This is the way Solzhenitsyn arrives at the conclusion that oppressive political institutions are not necessarily a supreme disaster, and that one can live a moral life within their confines even though they are not ideal. 'The state system which exists in our country is terrible,' he wrote, 'not because it is undemocratic, authoritarian, [and] based on physical constraint, [for] a man can live in such conditions without harm to his spiritual essence.'[30]

For that reason, too, Solzhenitsyn has uniformly maintained that protest in the USSR must be moral, not political; and this was also one of the major areas of disagreement between him and Andrei Sakharov.[31] When asked in 1974, 'How can your compatriots and youth show their support for you?' Solzhenitsyn answered:

> Definitely not by any physical acts but by rejecting the lie, and by refusing to participate personally in the lie. . . . In breaking with the lie, we are performing a moral act, not a political one, and not one that can be punished by criminal law.[32]

This explains also Solzhenitsyn's particular brand of 'passive resistance' to the powers, as well as his politics of 'non-politics'.[33] The intriguing question, of course, is whether the nationalist groups, which so eagerly adopt many of his views, will also follow him in his opposition to all kind of physical violence.

In his essay, 'Repentance and Self-Limitation', Solzhenitsyn says that it is a moral deformation always to put the blame on others for every mishap and misfortune: on the 'other fellow', on your neighbour, on other nations. Repentance, he believes, is a Russian national characteristic, but in the twentieth century Russians have lost this art

of repentance, and tended instead to take the most normal way out —
namely, blaming others, such as the White Guards, the kulaks, the
priests. 'Repent and do not blame the others!'[34] But Solzhenitsyn
himself does not always live up to this lofty principle. When he raises
the other perennial 'Russian' question, 'Who is to blame?' (*Kto
vinovat?*, the title of Alexander Herzen's novel), quite often his answer
is — the West. This approach colours several aspects of his world-
view, and provides a 'historical dimension' to and justification of
xenophobic attitudes among large segments of the nationalist right in
Russia.

In Solzhenitsyn's writings, 'the guilt of the West' is not a metaphor.
The West is responsible not only for its maladies which stem from its
own mistakes, but also for the historical fate of Russia, her sufferings,
and her slavery under communist rule. The linchpin of his outlook is
that Russia is the victim and has suffered most from the errings both
of the West and of communism, which is a 'Western invention' too.
(Needless to say that the other peoples of the Soviet Union and of
Eastern Europe, who see themselves as Russia's victims, have never
acquiesced to such a view of the course of history.) Speaking of the
aftermath of the two world wars, Solzhenitsyn says:

> Twice we helped save the freedom of Western Europe. And twice you repaid us by
> abandoning us to our slavery. It is clear what you wanted. Once again you wanted
> to extricate yourselves as quickly as possible from [a] terrible war; you wanted to
> rest . . . you wanted to forget, you wanted to go back to prosperity, to your
> fashions, to the latest dances . . . [35]

But a close reading of Solzhenitsyn's writings reveals that the 'West
betrayed Russia' not only twice, as he says above, but several times in
the span of half a century.

The first instance of the West's betrayal happened in August 1914,
when Russia entered the war not out of any self-interest. She did it
selflessly and only in order to save the Western democracies and to
honour her international obligations. In its plans and during the first
months of the war, the West did not take into consideration Russia's
needs and military situation, her unpreparedness for a rapid offensive
against the Germans, and her initial setbacks on the battlefield.

In 1915–16 Russia was betrayed again. She collapsed in the war
'out of loyalty to her Western allies', since Nicholas II prolonged the
senseless war with Germany instead of saving his country 'by
conducting a separate peace (like Sadat today)'.[36]

The West shared in the responsibility for Russia's destiny during the February Revolution. The latter was fomented by liberals and socialists — that is, people with *Western ideologies* par excellence — who 'overthrew the monarchy, elected themselves to power, and then led Russia into the abyss' of Bolshevism.[37] This event provided the occasion for another betrayal of Russia by the West. In October 1917, 'a dark and murky whirlwind descended on us from the West'. The Bolshevik's 'murderous coup' (*banditskii perevorot*)[38] was, in his view, a poisonous Western brew made out of German Marxism, German money, French Jacobinism and foreign revolutionaries — 'Latvians, Poles, Jews, Hungarians and Chinese'.[39]

Some of these elements, like 'German Marxism', need no elaboration. By 'German money' Solzhenitsyn means the subsidies purportedly funnelled to the Bolshevik Party by the German government and General Staff in 1916–17, a theory forcefully argued, albeit in pseudo-fictional form, in his *Lenin in Zurich*. The expression 'foreign revolutionaries' conveys his conviction that the October Revolution was carried out not by Russians, but by foreigners, and was directed against Russia. Even Lenin, he says, was to a great extent a foreigner, for only one-quarter of his blood was Russian, while the other three-quarters were a mixture of Kalmyk, German, Jewish and Swedish blood, or, as he put it more recently, 'Lenin . . . did not belong to any nation.'[40] Finally, French Jacobinism, elaborated in the West, and not some Russian doctrine or predisposition, was the model which, according to Solzhenitsyn, directed the action of the Bolsheviks:

> The similarities between Bolsheviks and Jacobins in both theory and tactics are utterly obvious to anyone who takes the trouble to study the historical evidence. . . .This is true to the smallest details: the prohibition of a free press; the crushing of rival factions; the proclamation of dictatorship as 'the highest form of freedom'; monolithic unity of the entire population; the merging of the state with the party, with the latter dictatorially controlled by a single individual; even food requisitioning detachments sent out to rob the peasants, the physical destruction of churches, the melting down of church bells, and the confiscation of church valuables.[41]

Surely, this kind of analogy is indefensible, and is not well served by the many factual inaccuracies of these 'similarities', but the basic idea is not new, for J.L. Talmon paved the way for such deductions with his grand scheme of the origins of 'totalitarian democracy' stretching over 150 years from Rousseau to Lenin. For Solzhenitsyn, too, these 'similarities' and the causes of the October Revolution were 'the logical result of doctrines' that originated in the West long ago and enjoyed considerable success.[42] These results are 'logical' because of the pernicious sequence (described above) that runs from the Renaissance and the Enlightenment through democratic societies, socialism, and the Bolshevik *putsch*. In Solzhenitsyn's hands, the unexpected effect of the theories which attribute the origins of Bolshevism to the Enlightenment, and see in Rousseau the precursor of Lenin, is that they exonerate Russia and the Russians from any wrongdoing and lay the blame for the Red Terror and the Soviet dictatorship squarely at the West's door: '. . . *c'est la faute à Rousseau*'. This sophism, generated by a pseudo-historical analogy, has already taken the form of an anti-Western nationalist slogan. François Furet was nearer the mark when he observed:

> The discovery in the twentieth century of an unprecedented form of despotism in no way implies that the Enlightenment was the cause of the gulag or even that democracy must necessarily veer towards totalitarianism.[43]

And speaking about a similar 'filiation', Richard Pipes is reported to have said: 'It is horrifying to blame a German scribbler [Karl Marx] who died a hundred years ago for what happened to Russia many years after his death.'[44]

The next infamy of the West occurred during the Civil War in 1918–20. When this 'apocalyptic storm was raging over the land that used to be Russia', says Solzhenitsyn, Western Europe was speedily extricating itself from the war in its haste to forget the ordeal and return to a life of prosperity, and it did not bother to help Russia. He quotes Lloyd George saying; 'Forget about Russia. It is our job to ensure the welfare of our own society,' and he comments:

> In 1914, when the Western democracies needed help, they were not averse to appealing to Russia. But in 1919 those Russian generals who, for three years, had fought to save the Marne, the Somme, and Verdun, straining Russian resources to the very limit, were refused military aid or even an alliance by their Western friends.[45]

This comment invites a few reminders. Firstly, the 'Russian generals' alluded to are Denikin, Wrangel, Kolchak and Yudenich: commanders whose political aims were confused (it is not enough to be 'for the Tsar' and against the Jews and the Bolsheviks), the behaviour of their troops inhuman, and who did not have the support of the mass of the Russian people (neither did the Bolsheviks, for that matter). Secondly, these generals, like the entire command of the Russian Imperial Army, did not fight mainly for the sake of Verdun. They had plans of expansion in the Balkans, control of the Straits, and seizure of Constantinople. They also had other political and strategic goals, far away from the Marne and the Somme, and totally unconnected with the Western front. That they finally had to fight in order to save Smolensk, Petrograd and Odessa (not Verdun) is the result of bad luck and military mismanagement: these were not the fronts of their choice, but of their incompetence. *Pace* Solzhenitsyn, it was not the West which had built the Russian army, devised its strategy, chosen its tactics. Nor did the West appoint Nicholas II as Commander-in-Chief in 1916, a fateful decision that increased Russia's misfortunes and sealed her war fortune; it was rather a decision taken by the same Nicholas for whom these generals were now fighting against their own people, a tsar who was and remained an incompetent political and military leader who never understood his task as head of state.

These are well-known and verifiable facts; they are maybe unpleasant for Solzhenitsyn, who has now undertaken the unenviable task of 'rehabilitating' Nicholas II under the pretext that in the Soviet Union he was 'characterized as less than human, as a monkey, as the ultimate scoundrel, but I described him [in *The Red Wheel*] as a real person, as a human being'.[46] But Solzhenitsyn should know that no such kind of ('monkey') portraiture of Nicholas is at stake. He should also know that for the serious reader and the educated public the real issue is not Nicholas II 'as a human being', but as a statesman, as the head of a big power, and as the ruler over the existence of millions of human beings and the destinies of many nations. Does Solzhenitsyn mean to invite us to a second look at Nicki's hobbies? At his exemplary behaviour as a father and husband? At his fondness of writing down in his diary the weather of the day? At his hopeless stupidity 'as a human being' *and* as head of state in his relations with charlatans like Rasputin and Prince V.P. Meshcherskii? If these biographical details have not been made public in the USSR, he should at least concede that in Western historiography, for which he has so much contempt, Nicholas's life has been amply documented in all genres of historical writing during the years since the brutal murder of the last tsar's family (which Pamiat publications now describe as a 'ritual murder', hinting thereby that it was perpetrated by Jews). Solzhenitsyn has often said that after the Soviets' falsifications of Russia's history, his greatest task is to rewrite her history and tell all things past as 'they really were'.[47] In this light, it is rather awkward that he takes such liberties with simple and elementary historical facts.

But if these White generals were refused an alliance by the West, says Solzhenitsyn, Lenin was not. Addressing an AFL-CIO audience on 3 June 1975, he explained that such an alliance is,

> at first glance, a strange and surprising one, but if you think about it, one which is well-founded and easy to understand: this is the alliance between our communist leaders and your capitalists. This alliance is not new. The very famous Armand Hammer, who flourishes here today, laid the basis for this when he made the first exploratory trip to Soviet Russia in Lenin's time, in the very first years of the Revolution. He was extremely successful in this reconnaissance mission and ever since then, for all these fifty years, we see continuous and steady support by the businessmen of the West for the Soviet communist leaders.[48]

The 'alliance between communists and capitalists' is a theme which Solzhenitsyn should handle with extreme caution, for words and slogans are not only what they say, but also what they mean in view of their past usage and indelible connotations. This would-be-alliance is only hinted at here, but is it surprising that in the minds of less sophisticated people in the Soviet Union it translates into the worn-out and alarming nationalist slogan of an 'alliance between Jews, plutocrats, and communists'?

The next instance of Russia's betrayal by the West happened in June 1941 when Hitler invaded the country. The aspirations of the peoples of the Soviet Union, he writes, were 'to cast off the scourge of communism and liberate themselves'. Lithuania, Latvia and Estonia, Byelorussia, the Western Ukraine and the first occupied Russian territories 'gave the Germans a jubilant welcome'. But the mood of the people was demonstrated most graphically of all by the Red Army:

> Before the eyes of the whole world it retreated along a 2,000-kilometre front, on foot, but every bit as fast as motorized units. Nothing could possibly be more convincing than the way these men, soldiers in their prime, voted with their feet. Numerical superiority was entirely with the Red Army, they had excellent artillery and a strong tank force, yet back they rolled, a rout without compare, unprecedented in the annals of Russian and world history. In the first few months some three million officers and men had fallen into enemy hands![49]

Thus, in Solzhenitsyn's rewriting of Russian history, it would appear that the 1941 rout of the Red Army was entirely due to its men's aversion for the communist regime, and (even after spending many years in the West) he has no use for works presenting more thorough and accurate explanations. For the question he wants to raise is, what did the West do under *these* circumstances (whether real or fictional)? Did it learn any lessons from *this* historic event? No, he says, it did not, and 'it has failed to grasp the point *to this very day*'.[50] If the West had been committed to the principle of universal liberty (including that of the oppressed peoples of the Soviet Union), here is what it should have done according to Solzhenitsyn. First, it should not have helped the war effort of the Soviet Union ('it should not have used Lend-lease to buy the murderous Stalin's help'). Second, it should not have helped Stalin to strengthen his dominion over the Soviet peoples. And third, it should have opened an independent front against Hitler and crushed him by its own efforts. 'In World War II against Hitler, instead of winning the conflict with its own forces, which would certainly have been sufficient', Western democracy relied on the Soviet Union which will prove to be a worse and more powerful enemy than nazi Germany,

> since Hitler had neither the resources nor the people, nor the ideas with broad appeal, nor such a large number of supporters in the West — a fifth column — as the Soviet Union possessed.[51]

According to Solzhenitsyn, the democratic countries had the strength to achieve the victory without Stalin's support, but they preferred to buy their liberty by sacrificing the peoples of the USSR and leaving them under communist rule: in so doing the West preserved its liberty 'at the expense of ours'.[52]

On this issue Solzhenitsyn's stand no longer pertains to the realm of history (however inaccurate), but of speculation and 'might have been'. Let us assume, for the sake of argument, that the West had followed Solzhenitsyn's policy: what might have been its consequences? For instance: how many years would the war have lasted beyond 1945 without the Red Army's participation? Two, three, four? How much deeper into the USSR would the Germans have penetrated without the dispatch of the West's war material to the Soviets (which Solzhenitsyn considers a blunder)? How much longer would the nazis have stayed in Eastern Europe? In Auschwitz, in Treblinka? Why does Solzhenitsyn think that the Russians' liberty (*if* it had been achieved by his strategy) has a greater value than the lives of millions of Jews, Poles and Czechs, of Serbian and Greek partisans, and of British, Canadian, Australian and American soldiers?

It would seem that Solzhenitsyn's scheme of how the second world war should have been conducted by the West has no greater moral weight than the one actually pursued. But it has, at least, a clear explanation: his belief that communism is the greatest evil, and that the West saved it instead of fighting it. In January 1982 he said: 'The danger for humanity in the twentieth century doesn't come from particular countries, nations or governments, but from the universal evil of communism'.[53] As a result, its extirpation from Russia and the USSR was even worth taking risks with immeasurable consequences — for Russia and for all mankind — in the struggle against nazism. Alexander Dallin rightly remarked:

> His angle of vision is a particular one; his own truth is that of the victim, a searing truth which pervades his outlook and his values, one which he passionately translates into his apocalyptic vision. The qualities which made him a hero and a prophet are not the same qualities that are needed for political analysis or for statesmanship.[54]

Neither, would I add, for historical writing.

The last stage of the story is summarized by Solzhenitsyn in one brief sentence:

> The selfish and ruinous mistake that the West committed during World War II has since been repeated time and time again, always in the fervent hope of avoiding a confrontation with communism.[55]

A confrontation with communism is what Solzhenitsyn thinks was appropriate during the second world war. His position, then, amounts to reproaching the West for not having waged war simultaneously against nazi Germany and Soviet Russia. Who knows for sure what might have been its outcome? He thinks also that an active confrontation with communism should have been the West's policy after the second world war. In the light of present events in the USSR and in Eastern Europe, one wonders whether such a strategy has been vindicated by the march of history. One may also wonder why Solzhenitsyn is advocating non-violent resistance to communism within the Soviet Union, while recommending an outright conflict with it in an age of nuclear weapons.

From these theoretical and historical premises stem Solzhenitsyn's views about Russia's future, and his programme for her national development. To start with the obvious, the features and institutions which he criticizes and disapproves of in the West are also those which have to be avoided in Russia. These are, above all, the developments that brought about the West's 'spiritual decadence' and lack of moral strength, namely, anthropocentrism and atheism in the realm of the spirit; liberalism, parliamentary democracy and the party system in the realm of politics.

The best political system for Russia is an authoritarian regime with moral foundations and the strength to restrain the divisive forces in society and in the nation; above all, a regime without political parties, as he clearly hinted in a rhetorical question: 'Are there no *extra-party* or strictly *non-party* paths to national development?'[56] Obviously, Solzhenitsyn holds that there are, and he rejects the multi-party democratic system as unsuitable for Russia. Apart from its harmful effects on the spiritual life of the nation, such a system would fail in Russia 'just as it failed after February 1917'. This 'historic precedent' supplies Solzhenitsyn with one more reason to prefer an authoritarian regime to a democratic one. All totalitarian regimes, in his view, have been generated by liberal democracies: this is what happened in Germany, Italy, and Kerensky's Russia. No authoritarian regime has ever led to a totalitarian one.[57]

Finally, spiritual considerations come to reinforce the conclusions arrived at from the 'lessons of history'. Authoritarianism, not democracy, is the shorter way to 'inner freedom', declared to be the goal of the 'historical development of the nation'. Since in democratic systems a man cannot live without harm to his spiritual essence, while in an authoritarian one he can, the latter should be preferred as being more favourable for 'inner freedom' and 'moral elevation'.

Solzhenitsyn's scheme for Russia's future political regime is the establishment of a 'law and order', benevolent, national and non-party authoritarian state. What would prevent it from the worst excesses of such regimes? Here is Solzhenitsyn's answer.

This regime would be characterized by the disestablishment of Marxism (which is anyway 'a dead dog', as Solzhenitsyn put it more than fifteen years ago, to the great shock and disbelief of many Western intelligentsias, who had to wait till 1989 to see it for themselves). It would secure freedom of political thought, religion, literature, speech, and would abolish all censorship. But is not the exercise of these liberties opposed to the essence of the authoritarian regime? It is not, says Solzhenitsyn, because two major factors would remove this formal contradiction. First, because this sort of social and political organization would be established after everybody had undergone a *moral* revolution. Second, because, as a result of this revolution, the government would use its powers with self-restraint; and the people would exercise freedom of thought with self-limitation.

Cynics may say that this scheme 'is too good to be true'; realists will see in it another utopian grand design. In any event, nobody could say — neither now nor in the future — that it was not known or clearly stated. We have been warned. The Russian people, too.

The same self-limitation also informs Solzhenitsyn's programme of economic development and foreign policy. He is against speedy and big-size industrialization which leads — under communism as well as under capitalism — to the exhaustion of the earth's limited resources. He advocates slow economic growth and moderate development by co-operatives, small-scale enterprises and advanced technology. He favours economic measures propitious to peasant society and the revitalization of agriculture. He criticizes the destruction of the Russian countryside by heavy machinery, large-scale projects, huge dams, dangerous nuclear plants and industrial effluent. As for the cities, he recommends eliminating excessive crowding, keeping down the number of cars, and refraining from adding more high-rise buildings. As an alternative to these harmful pursuits, Solzhenitsyn suggests the exploitation of the vast, almost virgin 'Russian North-East'.[58]

In line with this modest economic programme, Solzhenitsyn holds that military expenditure must be greatly reduced and directed only towards the needs of Russia's self-defence. Likewise, the country's foreign policy should be one of good neighbourhood and under-standing. All grandiose and wasteful foreign-aid programmes should be terminated, particularly the supply of arms to foreign countries, which entails enormous expenditure and a heavy burden on the national economy. In this light, Solzhenitsyn would appear as a mild isolationist, for he sees the main endeavour of the Russian people in moral elevation, and not in foreign policy and military adventures.

Indeed, with the economic programme he advocates, the Soviet Union (or Russia) could not remain a great power. In this sense, Solzhenitsyn implicitly raises an impertinent and sensible question rarely asked in Russia during the last 300 years, to wit: why should Russia be a great power in terms of military strength and international standing? In the past the people's sufferings and sacrifices have been justified by 'Russia's urge' to become, or to remain, a great power. But what justifies this urge? And whose 'urge' is it? The people's or the drive of megalomaniac tsars and of fundamentalist ideologists? Of course, the Russian people are not alone in this predicament, for they share it with other peoples on earth. But is that an incontrovertible curse on humanity and a *fatum* with no escape? In this respect Solzhenitsyn's doctrine of 'self-restraint' seems to be a more sensible way for the nations' life in the future, than the course of expansion, whether territorial or economic, or the policy of superpower bullying and mingling in the affairs of smaller nations.

In the light of this analysis, Solzhenitsyn's brand of nationalism appears to be oriented toward an internal regeneration of the Russian nation (conceived as a self-centred and closed entity) and the 'retrieval' of its culture and history. To that effect the best political regime is deemed to be an authoritarian one, based on 'law and order' and on religious values. His species of nationalism is devoid of visions of expansion and foreign aggression; nevertheless, it is nurtured by a strong resentment for the 'guilt' of the West (and of other nations) for the historic fate of Russia, and a deep contempt for its 'moral and political decay'. These are the main features of this specific species of nationalism.[59] But there is more to it, as Norman Podhoretz, a sympathetic author, put it:

> Solzhenitsyn's brand of Russian nationalism with its authoritarian coloration and its anti-semitic potential presents the most unpleasant and the most unsettling facet of a serious encounter with his life and his work.[60]

Less sympathetic critics have argued that Solzhenitsyn's nationalism (or 'neo-nationalism') 'is explicitly anti-democratic and . . . implicitly anti-semitic'.[61] However, with regard to his alleged anti-semitism (explicit, implicit or potential), opinions differ and the issue is still open.[62] It has been suggested that he is not 'particularly' an anti-semite, but since he does not like foreigners 'in general', then he does not like Jews either. This line of argumentation (which seems rather an excuse and an admission of the criticism) hints at a certain aspect in Solzhenitsyn's writings and utterances, namely the reference to features and behaviour of whole nations in a way which suggests a kind of sloppy thinking that informs all racialism and leads to a reflection on people in terms of essences and generalities. The nearest and most explicit example of this notion of 'a people's essence' is Solzhenitsyn's vision of the 'spirit of Russia' and of the Russians, their past and their future. The transfer of this notion to other peoples was, for Solzhenitsyn, easy and logical, and this explains his feeling — repeatedly stated — that on this particular issue he 'has not been understood' either by the West or by the new Soviet intelligentsia. In his view, he is just applying to other peoples a notion of 'specificity' and distinctiveness, which he uses for the Russians. Why, then, should that be wrong? The irony is that Solzhenitsyn does not understand indeed that *this*, precisely, is wrong. When asked by David Aikman what his response was to the accusations of anti-semitism (in connection with his depiction of Dmitrii Bogrov, Stolypin's assassin), Solzhenitsyn embarked on a tortuous definition of anti-semitism, instead of giving a clear and straight answer,[63] as if he did not understand what the accepted meaning of anti-semitism was.

How does Solzhenitsyn see himself within the context of modern Russian nationalism? As a rule he has defended his positions by denying that they are harmful or dangerous, both actually and potentially, and by pointing out that, in contrast to the denunciation of his views, similar positions of various contemporary thinkers in other nations are not criticized as 'nationalistic', but are greeted as constructive, 'progressive', and legitimate.[64] To those who consider him 'a symbol of extreme Russian nationalism', he retorts: 'I am not at all a "nationalist", but a patriot.'[65] This is also the stand now adopted by groups on the extreme right in Russia; as Bill Keller reported from Moscow:

> While much of the Soviet bloc seems to be lunging toward Western freedoms, the Russian nationalists — or Russian patriots, as they prefer to be called — deplore the chaos of Western-style democracy and the materialism of Western markets. They pine for a romanticized, patriarchal Russia.[66]

Is the similarity of this rejection of the 'nationalist' label both by Solzhenitsyn and by these 'patriots' entirely fortuitous? In any event, it appears that the whole Russian right has in common similar 'difficulties' with current concepts.[67] However, in spite of these 'difficulties' with terms, it does not hesitate to apply labels like 'racism' to others.[68]

Similarly, Solzhenitsyn can do nothing to prevent black-shirted thugs from opposing, like him, Western-style democracy and materialism. But the crux of the matter is that he has done nothing yet to dissociate himself from these movements. The blatant display of such similarities should have been for him a warning and an incentive to draw a clear demarcation line between him and them, lest he may appear to condone by omission their politics and activities. Public opinion in the West as well as in Russia is certainly curious to know his stand on this question.

What is the meaning of this nexus of views for Russia today? Standing against the West and the Soviet system, against socialism and capitalism, against gigantism and big industry, and cultivating attachment to the soil, the value of 'simple truths', and a nationalism which — although denied — is not devoid of potential dangers, Solzhenitsyn's blue-print for Russia's future is based on the concept of *another way* of national development. And the question is, what will be the shape and content of this 'other way'? For it seems that the latter is much clearer on its negative sides than on its mode of application in practical politics; and this is an additional feature which may also be breeding a potential danger — the danger of political and social programmes which state clearly what they stand against, but offer only generalities as to the alternatives they propose.

Solzhenitsyn's political message appears, then, as a complex and ambiguous one. By its function and content it is both political *and* ethical, for the two elements are almost inextricably intertwined in his thought. If applied to the reconstruction of Russia it may lead, on the one hand, to a sensible foreign policy based on restraint and respect for other peoples' aspirations, including the peoples of the USSR. But, on the other hand, it also contains features which may lead to, and breed, deplorable and even dangerous feelings and actions. These are, for instance, his religious fundamentalism; his impatience with particularistic political and social organizing; his deep-seated conviction that Russia was the victim of history as shaped by the West and by other nations. In his perspective Russia was not responsible for the many sufferings that befell her and other peoples between the first world war and 1945, through revolutions, Civil War, collectivization and Stalin's Great Terror; she was, rather, the greatest victim and casualty of these events. This psychological complex of 'others' guilt' is a powerful drive for a search for scapegoats, for demands that 'historical justice' be done, and for the myth of a widespread and insidious 'Russophobia' in the Soviet Union as well as in the West, a theory which Igor Shafarevich — whom Solzhenitsyn highly respects — has been forcefully arguing and spreading for nearly fifteen years with considerable success among ethnic Russians.[69] What kind of influence this theory may have is no longer a matter of speculation, for its main themes have been repeatedly voiced by rightist groups in Russia, and particularly by Pamiat, whose political orientation, proto-fascism, anti-semitism and use of violence need no elaboration here.

Solzhenitsyn's politics, his interpretation of the past and his vision of the future are based on a *historical myth*, or rather on a series of closely interconnected historical myths, each of which is both 'self-evident' and confirming of the others. This is a mighty amalgam which transforms 'history' into politics and makes it the 'locomotive' (to use this Marxian metaphor in a different context) of nationalism and chauvinism, as this has been the case (amply demonstrated) with all nationalisms during the last 150 years. Will Russians overcome this temptation when their way ahead is paved with still more political turmoil, moral tensions and economic austerity before the age of plenty and justice comes?

In this perspective, is it not the Russian moral leaders' greatest duty and responsibility — matters which Solzhenitsyn claims he understands well — to refrain, today more than ever, from giving encouragement and comfort to the forces, old and new, which threaten the freedom and dignity of man?

Notes

1. Thus, for instance, his seminal Nobel Lecture was published in *Novyi mir*, 7 (1989), 135–44.

2. John Bayley, 'God and the Devil', *New York Review of Books*, 21 December 1989, 11.

3. 'Solzhenitsyana' is growing constantly; for two inspired and solid works, see Michael Scammel, *Solzhenitsyn. A Biography* (New York and London 1984); Georges Nivat, *Soljénitsyne* (Paris 1980). After this article was sent to the editors, Solzhenitsyn wrote his appeal entitled *Kak nam obustroit' Rossiiu?* (How should we reconstruct Russia?). Published in *Komsomol'skaia pravda* and in *Literaturnaia gazeta* in September 1990, the appeal reiterated most of Solzhenitsyn's views voiced in the past, and cautioned again, *inter alia*, against excessive Western influence, decrying 'degraded pop, mass culture [and] vulgar fashions'. The main new ideas consisted in that Solzhenitsyn dropped his call to Russians to concentrate on the north-east of the

country, and now advocated dismantling the Soviet Empire, leaving Central Asia, and creating a federation of three Slavic Republics: Russia, the Ukraine and Byelorussia. These new points do not in the least affect the main themes and treatment of the present article. On this essay of Solzhenitsyn's, see David Remnick, 'Native Son', *The New York Review of Books*, 38, 4 (14 February 1991), 6–10.

4. See Paul Gray, 'Russia's Prophet in Exile', *Time*, 24 July 1989. The greatest part of Solzhenitsyn's answers in the interview conducted by David Aikman is a repetition of opinions elaborated in detail in the past. He explicitly endorses the ideas of his Harvard speech (*A World Split Apart*), his historiosophic conception regarding 'the decline of the moral life of the West during the last 300 years' (p. 60), and his views on the cataclysmic role of the first world war and the 1917 Revolutions, on Lenin, on the place of Christian faith in society, on nationalism and on anti-semitism. All these topics are discussed below.

5. A. Solzhenitsyn, *A World Split Apart* (New York and London 1978), 47; the same idea was developed also in his *Letter to the Soviet Leaders* (New York 1975), 26–31.

6. Ibid., 49.

7. Ibid., 49.

8. Ibid., 53–5; *The Listener*, 4 March 1976, 261.

9. *Vestnik russkogo khristianskogo dvizheniia*, 111 (1974), 67.

10. Solzhenitsyn, *A World Split Apart*, 57.

11. A. Solzhenitsyn, 'Rech' pri poluchenii premii 'Zolotoe klishe' soiuza italianskikh zhurnalistov', *Publitsistika. Stat'i i rechi* (Paris 1981), 176.

12. Solzhenitsyn has elaborated on this theme more than once, and most recently in the *Time* magazine interview with David Aikman, 24 July 1989, 57.

13. A. Solzhenitsyn, *Warning to the West* (New York 1978), 128.

14. See Jacob L. Talmon, *The Myth of the Nation and the Vision of Revolution: The Origins of Ideological Polarization in the 20th Century* (London 1981).

15. *Vestnik*, 111, 69.

16. A. Solzhenitsyn, 'Misconceptions about Russia are a Threat to America', *Foreign Affairs* (Spring 1980), 827–8.

17. Ibid., 829.

18. Ibid.

19. Ibid.; italics in original.

20. A. Solzhenitsyn, 'As Breathing and Consciousness Return', in A. Solzhenitsyn et al., *From Under the Rubble* (Chicago 1981), 19; italics in original. This article was written as a rebuke to Andrei Sakharov's treatise, *Reflections on Progress, Peaceful Coexistence and Intellectual Freedom* (New York 1968).

21. A. Solzhenitsyn, 'Nobel Lecture', in John B. Dunlop, Richard Haugh and Alexis Klimoff (eds), *Aleksandr Solzhenitsyn. Critical Essays and Documentary Materials* (New York and London 1975), 568.

22. Ibid.; italics in original.

23. Ibid.

24. Solzhenitsyn, 'As Breathing and Consciousness Return', 25.

25. Ibid., 22.

26. *Russkaia mysl'* (Paris), 24 April 1975, 3.

27. The *Letter* was sent to the Soviet government in 1973 and first published in 1974 in the West. It has been said that either this idea is utopian, or that in fact Solzhenitsyn is accepting the Soviet regime. Both criticisms are mistaken and unimportant for this discussion.

28. Konstantin S. Aksakov, 'On the Internal State of Russia', in Marc Raeff (ed.), *Russian Intellectual History. An Anthology* (New York 1966), 248.

29. Note that in this pattern of thought, while Western institutions are unsuitable for Russia, the 'Russian' path of salvation applies to all nations.

30. Solzhenitsyn, 'As Breathing and Consciousness Return', 24.

31. On this issue, see Donald R. Kelley, *The Solzhenitsyn–Sakharov Dialogue: Politics, Society, and the Future* (Westport, CT and London 1982); and also 'Conversation with Solzhenitsyn', *Encounter* (March 1975), 67–72, an interview with Janis Sapiets originally broadcast on the BBC Russian service.

32. *New York Times*, 22 January 1974. On the ambiguity of Solzhenitsyn's thought on the question of violence and non-violence, see Nivat, *Soljénitsyne*, 36, 104–5.

33. Solzhenitsyn explicitly disapproves of passive resistance, and insists that 'moral revolution' is not such a type of resistance. John B. Dunlop explains that the 'passiveness' of this revolution lies only, in Solzhenitsyn's words, in the fact that 'you don't have to take a machine-gun in your hands, you don't have to shoot and kill'. The 'ideological disobedience' Solzhenitsyn advocates has nothing in common with the 'insane boldness of Indian-style civil disobedience' where one goes out and sits on roadways or railway tracks; John B. Dunlop, 'Solzhenitsyn in Exile', *Survey*, 21, 3 (Summer 1975), 137.

34. Solzhenitsyn, 'Repentance and Self-Limitation in the Life of Nations', in *From Under the Rubble*, 108ff.

35. Solzhenitsyn, *Warning*, 136.

36. Solzhenitsyn, 'Misconceptions', 805.

37. 'Alexander Solzhenitsyn on the Russian Revolutions', *The Listener*, 15 February 1979, 240.

38. A. Solzhenitsyn, 'Skoro vsë uvidim bez televizora', *Russkaia mysl'*, no. 3412, 13 May 1982, 3.

39. Solzhenitsyn, 'Repentance and Self-Limitation', 126–7; see also, 'Alexander Solzhenitsyn on the Russian Revolutions', 240–1.

40. Interview with David Aikman, *Time*, 24 July 1989, 58.

41. A. Solzhenitsyn, 'The Courage to See', *Foreign Affairs* (Autumn 1980), 202.

42. Solzhenitsyn, *Warning*, 128.

43. François Furet and Mona Ozouf (eds), *A Critical Dictionary of the French Revolution* (Cambridge, MA 1989); quoted by Gwynne Lewis, 'New Views of Change', *Times Literary Supplement*, 26 January–1 February 1990, 93.

44. Quoted by Mikhail S. Bernstam, 'Letters from Readers', *Commentary* (June 1985), 12.

45. Solzhenitsyn, *Warning*, 131.

46. *Time*, 24 July 1989, 60.

47. See 'Alexander Solzhenitsyn on the Russian Revolutions', 240–1; and 'Solzhenitsyn: The Way Ahead', *The Listener*, 22 February 1979, 270–2.

48. Ibid., 10–11.

49. Solzhenitsyn, 'Misconceptions', 817.

50. Ibid.; Solzhenitsyn's italics.

51. Solzhenitsyn, *A World Split Apart*, 43.

52. Solzhenitsyn, 'Misconceptions', 817–18.

53. A. Solzhenitsyn, 'Glavnyi urok', *Russkaia mysl'*, no. 3396, 21 January 1982, 1.

54. Alexander Dallin, '[Letter] to the Editor', *Foreign Affairs* (Autumn 1980), 192.

55. Ibid., 819.

56. Solzhenitsyn, 'As Breathing and Consciousness Return', 19; italics in original.

57. Solzhenitsyn, 'Misconceptions', 828.

58. Solzhenitsyn, *Letter*, 32; italics in original.

59. For a cogent overview of recent Russian nationalism, see John B. Dunlop, *The Faces of Contemporary Russian Nationalism* (Princeton, NJ 1983).

60. Norman Podhoretz, 'The Terrible Question of Aleksandr Solzhenitsyn', *Commentary* (February 1985), 24.

61. Ibid. See also 'Solzhenitsyn and Russian Nationalism. An Interview with Andrei Sinyavsky', *New York Review of Books*, 22 November 1979, 3–6; the interview was conducted by Olga Carlisle.

62. This issue is addressed by Siniavsky in the interview quoted above, and in greater detail by Edith Rogovin Frankel, 'Russians, Jews and Solzhenitsyn', *Soviet Jewish Affairs*, 5, 2 (1975), 48–68; see also Mikhail Agursky, 'Syndrome of Hatred', *Jerusalem Post*, 20 December 1979, 8. The question of whether Solzhenitsyn is an anti-semite or not was heatedly debated in the 'Letters from Readers' on the pages of *Commentary* (June 1985, 4–16) following N. Podhoretz's article cited above.

63. Interview in *Time* magazine, 24 July 1989, 58.

64. The best example of this line of argument is to be found in his debate with several American historians, following the publication of his article 'Misconceptions about Russia are a Threat to America', 797–834. For the answer to his critics, see A. Solzhenitsyn, 'The Courage to See', 196–210.

65. Letter of A. Solzhenitsyn to President Ronald Reagan, 3 May 1982, *Russkaia mysl'*, no. 3413, 20 May 1982, 2. Exactly the same answer was given to David Aikman in the *Time* magazine interview, 24 July 1989, 60.

66. Bill Keller, 'Russian Nationalists. Yearning for an Iron Hand', *New York Times Magazine*, 28 January 1990, 19. He writes also: 'The Russian patriots consider themselves not the perpetrators of communism, but its most punished victims. . . . Self-pity is the life-juice of Russian patriotism. In their self-pity, the Russian nationalists look for culprits and they usually find the scapegoats of history: the Jews' (ibid., 20, 48).

67. Thus, for example, when interviewed by *Newsweek*'s Carroll Bogert in Moscow, Igor Shafarevich answered the question 'Are you an anti-semite?' as follows: 'I used to be accused of anti-Sovietism, now it's anti-semitism. I don't really understand either term. They're vague and propagandistic.' He says also: ' "Pogrom" is a kind of slogan of the Jewish national movement' ('A Slander Against Russians', *Newsweek*, 12 February 1990, 52). All of a sudden, terms like nationalism, anti-semitism, and pogrom become 'vague'. One would expect that Shafarevich, author of the theory of 'Russophobia' and 'anti-Russianism' (about which more will be said below), should know better about topics like 'anti-semitism', or else, as he says about others, his theory is just 'propaganda'.

68. Thus, for instance, elaborating on Solzhenitsyn's criticism of Richard Pipes's book *Russia Under the Old Regime* (London 1974), Irina Ilovaiskaia, Solzhenitsyn's former associate and editor of the émigré weekly *Russkaia mysl'*, charged Pipes's views on Russia's history as being 'a form of racism'. See Irina Ilovaiskaia, 'Rossiia v otritsatel'no-mesticheskom osveshchenii', *Vestnik russkogo khristianskogo dvizheniia* 126 (1978), 193–206.

69. In 1989, Shafarevich published in the monthly magazine of the Russian writers' Union, *Nash sovremennik*, a two-part serialized manifesto entitled

'Russophobia' in which he accused the Jews of being responsible for the present outburst of anti-Russian feelings. See also Igor Shafarevich, 'Socialism in Our Past and Future', *From Under the Rubble*, 26–66; and *The Socialist Phenomenon* (New York 1980), with a foreword by A. Solzhenitsyn. For one of Solzhenitsyn's utterances on Russophobia, see 'Repentance and Self-Limitation', 125–6.

Michael Confino
is Samuel Rubin Professor of Russian and
East European History and Civilization at
Tel Aviv University. His most recent book is
*Société et mentalités collectives en Russie sous
l'Ancien Régime* (Paris 1991). He is currently
working on two book-length studies: *Estates
and Social Classes in Imperial Russia* and
*Historians and Historical Consciousness in
Contemporary Culture and Society.*

Shlomo Avineri

Marxism and Nationalism

One of Hannah Arendt's more surprising observations in *Origins of Totalitarianism* is her statement that 'modern anti-semitism grew in proportion as traditional nationalism declined'.[1] Rather than identify anti-semitism, and racism in general, as the most extreme and pernicious excrescence of nationalism, Arendt chose to see anti-semitism as something extraneous to nationalism, a reaction to its failure. Elsewhere in her book she argues that each class in European society became infested with anti-semitism when it came into conflict with the state, 'because the only group which seemed to represent the state were the Jews'.[2]

This surely is an extraordinary view. This is not the place to discuss in detail the question how far Arendt's overall thesis about the role of Jews in European economic life and their power in the modern state is itself an internalization, by a Jewish thinker, of anti-semitic images and theories; nor can such an affinity of views be merely ascribed to her close relationship with Heidegger. On a much more fundamental level, Arendt would be the first to concede that sometimes victims of totalitarian ideologies adopt — albeit unknown to themselves — images, stereotypes and identities projected onto them by their persecutors. In *Eichman in Jerusalem*, Arendt argued forcefully along these lines, perhaps pushing the argument to its extreme; her analysis of modern Jewish life — and the causes of anti-semitism — may be another instance, sophisticated, scholarly and urbane as it is, of such a brutalization of the victim.

Be this as it may, Arendt's apparently idiosyncratic view of the relationship between the rise of anti-semitism and the decline of nationalism is linked to her general understanding of the phenomenon of nationalism, and it is directly connected with our main topic, viz. the Marxian attitude to nationalism. For in the course of her

study of totalitarianism, Arendt maintains that 'the body politic of
the nation-state came into existence when no single group was any
longer in a position to wield exclusive political power'.[3]

There are obvious echoes here of Marx, but they are complex and
not explicitly stated. In his 'Eighteenth of Brumaire of Louis
Bonaparte', Marx postulated a sophisticated analysis of the class
relations that had given rise to Louis Napoleon and his curious blend
of conservatism and radicalism. In certain moments in history, Marx
argues, class relations are so finely balanced that no single class can
attain exclusive political power: every class is strong enough to
prevent any other class from controlling political power, but no class
is so strong as to arrogate to itself exclusive control over the state. In
such a situation of balance, a person like Louis Bonaparte, being all
things to all people, symbolizing both a historical myth and a radical
message, can appeal to various and conflicting class interests and thus
emerge 'as the executive power which has made itself an independent
power'.[4] This quasi-autonomy from social and economic class
structure is to Marx the secret of the unique nature of the
'bastardized' form of government epitomized by Napoleon III.

What to Marx was a unique exception, unsettling and certainly not
fitting into the general pattern of the Marxian thesis about the
relation between economic infrastructure and political superstructure, is made by Arendt into a general explanatory model for the
rise of the modern nation-state. It points to both the creative potential
of Marx's essay on Louis Napoleon (certainly one of the more
nuanced and differentiated pieces of social and political analysis ever
to have been written by him): it also suggests the dilemmas within
Marx's own attitude to questions relating to the emergence of the
modern state — and of modern nationalism.

Of all the historical phenomena discussed by Marx, his treatment of
nationalism, nationalist movements and the emergence of the nation-
state is the least satisfactory. It also left a problematic heritage to the
socialist movement, with a veritable 'black hole' where a confrontation with one of the most potent social and political forces of the
nineteenth and twentieth centuries should have been.

Marx never discussed nationalism in any systematic way, and what
we have are a number of disjointed statements, dealing with the issue
sometimes on a very general level, sometimes in response to specific
historical events on which he had commented in newspaper articles.

A careful study of these scattered references will show that there are two distinct analyses of nationalism in Marx, one pre- and one post-1848. I call pre-1848 'the pre-modern paradigm', the post-1848 'the bourgeois paradigm'.

The *locus classicus* for the 'pre-modern paradigm' (paradigm I) is to be found in *The Communist Manifesto*, where the universalizing power of the capitalist market is sketched by Marx in memorable and pithy language. This universalizing thrust, according to Marx, does away with everything that is particular, be it regional or national. The capitalist mode of production is to Marx the first to have

> given a cosmopolitan character to production and consumption . . . .To the great chagrin of reactionists, it has drawn from under the feet of industry the national ground on which it stood. All old-established national industries have been destroyed or are daily being destroyed. They are dislodged by new industries, whose introduction becomes a life and death question to all civilized nations, by industries that no longer work up indigenous raw material, but raw material drawn from the remotest zones; industries whose products are consumed not only at home but in every quarter of the globe. In place of the old wants, satisfied by the productions of the country, we find new wants, requiring for their satisfaction the products of distant lands and climes. In place of the local and national seclusion and self-sufficiency, we have intercourse in every direction, universal interdependence of nations. And as in the material, so also in the intellectual production. The intellectual creations of individual nations become common property. National one-sidedness and narrow-mindedness become more and more impossible, and from the numerous national and local literatures there arises a world literature . . . [5]

And furthermore:

> National differences and antagonisms between peoples are daily more and more vanishing, owing to the development of the bourgeoisie, to freedom of commerce, to the world market, to uniformity in the mode of production and in the conditions of life corresponding to them.[6]

Hence Marx's famous dictum that 'the workingmen have no country' and his postulate that in the future 'the supremacy of the proletariat will make [these differences between the nations] vanish still further'.[7]

National differences thus are likened in this paradigm to other *pre-modern* traits, like local customs and dress: they are all due to disappear before the universalizing onslaught of the bourgeoisie and be even more perfectly integrated into a world-culture by the proletarian revolution.

It was this aspect of paradigm I of Marx's thoughts on nationalism which came to characterize the cosmopolitan and internationalist heritage of the socialist movement. Yet Marx himself subtly changed his views — though without ever admitting that he had done so. The experience of the revolutions of 1848/9, during which nationalism appeared as a major force for the first time on a a massive scale, occasionally proving to be much stronger than class interests, was followed very closely by Marx as editor of the *Neue Rheinische Zeitung*, and his journalistic writing of this period abounds with many insights into the emergence of, and clashes between, various national movements — in Germany and Italy, in Poland and Bohemia, in Hungary and Croatia. Obviously such a powerful force evidently changing and redrawing the map of Europe, reordering borders and state structures, could no longer be subsumed under the pre-modern paradigm as a mere appendix of pre-modern economic formations, about to be swept into the dustbin of history by the universalizing forces of market capitalism.

What Marx developed after 1848/9, and mainly in response to the developments leading towards the unification of Germany and Italy, was paradigm II — the explanation of nationalism as a *modern* superstructural expression of the bourgeois need for larger markets and territorial consolidation. In this paradigm, far from being an exotic and romantic — or romanticized — relic of the pre-industrial age, nationalism is (to use Eric Hobsbawm's later phrase) a 'building block' of capitalism.

According to this paradigm, capitalism needs large economic entities: it cannot function and develop properly when Germany, for example, is divided into thirty-seven states, mini-states and city-states, each with its own laws, customs arrangements, political structures and currency. The unification of Germany — and of Italy — is no longer just a dream of the romantics, yearning for elusive and imaginary Teutonic forests or Roman glory: it is in the direct economic interest of the bourgeoisie, and nationalist ideologies are nothing other than superstructural strategies of legitimation for these economic interests. The *Zollverein* — the mainly north German customs union which preceded the political unification of Germany under Bismarck — is the model for the emergence of modern nation-states. Nationalism is no longer pre-modern for Marx — it is the epitome of the processes of capitalist development and industrialization.

Because of this, Marx now supported, for instrumentalist but not immanent reasons, the unification of Germany and Italy: whatever helped develop capitalism was, of course, ultimately hastening its demise. Furthermore, only in large, unified entities could the proletariat develop an adequate class consciousness and not be sidetracked into secondary efforts. Marx's support for Prussia in the 1870–1 Franco-Prussian War, for example, was argued in terms of the instrumentality of this war toward Germany's unification and as an important step in the development of industrialization, capitalism and the ensuing strengthening of the working class. As one could imagine, such a view, overlooking the immediate causes of the war, did not always sit well with others within the radical movement, with its emphasis on ethical considerations and opposition to the kind of regime epitomized by Bismarck. Yet Marx never wavered from this instrumentalist approach, eschewing merely 'moral' approaches.

It was, therefore, wholly consistent with the consequences of paradigm II that Marx opposed the various national movements in Central and Eastern Europe of those people who tried to secede from the Austro-Hungarian Empire or achieve autonomy within it — mainly the Czechs and the Croatians. They, and other Slavonic groups, by trying to 'Balkanize' the Habsburg Empire were 'reactionary' in the sense that should they succeed, industrialization and economic development in Central and Eastern Europe would be slowed down, and hence the eventual victory of the proletariat would be hampered. Czechs, Croatians and Serbs should not set up separate states but be integrated into the one, larger market of Germany/Austria. Similarly, Marx argued on another occasion, Denmark should ultimately be absorbed by Germany — and Mexico by the more developed, and capitalist, United States. What hastens capitalist development is 'progressive', what hinders it is 'reactionary', and should be opposed.[8] Less developed areas and populations should be integrated into the more developed ones, and thus the Czechs, who had no bourgeoisie, would eventually be able to develop an industrial society only in connection with the German-Austrians. Nowhere in Marx's writings is there any mention of a right to self-determination or support for 'national liberation' as such.

This appears as a straightforward view, which, while wholly instrumental, and devoid of any substantive assessment of nationalism, is consistent with Marx's general view about the relations of 'developed' to 'non-developed' societies.[9]

Yet a curious inconsistency becomes apparent. Given the theoretical argument in favour of larger economic entities and the absorption of less-developed regions within the larger, more developed ones, one would have expected Marx to support the integration of the Polish lands into the three Empires (German, Austrian and Russian) that had divided the historical Polish Commonwealth among them. If Marx had been consistent, the fate of the Poles should have been no different from that of the Czechs, Slovenes and Croatians. After all, the Poles had a highly archaic, feudal social structure, there was no ethnic Polish bourgeoisie, commerce was in the hands of Jews and Germans. Yet throughout his life, Marx strongly supported Polish independence and the restoration of Polish political integrity.

It could be argued that Polish independence was so central a platform of the European left in the nineteenth century that it would have been extremely difficult, if not politically impossible, for Marx to dissociate himself from it, regardless of whatever theoretical grounds he might have had that militated against it. But it appears that other considerations were at work — considerations that were related to an overall revolutionary strategy which eventually overruled Marx's own theoretical considerations.

Ever since the failure of the 1848/9 revolutions, Marx had become obsessed with the fear that a tsarist Russian military intervention might frustrate any gains achieved by a revolutionary movement in Western and Central Europe. This was not an imaginary or groundless fear: both in 1812–14 and 1848–9, Russian military forces secured the victory of reactionary and conservative regimes in Europe — first against Napoleon and the heritage of the French Revolution, later against liberal uprisings in Vienna, Prague and Budapest. In both instances, the reactionary regimes in Europe were able to maintain or regain their hold on their people by calling on the Russians and thus tipping the balance of forces. In the 1850s, this fear of a Russian intervention became one of Marx's central concerns — and it was for this reason that he supported the independence of Poland. The very re-emergence of an independent Poland would be a severe setback to Russia, and — this was central to Marx's thinking — it would set up a buffer state between a weakened Russia and the West, thus making Russian counter-revolutionary intervention more difficult and less likely. It was for similar reasons of containing Russia that Marx in the 1860s and 1870s supported the British policy of propping up the Ottoman Empire: the emergence of Slavonic nation-states in the Balkans would greatly strengthen Russia, and the dissolution of the Ottoman Empire would also bring Russia to Constantinople and the shores of the Bosphorus. This would greatly enhance Russia's power to intervene and frustrate revolutionary developments in Europe. In this context Marx saw pan-Slavism as a mere Russian imperial device, and hence opposed Czech and Serbian nationalism also because of their connection with pan-Slav ideologies.

These views made Marx into a strange ally of British conservative politicians who were basing their policies on the 'Eastern Question' in an attempt to curb Russian influence in the Levant. This position also moved Marx in the wake of the initial Russian defeats in the Russo-Turkish war of 1877/8 to postulate the possibility of a revolutionary situation in Russia and the eventual dissolution of the tsarist Empire, thus liberating the European revolutionary movement from the nightmare of another Russian counter-revolutionary military intervention.

The complexities of Marx's attitude to the question of nationalism left the socialist movement an ambiguous heritage, in so far as it relied upon Marx as a guide to its policies towards the national question. The fact that there were two paradigms in Marx's own thinking, and that paradigm II had been mitigated and greatly circumscribed by strategic considerations, did not make it easier to come up with a coherent theory of nationalism.The intensification of the development of nationalist movements towards the end of the nineteenth century also made the articulation of a socialist policy towards these phenomena an exercise in frustration and sometimes incoherence.[10]

By and large, however, the instrumentalist approach as expressed in the 'bourgeois paradigm' (paradigm II) remained dominant. It was to be summed up in perhaps the most succinct way by Trotsky, who maintained that 'the national state is erected as the most convenient, profitable and normal arena for the play of capitalist relations'.[11]

Yet in the process of the political struggles of the various socialist movements, especially in Eastern Europe, and the emergence, through civil war and outside intervention, of the Soviet state, this general theory and its proponents found themselves facing a recalcitrant political reality which pushed them in opposite directions. The conditions of the multi-ethnic tsarist Empire introduced into Lenin's thought and revolutionary strategy the notion that all the nations of the old Empire — come the revolution — would have the right to self-determination and secession. Such a view, which still failed to define what was a nation, and basically had no grounding in Marx's own thought, proved extremely difficult to maintain, given the vicissitudes of the political realities of the Bolshevik revolution — as the history of the Ukraine and the Transcaucasian Republics would show in the years 1917–23.

Yet even before this, Lenin had to clarify his position on the national question within the socialist movement, and this came to a head in relation to such disparate issues as the place of the Jewish and Polish socialist parties within the structure of the overall Russian socialist movement. The details of Lenin's controversy with the Jewish Socialist *Bund*, and to what degree it determined later Soviet attitudes to the Jewish question and to Zionism, do not need to detain us here.[12] Suffice it to say that some of the more convoluted arguments used by Lenin and his followers, in combining highly theoretical constructs with crude political necessity, amply show how inadequate the legacy Marx left his followers on the national issue really was.[13]

The same could be seen in the controversy between Lenin and Rosa Luxemburg on the question of Polish independence. Lenin advocated the establishment of an independent Poland and advised Polish socialists to fight for the victory of the working class within a future independent Polish state; to him, the Poles, like the Finns and the Baltic nations, had the right to secede from Russia (as well as, in their case, from the German and Austrian Empires). Rosa Luxemburg and her party (with the carefully chosen name of the Social Democratic Party of the Kingdom of Poland and Lithuania, clearly excluding the Polish lands under German and Austrian rule) opposed Polish independence. They argued — following the bourgeois Marxian paradigm — that it was in the interest of capitalist, and hence proletarian, development not to break up large economic entities, and that the underdeveloped structure of Polish society would hinder economic and social development if Poland became independent. The paradox was that while the Luxemburgian conclusion about Poland was the exact opposite of that of Marx (who, as we recalled, saw an independent Poland as a corner-stone of his revolutionary strategy), its argument in favour of large economic entities could be presented as being truly within the Marxian theoretical construct of paradigm II. To Luxemburg, nationalism was nothing more than a 'false consciousness' exploiting genuine feelings of solidarity based on a common culture cynically manipulated by bourgeois demagogues.[14] However, the main Polish socialist party (PPS) took a different path — in a way following the Leninist approach, but from different (i.e. Polish national) motivations. That the PPS leader, Josef Pilsudky, eventually left his own party on the issue of nationalism and later, as commander of the Polish army, confronted the Red Army at the gates of Warsaw, only proves once more how extremely malleable the Marxian attitudes to nationalism really were. As a guideline to politics, and especially in the highly charged and volatile atmosphere of a revolutionary situation, they were of hardly any use.

Yet Lenin's main contribution to the Marxian theory of nationalism and its adaptation to twentieth-century conditions appears in his theory of imperialism. It is here that he widens the scope of the Marxian paradigm II and argues that nationalism appears not only with the emergence of capitalism, but is intensified in the era of imperialist expansion to universal dimensions. In this process, however, nationalism dialectically becomes an anti-capitalist force, as the national movements in the non-European colonies emerge as a response to the exploitation of the colonial people by the European capitalist powers. On the other hand, a 'chauvinistic' form of nationalism appears within the imperialist societies themselves, in response to these national liberation movements.[15]

While this is obviously an elaboration of the basic ideas underlying the Marxian paradigm II, it gives rise to a new ambivalence about the political classification of national movements. While in Marx the national movements calling for political unification of large units (Germany, Italy) were called 'progressive', whereas the nationalism of small nations (Czechoslovakia) was 'reactionary', Lenin now called Asian and African nationalism 'progressive', while European nationalism came to be seen as 'reactionary'. While this distinction may have been politically helpful despite the strange bedfellows with which it occasionally saddled the communists (like the communist–Islamic alliance in Palestine, when in the 1930s the Soviets supported the Mufti of Jerusalem), it is intellectually problematic from the Marxist class analysis point of view: most European socialist movements did not dissociate themselves, until the second world war, from the imperialist nationalism of their countries, and in the case of the French Communist Party it continued to support French rule in Algeria well into the 1950s.

This allows one author of a recent attempt to vindicate the Leninist position to maintain that the strength of Lenin's views was due to his 'leaving open the question of the nature and role of nationalism and its relationship with socialism'.[16] The intent of this observation is obviously laudatory: it is, however, an admission of Lenin's failure to develop a general theory of nationalism and its relationship to a Marxist socialist analysis.

The past decade has seen some serious attempts, within Marxist circles, to restate and reformulate what became known as the Marxist-Leninist theory of nationalism. These attempts were part of a wider effort to restructure Marxism and salvage some of its theoretical constructs and radical emancipatory vision from the detritus of Soviet reality. The inadequacies of the Marxian paradigm with regard to nationalism were discussed with a candour and open-mindedness rare in previous discussions of the subject within the socialist and communist movement.

Thus we find a number of Marxist theoreticians, affiliated with different groups of the New Left, admitting for the first time that Marx — and Marxism — never *had* a theory of nationalism, or that whatever theory of nationalism Marxism did develop had been inadequate and utterly wrong. Thus John Ehrenreich, in two different articles, maintains that, 'It is time to admit that as Marxists we simply have no understanding of the phenomenon [of nationalism].'[17] Calling his studies 'a work of destruction',[18] Ehrenreich does not offer an alternative theory, but hopes to stir up a debate and shock orthodox Marxists out of their complacent reiterations of pious platitudes about 'proletarian internationalism'. Similarly, Regis Debray, in a long interview in which he tries to trace his disillusionment with Marxism, points out that the inadequacy of Marxist theory with regard to nationalism was the first issue which raised doubts in his mind about Marxism in general.[19]

Nicos Poulantzas, apparently totally despairing of salvaging any Marxian component for a theory of nationalism, reverts to what appear as echoes of Levi-Strauss — but are ultimately a mere tautology — when he says that 'territory and tradition are inscribed in the underlying conceptual matrix of space and time', and postulates a total autonomy of the state — via nationalism — from class structures.[20]

Horace Davis, on the other hand, tries in his studies to retain some of Lenin's theses by arguing that while in general national liberation movements are 'emancipatory', there are cases in which a national struggle does not possess class components (as in some 'classless tribal societies in Africa'), while in others a national struggle becomes the struggle of all classes (as in the case of Castro).[21] While admitting that Lenin's analysis of the class basis of nationalism is 'in need of reformulation', the pattern emerging from Davis's serious and detailed study is so fraught with reservations and exceptions as to verge on the incoherent. This leads another Marxist scholar, John

Blaut, to argue that if one tries to tinker with the Leninist model, the consequences leave Marxism with no adequate guidelines whatsoever for political action.[22]

A versatile new chord was struck in the late 1970s and early 1980s by Marxist writers who were labouring under the impact of development in Northern Ireland — and to a lesser degree with the emergence of nationalist tendencies in Wales and Scotland (as well as in Quebec), which were associated with left-wing ideologies. Jenkins and Minnerup argue in their book that while Marxism has 'converted progressives of all shades into the cosmopolitan dream of One World as the antidote to the nationalist fever', it can no longer avoid admitting the autonomous power of nationalism in terms of class structure, nor the emancipatory power of nationalism as such, not as a mere adjunct of the class struggle:

> Far from being the dark source of most modern evil, the nation state actually represents the pinnacle of human development in the field of political emancipation.
>
> The common view that the nation state is an anachronism which has been long outstripped by the development of productive forces . . . [is shared] by bourgeois liberalism and Marxist socialism.[23]

Such iconoclastic revisionism is shared by Tom Nairn, perhaps the most radical of the thinkers on nationalism among the New Left. In a number of publications he presents a complex — and perhaps confusing — picture of how to fit nationalism into Marxism. On the one hand, he calls nationalism 'the pathology of modern development' and in a Marxist orthodox fashion sees it as traceable to economic factors — but in a novel way: nationalism is the outcome of the *uneven* development of capitalism (hence the 'pathology'). Its sources are transnational in the sense that the upper classes of less-developed societies, who are most directly hit by the unevenness of economic developments, succeed in sweeping with them the other classes of colonial societies into the national liberation movements. On the other hand, *all* nationalisms are reduced to this model, and therefore fascism as well as Castroism belong to the same category and are merely two facets, albeit with clearly distinguishable consequences, of the same 'inherent unity', to be judged, however, differently from the revolutionary point of view. For a Marxist scholar thus to claim that 'fascism is the archetype of nationalism'[24] and yet support some forms of nationalism suggests an admission that nationalism has no fixed class matrix, and therefore Nairn still has to agree that the theory of nationalism is 'Marxism's greatly historical failure'.[25] All this is then used as a pedestal for an edifice which plays around with the idea of advocating the break-up of Britain and the possible emergence of independent nation-states on its Celtic fringe as being in tune with such a reading of Marxism.

As one can imagine, such a complete breakdown of the Marxian paradigm evoked a response, and the most sophisticated attempt at restating, though in a nuanced way, the classical Marxian position came from Eric Hobsbawm. With his erudition and combination of historical analysis and theoretical sophistication, Hobsbawm set out to demolish what he considered the revisionist outpouring of sheer nonsense. This was done with verve, wit and obvious impatience, and while sometimes caricaturing his opponents' views, he pointed out that when speaking within the Marxian tradition, one cannot go beyond certain conceptual boundaries. Hobsbawm argued that the revisionists — and especially Nairn — had totally misunderstood the historical function of nationalism. Yet he had to admit that Marxism itself does not and should not offer overall theoretical political answers to the phenomenon of nationalism. It is worthwhile to quote him at some length:

> Marxists . . . have to come to terms with the *political fact* of nationalism, and to define their attitudes towards its specific manifestations. Ever since Marx, this has for the most part and *necessarily*, been a matter not of theoretical principle (except for the Luxemburgian minority which tends to suspect nations *en bloc*) but of *pragmatic* judgement in changing circumstances. In principle, Marxists are neither for nor against independent statehood for any nation.[26]

In the nineteenth century, Hobsbawm argued, the emergence of nationalism in Europe created the 'building blocks' of capitalism — though even in Europe there had been cases of 'Ruritanian' nationalism. In the twentieth century, things changed. First of all, the further development of capitalism — which needed in its *first* stage national states — now tended towards multinational developments, and the salience of nation-states decreased. The disintegration of the European empires had now totally shattered the link between anti-imperialism and national liberation movements, and opposition to neo-colonialism was not a struggle for self-determination, which had already been achieved through decolonialization.

In this changed world, Hobsbawm continued, the nationalist movements — like those defended and advocated by Nairn — were very different from those of the nineteenth century: the classical nationalism of the nineteenth century aimed at *uniting* different provinces and regions into one nation-state and one economic market. The new nationalisms of the second half of the twentieth century were not unifying, but, on the contrary, aimed at the *fission* of developed capitalist states (Britain, Spain), and as such were reactionary. This new nationalism led to absurd concepts of national sovereignty that had nothing to do with Marxist principles. In a scathing set of commentaries on what had become a new fetishism of sovereignty, Hobsbawm wrote:

> The majority of the members of the United Nations is soon likely to consist of late twentieth-century (Republican) equivalents of Saxe-Coburg-Gotha and Schwarzburg-Sonderhausen . . . .
>
> Any speck in the Pacific can look forward to independence and a good time for its president, if it happens to possess a location for a naval base for which more solvent states will compete, a lucky gift of nature such as manganese, or merely enough beaches and pretty girls to become a tourist paradise . . . .
>
> If the Seychelles can have a vote at the United Nations as good as Japan's, then only the sky is the limit for the Isle of Man and the Channel Islands . . . [27]

Hobsbawm's critique certainly restored to the debate its historical seriousness and extricated it from the narrower sectarian interests of some of the previous participants. Yet despite all this, Hobsbawm was not able to suggest a more fundamental Marxian attitude to nationalism beyond the merely instrumental approach postulated by Marx's paradigm II. The problem remained where it had been since Marx left his followers with his unwillingness to discuss nationalist phenomena on their own merits.

Where does all this leave Marxism today? The basic flaw of the Marxian analysis of nationalism has been the attempt to reduce all its phenomena — including the cultural aspects of nationalism — to socio-economic causes and deny nationalism, and culture in general, an autonomous status in the scheme of human things. Viewing nationalism as merely superstructural is, of course, only one facet of the general Marxian analysis of historical development — yet it makes it extremely difficult for Marxists to assess concrete nationalist movements. There is truth in the feeling that the Marxian paradigm II limited the scope of nationalism to generalizations based on the example of the *Zollverein* — and the *Zollverein* happens to be a very limited model for the explication of such an enormously powerful and universal social phenomenon usually subsumed under the general heading of nationalism.

But just as one can find in Marx himself more differentiated views in some of his *obiter dicta* on literature (e.g. the excursus on the Greek classics in the *Grundrisse*, where Marx admits that they have validity beyond the concrete class structure which gave rise to their writing), so the socialist movement itself, both within the Marxist tradition and on its periphery, did bring up alternative, non-reductivist models. Any attempt to revive interest in a socialist theory of nationalism must take these into account, and a few of these attempts will be mentioned here as the possible context within which a future debate about socialism and nationalism will have to take place.

(1) In the writings of Moses Hess, one can find a complement to Marx's reductivism. Despite Marx's disparaging remarks about Hess in *The Communist Manifesto*, the confluence of many of their ideas continued throughout their lives, though Hess never developed a theoretical edifice comparable to the one erected by Marx. Perhaps because he was no system-builder, Hess could be more attuned to social developments happening in his own time, while Marx occasionally had to force all phenomena into the Procrustean bed of his theoretical matrix. While Hess later became known for his proto-Zionist *Rome and Jerusalem* (1862), his views on nationalism were not limited to Jewish issues, but rather the other way around; because he had a general awareness of the rise of nationalism, he applied it also to things Jewish.

In his views on nationalism, Hess was close to Mazzini's thinking, which saw the nation as a laboratory for solidarity, as the fulcrum where human beings are educated to behave in non-egotistical ways, learning how to transcend their merely individual interests for the sake of communal other-directedness. Hess also viewed the national community as an element of mediation, and thus introduced a Hegelian theoretical dimension which was curiously lacking in Marx, for whom mediation was exclusively focused on class solidarity on a universal level — hardly the kind of concreteness called for by a Hegelian understanding of mediation. Moreover, with the victory of the proletariat and the abolition of class differences, even this aspect would be eliminated with only a very abstract notion of humanity holding together all mankind. Hess, on the other hand, maintained that:

> Nationality (*Nationalität*) is the individuality of a people. It is this individuality, however, which is the activating element; just as humanity cannot be actual

(*wirklich*) without distinct individuals, so it cannot be actual without distinct, specific nations and peoples (*Nationen und Volksstamme*). Like any other being, humanity cannot actualize itself without mediation, it needs the medium of the individuality.[28]

To Hess, the revolution, which would abolish classes, would also abolish national conflicts — but not the existence of nations. Culture — mores, tradition — all had an autonomous existence, related to class structure (as in the case of the uneven socio-economic structure of the Jews in the diaspora), but not exclusively reducible to it. The emancipation of subject nations was itself a corner-stone of the cause of proletarian revolution according to Hess, and while Marx envisaged the disappearance of most nations into the larger economic units dominated by the two or three large European cultures, Hess postulated a post-revolutionary future in which all nations would be free and able to develop their own culture, and this would include 'even the smallest nation, whether it belongs to the Germanic or Romance race, to the Slavonic or Finnish, to the Celtic or the Semitic'.[29]

(2) Hess's views did not have much impact (except eventually within the limited sphere of the socialist Zionist movement), yet a similar challenge was posed on a much wider scale to the Austrian Socialist Party. The unique contribution of Austro-Marxism to socialist theory by introducing non-reductivist aspects into historical and economic analysis has often been noted, though for obvious historical reasons it is today much less acknowledged than it should be.[30] But on the national question, the Austrians had to face a specifically complex situation, growing out of the fact that with industrialization in Austro-Hungary, the majority of the proletarianized former peasants who crowded into Vienna were not of German stock and did not speak German: they were Czechs, Slovaks, Hungarians, Croats, Slovenes, Poles and Jews. For a socialist party (based as it originally was on German-speaking, Viennese activists) to carry out its political propaganda in German among such a polyglot non-German proletariat, posed a number of excruciating problems. The party leaders realized that they might not be understood at all, literally, but worse, that they might be perceived by the non-German workers as just another example of German-language hegemony, and the socialist message might be totally lost in this misconception. As a consequence, the Austrian party decided to organize itself in different language sections, so that a worker in Vienna could join a Czech, or

Slovenian socialist club in which his language, and not German was used. This gave the overall party organization a federalist structure, in which cultural pluralism became the corner-stone of political organization and practice.

Moreover, on the theoretical level, some of the Austro-Marxists like Otto Bauer and Karl Renner also tried to relate class structure to national problems in a sophisticated historical approach. They argued, for example, that subject nations like the Czechs lost their upper classes when conquered by the German Habsburgs — either through massacres or cultural assimilation. As a consequence, the disappearance of such national élites meant that the Czech nation remained a nation of peasants — with no social and political leadership and no literary élite, and economically dependent on German-speaking landlords. Capitalist development thus started with the German-speaking traditional élites, and the Czech peasant-turned-proletarian found himself subjected to both economic and cultural exploitation. It was the impoverished cultural sphere of the Czech lower classes that the Austrian Socialist Party set out to salvage through its political and cultural activity, thus giving the Czech (or Croatian) working man both his economic and cultural empowerment.

This was obviously an attractive project, and in the Austro-Hungarian context it tried also to supply a 'third way' between German-speaking hegemony and the xenophobic nationalism of the various nationalities of the Empire, whose nationalist movements were calling for the break-up of the Dual Monarchy and the establishment of numerous nation-states on its ruins. The Austro-Marxist alternative was to preserve the old Empire but transform it from a hegemonic structure of national and social subjection into a federation of national and cultural groups — a model for a truly internationalist socialism, in which nations were not subsumed under each other but co-existed in a pluralist structure. Bauer and his colleagues also envisaged that in such a socialist federative commonwealth there would be two tiers of representation: one territorial, the other national-linguistic. The first would deal with the obvious issues common to all citizens of the territory; the second, election to which would be reserved for members of each specific group, would deal with problems of education, language, culture, historical heritage, etc. It was in this pluralistic system that the Austro-Marxists saw a guarantee against a hegemony imposed by the economically stronger groups (like the German-Austrians) over the weaker and less developed national entities.

The impact of these ideas can, of course, be identified in different ways in such disparate areas as the Soviet nationalities policy, the Yugoslav model, socialist Zionism and some aspects of Quebecois and Basque nationalism.

(3) It is in this context that Joseph Stalin deserves to be mentioned. While the political consequences of his nationalities policies as carried out by Lenin and then by himself have been catastrophic in many cases and brutally repressive, it cannot be denied that on the cultural level some of the smaller peoples of the Soviet Union owe a cultural revival to these principles. While in his 1913 brochure on the nationalities problem Stalin disagreed with the Austro-Marxists with regard to the non-territorial aspects of their nationality policy, his very definition of a nation — not always adhered to in Soviet practice — does, however, evince a sensitivity to the cultural aspects of nationalism and goes beyond the classical Marxian reductivist paradigm. It is worth quoting Stalin's definition of a nation:

> A nation is an historically evolved stable community of language, territory, economic life and psychological make-up manifested in a community of culture.[31]

While one should obviously be careful not to advocate a revival of interest in Stalin, this aspect of his thought should not altogether be forgotten, especially as it is so near in its openness to the pluralist approaches realizing the autonomy of cultural dimensions as evinced by the Austro-Marxist tradition.

(4) Lastly, we should mention a relatively unknown contribution (outside of Israel) of a Zionist socialist thinker, Chaim Arlosoroff. Born in the Ukraine, educated in Germany, Arlosoroff emigrated in the 1920s to Palestine and tried to define his Zionism in terms of a general theory of the relationship of socialism to the national question. At the age of twenty he wrote a pamphlet called *On Jewish People's Socialism* which owed its terms of reference both to the Russian populist as well as the German youth movement tradition. Before dealing with the specific Jewish problem in post-1918 Europe, Arlosoroff addressed the wider problem of the failure of the Socialist International in the summer of 1914 to maintain internationalist class solidarity. According to Arlosoroff, the blame lay with the abstract internationalism of the Marxist tradition, where general commitments to international solidarity across national boundaries were reiterated again and again — but without being anchored in a concrete mediation of institutions and behaviour patterns (an

argument reminiscent of Hess's insistence on mediation). Consequently the workers did not find in the socialist movement a response
for their concrete consciousness regarding their culture and heritage
— and hence went somewhere else. In the charged atmosphere of
1919, Arlosoroff warned the socialist movement, almost prophet-
ically, to substitute its abstract universalism with a universalism
mediated by concrete identity with historical cultures, otherwise it
might lose working-class support to the right wing. For even if the
worker is alienated from the élites of his society and its high culture,
he does have a concrete cultural consciousness which binds him to the
language and culture of his national environment:

> The community of national life and destiny moves the hearts of the workers as
> strongly as it does that of any other member of society. He too loves his mother's
> tongue, in which the sparse lullabies were sung to him, in which the spirit of his
> parents lived and created. He too loves his homeland, the people of his homeland,
> their manifold manners and traditions, *Sitten*, their multicoloured artifacts, the sky
> of his homeland and the fields and towns of his fatherland. He too carries the
> culture of his nation within himself: his being, his emotional life, is its being, its
> life.[32]

According to Arlosoroff, the Second International, on the other
hand, overlooked this aspect of the concrete consciousness of the
working class, and substituted it with an abstract universalism, which
was never anchored in the actual praxis of the proletariat. Hence its
brittleness in the face of the nationalist onslaught of the summer of
1914.

Arlosoroff further warned that if the newly organized socialist
movement, trying to resurrect itself after the war, did not take into
account this cultural content of the concrete consciousness of
proletarian life, the working class might go somewhere else — to a
movement or a leader who would address these issues. Bearing in
mind that this was written in 1919, the prophetic force of this
statement cannot be overlooked.[33]

Socialism has thus been burdened with an anti-national bias, which,
drawing on the universalist ideas of the eighteenth-century Enlightenment, did not make it especially capable of meeting the challenges
of the late nineteenth and twentieth centuries. In this blindness and in
a very profound sense, Marxism shares this poverty with its rival,
classical liberalism. Both, being offspring of the universalist ideas of

the Enlightenment, have difficulties in perceiving and granting legitimacy to historical entities which cannot be subsumed under purely universal criteria. Even the proletariat is central to Marx because it is a 'universal' class, and the market is, of course, for liberalism the epitome of universal modes of human conduct.

Nationalism relates to the particular, but this particular can be woven — as it has been by the Austro-Marxists — into the universal realm. It is a human mode of communication, perhaps the strongest mode because it relates directly to language, and modern communication, far from obliterating it, by being so verbal, is anchoring it even deeper in the concrete consciousness of human beings. For anyone thinking in communitarian terms, this is a veritable challenge.

Notes

1. Hannah Arendt, *Origins of Totalitarianism*, new edn (New York 1973), 3.

2. Ibid., 25.

3. Ibid., 38.

4. Karl Marx/Friedrich Engels, *Basic Writings on Politics and Philosophy*, ed. Lewis S. Feuer (Garden City, NJ 1959), 345.

5. Ibid., 11.

6. Ibid., 26.

7. Ibid.

8. In the case of Engels, some condescending remarks on the 'non-historical' nature of Slavonic nations added some venom to these comments. For some Yugoslav critical comments, cf. France Klopcic, 'Friedrich Engels und Karl Marx über die "Geschichtslosen" slawischen Nationen', *Marxismus und Geschichtswissenschaft*, ITH Tagungsbericht, vol. 19 (Wien 1984), 217–49.

9. See the introduction to my edition of Karl Marx's *On Colonialism and Modernization* (Garden City, NJ 1968), 3–31.

10. For some of the recent critical literature see Walter Connor, *The National Question in Marxist-Leninist Theory and Strategy* (Princeton, NJ 1984); and Roman Szporluk, *Communism and Nationalism* (New York and Oxford 1988), esp. parts I and III.

11. Leon Trotsky, *The History of the Russian Revolution* (London 1967), III, 39. That Trotsky is aware that such a theory does not fit into any concrete analysis of the historical emergence of capitalism is evident from the fact that he immediately remarks in the following sentence that the rise of the capitalist mode of production in the Netherlands and in England preceded the formation of national states, and that basically his generalization is drawn from the example of the German *Zollverein*.

12. See Jonathan Frankel, *Prophecy and Politics: Socialism, Nationalism and the Russian Jews 1862–1917* (Cambridge 1981), esp. 171–257.

13. A detailed list of Lenin's writings on the national issue can be found in James M. Blaut, *The National Question* (London and New York 1987), 220–1.

14. For a useful collection of her writings in English on these issues, see Rosa Luxemburg, *The National Question — Selected Writings*, ed. H.B. Davis (New York and London 1976).

15. The most important texts are 'Report of the Commission on the Nationalities and Colonial Question', in V.I. Lenin, *Works* (Moscow 1965), XXI, 240–5; 'The Question of the Nationalities', ibid., XXXVI, 605–11; and notes for a lecture on 'Imperialism and the Right of Nations to Self-Determination', ibid., XXIX, 735–42.

16. For a recent Soviet restatement of Lenin's position, cogently argued and trying to distinguish national liberation movements from 'bourgeois' nationalisms, see K.N. Brutens, *National Liberation Movements Today* (Moscow 1977), 2 vols. An earlier attempt by a sympathetic Western observer to vindicate internal Soviet policies on the nationality problem can be found in an almost forgotten volume by Hans Kohn, *Nationalism in the Soviet Union* (New York 1933).

17. John Ehrenreich, 'The Theory of Nationalism: A Case of Underdevelopment', *Monthly Review*, 27, 1 (1977), 67. See also his 'Socialism, Nationalism and Capitalist Development', *Review of Radical Political Economists*, 15, 1 (1983), 1–40, where he says that 'Marxists have failed in their efforts at incorporating the reality of nationalism into their theoretical understanding, and . . . this failure is deeply rooted in the nature of Marxist thought itself' (p. 1).

18. Ibid., 29.

19. Regis Debray, 'Marxism and the National Question', *New Left Review*, no. 105 (1977), 25.

20. Nicos Poulantzas, *State, Power, Socialism* (London 1978), 97ff.

21. Horace B. Davis, *Towards a Marxist Theory of Nationalism* (New York and London 1978), 202–40, 189–91.

22. Blaut, op. cit., esp. 68ff.

23. Brian Jenkins/Gunter Minnerup, *Citizens and Comrades — Socialism in a World of Nation States* (London and Sydney 1984), 144–5.

24. Tom Nairn, 'The Modern Janus', *New Left Review*, no. 94 (1975), 17.

25. Tom Nairn, *The Break-Up of Britain?* (London 1977), 329.

26. Eric Hobsbawm, 'Some Reflections on *The Break-Up of Britain*', *New Left Review*, no. 105 (1977), 9.

27. Ibid., 6–7.

28. Article in the *Kölnische Zeitung*, 14 October 1843, in Moses Hess, *Philosophische und sozialistische Schriften 1837–1850*, ed. W. Monke, 2nd edn (Berlin-DDR/Vaduz 1980), 251.

29. *Rom und Jerusalem*, in Moses Hess, *Ausgewählte Schriften*, ed. H. Lademacher (Köln 1962), 320. In his vision of a Jewish socialist commonwealth in Palestine, Hess accompanies this with a call for the resurrection of independent Arab states in Syria and Egypt. Cf. my *Moses Hess — Prophet of Communism and Zionism* (New York 1985), 228.

30. See Tom Bottomore and Patrick Goode (eds), *Austro-Marxism* (Oxford 1978), esp. 102–35; Norbert Leser, *Zwischen Reformismus und Bolschewismus: Der Austromarxismus als Theorie und Praxis* (Wien 1968).

31. Quoted according to the German text of Stalin's brochure, *Der Marxismus und die nationale Frage* (Vienna 1913), 10–11.

32. Viktor Chaim Arlosoroff, *Der jüdische Volkssozialismus* (Berlin 1919), 11.

33. Ibid., 37. See my *Arlosoroff* (London 1989), esp. chaps 2 and 4.

Shlomo Avineri
is Herbert Samuel Professor of Political
Science at the Hebrew University of
Jerusalem. Amongst his publications are:
*The Social and Political Thought of Karl
Marx*; *Hegel's Theory of the Modern State*;
The Making of Modern Zionism; *Moses
Hess: Prophet of Communism and Zionism*,
and *Arlosoroff — A Political Biography*.

Jehuda Reinharz

European Jewry and the Consolidation of Zionism

The idea of Jewish national sovereignty, and elaborate strategies for achieving it in Palestine, were anticipated by proto-Zionist enthusiasts long before the Zionist movement arose. The same may be said about the other special Zionist objectives, that were ultimately embodied in Israel's major domestic institutions.

The Haskala, a movement to transform the Hebrew language from a sacred tongue to a medium of modern secular enlightenment, had existed for about a century before the 1880s. Its aims also included reforming the Jewish occupational distribution. Haskala projects of occupational transfer were not directed toward resettlement in Zion, but were intended to prepare ghetto Jews, wherever they lived, for civic equality and social acceptance. However, since the 1840s, general education, vocational retraining and a shift to 'productive' occupations were also proposed as the way to build a sound social and economic base for the growing Jewish community in Palestine.

Jewish settlement in Zion was continually stimulated by organized groups of sponsors; since the 1860s at least, their aim was not merely to encourage prayer and study but to establish *self-supporting* settlers in the Holy Land. Yet their motivation remained religious rather than strictly nationalist. Such proto-Zionists did not hope to solve the problems of Jews in Europe by emigration, but to build a community in Zion that would carry out Biblical social, economic and, eventually, political commandments that could not be observed in Exile. By this means they believed the advent of the Messiah might be prepared.[1]

The proto-Zionists had little or no success in building self-supporting settlements in Palestine, and the number of migrants to Zion encouraged by them was minuscule. However, on several occasions when oppression became acute in some country during this period, there were also attempts to apply mass emigration — though not necessarily to the Holy Land — as a solution to the Jewish problem.

Thus, the major elements of a Zionist ideology — emigration to solve the Jewish problem, the return to Zion, occupational retraining and redistribution and the revival of Hebrew as a medium of secular culture — were present long before the movement arose; but they were espoused in fragmentary, sometimes mutually opposed, forms by diverse Jewish groups. This remained true even in the 1870s, when a series of crises challenged all existing Jewish attitudes, traditionalist or modern, and strongly suggested a nationalist alternative. In Russia, a reactionary mood set in following the Polish insurrection of 1863, and was given sharp point for the Jews by a pogrom in Odessa in 1871. At the same time, expulsions and persecution of Rumanian Jewry forced the Western Jewish communities to meet in international conferences, at which radical proposals to solve the problem by mass emigration were seriously discussed. Thereafter, the Balkan wars and the Congress of Berlin in 1878 raised simultaneous questions concerning the future of Palestine, should the Ottoman empire collapse, and concerning the future of Balkan Jews under conditions of mounting oppression. But even after all this, inhibitions against a full-blown nationalist stand remained powerful. Nobody demonstrated this better than some of the men who were soon to be counted among the forefathers of the Zionist movement.

The idea that Palestine should be among the havens considered when Jewish refugee problems arose, had become familiar ever since the famine years of 1867–9, which severely affected the Pale of Settlement. Russian Jewish spokesmen of an enlightened Orthodoxy, like David Gordon or Yehiel Mikhal Pines, argued that the refugees should be settled not only in America or in agricultural colonies in southern Russia, but also, or primarily, in the Holy Land. The Alliance Israélite Universelle, under the influence of Charles Netter, at that time showed sympathy toward this view. An agricultural school, Mikve Israel, was founded in the plain near Jaffa for any Jewish settlers, but especially for already established residents, who could be induced to train for agricultural colonization in Palestine. However, active interest in fostering settlement in Zion was still largely confined to Orthodox elements, long dedicated to this purpose on religious grounds and, for that very reason, the maskilim maintained a lukewarm, if not cool, attitude.

In 1874, admirers of Sir Moses Montefiore planned to raise a testimonial fund in honour of the venerable philanthropist's ninetieth birthday and, in view of his long interest in Palestine Jewry, it seemed appropriate to apply the contributions toward improving the cultural and economic position of that community. The outstanding contemporary poet of the Russian Haskala, Judah Leib Gordon, was asked if he — or, alternatively, Yehiel Mikhal Pines — would raise the funds in Russia, and also how he thought the contributions should be used. He replied that if the goal were merely to build a school or hospital commemorating Montefiore, then — considering conditions in Russia — it would be better not to expose any Russian Jew to the risk of heading the committee. But if it had a more significant aim, such as purchasing land in Palestine for a settlement that might become the nucleus of a national revival, he himself would gladly serve — and he also highly recommended Pines for such a post. However, his agreement was conditional: he stipulated that the Jews already living in the Holy Land should first be removed, for their fanatical obscurantism could cripple the enterprise.[2]

Even the pogroms, which produced an upheaval in the spirit of so many Russian Jews, failed to alter Gordon's cool and sober habit of mind. His nationalist views remained subject to the earlier reservations, and no sudden access of enthusiasm caused him to overlook the obstacles to colonization in Palestine. He was, consequently, regarded as unsympathetic or insufficiently sympathetic to the cause by ardent new adherents. But right up to the traumatic pogrom experience that radicalized their whole view, some of those most prominently identified with the movement after 1881 had a similarly qualified and restricted sympathy for nationalism.

A striking example is the famous exchange between Eliezer Ben-Yehuda (Perlman) and Peretz Smolenskin. Ben-Yehuda, teacher, propagandist, lexicographer of spoken Hebrew, to which cause he devoted his whole life from the day he set foot in Palestine in 1881, had the direct, single-minded approach of a Russian radical. He was a disciple of Smolenskin's cultural nationalism, heightened by the vogue for Slavophilism during the Russo-Turkish war of 1877–8. In 1878, while studying medicine in Paris, he wrote an outspoken, full-blown nationalist manifesto entitled 'A Burning Issue', which Smolenskin renamed more moderately 'A Significant Issue' when he published it in 1879 in his journal *Hashahar*, a recognized organ for many varieties of proto-nationalist opinion. Ben-Yehuda argued that religion and Jew-hatred, which had preserved Jewish solidarity in the past, could no longer do so. In order to survive, the Jewish people would have to resettle en masse on the soil of Palestine and there create an autonomous national centre and revive spoken Hebrew as the vehicle of a secular Jewish culture.

Smolenskin published this youthful effusion in *Hashahar*,[3] but he was far from agreeing at that time with such a radical, simplistic stand. An exchange of articles and open letters took place between the two in the period immediately before the pogroms; the last interchange, in fact, did not appear until after that turning-point, although written before it. Smolenskin's views then included the following: a return to farming — as was being advocated by proponents of colonization in southern Russia — would solve no Jewish problem, for if Jews had civil rights they would enter all occupations, and without such rights they could not be aided materially; the Hebrew language would never revive as a spoken vernacular, but should be cultivated as the literary organ of a spiritual Jewish nationality; and while the resettlement of Jews in Zion was a Messianic vision essentially bound up with Jewish history, and those who returned at any time deserved sympathy and support, the people were not prepared to undertake this as a practical, political plan for solving the Jewish problem.

The last interchange between Ben-Yehuda and Smolenskin was published, as noted, after the pogroms, although written earlier. In the very same issue of *Hashahar* Smolenskin also published another article, written *after* the pogroms, which directly reversed his position on Palestine and was imbued with a totally different spirit. He began by attacking bitterly all those Russian Jewish leaders who had placed their faith in emancipation and enlightenment. The Jews were to blame for their own sorry plight, because they refused to see themselves as a nation and act accordingly. Their leaders had merely echoed antisemitic charges against their own people and, even though forewarned by himself (as Smolenskin acidly points out), they failed to anticipate the pogroms or do anything to forestall them. Even now they were resisting the necessary remedy, which a nationally-minded leadership would readily understand: namely, mass migration of the Russian Jews to the only country where a better Jewish future was conceivable, the ancestral Zion.[4]

The radical effect of the pogroms is equally evident in the changing views of Moshe Leib Lilienblum, an even more important pioneer of Zionism. As already noted, he had become prominent in his early twenties through his battle for an essentially conservative doctrine of religious reform. He then turned increasingly agnostic and cosmopolitan under the influence of Russian positivist writers but, by the mid-1870s, gradually reverted to the loyalties of his youth. At this point, he attacked the assimilationist inclinations of Russo-Jewish circles, and showed a moderate sympathy toward projects for Jewish resettlement in Palestine which were being discussed in the press.

In 1874, an article in the *Odesskie Vestnik*, ridiculing a reputed Rothschild plan to buy Palestine for Jewish resettlement, evoked a letter to the editor from Lilienblum defending the idea.[5] In 1875, an actual project of this kind gained widespread attention. Chaim Guedalla, head of an association of bondholders affected by reduced payments on the Ottoman loan, proposed that the debentures be redeemed by the transfer of lands in Palestine and other Ottoman regions for Jewish settlement.[6] At this time, too, a group of pious Jerusalem residents organized for colonization on the land; from which beginning came later the initial (abortive) settlement of the village of Petach Tikvah in 1878. A critical observer reported these events with measured approval in the Haskala journal, *Hatzefirah*; but he suggested that it would be a highly desirable preliminary step to convoke a Sanhedrin in order to reform traditions which, he said, precluded success in founding a modern Jewish state.[7] Lilienblum, the erstwhile champion of religious reform, wrote, in a sharp rejoinder to the author, that this question should be shelved at a time when it might stand in the way of acquiring Palestine for Jewish settlement.[8] Nevertheless, for Lilienblum, too, Palestine was not yet a clear, ideologically defined goal, nor did he see mass resettlement and territorial concentration in a Jewish country as *the* solution to the Jewish problem. When it was reported, in 1878, that the Alliance Israélite Universelle proposed to purchase land in Russia for Jewish colonization, Lilienblum was a vigorous supporter of the project.

Lilienblum has given direct testimony, in his diary notations, of the emotional impact the pogroms had upon him. He was glad to have lived through the Odessa pogrom, he said, this intimation of what his forefathers had suffered served to reunite him with them. During this time, too, he came to a new intellectual conviction about the roots of the Jewish problem. Jewish alienness, he now believed, was the fundamental cause of antisemitism, which, accordingly, was inevitable and ineradicable in the Diaspora. The only remedy was resettlement in the historic Jewish homeland.[9]

Sharing similar emotional and intellectual experiences, Lilienblum and men like him now felt themselves identified with a distinct party and ideological movement in Jewry. This group identity served the new Zionists as a common fixed point from which — each in accordance with his other predispositions — they severally took their bearing on current Jewish issues.

A group identity *may arise* out of a shared traumatic experience, but it is most effectively *defined* by opposition to the specific attitudes of rival groups. The role of ideological antagonist was performed, for the new Zionist movement, by the Western European Jewish organizations and the Russo-Jewish leadership; so too, the rise of a self-conscious Zionist opposition led these anti-nationalists to take a firmer, more ideological stand on current issues.

The questions debated in Russia in the 1880s were similar to those argued in relation to Rumania a decade earlier, under similar circumstances. In both cases, a government indicated its deliberate intent to reduce the Jewish population by encouraging, if not compelling, emigration. In both cases, the Western and local Jewish leaders had to choose between opposing emigration — because it might imply abandoning a civil rights struggle — or aiding resettlement in order to solve the immediate problem. In both cases, the question arose whether America or Palestine should be the destination for assisted emigrants.

But the debate over the Rumanian problem in the 1870s did not line up nationalists and anti-nationalists in clear and consistent opposition. The idea of a mass evacuation from Rumania was favoured not by a nationalist, seeking to restore the Jewish State in Palestine, but by Benjamin Franklin Peixotto, an American Jew. He renounced hope only in the specific case of Rumania, not in the tolerance of Gentiles in general, and what he proposed was not auto-emancipation in Zion but emancipation in America.[10] A proto-Zionist like Rabbi Zvi Hirsch Kalischer, who preferred Zion to America as a haven for Rumanian Jewish emigrants, was far less radical than Peixotto in his support of emigration. He did not think in terms of an evacuation but of a minor movement; thus, one of his arguments in favour of resettlement in Zion was that, by proving Jews could become productive workers, the emigrants might induce the Rumanian government to grant civic rights to those who remained behind.

The Russian crisis consolidated opposed attitudes into rival ideologies. For all the reluctance of Western Jews to accept mass emigration from Rumania in the 1870s, the Israélite Universelle had not been disinclined to help immigrants to Palestine. Charles Netter, who founded the Mikve Israel farm school at that time, was ready, as were other leaders, to co-operate with proto-Zionists. But in the

1880s, the resistance of Western and Russo-Jewish leaders to the whole notion of mass emigration was much stiffer and — what is more important — far more public. As emigration continued on a mass scale in spite of their efforts, they aided those who went to America or other places of refuge, but they resolutely refused (with minor exceptions) to help those who tried to reach Zion. The nationalists were thereby provoked to sharp protest and they campaigned energetically, by circulating petitions and publishing open letters, to *compel* the Jewish organizations to change their attitude.

They reacted to such pressure in a letter to the London *Jewish Chronicle*, signed by none other than Charles Netter, and the reasons for *not* assisting Palestine immigration were given in detail. All the healthy and fertile areas, Netter argued, were already cultivated by Arabs. The Turkish administration was oppressive. In America, only lack of farm experience and capital had to be overcome, but in Palestine an additional handicap, the probable revival of Biblical agricultural laws, doomed the project from the start. And, finally, he pointed out that, if unsuccessful as farmers, immigrants to America would find a way to support themselves in the cities, while in Palestine they would simply be added to the existing pauperized community supported by pious donations.[11] So sharp and decisive a tone encountered an equally partisan nationalist response. Leib Gordon, formerly a warm admirer of Netter, could find no other parallel than the following to describe Netter's betrayal: 'In these words he defames the Holy Land more than did the spies in ancient time.'[12]

Thus, the lines were drawn, and henceforth positions were defined polemically — that is, increasingly in terms of principle, not of the particular case. Before this time, proto-nationalists had been deviant individual voices, in either the modernist or traditionalist camp. Their opinions were perceived as erratic departures from one or another of the ideological axes around which discussion revolved. With the pogroms, nationalism emerged as an independent axis of Jewish opinion. Particular views on the cultural, social and economic reforms needed in the Jewish community were now related to the central nationalist end. Moreover, opposing non-nationalist views had to be redefined ideologically in relation to the new Zionism.

For the nationalists themselves, what was now primarily important was their (essentially emotional) identification with the group, not the particular attitudes they adopted. As nationalist opinion was no longer a matter of individual rebellion, but an established ideological position, its definition was no longer an individual matter but a collective process, arising out of a group polemic against other groups. Accordingly, the new nationalists began immediately to adjust their personal opinions on particular issues to the needs of their group identity, leading in many cases to rapid shifting of lines.

The case of Lilienblum is characteristic. The immediate impact of the pogroms left him one certainty — his identification with his people's historic fate and destiny — but with no fixed opinion on how to achieve the national aim. He knew only that Jews could no longer rely on others, but solely on themselves, that they must emigrate and set up their own autonomous state in their own ancestral land. When, shortly after the Odessa pogrom, university students asked his help in raising funds to purchase Palestine from the Sultan, he said that was a task for Western European Jews. Soon after, he was urging the Russian Jews to repair the omissions of their ancestors and raise funds to buy back Zion. Jews of all persuasions should settle there, without disputing religious issues, and they must build not only individual settlements, but a state — for 'if we do not get the right to set up a shadow government, we should do better to establish colonies in America, a country more settled and with better commercial prospects than the land of our fathers.'[13] Not long after this, he reached his conclusions about the causal connection between Jewish alienness and Jew-hatred. He then decided that *only* in Zion — *no matter under what political conditions* — could the Jews ever be other than alien. His support for resettlement in the Holy Land had become absolute and unconditional.

Among the Russian-trained intellectuals converted to Jewish loyalty by the pogroms, it was not Zion but America that had the most immediate and widest appeal as the goal of a mass migration, but the rationale was distinctly nationalist even in this case. Such men founded the *Am Olam* (Eternal People) movement, which sought national Jewish liberation by agricultural co-operative settlement, especially on the American frontier. Russian and Hebrew periodical articles on this subject stressed the possibility, under American laws, of qualifying for territorial home rule by settling 5000 Jewish families in a frontier region, or even of constituting a state in the federal union, if 60,000 families could be settled contiguously.

However, some young students preferred Palestine rather than America from the outset because historical attachment gave *any* settlement there national significance, whatever its size, and the return to Zion made an immediate appeal to national sentiment. This was the most prevalent point of view among nationalist maskilim;

and there is no need to say it was the ruling opinion among the proto-Zionist traditionalists who welcomed the new recruits to a cause they had maintained alone until then.

In the end, the course of events settled the issue between America and Palestine for nationalists. The return to Zion became the only emigration policy with which a Jewish nationalist of that generation could identify himself. The migration to the United States continued and grew steadily more massive, but the dreams of Jewish autonomy, based on a dense Jewish co-operative farm settlement on the frontier, quickly proved chimerical. The *Am Olam* movement disappeared, and no national significance was thereafter attached by any ideological group to the mass exodus to America. The migration to Palestine, on the other hand, remained small and was repeatedly checked by Turkish opposition. Nevertheless, the idea of resettlement in Zion as the solution of the Jewish problem remained the central belief of a new, distinct ideological group.

In this group were united Russian-trained Jewish intellectuals, modernist maskilim who combined a self-taught European culture with traditional schooling, and some of the Orthodox laymen and rabbis who had long been involved with the project of resettlement in Zion. For the Russified intellectuals, as already noted, their conversion to nationalism was an effect of the pogrom trauma, which shattered fully and finally their reliance on Gentile liberalism and Russo-Jewish enlightenment. What they felt was, first and foremost, sheer revulsion against attitudes they had previously shared. To use a current parallel, the pogroms made them see themselves as 'Uncle Toms'.

The Hebrew maskilim, who had distrusted the assimilationist attitude even before, also experienced the pogroms as a severe emotional shock; but it produced not so much a conversion as a radicalization and politicization of their previous attitudes. Their views on all the cultural, social, economic and political issues current among Eastern European Jews were no longer voiced as a form of marginal dissent on particular points, but now expressed a distinct group identity. Opinions on specific issues therefore had to flow organically from a common nationalist ideology, which remained to be positively articulated.

Traditionalists who became Zionists suffered no trauma because of the pogroms. The direct and empathetic pain experienced was certainly no less for them than for other Jews. But they needed no intellectual or emotional reorientation to cope with it, for such trials and troubles were part of the familiar pattern of Exile. That modernist Jews now became nationalists gave them new hope, for they saw this as a return of the prodigals to positions they themselves had long occupied.

A Zionist grouping thus emerged as a major ideological component of the Jewish community. Not all who joined it shared every position implied or expressed in the common programme, as defined at a given moment, and many who would not join nevertheless sympathized with particular Zionist viewpoints. The varied initial composition and leanings of the group were favourable to divergent definitions of the nationalist aims from the outset. Such divergences, crystallized by the critical experiences of successive Zionist generations, resulted in a variety of ideological factions, each devoted to a particular nationalist purpose it held to be most essential.

Eastern Europe was the cradle of Zionism, but from its earliest days the movement developed significant relations with Jewish communities in the West. Oppressive conditions in its original Russian base hampered the movement in its work and compelled Zionism to seek support in countries of greater freedom. The waves of emigration from Russia, Rumania and Austro-Hungary included a scattering of Zionist adherents who came to Western cities like Berlin, Paris, London and New York and built Zionist cells wherever they settled. Such societies were founded in the West from the beginning of the movement in Eastern Europe.

Western Zionism always had in its ranks — and often as its local leaders — native-born or fully integrated Western Jews. Such recruits shared, broadly speaking, their Eastern comrades' assumptions about the general nature of the 'Jewish problem', but they came to Jewish nationalism by a different route, from a background of experience which they shared with some of their non-Zionist Western contemporaries.

One source of Western sympathy for Zionism was the tradition of supporting the Yishuv in the Holy Land. Western philanthropists who carried on the tradition in the nineteenth century did so in a new, modernizing spirit. Their benefactions were not simply acts of pious charity but also an extension overseas of the programme of enlightenment and socioeconomic 'amelioration' that they pursued on behalf of fellow Jews at home in the campaign for civic emancipation. The traditionalist community in Palestine, however, showed a stiff resistance to modernization, particularly in its opposition to secular studies, the mainstay of the Westerners' programme. The Zionists, on the other hand, were no less committed than the philanthropists to projects of secular education, vocational retraining and agricultural settlement. This made co-operation with them an attractive option — but only if the Zionists would downplay their dangerous nationalist political intentions. When Zionists did so, under the pressure of Ottoman restrictions, co-operation with Western non-Zionists was indeed achieved. At the same time, there were from the beginning Western Jews who found ideological Zionism itself basically acceptable. Such men joined and frequently became leaders in early Zionism in such countries as Germany, England and the United States.

One factor that predisposed such Western Jews to become Zionists was the tendency toward a more militant self-assertive style in the defence of Jewish rights and interests that was increasingly manifested in the nineteenth century. Early Jewish protagonists of Western enlightenment and civic emancipation had usually accepted that Jews must earn their equal rights by reforming their traditional ways, economic and social as well as religious. This attitude led many — notably in America — to eschew separatist Jewish political activity such as was clearly implicit in Zionism when it later arose. But by then a different, activist attitude was held by a generation of self-assured Jewish liberals. They considered civic equality to be an absolute right that must not be made conditional and withheld until Jews fulfilled demands for 'amelioration'. Moreover, it became clear by the 1870s that not only legal discrimination but social prejudice against Jews, culminating in the rise of political antisemitism, required militant Jewish action, and therefore Jewish organization for self-defence.

The Alliance Israélite Universelle, formed in France in 1860 as an international Jewish body, and the Centralverein deutscher Staatsbuerger juedischen Glaubens, organized in Germany in 1893 to combat antisemitism, were founded by leaders of this activist inclination. Their avowed commitment to emancipation according to the principles of the French Revolution was, of course, in direct conflict with the Zionist slogan of auto-emancipation; their anti-Zionism became outspoken when this Zionist ideological position was proclaimed with special emphasis. But when they opposed certain other expressions of Zionist militancy it was rather because of the challenge to their own dominance in the activist, militant and implicitly political defence of Jewish interests. The conflict on these grounds frequently took the form of differences over tactics, but this kind of non-Zionist Jewish leadership shared with Zionists a fundamental strategy of activism rather than of passive, inner-directed accommodation in seeking to define the Jewish position in a Gentile world.

Theodor Herzl belonged to a generation of young Jews in German lands whose sensitivity to the insults of antisemitism was strongly implanted in them in their student years. The 1880s saw German and Austrian political parties rise to heights of menacing strength. Even if the antisemites' electoral strength receded in Germany in the 1890s, students at the universities continued to be harassed and humiliated by antisemitic fraternities. In consequence of the rejection they encountered, Jews organized their own student societies: some were professedly non-sectarian, though overwhelmingly Jewish in composition; others were proudly, if not defiantly, committed to positive programmes of Jewish self-assertion. The founders of the Centralverein, as well as German Zionists like Max Bodenheimer and the sociologist, Franz Oppenheimer, not to speak of Herzl himself, came from this background. The wounded pride which those of that generation shared in common was expressed by the Centralverein's leaders in their militant defence of Jewish rights and by men like Bodenheimer, Oppenheimer and Herzl in their Zionism.[14]

With the rise of Herzl, Zionism emerged as no longer an essentially East European movement with marginal Western supporters and sympathizers. To be sure, even before Herzl, Western sympathizers played a vital role in the proto-Zionist movement (*Hibbat Zion*); the Parisian Baron Edmond de Rothschild had taken over the financial sponsorship of nearly all the Palestinian settlements founded by the movement and *Hibbat Zion* had tried to overcome the handicaps the Russian government imposed on it by setting up headquarters in Paris. But what Herzl did in convening the Zionist Congress in 1897 was to project the Zionist movement boldly and effectively into the domain of international affairs — not as a pragmatic solution to the local problems of certain oppressed Jewish communities in Eastern Europe, but as the claim of Jews throughout their dispersion to be liberated as 'a nation, one nation'. In this bold manoeuvre he was able both to revive the original impulse of auto-emancipation among the Zionists in the East and — by a positive expression of Jewish pride — to attract a following among men like himself in the West. He posed Zionism once again as an ideological challenge to all Jews and as a solution for a problem that affected them all alike.

For Westerners, however, this meant identifying with an ideology and a prescription for action that found its clearest application in the situation of East European Jews. Herzl did not boggle at this conclusion, arguing that the crisis that was clearly approaching in the case of Russian and Rumanian Jews was bound eventually to befall Jews everywhere in Gentile lands. Others, like Bodenheimer (a proud German Jew who became a Zionist by identifying with the plight of Russian Jewish refugees in 1891), might agree that in principle the basic Jewish situation was most clearly exemplified in Eastern Europe, but would regard the case of Germany as a fortunate exception. The plea of exceptionalism was one that Western Jews in many countries, and Western Zionists among them, made in respect of their own case, but in their understanding of the situation of the Jews generally, as a single people, such Zionists accepted the East European situation, and the diagnosis and prescription appropriate to it, as the paradigmatic case.

One further element that made Zionism attractive to some Western Jews was their growing disquiet over the effects of the rationalist universalism of Jewish religious reform and of secularist liberalism in Western countries. Young Jews brought up in such a milieu too frequently dismayed their parents by abandoning their tribal loyalties; or, alternatively, the young might themselves find their parents' secularism or reformed religion to be distasteful expressions of a bourgeois life-style. Both situations could lead, among other deviations, from the established Western Jewish consensus to a heightened appreciation of the solid ethnic-rootedness believed to characterize the East European Jewish community. Zionism, as an expression of this quality, drew some German Jews of Orthodox religious background in the early years. Later, especially after closer contacts with Eastern Europe during the first world war, an avant-gardist group of young Zionists in Berlin, Prague and other centres of German modernist culture came to lead the German Zionist movement. Both there and in America and other Western Jewish communities, Zionism was taken up, like the vogue for neo-Hassidism inspired by Martin Buber and others, as part of a broader rebellion of the young against the older Western Jewish establishment.

Notes

1. Lucy Dawidowicz, *The Golden Tradition: Jewish Life and Thought in Eastern Europe* (Canada 1967), 52.

2. Michael Stanislawski, *For Whom Do I Toil: Judah Leib Gordon and the Crisis of Russian Jewry* (New York 1988), 122.

3. *Hashahar*, IX, no. 7 (1879), 359–66; ibid., X, no. 2 (1880), 57–64; ibid., no. 3 (1880), 105–14; ibid., no. 4 (1880), 153–60; ibid., no. 5 (1881), 241–9; excerpt translated in Hertzberg, *The Zionist Idea* (New York 1969), 160–5.

4. *Hashahar*, X, no. 5 (1881), 209–29; excerpt translated in Hertzberg, op. cit., 148–53, substantially compressed.

5. Moshe Leib Lilienblum, *Derekh letshuva* (1899), 7, 33–5.

6. *Encyclopaedia Judaica*, Vol. 7 (Jerusalem 1971), 958.

7. Israel Klausner, *Behitorer am: haaliyah harishonah mi-Russyah* (Jerusalem 1962), 51–5.

8. Ibid., 58.

9. Hertzberg, op. cit., 168–70.

10. Israel Klausner, *Hibbat zion be-Rumania* (Jerusalem 1958), 20.

11. *The Jewish Chronicle* (London, 24 March 1882).

12. Yehuda Leib Gordon, 'Yishuv Eretz Israel', *Hamagid* 26, no. 13 (1882), 107; cited in Israel Klausner, op. cit., 181.

13. Moshe Leib Lilienblum, 'Al Israel veal artzo', *Hashahar* X, no. 8 (1882), 403.

14. Ismar Schorsch, *Jewish Reactions to Anti-Semitism, 1870–1914* (New York 1972), 179–202; Jehuda Reinharz, *Fatherland or Promised Land? The Dilemma of the German Jew, 1893–1914* (Ann Arbor 1975).

Jehuda Reinharz
is Richard Koret Professor of Modern
Jewish History and Director of the Tauber
Institute for the Study of European Jewry at
Brandeis University. He is the author/editor/
co-editor of numerous books, among them
*Chaim Weizmann: The Making of a Zionist
Leader* (1985) and *Chaim Weizmann: The
Making of a Statesman* (1992).

George L. Mosse

The Jews and the Civic Religion of Nationalism

Nationalism is not simply good or evil but contains many layers of meaning. This statement is especially relevant for Jews in Western and Central Europe after emancipation. For while it was the state, then in formation, which emancipated them, it was the nation they faced once they were emancipated. Jews up to that time had been treated as an altogether separate nation, referred to as the 'Jewish nation' in distinction to the nation in which they lived; now they had to leave their own nation and integrate themselves into the host nation. The adjustments and the problems of such integration have been analysed many times in religious, social and economic terms, and indeed these factors were crucial to Jewish assimilation. But on another level as well, Jews had to come to terms with the modern nation as a unifying force, which tried to assimilate not only the Jewish nation but many other diverse groups of the population.

The civic religion of nationalism, with its liturgical rites and ceremonies, seemed one important factor through which the people could be united with the nation. During most of the nineteenth century this civic religion helped to integrate the Jews into the nation. They took part in its festivals, sang its anthems and admired national monuments. Here, as for example in Germany, the nation was defined primarily in cultural terms and many of its national heroes like Goethe and Schiller came from the Enlightenment with its promise of toleration in return for good citizenship.[1] Nationalism itself was not one-dimensional, it could make alliances with Liberalism and even socialism, it was not yet mainly conservative or chauvinistic. A liberal and rather tolerant nationalism characterized the period of Jewish emancipation, and the Jews themselves supported this nationalism which continued to make their assimilation possible. Nevertheless, certain foundations of national identity were taken for granted regardless of the variety of politics which nationalism could accommodate.

The belief in the existence of a 'national character' was present from the beginning of modern nationhood.[2] Romanticism, with its emphasis on organic development, upon the totality of life, was at the root of this search. It meant that regardless of the unity in multiplicity which some nationalisms advocated, cohesion and uniformity were always potentially present. The foundation upon which national character was built did not differ greatly from nation to nation: a certain morality, comportment and looks were crucial, usually linking the nation with the moral attitudes of the newly triumphant middle classes.[3] The wars of liberation in which so many nations found their national identity in the nineteenth century added ideals of manly strength, of heroism and of camaraderie. At the same time, the preoccupation with ideals of beauty in an ever more materialistic and urban civilization gave shape to such ideals through the elaboration of a national stereotype. The important role which the admiration of art played among the nineteenth-century bourgeoisie is well known. Art as a projection of beauty stood for the true, the good and the holy, and so did the national stereotype which reflected and personalized the character of the nation.

Here the civic religion of nationalism set additional conditions of Jewish assimilation and, though the now dominant manners and morals were no real obstacle, the national stereotype was potentially dangerous. For in all constructions of a national character the distinctions between insider and outsider were more or less sharply drawn. The antisemitic literature opposed to Jewish emancipation cast the Jew as the very opposite of national ideals as reflected in the national character: lacking in respectability, truthfulness and beauty. The Jew, and indeed all of those who stood outside respectable society and therefore the national ideal, were always characterized for what they were not rather than for what they were, measured against the ideals represented by the nation.

Within the evolution of nationalism the relationship between insider and outsider needs closer examination. How important was the counter-image, the stereotype of the Jew, to the image of nationalism, the outsider to the very existence of society itself? Nationalism had its origins in the needs of the times but its evolution was sharpened and further defined as it faced real and putative enemies. These enemies, whether so-called unassimilable Jews or, for example, those who in Germany were called the scoundrels without a

Fatherland — namely the socialists — were given the identical morals, manners and looks — directly opposed to the national stereotype. Here we may have touched upon a hidden need of all modern society: insider and outsider are indissolubly linked.

Most Jews before the 1930s entered fully into the civic religion of nationalism: within the ever narrower nationalism of Germany or, much easier, into what remained of the liberal nationalism of Italy or France. Jews accepted this civic religion and kept their identity through their faith. The barriers to such assimilation were potential rather than actual warning signs: where the civic religion expressed itself largely through comportment and looks, conditions were created which eventually encouraged antisemitism and even racism — in the end this could mean total integration or total exclusion.

The civic religion of nationalism was a secularization of revealed religion, and yet Christianity remained present, another indication that Jews might easily become outsiders. The connection between nationalism and Christianity was most obvious, so it seems to me, at the start of modern nationalism and then again during the first world war. During the first part of the nineteenth century, national monuments were proposed in which crosses played a part, churches themselves were designed as national monuments, such as the Cathedral of Cologne in Germany, and churches could provide the settings for national festivals. But the influence of Christianity was mostly felt in less obvious ways; for example, in the production and choreography of national festivals. After all, the civic religion was a secularization of revealed religion and always kept something of its origins. This problem has not yet been properly investigated, except for Germany,[4] and until the first world war all statements must be tentative. But in that war as hundreds of thousands sacrificed themselves for the nation, the link between nationalism and Christianity became obvious. Christian symbols, indeed the very figure of Christ, were present in the cult of the Fallen Soldier — and in Germany, Italy and France, familiar Christian symbols represented national sacrifice.[5] The first world war was a climax in the evolution of modern nationalism, and in its quest for totality it sought to co-opt Christianity. I am concerned here with modern nations which practised their own civic religion, and not with nations like Rumania where nationalism and Christianity were virtually identical in a predominantly peasant society, and where, during the second world war, the Legion of the Archangel Michael, better known through its

Iron Guard, staged bloody pogroms against the usurious and infidel Jews who had killed Christ.

For many Jews, the first world war seemed to present a new opportunity for a more perfect integration into the nation at the precise time that the civic religion of nationalism became ever more menacing through its cultural imperatives, which tended to homogenize its members. This civic religion, especially after the first world war, was supported by much of the centre and all of the political right. Now its effect in many nations with an antisemitic tradition was a de-emancipation of the Jews rather than the integration of outsiders into the nation. Most European Jews were patriots and remained liberals. This meant a certain reluctance to participate in a nationalism which had shed its earlier tolerance and which was becoming increasingly militant, an integral nationalism which sought control over all aspects of life and thought. The more developed the religion of nationalism, the greater the need for external and internal enemies against which it could define itself and strengthen its resolve, and here the Jews were a ready-made target.

But what about the civic religion of nationalism among the Jews themselves, as some attempted and then succeeded in founding a Jewish nation? The Zionist movement, similar to other European nationalisms, contained many social and political attitudes; it could absorb socialists, liberals and conservatives. And yet, at first, Liberalism predominated, reflecting the self-interest of Jews in their period of assimilation. But this liberal impetus did not entail a neglect of the civic religion of nationalism. Theodor Herzl himself is a good illustration of how both a liberal attitude and the civic religion were joined. Herzl, in 1902, published his Zionist Utopia, *Altneuland*. The Palestine of the novel is a land where 'supreme tolerance' reigns, where Arabs and Jews live harmoniously side by side, and where religion is largely removed from public life. To be sure, a chauvinist faction led, typically enough, by an orthodox rabbi, struggles for power in *Altneuland*. But the hero of the book strongly affirms that there can be no distinction between one man and another, that one should not inquire after a man's religion or race. And indeed, the hero's best friend is an Arab of an old Palestinian family.[6] Herzl's departure from liberal dogma comes only in his praise of an economy based on the model of the English co-operative movement.

National symbols and national rites were an integral part of the Palestine of Herzl's imagination. The care with which Herzl personally designed the symbols of Zionism and the staging of his Zionist congresses are now well known; as he put it in his *Judenstaat* (1896): '. . . if anyone wants to lead many men he must raise symbols over their heads.'[7] He paid close attention to the creation of a flag for the movement, and devoted his energies to the design for a new parliament building. Many more examples of the conscious creation of national symbols could be given: from creating songs for the movement to attempts to found a specific secular culture. The invention of national festivals also engaged Herzl's attention, and Martin Buber's call in 1899 for a national rite which would link the victory of the Maccabees to the new Jewish national movement reflected his own intentions. But in this particular case the Maccabees did not stand for an aggressive spirit, indeed the nationalism which accompanied the creation of a civic religion was centred upon the inner renewal of the Jew, a renewal which would make the Jew one with the land and his people. Hans Kohn, an important early theoretician of the Zionist movement, called this the 'nationalism of inwardness'. An inner spiritual reality would be created through membership in a real community based upon shared experience. Martin Buber and his Zionist friends considered this the true 'Hebrew Humanism'.[8] For Herzl as for Buber, the civic religion of nationalism was not a call to battle but an educational process for the individual Jew who must recapture his dignity as a human being.

Martin Buber and many other Zionists saw national unity as a prerequisite for a larger unity between peoples, between humanity and all living creatures, between God and the world. The creation of a civic religion was accompanied by a certain cosmopolitanism — it was more like the old liberal nationalism which had stood at the beginning of the rise of modern nationalism, than the all-encompassing and chauvinistic nationalism which was reaching for victory after the turn of the century.

The first world war strengthened so-called integral nationalism all over Europe, and it penetrated Zionism as well. Vladimir Jabotinsky founded his revisionist movement in 1923, and this movement subordinated considerations of justice and morality to the central goal of founding a sovereign and exclusively Jewish state in all of Palestine. For Jabotinsky, old fashioned Liberalism was irrelevant, as good as dead in a world which knew no mercy. The result was a Zionism which called itself a movement rather than a party, and which attempted to rely upon a mass base. Jabotinsky, in his novel *Samson the Nazarite* (1930), said of his hero that in the spectacle of thousands obeying a single will, '. . . he had caught a glimpse of the great secret of the builders of nations.'[9] The movement itself, and especially its youth, set store by a paramilitary spirit and discipline. Revisionism projected a modern nationalism as over against the kind of liberal nationalism which the majority of Zionists at that time advocated. Here Zionism caught up with the normative nationalism of the post-war age. Jabotinsky also believed in political ritual and ceremonies centred in this case upon Trumpeldor and other heroes of a Jewish militant and heroic past. Tel Hai, the Jewish settlement which Trumpeldor had defended against Arab forces, and where he had been killed in 1920, became the centre of a revisionist cult, a place of Jewish heroism and bloody sacrifice, while for Socialist-Zionists Trumpeldor remained above all a committed socialist, a symbol of work and toil on the land.[10]

However, modern integral nationalism was latent even in those liberal attitudes which the Zionist movement cherished over so long a time. Here, once more, the civic religion of nationalism played its part and especially the search for a national character which, as we have seen, entailed the belief in an ideal type — in the stereotype of rooted men and women. It is not astonishing that Zionism was concerned with creating a 'new Jew', for other national movements towards the turn of the century also wanted to create their own 'new man': a national stereotype, strong, filled with energy, well proportioned according to Greek models.

Max Nordau's famous speech at the second Zionist Congress of 1898 set the tone for Zionism with its distinction between 'muscle' and 'coffee-house Jews', the latter pale and stunted, the former deep-chested, sturdy and sharp-eyed men. This was an effort to shake off the stereotype of the ghetto Jew and to normalize Jewish men, to construct them in contrast to those avant-garde artists and writers who fill Nordau's famous book, *Degeneration* (1892). His ideal were what he called normal men, those 'who rise early and are not weary before sunset, who have clear heads, solid stomachs and hard muscles.'[11] The same year in which Nordau made his speech, the Bar Kochba Gymnastic Club was founded in Berlin.

All national movements had stressed bodily rejuvenation and founded gymnastic clubs as a means of forming a 'new man'. The Zionists, however, had a special urgency in creating a 'new Jew', who would signal a break with the so-called physical weakness and nervous condition of Jews in the diaspora. Jews must reconnect with their ancient and heroic past, symbolized, for example, by Bar Kochba's uprising against Rome. The bodily degeneration among

Jews caused by shattered nerves became a popular topic in Zionist publications — indeed, physicians at the time considered nervousness the chief sign of degeneracy. Zionists added over-intellectualizing as another cause typical of city life where men sat up all night in coffee houses: neurasthenia was the result, symbolized through pale figures who slink home at dawn.[12]

Zionism, like all modern national liberation movements, was hostile to the modern city, the 'whore of Babylon', which encouraged rootlessness. Here, once more, Zionism felt a special urgency as most Jews were indeed city dwellers and therefore exposed to temptations which would lead to shattered nerves and the destruction of strength and beauty. The coffee house served as a symbol for the rootlessness of the city, for German as well as for Jewish nationalism, however different their evolution proved to be in the end. Coffee-house Jews were said to lack will power and courage, exactly the two characteristics thought indispensable for those who wanted to build a nation. Nervousness marked all those who stood outside or were marginalized by European society and the nation — Jews, the insane, habitual criminals, sexual deviants and gypsies by and large shared the same stereotype, the counter-type to the normal, healthy, vigorous and self-controlled male as Max Nordau had described him. Zionism was no exception in the way it marginalized those who did not conform to national ideals, in this case the ghetto and the coffee-house Jew. Here also it was the belief in a Jewish 'national character' which mattered, symbolized through outward appearance. The ideal of manly strength and beauty, represented through a well-proportioned, steeled and muscular body, was celebrated in much of Zionist literature and art, just as it was propagated, for example, in England and Germany as their national stereotype at the same time. As a recent historian of Zionism has written: 'The physical ideal was entailed by the national ideal to the point where it was impossible to separate the two'.[13]

Despite the influence of a more cosmopolitan and liberal nationalism, the iconography of Zionist nationalism did not differ markedly from that of other nations, not only in the importance assigned to the 'new man', but also in its flag, national anthem and sacred flames — in the use of nature, its sunsets and dawns to arouse a national spirit. After all, Theodor Herzl saw no contradiction between the tolerance and openness of *Altneuland* and the necessity of creating a civic religion in order to integrate a disparate people into one nation.

However, in the history of the Zionist movement the uniformity latent in the civic religion of nationalism never quite won a victory over that individualism which Herzl had praised. It is true that between the two world wars nationalism easily became racism and Jabotinsky, for example, came close to advocating such a nationalism. And yet, the individualism of a liberal nationalism retained its hold for a long time, first upon Zionism and then in the State of Israel even as it fought wars which might have foreclosed this option. Certainly, one crucial part of the civic religion of the State of Israel reflects this tradition and not the militancy or integral nationalism which might have been expected. War monuments, the commemoration of its fallen soldiers, are close to the core of the civic religion of all nations. In Europe, the commemoration of fallen soldiers was usually combined with praise for their heroism and the glorification of the nation. There are about 1000 war memorials and memorial sites all across Israel and from the vast majority any kind of aggressiveness, glorification of the nation or hero-worship are absent.[14] The astonishing density of memorials and memorial sites (about one for every 16 fallen soldiers) does not mean, as it would have in Europe, an effort to make war acceptable through masking or disguising its horror.

Indeed, heroic abstraction or patriotic inscriptions are avoided by most Israeli war monuments, though some existed after 1967, nevertheless the individualism present even in the most nationalistic approaches shines through. Thus there are some memorials of naked youths, but they are not presented as ancient Greeks or as symbols of heroism as, for example, in Germany, but as individuals instead. Just so, the nicknames of soldiers are inscribed together with their proper names on even the few aggressive monuments, depriving them of an aura of sanctity. Here also the latitude allowed to graves in the national military cemetery in Jerusalem is startling. The graves in European military cemeteries, from the first world war onwards, are uniform, subordinated to the symbolism of the nation and of Christianity, which promises the resurrection of the fallen. The decoration and, for the most part, the inscriptions on the gravestones are laid down by the War Graves Commissions of the respective nations. But, while the form of the Israeli war graves in the national military cemetery in Jerusalem is uniform, their decoration is entirely up to the families of the soldiers themselves. They choose the flowers and even the artifacts which can be placed upon the grave — this in contrast to the British Military Cemetery on the other side of Jerusalem, on Mount Scopus, where uniform gravestones are embedded in a well manicured impersonal lawn.

The Memorial Books (*Yiskor Books*) which families or comrades assemble for the fallen soldier are unique; thus, for example, every one of the 1200 soldiers of the famed Golani Brigade who were killed in Israel's wars is commemorated in such an album. The format of these booklets is uniform but their contents are highly personal: pictures, diplomas, reminiscences by friends, essays and poems written by the fallen soldier himself. The culture of commemoration in Israel projects a feeling of personal mourning rather than national triumph.

The fact that Zionist nationalism had managed to retain some of the liberal nationalism of its birth is one factor which made it possible to combine individualism and the cult of the fallen soldiers — a centrepiece of the civic religion of nationalism — in this almost unique manner. Yet other specific factors also went into this retention of individualism in the face of a nationalist imperative. The tradition of Judaism encouraged such personal mourning; here there is no Christian linkage between death and resurrection so crucial for the mythology of the fallen in European nations. Moreover, the country itself is small and intimate, practically everyone knew some fallen soldier or his family. Still, the broader historical considerations related to the history of nationalism must not be lost from sight. Even when it came to building their own Zionist nation, the nationalism involved for a long time tended to remain archaic in contrast to that modern nationalism which dominated Europe after the first world war.

Yet, through the revisionist movement, modern nationalism made inroads into Zionism as well, while the attempt to form a stereotype which would symbolize the national character seemed — together with other elements of the civic religion — to contradict the openness and relative tolerance of the older liberal nationalism. Clearly, a people's history and present situation decide what kind of nationalism is going to triumph, and a newly built nation living in a state of permanent war — with a cohesive civic religion already in place — may well feel the pull towards modern integral nationalism. That in Israel the battle between the old and the new nationalism was joined for such a long time, that the urge towards uniformity always inherent in a civic religion of nationalism has not yet won out, points to the strong heritage of an open and tolerant nationalism, which in the diaspora had given the Jews their chance at citizenship. Here the tradition of the age of Jewish emancipation — of the enlightenment — however beleaguered and challenged by modern nationalism, continued to have its effect.[15]

Notes

This is a somewhat amended version of an essay first given at a symposium, 'Stato Nazionale, Societa Civile e Minoranze Religiose', at the University of Rome, 'La Sapienza', October 1991.

1. Thomas Nipperdey, *Deutsche Geschichte 1800–1866* (München 1983), 300.

2. Thomas Nipperdey, *Nachdenken über Deutsche Geschichte* (München 1986), 140.

3. George L. Mosse, *Nationalism and Sexuality* (New York 1985), chaps 1, 4.

4. George L. Mosse, *The Nationalization of the Masses* (New York 1975), passim.

5. George L. Mosse, *Fallen Soldiers, Reshaping the Memory of the World Wars* (New York 1990), chaps 3, 5.

6. For Herzl and the problem of Jewish–Arab relations, see Walter Laqueur, *A History of Zionism* (New York 1972), chap. 5.

7. Theodor Herzl, *Der Judenstaat* (Leipzig-Wien 1896), 76. For a good discussion of Theodor Herzl and the civic religion of nationalism, see Amos Elon, *Herzl* (New York 1975).

8. Paul Mendes-Flohr, *Divided Passion. Jewish Intellectuals and the Experience of Modernity* (Detroit 1991), 189.

9. Vladimir Jabotinsky, *Samson the Nazarite* (London 1930, first published in Russian in 1927), 180. Yet in some ways Jabotinsky was uneasy about a leadership cult, see Yaacov Shavit, *Jabotinsky and the Revisionist Movement 1925–1928* (London 1988), passim.

10. Charles S. Liebman and Eliezer Don-Yehia, *Civic Religion in Israel* (Berkeley and Los Angeles 1983), 74.

11. Max Nordau, *Degeneration* (New York 1968), 541.

12. Erich Burin, 'Das Kaffeehaus Judentum', *Jüdische Turnerzeitung*, vol. IX (1908), 33ff.

13. Shmuel Almog, *Zionism and History* (New York 1987), 109.

14. The Israeli Ministry of Defense published *Gal-Ed, Memorials to the Fallen* (1990, in Hebrew) where these monuments are reproduced. I am grateful to Tom Segev who visited some of them with me and then published my analyses in 'What do the Monuments do at night? A Travel Report' (in Hebrew), *Ha-Aretz*, 27 April 1990.

15. Vicki Caron's interesting essay, 'The Ambivalent Legacy: The Impact of the Enlightenment and Emancipation on Zionism', *Judaism*, vol. 38, no. 4 (Fall 1989), centres upon the idea of regeneration but says nothing about nationalism.

George L. Mosse
is Bascom-Weinstein Professor of History,
Emeritus, at the University of Wisconsin in
Madison, and Koebner Professor of History,
Emeritus, at the Hebrew University of
Jerusalem. His previous books include,
among others, *The Crisis of German
Ideology, The Nationalization of the Masses,
Nationalism and Sexuality* and *Towards a
Final Solution.* His latest book is *Fallen
Soldiers: Reshaping the Memory of the World
Wars.* He is co-editor of the *Journal of
Contemporary History.*

Index